KNOWLEDGE-BASED SYSTEMS IN ENGINEERING

KNOWLEDGE-BASED SYSTEMS IN ENGINEERING

Clive L. Dym
University of Massachusetts

Raymond E. Levitt
Stanford University

McGraw-Hill, Inc.

New York St. Louis San Francisco Auckland Bogotá Caracas Hamburg
Lisbon London Madrid Mexico Milan Montreal New Delhi Paris San Juan
São Paulo Singapore Sydney Tokyo Toronto

KNOWLEDGE-BASED SYSTEMS IN ENGINEERING

2 3 4 5 6 7 8 9 0 DOC DOC 9 5 4 3 2 1

ISBN 0-07-018563-8

This book was set in Palatino by the authors using Microsoft® Word on an
Apple® Macintosh II.
The editors were B. J. Clark and Margery Luhrs;
the designer was Clive Dym;
the production supervisor was Louise Karam.
The cover was designed by Amy Becker.
R. R. Donnelley & Sons Company was printer and binder.

Library of Congress Cataloging-in-Publication Data

Dym, Clive L.
    Knowledge-based systems in engineering / Clive L. Dym, Raymond E.
    Levitt.
            p.   cm.
    Includes bibliographical references.
    ISBN 0-07-018563-8
    1. Computer-aided engineering.   2. Expert systems (Computer
    science)   I. Levitt, Raymond E.   II. Title.
TA345.D95   1991
620'.0042'0285—dc20   90-5768

CONTENTS

Preface   xv

1 INTRODUCTION   1
  1.1   The practice and tasks of engineering   1
  1.2   Modeling and problem solving   4
  1.3   The role of computation in engineering   7
  1.4   Knowledge-based systems defined   10
      1.4.1   Knowledge in AI   10
      1.4.2   Definitions of knowledge-based systems   11
      1.4.3   Basic architectures of knowledge-based systems   14
  1.5   Knowledge-based systems in engineering   18

I CONCEPTUAL UNDERPINNINGS   21

2 PROBLEM FORMULATION AND SEARCH   23
  2.1   Introduction   23
  2.2   Formulation and representation of problems   24
      2.2.1   Missionaries and cannibals   24
      2.2.2   The 8-puzzle   30
      2.2.3   Search and engineering problems   33
  2.3   State space search   34
      2.3.1   Search trees and graphs   34
      2.3.2   Data- and goal-driven reasoning   36
      2.3.3   Problem characteristics   38
      2.3.4   Strategies for solving problems   39
      2.3.5   Stopping criteria; satisficing and optimizing   40
  2.4   Exhaustive search   41
      2.4.1   Weak methods   42
      2.4.2   Breadth-first search   42
      2.4.3   Depth-first search   43
      2.4.4   Depth-first iterative-deepening search   44
      2.4.5   Generate-and-test   46
      2.4.6   Constraint satisfaction   47

	2.5	Directed search	49
		2.5.1 Strong methods; heuristic search	49
		2.5.2 Hill-climbing	50
		2.5.3 Best-first search	52
		2.5.4 Branch-and-bound search	53
		2.5.5 The A* algorithm	54
	2.6	Summary	56
3		**DEDUCTION WITH FORMAL LOGIC**	57
	3.1	Introduction	57
	3.2	Formal logic systems	58
		3.2.1 Propositional logic	60
		3.2.2 First-order predicate logic	65
		3.2.3 Unification and resolution	73
		3.2.4 Interpretation in logic systems	75
	3.3	How deduction can be used by engineers	76
	3.4	Summary	79
4		**LANGUAGES FOR SYMBOLIC COMPUTATION**	81
	4.1	Introduction	81
	4.2	Lisp	82
		4.2.1 Atoms and lists in Lisp	82
		4.2.2 Evaluation of expressions in Lisp	83
		4.2.3 Defining functions in Lisp	83
		4.2.4 List processing in Lisp	84
		4.2.5 Defining classes and their properties	84
		4.2.6 Conditional statements	85
		4.2.7 Recursion in Lisp	86
		4.2.8 Variables and dynamic memory management in Lisp	86
		4.2.9 Summary and discussion of Lisp features	87
	4.3	Prolog	88
		4.3.1 The architecture and philosophy of Prolog	89
		4.3.2 Facts, variables, and queries in Prolog	89
		4.3.3 Rules in Prolog	89
		4.3.4 Illustration: A Prolog system to support design	92
		4.3.5 Summary of Prolog's features	93
	4.4	Higher-level languages for computer reasoning	93
	4.5	Summary	95
II		**IMPLEMENTATION TECHNIQUES**	97
5		**RULE-BASED REPRESENTATION**	99
	5.1	Logic and plausible inference	99

5.2	Forward and backward chaining		101
5.3	Writing and organizing rules		105
	5.3.1	Rule syntax	105
	5.3.2	Organization of rule-based knowledge bases	108
	5.3.3	Rule sets and metarules	111
	5.3.4	Rule selection and conflict resolution	112
5.4	Architecture of a rule-based system		113
	5.4.1	Organization of a rule-based system	113
	5.4.2	Attributes of a rule-based system	115
5.5	Representation of uncertainty		116
	5.5.1	Sources of uncertainty	117
	5.5.2	Probability theory and measures of uncertainty	118
	5.5.3	Certainty factors in EMYCIN	122
5.6	Inference nets for reasoning with uncertainty		124
5.7	Summary		127

6 SEMANTIC NETS, FRAMES, AND OBJECT-ORIENTED PROGRAMMING

			129
6.1	Semantic nets		129
	6.1.1	Taxonomic hierarchies	130
	6.1.2	Properties of entities	132
	6.1.3	Subsystem/component hierarchies	136
	6.1.4	A cautionary word	138
	6.1.5	Computer reasoning with semantic nets	138
6.2	Frame-based representation		140
	6.2.1	Information hiding in frame hierarchies	140
	6.2.2	The internal structure of a frame	141
	6.2.3	Inheritance of attributes in frame-based systems	142
	6.2.4	Facets: Attributes of slots	144
	6.2.5	Inheritance of behavior by subclasses	145
6.3	Object-oriented programming		146
	6.3.1	Syntax of methods in OOP	146
	6.3.2	Control in OOP languages	147
	6.3.3	Programming languages for OOP	150
6.4	Integrating rules, frames, and procedures		151
	6.4.1	Production rules as slot values of rule frames	153
	6.4.2	Attribute values point to rules	154
	6.4.3	Attribute values obtained by rules or procedures	155
6.5	Explanation in a KBES		156
	6.5.1	Frame hierarchies	156
	6.5.2	Rule traces	156
	6.5.3	Automatic explanation (transparency of reasoning)	157
	6.5.4	Rule graphs	159
	6.5.5	Knowledge-based interactive graphics	160

6.6   Summary   161

7   ADVANCED TOPICS IN REPRESENTATION   163
    7.1   Qualitative reasoning   163
        7.1.1   A taxonomy of engineering knowledge   164
        7.1.2   Qualitative physics: Some definitions   166
        7.1.3   Qualitative physics: A simple model   168
    7.2   Belief revision systems   169
    7.3   Spatial and temporal reasoning   173
        7.3.1   Spatial reasoning   174
        7.3.2   Temporal reasoning   176
    7.4   Summary   177

8   KBES ARCHITECTURES FOR ENGINEERING APPLICATIONS   179
    8.1   Architectural requirements of engineering KBESs   179
    8.2   An architecture for model-based reasoning   181
        8.2.1   Obtaining component descriptions from CADD databases   182
        8.2.2   How components can inherit behavior   184
        8.2.3   How components can deduce their function   185
        8.2.4   Generating system behavior in MBR   186
        8.2.5   Engineering applications of MBR   189
    8.3   Blackboard architectures   190
        8.3.1   A human organizational analogy   191
        8.3.2   The blackboard metaphor in BB1   193
        8.3.3   Representation in a blackboard system   194
        8.3.4   Reasoning in a blackboard system   194
        8.3.5   Control in a blackboard architecture   195
        8.3.6   Suitability of blackboard architectures
                 for engineering KBESs   196
    8.4   Cooperative distributed problem solving (CDPS)   198
        8.4.1   Motivations and applications   199
        8.4.2   Characteristics of CDPS systems   202
    8.5   Architectural considerations in CDPS   203
    8.6   Summary   208

III ENGINEERING APPLICATIONS   211

9   KNOWLEDGE-BASED SYSTEMS FOR CLASSIFICATION   213
    9.1   Characteristics of classification problems   213
    9.2   Diagnosis   215
        9.2.1   The inference structure of diagnostic knowledge   215
        9.2.2   Examples of KBESs for diagnosis   217
        9.2.3   Recapitulation of KBESs for diagnosis   217

9.3   Diagnostic evaluation: The LSC Advisor   218
   9.3.1   The LSC Advisor: Binary evaluation against safety codes   218
   9.3.2   Origins of the LSC Advisor   219
   9.3.3   Architecture of the LSC Advisor   220
   9.3.4   Representing provisions of the Life Safety Code   222
   9.3.5   Representing and reasoning about a floor plan   223
   9.3.6   Travel distance algorithms   225
   9.3.7   Control issues in the LSC Advisor   227
   9.3.8   A unifying database   228
9.4   Scaled evaluation: SafeQual   229
   9.4.1   Motivation for SafeQual   230
   9.4.2   Architecture of SafeQual   230
   9.4.3   Reasoning in SafeQual   231
   9.4.4   Control in the SafeQual system   232
   9.4.5   Present status of SafeQual   234
   9.4.6   Recapitulation of evaluation KBESs   234
9.5   Monitoring and control: PLATFORM   235
   9.5.1   Goals of the PLATFORM project   235
   9.5.2   Representation in PLATFORM   236
   9.5.3   Reasoning in PLATFORM   237
   9.5.4   Control in PLATFORM   237
   9.5.5   Knowledge-based interactive graphics in PLATFORM   238
9.6   Real-time monitoring and control: Guardian   239
   9.6.1   Goals of the Guardian system   239
   9.6.2   Guardian's architecture   239
   9.6.3   Representation in Guardian   239
   9.6.4   Reasoning in Guardian   240
   9.6.5   Control in Guardian   241
   9.6.6   Status of Guardian   241
9.7   Summary   241

10 KNOWLEDGE-BASED SYSTEMS FOR DESIGN   243
10.1   Engineering design: Taxonomies and prescriptions   243
   10.1.1   Definitions of engineering design   243
   10.1.2   The spectrum of engineering design tasks   245
   10.1.3   A taxonomy of design: Routine versus creative design   246
   10.1.4   The design process: Phases and prescriptions   248
   10.1.5   An information-processing model of design   252
10.2   KBES-based approaches to engineering design   254
   10.2.1   Solution methods for design problems   254
   10.2.2   Roles for knowledge-based tools in engineering design   257
10.3   Configuration: The PRIDE system   259
   10.3.1   PRIDE: A sophisticated configuration system   259

	10.3.2	The origins of PRIDE	261
	10.3.3	Architecture of PRIDE	261
	10.3.4	Representation issues in PRIDE	262
	10.3.5	Control issues in PRIDE	271
	10.3.6	Current status of PRIDE	273
10.4	Synthesis: The SightPlan system		274
	10.4.1	The origins of SightPlan	275
	10.4.2	Architecture of SightPlan	277
	10.4.3	Representation issues in SightPlan	278
	10.4.4	Control issues in SightPlan	280
	10.4.5	The GS2D constraint engine	282
	10.4.6	SightView: An interactive graphic interface for SightPlan	283
	10.4.7	Current status of SightPlan	287
10.5	Synthesis: Intelligent Boiler Design System (IBDS)		289
	10.5.1	Background of IBDS	289
	10.5.2	Architecture of IBDS	290
	10.5.3	Representation in IBDS	291
	10.5.4	Reasoning in IBDS	291
	10.5.5	Explanation in IBDS	291
	10.5.6	Current Status of IBDS	292
10.6	Summary		293
11	**KNOWLEDGE-BASED SYSTEMS FOR PLANNING**		**295**
11.1	Overview of AI planning research		295
11.2	General-purpose AI planning systems		297
	11.2.1	The evolution of AI planning systems	297
	11.2.2	Limitations of classical AI planners	299
	11.2.3	Representation: The Achilles heel of AI planners	301
11.3	Narrowly scoped expert planning systems		302
	11.3.1	Molgen	303
	11.3.2	LIFT	303
11.4	Toward KBES planning shells		304
	11.4.1	ISIS and Callisto	305
	11.4.2	CONSTRUCTION PLANEX	306
11.5	MBR planning systems		307
	11.5.1	SIPE-2/SIPE	307
	11.5.2	GHOST: Using critics to constrain a plan	308
	11.5.3	PIPPA: A hierarchy of actions applied to objects	309
	11.5.4	OARPLAN: Planning as model-based reasoning	310
11.6	Molgen: Hierarchical planning with constraints		310
	11.6.1	Philosophy of Molgen	311
	11.6.2	Representation in Molgen	311
	11.6.3	Reasoning in Molgen	311

	11.6.4	Control in Molgen	312
	11.6.5	Contributions of Molgen	313
11.7	OARPLAN: The Object-Action-Resource Planner		313
	11.7.1	Representation in OARPLAN	314
	11.7.2	Reasoning in OARPLAN	319
	11.7.3	Control in OARPLAN	326
	11.7.4	Essential features of OARPLAN	327
11.8	Summary		328

IV INSTITUTIONAL AND SOCIOLOGICAL ISSUES

329

12 THE LIFE CYCLE OF A KBES

			331
12.1	Introduction		331
12.2	The stages of development of a KBES		332
12.3	Task selection criteria		333
12.4	Knowledge acquisition		334
	12.4.1	Working with several experts: The PRIDE project	336
	12.4.2	Working with one expert	339
	12.4.3	The interviewing process; protocol analysis	341
	12.4.4	Trends in knowledge acquisition	343
12.5	KBES verification and validation		344
	12.5.1	Verification	345
	12.5.2	Validation	346
12.6	The "maximum anxiety" heuristic		348
12.7	Delivering a KBES		349
	12.7.1	Hardware and software environments	349
	12.7.2	Maintenance and support	354
12.8	Institutional and social impacts of KBESs		356
	12.8.1	Institutional costs and benefits	356
	12.8.2	Who owns the knowledge in a KBES?	360
	12.8.3	Who is responsible for the knowledge in a KBES?	360
	12.8.4	The changing roles of KBES users	362
12.9	Summary		363

| **References** | 367 |
| **Index** | 391 |

PREFACE

This book is devoted to the use of a specific artificial intelligence (AI) technique, knowledge-based (expert) systems, as a research and application tool for engineering analysis, design, and project management. The very recent introduction of AI into engineering has uncovered many exciting opportunities for improvements in the art of engineering and for interesting research.

Aims of the Book

This book is intended to explain

❑   What is meant by the term *knowledge-based (expert) systems (KBESs)*;

❑   What the underlying AI concepts are; and

❑   How these concepts and systems can be applied to engineering.

In the process of achieving these goals, we will list and abstract from much of the applied literature on knowledge-based systems and some of the more fundamental work in AI. However, we assume no prior AI knowledge on the part of the reader; the explication is self-contained and is intended to be accessible to engineering students and practitioners who have some familiarity with conventional procedural programming techniques and tools.

Organization of the Book

The book is made up of four major parts preceded by an introductory chapter (see the Table of Contents for greater detail). Chapter 1 serves as the introduction to both the book and its subject. Here we explain why AI is important to engineering and what our intentions and objectives are, and we give an account of why this book came into being. We provide a description of the major tasks of engineering, explaining how engineering practice differs from other disciplines, and we give an overview of the role that computers have played in engineering over the past three decades. We also present a detailed definition of knowledge-based (expert) systems and illustrate how such systems can be used in support of different kinds of engineering tasks, from the derivation or classification type to the formation or synthesis kind. This discussion is coupled to a preview of existing engineering knowledge-based systems.

Part I is intended to provide the conceptual underpinnings for all that follows. In Chapter 2 we introduce the notions of alternative representations for problem solving, and we provide a basic introduction to the crucially important ideas of search. The emphasis here is on representation as a choice to be exercised in the formulation and consideration of any particular problem. We pay special attention to state space representation and tree search. In our discussion of search, we develop the distinction between blind, exhaustive search, on the one hand, and guided, heuristic search, on the other, and we present algorithms for conducting such searches. Also, we identify strategies for problem solving and we relate them to the procedures for executing state space search.

In Chapter 3 we introduce the concepts underlying deduction in systems of formal logic. We show that deduction complements search in problem solving by humans and computers. Deduction also adds to the arsenal of implementation techniques for knowledge-based systems by providing the underpinnings for various techniques, particularly rule-based inference and inheritance of class properties. In Chapter 4 we describe programming languages that implement high-level capabilities for deduction and search in applications of knowledge-based systems.

Part II of the book (Chapters 5 through 8) is devoted to those AI fundamentals that are especially relevant to the implementation or programming of knowledge-based systems. This part of the book is a serious examination of the ways we can represent knowledge in symbolic terms, with an eye toward computability, an absolute prerequisite for knowledge programming. Here we cover representation of knowledge through production rules, including uncertainty (Chapter 5), and semantic networks, frames, and structured objects (Chapter 6). In Chapter 6 we also describe the exceptional capabilities knowledge-based systems have for explaining their solutions and the reasoning processes used to derive them.

In Chapter 7 we deal with some advanced topics in representation, including qualitative reasoning, belief revision systems, and spatial and temporal reasoning. We conclude Part II with discussion of architectural issues which are of special interest to engineers. In Chapter 8 we first present an overall engineering-oriented architectural approach, sometimes called model-based reasoning. We then go on to describe architectures for concurrent or simultaneous engineering, including both blackboard architectures and cooperative distributed problem solving. These are ideas that offer great potential for future engineering application, but they have not yet been as fully exploited as the basic representation paradigms in Chapters 5 and 6.

Part III of the book (Chapters 9 through 11) builds on the previous material to illustrate how knowledge-based systems have been applied to major engineering problems. We present here detailed discussions of important knowledge-based system applications for each of the major types of problem-solving tasks introduced in Chapter 1. The examples have been carefully chosen to reflect problem types that are common to several of the engineering disciplines as well as to the management of engineering projects. Moreover, in many of the examples we are writing about knowledge-based systems projects that we have personally initiated and/or directed.

Part IV of the book (Chapter 12) is devoted to a discussion of how KBES applications are brought into being and to some thoughts about their use. In our discussion of implementation issues we cover both technical and institutional/social issues, for the latter are quite important and often interact with technical considerations; again we draw on our own experience in system building as the basis for these perspectives. Also included are discussions of the life cycle of knowledge-based systems and of some of the legal, professional, and social issues attendant to their development and use. We conclude with some suggestions and speculations about the future of knowledge-based systems, both as a technology and as a tool to be used in support of enhancing engineering practice, education, and research.

What This Book Is and What It Is Not

Having outlined what we do cover in this text, let us also note what we omit. One important point is that this book is not intended to be a full-fledged introduction to AI for computer scientists. First of all, we do not even begin to examine such topics as natural language processing (NLP), knowledge-based (computer) vision, learning, or cognitive science. Second, our discussion of the relevant essentials of AI is designed to be correct and properly grounded and motivated, but bare rather than comprehensive. Our explications of search, deduction, programming languages, and representation paradigms are utilitarian rather than exhaustive. And third, while on occasion we note some of the history of the development of AI, in the main we leave that to others. (In particular, see the oft-cited works [Barr 1981; Rich 1983; Winston 1984a; Charniak 1985].)

Another point is that we do not teach the programming conventions and syntax of a particular KBES development tool; these are readily and more appropriately found in software user's manuals. Our discussion of AI fundamentals and basic expert system implementation techniques is intended to provide the reader with the necessary fundamental undertanding of alternative representation and reasoning schemes needed to choose the most appropriate programming tools for any given KBES application. Consequently, the reader who has mastered the material in this book will be able to use a wide range of KBES development tools with insight and understanding.

We stress again that this book is being written for engineers by engineers. Although as individuals we have devoted substantial time and effort to working with and learning from serious AI researchers and practitioners, our viewpoint remains unrepentantly that of engineers: Knowledge-based systems represent an exciting new technology that will be a major engineering tool over the next decade and beyond. We are enthusiastic about the potential, and we want our colleagues and students to learn about knowledge-based systems and apply them in support of the art of engineering.

Using This Book in a Class

This book is designed for use in a one-quarter or one-semester course that introduces upper division undergraduate or graduate engineers to KBES concepts and their application. (The Expert Systems Committee of the American Society of Civil Engineers has produced a monograph aimed at helping new instructors develop this kind of introductory class; it is a valuable reference for sample assignments and exams [Mohan 1989].) We have successfully covered collections of readings whose scope approximates that of this book in a single four-quarter-hour or three-semester-hour course. The conceptual material in the book can be covered in about 30 one-hour lectures, with students reading chapters in advance of lectures. For the one-quarter option, instructors may choose to omit Chapters 7 and 8.

We recommend that an introductory KBES class taught with this book also include one hour per week of parallel laboratory time in which students are taught to use a series of progressively more challenging software tools in a computer teaching classroom environment. With these tools, students can gain hands-on experience at encoding knowledge in rules, frames, and perhaps one object-oriented programming (OOP) language through a series of assignments that parallel the lectures. We have successfully used a variety of tools and platforms: a production rule (see Chapter 5) shell running on a Macintosh computer; an inference net (see Chapter 5) package running on IBM AT–class computers; and a general-purpose representation language (see Chapters 4 and 12) that integrates rules, frames, and objected-oriented programming (see Chapter 6) and runs on a range of engineering workstations. There are many tools that can serve this function.

We also recommend that evaluation in a class of this type be based in part on a final project in which students work in small groups to incorporate some significant real-world expertise (perhaps acquired from local engineering practitioners) into a KBES over the duration of the class. This requires an early start and especially good follow-through in a one-quarter class, but it can be done.

A more leisurely pace which might suit some instructors and students better would be a two-quarter or two-semester sequence in which the fundamentals could be covered more thoroughly in the first part of the course, incorporating some of the additional readings referenced in the text and with example problems used to reinforce the concepts. A more significant project could then be undertaken in the second quarter or semester, with a sequence of deliverables: proposal development and submission, prototype development, implementation, and validation.

Some Comments on Usage

Some minor notes on usage are appropriate here. The first is that the phrase *knowledge-based (expert) systems* will appear throughout this book. In order to save a little space and enhance the readability of the text, we will generally use the acronym KBES to stand for one of those systems about which we are so excited and which hold so much promise. However, we will also—albeit less frequently—use the more popular phrase *expert systems* where we think it "sounds" better, although we do not intend thereby to draw any distinction—as some authors are inclined to do—between an expert system and a KBES. The second note concerns the style of citations and references. For the former we have adopted the style generally used in the AI literature, referring to works by first author and date, these being within a pair of brackets. (See, for example, the citations to standard works given above.) The references are all gathered at the end of the book, ordered alphabetically by first author.

The third note concerns typeface styles. There is more than a little diversity in the typeface conventions used in the literature to denote logic statements and connectives; rules, frames, and frame slots; mathematical terms; and so on. We have generally applied a fairly simple convention that is designed to distinguish these items from neighboring text. This convention also allows us to distinguish logic statements from frames by the context of the discussion in which they appear. The convention is that all such terms appear in capital letters in a SANS_SERIF typeface, with underscores used to connect words in phrases. There are some instances, however, where we have modified or ignored this convention for the sake of clarity. In the discussion of some aspects of qualitative reasoning in Chapter 7, for example, we have used conventional mathematics notation because it seemed more appropriate. Similarly, when we have used screens or other results from particular KBESs, we have modified the case and connections of the notation (e.g., SansSerif) to match that used in the particular application being described. We have done this in Chapters 6, 9, 10, and 11.

Some Key References

Several works on AI have been seminal for us in that they have provided us with an understanding of the field, some directions for its implementation, and some notions of its potential. For thorough introductions to AI we recommend [Charniak 1985] and [Winston 1984a]. A treatise by Stefik [1990] provides a thoughtful and eminently readable overview of the process and techniques of encoding knowledge for computation. For lucid discussions of search we have found [Nilsson 1980] and [Rich 1983] to be particularly helpful, while [Pospesel 1974] and [Pospesel 1976] present excellent and clear introductions to logic.

Acknowledgements

Although this book represents the fruits of a joyous and enlightening collaboration, we each have some individual acknowledgements that we would like to make in addition to those we render jointly.

For CLD: My introduction to KBESs came from an after-luncheon talk given in 1982 by a longtime colleague and friend, Steven J. Fenves, Sun Company Professor at Carnegie Mellon University. He sparked my interest and has provided sustained encouragement and support ever since. In 1983, through the good offices of Dr. M. J. Stefik, I was invited to spend a year at the Xerox Palo Alto Research Center (PARC), where I learned an approach to modeling qualitative knowledge that was not only complementary to long-held beliefs about modeling engineering tasks; it was also intensely stimulating and challenging. Drs. D. G. Bobrow and Sanjay Mittal joined with Mark Stefik to make that year interesting and exciting, and PARC provided a wonderful environment. While at PARC I initiated the PRIDE project and teamed with Sanjay to complete the knowledge acquisition and sketch out the user interface. Sanjay made PRIDE his project when I left PARC, and he made it the success it is today. In doing PRIDE, we both were supported and influenced by Mahesh Morjaria, an engineer with the Xerox Reprographics Business Group. Also while at PARC, and facilitated by a parallel appointment at Stanford University, I met another civil engineering professor who saw the same vision that I did—and there were not too many of us then. We formed the basis of the friendship and collaboration whose partial fruits you now hold in your hands.

I am also very pleased to acknowledge copious help offered—and gratefully received—over many years, and for far more than the specifics of this project. Dr. Thomas A. Cruse of Vanderbilt University has been a friend and colleague for two decades and has consistently encouraged and supported my intellectual meanderings. Tom and Steve Fenves have given shape and focus to my professional life in ways that have nurtured every aspect of my life.

Other close friends have made me feel that my writing and thinking were good and useful. Unless otherwise noted, they are at the University of Massachusetts: Professors Robert H. Allen (University of Delaware); Bernard B. Berger; James W. Male; A. B. Perlman (Tufts University); Daniel R. Rehak (Carnegie Mellon University); Barbara A. Schreier; and Linda S. Slakey.

For REL: The best way to learn a subject may be to write a book about it, but would-be writers have to start somewhere. My exploration of KBESs over the past ten years has been inspired and guided by three remarkable friends and mentors.

Dr. Alan Campbell was the geologist on the original PROSPECTOR expert system project at Stanford Research Institute during the mid-1970s when we were both doctoral students at Stanford. Alan's long-range vision of the potential of KBES technology for distributing knowledge more widely in the world; his development of the Deciding Factor (an early PC-based, inference net KBES shell); and his guidance in its use provided my introduction to this exciting and rewarding field. In 1984, I had the opportunity to spend a sabbatical leave with IntelliCorp and work beside Dr. John Kunz, the company's chief knowledge systems engineer, in exploring the applicability of AI techniques to problems in the management of engineering projects. John is not only one of the world's most experienced and capable knowledge engineers; he is also a master teacher. From John I learned how to tap the enormous power of integrated rule/frame/OOP environments for engineering applications. Dr. Barbara Hayes-Roth at Stanford's Knowledge Systems Laboratory is another friend and colleague who educated me in the ways of KBES research. From Barbara I learned about the power of blackboard expert system architectures for opportunistic problem solving, and about the power of scheduled software demonstrations for motivating graduate students. Our three-year collaboration on the SightPlan project has been the high point of my academic career to date. I thank each of these special friends for their guidance and their friendship.

A group of exceptionally talented Finnish engineers taught me some "object lessons" about the use of AI in design automation. Matti Katajamäki, Tapio Karras, and Hannu Lehtimäki of Design Power, Inc., and Asko Riitahuhta of Tampella Power Division developed the pathbreaking boiler design application described in Chapter 10 and gave generously of their time in explaining it.

Iris Tommelein—civil engineering and computer science student extraordinaire, and now assistant professor at the University of Michigan—worked with me for four years in developing and refining a course, Expert Systems in Civil Engineering, in which many of these ideas were clarified and honed. This collaboration, along with our work on the SightPlan project, provided me with valuable insights about KBES concepts and ways to teach them to engineers.

My friend and assistant at Stanford, Margaret Gelatt, helped with this book in more ways than I could ever recall or recount. Many thanks, Margaret.

The majority of my writing on this book took place during a beautiful and exciting autumn quarter at the Oregon Graduate Institute. My warmest appreciation goes to Dwight Sangrey, president, who invited me to work at OGI; Jim Huntzicker, provost, who kept me running; Nike Horton of the computer science department, who kept me "on line"; and Carole Hendrickson, Julie Wilson, Kristi Angevine, Joe Sandaal, Kelly Atkinson, and Beverly Kyler, who provided the infrastructure for writing.

A future AI scientist, Benjamin Levitt, provided his father with much needed assistance—and emotional support—in the final stages of page layout. Thanks, Ben!

Finally, I want to thank a superb group of research students at Stanford whose work on KBES over the past ten years has provided much of the grist for my writing: Alan Axworthy, Weng-Tat Chan, Paul Chinowsky, Lai Chua, Tony Confrey, Adnan Darwiche, Bruce Fink, Martin Fischer, Thomas Froese, Deepak Jain, Nabil Kartam, Damien Kelly, Charlie Koo, Michelle Lamarre, Yichin Lee, Greg Luth, Hooman Sotodeh-Khoo, Iris Tommelein, and Lloyd Waugh.

We are *jointly* grateful to Mark Stefik for making available to us advance drafts of several chapters from his treatise on knowledge systems; to Dan Rehak, Deepak Jain, Steve Salata, Iris Tommelein, and Tom Richards for providing us with meticulous reviews of various chapters of the manuscript; to B. J. Clark and Eric Munson, our editors at McGraw-Hill, Inc., whose faith in this project provided us with the needed encouragement and resources to take the time to write the book; to Kathryn Graehl for a superb job of copy editing; and to Margery Luhrs for managing the editorial production of the book with exceptional skill and patience.

Finished and complete; praised be the Creator of the Universe.　　　　תושלב"ע

Clive L. Dym　　　　　　　　　　　　　　　　　　Raymond E. Levitt
Northampton, Massachusetts　　　　　　　　　　Stanford, California

KNOWLEDGE-BASED SYSTEMS
IN ENGINEERING

Chapter 1

INTRODUCTION

In this chapter we begin our odyssey by looking at engineering in a larger context, defining and characterizing the intellectual tasks that make up the practice of engineering. We also include in this introductory discussion a review of the underlying notions of modeling because this book is really about new ways—different from our traditional mathematical ways—to model or represent both the artifacts that result from engineering design and analysis and the processes that lead to those artifacts. Inasmuch as we are interested in computer-based modeling of these processes, we find it useful to review the role of computation in engineering. And here, too, we shall be contrasting the "traditional" ways we have used the computer to perform numerical algorithms with the new style of programming implied by the representation ideas that we bring forth in this book. These discussions serve to set the stage for the particular kind of computer-based modeling and reasoning that is the central theme of this book, knowledge-based (expert) systems, abbreviated as KBESs. Thus, in Sections 1.1 and 1.2 we define what we mean by knowledge-based systems and we describe the basic architectural building blocks of which such systems or programs are made. We then complete our introduction by describing some of the ways in which knowledge-based systems have been applied to various engineering tasks.

1.1 THE PRACTICE AND TASKS OF ENGINEERING

What is engineering? What does an engineer do? These are two questions that are not uncommon and to which the usual answers seem perhaps superficial and a bit abstract. For example, Webster's gives the following definitions of engineering: "the art of managing engines" and "the application of science and mathematics by which the properties of matter and the sources of energy in nature are made useful to people in structures, machines, products, systems, and processes." The first of these we would regard as too narrow a definition (and perhaps a bit insulting to those highly conscious of their professional status), while the second sounds like a good dictionary definition but is still vague enough to elicit the follow-up question, Yes, but what do engineers really *do*?

Another response, somewhat more definitive, would be that engineers design, analyze, and build things, artifacts, objects, and so on. This seems consistent with the second dictionary definition and it uses comfortable and familiar terminology, words like *analyze* and *design*. We *know* what they mean, don't we? We could go back to the dictionary, but we still find that the definitions given are not quite precise enough. For example, the verb *design* means, among other things, to "draw the plans for" and to "create, fashion, execute, or construct according to plan." The problem that we have is that in order to think about replicating the tasks of engineering on a computer within any sort of computer program, we need to have better specifications of what really are the tasks of engineering.

In order to focus this discussion more narrowly, and to provide a basis for discussing all the tasks of engineering within a common framework, we adapt here the spectrum of problem-solving tasks outlined by Amarel [1978] and depicted in Figure 1-1. In this model, there are two broad classes of problem-solving activity. The first is the set of **derivation** or **classification tasks**, in which solutions are *derived* from given facts and data. This class includes diagnosis, in which we seek to identify the reasons for a failure or malfunction; interpretation, in which we try to discern a pattern among a set of facts or readings so that we can understand their meaning; and monitoring, in which we track the changes in a system dynamically with a view toward intervening if something critical is about to happen. The following engineering classification tasks are given by Dym [1985a] and Stefik [1990].

Diagnosis. Identify the causes that might explain the observed symptoms in a failed structural system.

Diagnosis/selection. Find an analysis strategy and select the corresponding tool(s) to analyze a structure, given certain constraints on time, cost, and the degree of accuracy required of the answer.

Interpretation. Locate the source and determine the magnitude of an earthquake from ground motion data recorded at several remote seismometers.

Monitoring. Decide on the timing and nature of specific actions that must be taken during the processing of polymers in a chemical plant.

The second set of tasks are the **formation** or **synthesis tasks**, in which a problem is solved by *forming* or creating an object or a set of plans for

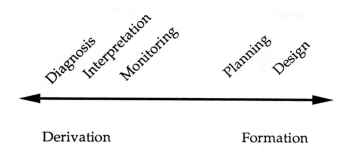

Figure 1-1 Amarel's spectrum of problem-solving tasks.

making an object. This class includes both planning, in which we seek to lay out the sequence of steps required to achieve some objective, and design, in which we seek to create an artifact or set out a plan for making that artifact. Some engineering examples of synthesis tasks are taken from [Dym 1985a].

Planning. Plan the delivery of construction equipment of the appropriate type and capacity to arrive at a building site so as to ensure that there will be no construction delays.

Design. Lay out a path that paper can travel through a copying machine, and design all the requisite devices needed to physically move the paper along that path in terms of their type, dimensions, materials, and locations.

We will see, as this book unfolds, that all of the examples given above are real and relevant, not only in the sense that they are legitimate engineering tasks, but also in that they have been encapsulated in various knowledge-based systems.

Another way of distiguishing between derivation (classification) tasks and formation (synthesis) tasks is the following [Dym 1985a; Stefik1982a]. In derivation tasks we are intent on classifying data (which is presumably available to us). However, in general we must be prepared to handle both unreliable data and time-varying data in order to be able to do diagnosis, monitoring, and so on. When synthesizing something, on the other hand, the task requirements may involve evaluating partial solutions (e.g., incomplete designs); dealing with interacting—or even conflicting—subgoals; and perhaps guessing at or generating multiple candidate solutions, especially where a complete specification of the form of the solution may not exist. The point is that the requirements vary with each type of task in Amarel's spectrum and so we would expect—and we will see in both Chapter 2 and Part III—that the solution prescriptions will vary as well. And, among other things, we shall see that far more is known about representing derivation tasks than about representing planning and design, a true reflection of the state of engineering practice today, where we can formalize much more of what we know about analysis than we can of what we know about design.

1.2 MODELING AND PROBLEM SOLVING

Section 1.1 has provided us with a vocabulary for talking about the process or tasks of engineering, but as yet we do not have a clear idea of the language which we can use to describe the artifacts or plans that are the results of engineering tasks. The next step in our discussion must therefore be to focus on **modeling**, on how we actually represent or describe something so that we can describe a phenomenon or object, make predictions about it or with it, analyze it, design it, and so on. The idea of modeling is inherent in the scientific method and is a central feature of engineering [Dym 1980]. We use models all the time, generally in an unconscious fashion in which we take them for granted. We use verbal models to describe thoughts and feelings as well as objects and plans. And in engineering we use a technical vocabulary and various kinds of mathematical and numerical models to do our work. For example, we model structures, circuits, chemical processes, and mechanical parts, and for all of these we have a set of terms, both verbal and mathematical, that we use to describe the immediate objects of our attention. However, the main point we wish to emphasize here is that our most familiar models are mathematical ones in which we describe objects in the language of continuous mathematics, such as differential and integral calculus. These models serve us quite well in many ways, and they can also be extended into algorithms that can be effectively manipulated on computers by processing symbols that represent numbers (see Section 1.3).

In this book we shall be introducing new models for describing and solving engineering problems, together with a new language for representing the problems and their constituent pieces and methods. We do this because there is much more to engineering than can be described in (continuous) mathematical and numerical terms. For example, in Chapter 7 we shall present a preliminary but detailed taxonomy of engineering knowledge in which we identify and order the kinds of knowledge that we bring to bear when we do engineering. An outline of that taxonomy would have the following elements:

First principles. These are the basic physical laws of an engineering field. In structural engineering, the field of mechanics (a branch of physics) and the discipline of engineering mechanics would embody the first principles. Examples include Newton's laws of motion, conservation of momentum, and conservation of mass.

Phenomenological models. These are models—typically expressed as ratios, differential equations, or other nondiscrete mathematical forms— often based on experimental results or on compiled high-level extrapolations of the fundamental laws. Examples of such models include pressure-volume relations, stress-strain laws, and generalized force-deflection and mass-stiffness-frequency relations.

Analytical models. These are models, both exact and approximate, used to represent specific "cases" or subsets of the more general first principles and phenomenological models. These models typically employ continuous mathematics as their language for stating and manipulating the models. For example, in modeling elastic continua, we would apply special-case models to analyze the behavior of beams, columns, plates, and shells.

Numerical representations. These are the "numerical versions" of the analytical models just described. Perhaps the best-known examples in structural mechanics are the finite element codes that are in widespread use in structural and mechanical engineering, wherein polynomials are used to approximate continuous and compatible displacement and strain fields.

Heuristics. Inasmuch as heuristics or rules can be used to represent many different kinds of knowledge, this type of information transcends, in some sense, the entire hierarchy just listed. For example, rules may be used to express aspects of fundamental principles, compiled versions of both phenomenological and analytical models, preferences and assumptions about the use of numerical codes, experiential rules of thumb, and high-level knowledge about how to use other kinds of knowledge.

We can see from this list that while mathematical representations would be useful—if not absolutely essential— to the intelligent use of much of this knowledge, they are inadequate for other kinds of knowledge. In particular, much of the knowledge that we categorize as heuristic is simply not expressible in continuous mathematical formulas, although (as we will see in Chapter 3) they can be expressed in the "discrete" mathematics of formal logic. Thus, we must look to other ways to represent the kind of experiential and strategic knowledge that experts use to solve problems. For example, the choices made by an expert about *how* to solve a particular structures problem, choosing among analytical methods, numerical schemes, back-of-the-envelope calculations, experiments, and so on, are choices (with corresponding attributes) that cannot be described in formulas or with a numerical code. And while we might have a finite element model of a part we are designing, we typically cannot represent the function of the part within the product to which it belongs in such an algorithm, and there may be other attributes (e.g., color, fit, manufacturability) that also cannot be described in numerical symbols.

Thus, in order to capture other kinds of knowledge, we need some additional language tools. And we shall look at such tools in two ways.

❑   We will broaden the discussion of how we represent problems and the methods available to solve problems.

❑   We will introduce the notion of symbolic representation of the knowledge of an engineering domain.

In the first category we will present in Part I the ideas of search and of logic as ways of formulating problems. These techniques for formulating problems and solution approaches move us away from the idea of seeing every problem as the solution to a differential equation, whether analytical or numerical, and toward representing problem states as discrete elements in a space that must be searched in order to find a solution. As we shall see in Chapter 2, search gives us a new way of formulating problems so that we can look at problems in a way that classical methods do not permit. Similarly, the exercise of logic (see Chapters 3 and 4) allows us to apply formal techniques, especially deduction, to derive new facts from those currently believed to be true or to test the consistency of a proposed new fact with respect to an existing base of facts.

In the second category we shall introduce ways of representing the detailed knowledge that we use in search and logic. The new representation ideas will include rules to describe situations and consequent actions, semantic nets to order elementary objects into a meaningful organizational network, and frames or structured objects to characterize more complex objects and concepts and their attributes and relationships. These ideas are based on symbolic representation, in which we use a symbolic language for the objects, concepts, and so on. We shall then be able to describe nonnumerical characteristics and purposes for objects in addition to their mass and dimensions. Thus, we shall have a whole new way of modeling artifacts and of reasoning about them.

There are two final points that ought to be made here. The first is that we are acknowledging in the foregoing discussion that we have options about how we choose to represent and use knowledge. Indeed, we might borrow a wonderful quote from Stefik [1982b] to express the central theme of this book: "Knowledge is an artifact, worthy of design." That is, it is worth thinking about how we choose to express and exploit knowledge. There are choices to be made, and it is worth choosing wisely and well.

The second point is also somewhat philosophical, and it is important in a practical sense as well. One of the ideas that emerges rather explicitly in the discussion of symbolic representation is that of **abstraction**, in which we look at descriptions at various levels of detail and try to abstract at a given level just that set of details or attributes or ideas that are needed to answer a given question. Thus it is important to keep in mind the questions being asked and the kinds of information required to answer those questions. In a similar vein, it is quite important that we remember, in all kinds of modeling, both in the traditional mathematics-based approaches and those presented in this book, that we are dealing with realizations or abstractions of reality, not with reality itself. As noted by the semanticist Korzybski (see [Hayakawa 1978]), "The symbol *is not* the thing symbolized. The map *is not* the territory. The word *is not* the thing." We must constantly be aware as we model things, numerically or symbolically, that we are invoking assumptions and implying restrictions as we create or apply our models. Thus we must always be on guard that we do not violate our assumptions and premises, and that our results are consistent with our starting assumptions.

1.3 THE ROLE OF COMPUTATION IN ENGINEERING

What is the role of computation in engineering? The standard answer would no doubt reflect advances in numerical codes and algorithms, graphics, and the manipulation of large spreadsheets and databases. Indeed, it may well be said that advances in computer science go hand in hand with advances in engineering, as it is often applications that motivate and drive progress in computational technique. A very obvious example has been the advent of large-scale finite element method (FEM) codes, which have roots in applied mathematics and numerical analysis and whose conceptual development proceeded along parallel paths in structural analysis, algorithm development, and hardware advances. We show in Figure 1-2 a pictorial view of these interactive developments.

Computers have become ubiquitous and are involved in every phase of engineering. The kinds of computers used range from desktop personal computers through mainframe supercomputers. The kinds of tasks range from elementary modeling for analysis and design, through the preparation of documents and drawings, to highly developed supercomputer and parallel algorithms used for numerical modeling such things as weather patterns and complex fluid flow problems involving highly nonlinear partial differential equations. In all of these applications, notwithstanding the use of word processing and graphics, the principal element of representation for computing is the representation of numbers.

From a broader perspective, computers have allowed us—as engineers—to assimilate and exploit much more knowledge than we could just a few years ago, and at a much faster rate. Thus we can model more complex phenomena, in a more satisfying way, and as a result we can design more complex and sophisticated artifacts. In some sense, as we have developed and applied more powerful algorithms and graphics packages, we have really applied a powerful idea about computing: "It has often been said that a person really doesn't understand something until he teaches it to someone else. Actually a person doesn't really understand something until he can teach it to a computer, i.e., express it as an algorithm. . . . The attempt to formalize things as algorithms leads to a much deeper understanding than if we simply try to understand things in the traditional way" [Knuth 1973].

Knuth's quote is quite relevant to our present concerns, even though the focus is different than the development of (numerical) algorithms. Indeed, the idea of "teaching" something to a computer is central to the idea of knowledge-based systems, as the definitions presented in Sections 1.4 and 1.5 make abundantly clear. We now have an increasing capability to teach the computer knowledge that is representable in symbolic terms so that we can introduce the qualitative aspects of engineering which cannot be captured as numbers or algorithms. That is, we can now program conceptual reasoning, rules of thumb, judgement calls, and so on. And, in fact, the entire thrust of this book is that we now have the ability to do better engineering because we can encode much more knowledge and in much more accessible and useful ways. We will see, especially in the detailed discussions of engineering knowledge-based systems (Chapters 10 through 12), that we can go well beyond the algorithmic black boxes which are in widespread and daily use. We can now think in terms of **intelligent assistants** which incorporate useful forms of human expertise that can be

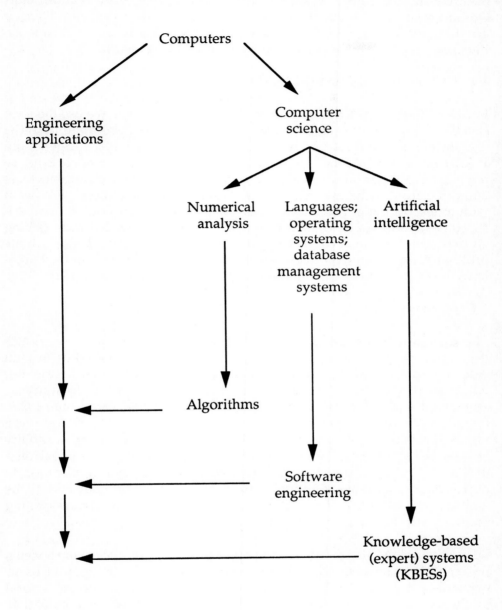

Figure 1-2 A pictorial view of the relation between developments in computer science and engineering applications (adapted from [Fenves 1982]).

applied in different ways and that can produce advice about and explanations for the problems they are called upon to solve. Thus, if anything, computers will become even more central to our ability to do intelligent engineering in an increasingly technological world.

1.4 KNOWLEDGE-BASED SYSTEMS DEFINED

In this section we describe and define what we mean when we use the term *knowledge-based (expert) system*. Definitions of such systems abound in the literature (see [Bobrow 1986b; Brachman 1983; Dym 1985a; Feigenbaum 1983; Fenves 1982; Maher 1987a] as well as the references cited in these papers). However, all the definitions are similar in their basic structures and differ from each other only in slight nuances and variations. We begin with a description of human expertise, which we then follow with an AI-based description of types of knowledge. This sets the stage for describing an expert system and contrasting it with the more familiar algorithmic programming. Then we will present some formal definitions of knowledge-based systems. Much of the discussion parallels that of Dym [1985a].

1.4.1 Knowledge in AI

The roots of knowledge-based programming lie in the field of AI, which may be said to be the science that tries to replicate intelligent human behavior on computers. (For a historical perspective of the development of AI, see [Dreyfus 1986; Feigenbaum 1983; McCorduck 1979]). In studying knowledge and its use, we find many interesting features [Brachman 1983]. It turns out, for example, that human expertise tends to be narrow and highly specialized. Further, what distinguishes the true expert is the ability to rapidly recognize patterns in and bring appropriate rules to bear on a problem. Although the rules are often heuristic, it is their application to narrow the search of a solution space that is important. But one of the hallmarks of expertise is the ability of an expert to explain the reasoning that was used to solve a given problem.

Researchers in AI also divide knowledge into surface and deep components [Hart 1982]. The term **deep knowledge** refers to reasoning from basic principles, that is, from basic laws of nature or structural and behavioral models. **Surface knowledge** is that heuristic, experiential knowledge that comes from having successfully solved a large number of similar problems. In current usage, surface knowledge, although very often useful, is regarded as being based on experience rather than being grounded on first principles or based on deep knowledge. The distillation of deep knowledge into an efficient, optimized form results in **compiled knowledge**, which is often confused with surface knowledge [Chandrasekaran 1984]. The ability to explain heuristics in terms of first principles, for example, indicates compiled knowledge, while the application of the same rules simply because they work is typical of surface knowledge.

In our own work in engineering, we might recognize here a very loose analogy between having access to a full-blown finite element package which might solve any well-posed mechanics problem, on the one hand, and, on the other hand, having available an experienced consultant who can identify and provide acceptable solutions for critical problems on the back of an envelope. Although is is sometimes wrongly—and unfortunately—characterized as surface knowledge, it is just that compiled expertise which is most useful—and therefore most prized—for knowing when and how to apply deep knowledge. At the same time, compiled deep knowledge is also prized because it alone can often be successfully applied beyond the limits of existing formal theory. One example is that an auto mechanic can diagnose and repair an automobile engine, but only a mechanical engineer can design a new engine.

1.4.2   Definitions of Knowledge-Based Systems

A **knowledge-based (expert) system** (**KBES**) is a computer program that performs a task normally done by an expert or consultant and which, in so doing, uses captured, heuristic knowledge. If we think of a computer program as being a collection of rules that describe actions to be taken, then the familiar algorithmic program may be viewed as one where the sequence of **firing**, or testing and applying, the rules is determined in advance and where each rule premise or condition leads to one—and only one—action. That is, progress in such a program is controlled by a tightly knit algorithm. Further, in a conventional algorithmic program, the processing is done using symbols to represent numbers, arithmetic properties (e.g., inequalities), and mathematical operations.

In contrast, in a knowledge-based system, the sequence of rule firing is determined by an inference engine that is contained within the program, and the conditions required to fire any rule(s) may lead to multiple actions or to no action at all. The collection of rules in such a system may incorporate heuristics or rules of thumb that are accumulated by an expert over years of problem solving. This allows the expert system to reason as it performs a task, as well as adapt to new data or new situations.

The symbols in a knowledge-based system are used to represent virtually any kind of object, including artifacts, people, materials, biological organisms, classes of objects, concepts, and so on. We shall see many examples of this throughout the text (see especially Chapters 5 through 7), but the really interesting point is that we are intent on seeing and manipulating symbols as something other than numbers, hence we need very different programming language features and facilities.

Another distinction between conventional algorithmic programming and the AI-based programming that is reflected in knowledge-based systems could be said to be in the programming style [Bobrow 1986a]. In conventional programming, which is often called **procedural programming**, we tell the computer what must be done with the data subsequently entered. Thus, in procedural programming the procedures are our representation of *how* we want something done. In knowledge-based programming, on the other hand, we are representing **declarative knowledge** about a domain; that is, we are representing *what* we know without deciding in advance precisely how that knowledge will be used.

There is, in fact, something to be said for the idea that knowledge-based systems can be viewed as "nothing more" than a new style of programming [Bobrow 1986a]. In this context, we summarize in Table 1-1 the distinctions between the two programming styles. Two points are particularly worth noting here. The first, consistent with the dichotomy of procedural versus declarative styles just mentioned, is the fact that in procedural programming we talk about manipulating *data*, while in declarative programming we are concerned with representing *knowledge*. The second, and more important, point is the attribute of *separating knowledge from control* that is characteristic of knowledge-based programming. In procedural programming we reflect our knowledge in the explicit content and ordering of the procedures and subroutines that are the very fabric of the algorithm, so that changing the way a problem is handled—say, from modeling an inviscid fluid to modeling one that is highly viscous—requires a major rewriting of the program. We will see that in a knowledge-based system, the knowledge of the model about which we are reasoning is stored as declarative knowledge in a **knowledge base**; the use of that knowledge is governed by a control strategy stored in a separate **inference engine**. This gives us a great deal of flexibility, both in adding knowledge or otherwise changing the knowledge base and in exploring how different inference schemes might be exercised in order to achieve a solution.

One widely quoted definition of expert systems is given in [Gaschnig 1981].

> Expert systems are interactive computer programs incorpor-
> ating judgement, rules of thumb, intuition and other expertise
> to provide knowledgeable advice about a variety of tasks.

Table 1-1 Comparison of characteristics of conventional (procedural) and knowledge-based (declarative) programming (after [Maher 1987b])

Conventional Programs	KBESs
Representation and use of data	Representation and use of knowledge
Integration of knowledge and control	Separation of knowledge and control
Algorithmic processing	Inferential processing
Manipulation of large databases	Manipulation of large knowledge bases
Programmer ensures uniqueness, completeness	Relaxation of uniqueness, completeness
Run-time explanation is impossible	Run-time explanation is a (desirable) characteristic
Orientation: Numerical processing	Orientation: Symbolic processing

Another, and more extensive definition of an expert system is to be found in [Brachman 1983].

> An expert system is one that has expert rules and avoids blind search, reasons by manipulating symbols, grasps fundamental domain principles, and has complete weaker reasoning methods to fall back on when expert rules fail and to use in producing explanations. It deals with difficult problems in a complex domain, can take a problem description in lay terms and convert it to an internal representation appropriate for processing with its expert rules, and can reason about its own knowledge (or lack thereof), especially to reconstruct inference paths rationally for explanation and self-justification.

Brachman's definition is much more ambitious and, in addition, contains terms that are familiar to the AI community but not, as yet, to us. For example, we have yet to explicitly define *domain knowledge*, although we can readily infer the meaning of this phrase, nor have we defined *weaker reasoning methods*, although we will do so in Section 2.4.1. However, in its reference to an *internal representation*, this definition gives us a strong hint about what is a central focus of this book. It is this internal representation which allows a computer to manipulate those objects, concepts, and rules that are the basis for representing the knowledge we expect an expert system to have and display.

One drawback of Brachman's definition is its very emphasis on rules, because even though rules are very important to this enterprise both historically and practically, it is equally important that we always be aware of the roles to be played by other schemes for representing knowledge. Perhaps the most common misunderstanding of expert systems is the tendency—which should at all costs be avoided—to equate knowledge-based systems with rule-based systems. As we have already noted, much of this book is devoted to ways of representing knowledge, and while rules are important (see Chapter 5), there are other paradigms for representation and reasoning that serve to greatly extend the power and reach of KBESs (see especially Chapters 6 and 7).

1.4.3 Basic Architectures of Knowledge-Based Systems

The basic structure of a knowledge-based system is shown in Figure 1-3. We will describe first the components and second the actors that bring such a system into being. The components include

Input/output facilities that allow the user to communicate with the system and to create and use a database for the specific case at hand;

A **working memory** that contains the specific problem data and intermediate to final results produced by the system;

An **inference engine** that incorporates reasoning methods, which in turn acts upon the input data and the knowledge in the knowledge base to solve the stated problem and produce an explanation for the solution;

A **knowledge base** that contains the basic knowledge of the domain, including facts, beliefs, and that heuristic lore unique to the expert; and (perhaps)

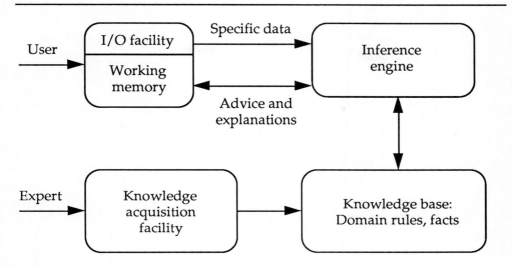

Figure 1-3   The components of a basic knowledge-based (expert) system (after [Dym 1985a; Feigenbaum 1983]).

A **knowledge acquisition facility** that allows the KBES to acquire further knowledge about the problem domain from experts, or even automatically, from libraries, databases, and so on.

The inference engine acts as the executive that runs the system. For example, in a rule-based system it selects rules according to a set of built-in criteria (we will discuss this in greater detail in Sections 5.3 and 5.4) and fires them in accordance with a built-in reasoning protocol. By so doing, the inference engine performs actions that lead to a solution of the problem and, at the same time, may change the knowledge base by adding to or otherwise modifying the knowledge contained therein. The knowledge base contains the **domain knowledge**, that is, the knowledge specific to the domain or field in which the problem is defined—knowledge which has typically been elicited from one or more experts. (We will discuss the knowledge engineering process in extenso in Chapter 12.) The inference engine and the knowledge base are generally viewed as separate components, but we will see that there is much overlap and interaction between the concepts underlying both.

In Figure 1-4 we display a more elaborate structure for a KBES in which we highlight in particular the **explanation facility** that explains to the user the

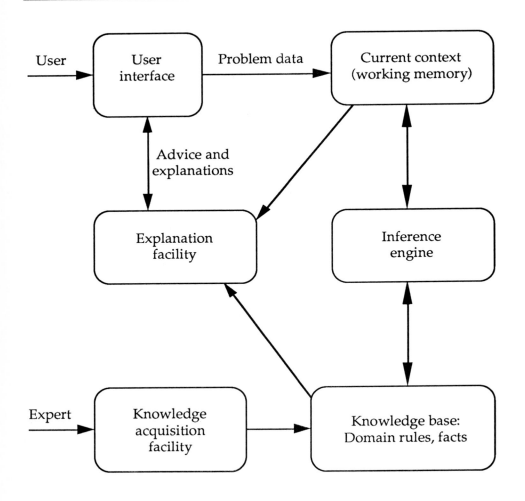

Figure 1-4 The components of a more elaborate knowledge-based (expert) system (after [Maher 1987b]).

reasoning behind any particular problem solution. In the same way that we ascribe credibility to human experts on the basis of their ability to explain their reasoning, we look to expert systems to exhibit the very important quality of **transparency**, that is, of making their chain of reasoning explicit so that the user may judge its plausibility. (See Chapter 6 for a detailed discussion of how transparency is achieved in a KBES.)

The separation of the domain-specific knowledge from the control strategy of the inference engine has provided an interesting and powerful incentive to builders of KBESs: the same inference engine can be used in conjunction with knowledge drawn from different domains to make different expert systems from the same basic building blocks. This idea has been quite advantageously exploited in many areas, and we shall describe in detail an application in structural mechanics when we discuss rule-based systems in Chapter 5. The same notion has led to research in and development of system-building environments, or shells, which can be used in different domains to build systems that do different kinds of tasks (see Chapters 4, 7, and 12).

What types of actors are involved in the building of expert systems? There are three, two of whom—the user(s) and the expert(s)—are depicted in Figures 1-3 and 1-4. What is not shown is the role of the **knowledge engineer**, the one who historically has been the architect and builder of the KBES. This is typically someone who is skilled in AI techniques, especially knowledge-based programming, who elicits, models, and structures the expert's expert knowledge so that it can be encoded in a KBES for access by one or more users. We shall devote a good part of Chapter 12 to discussion of the knowledge engineering process by which these systems are built, but for now we note that the distinctions between the various roles are becoming blurred as increasing numbers of domain experts are learning knowledge-based programming. Thus, we are seeing more KBES applications built by domain experts themselves. This tendency is also being hastened along with the development of increasingly powerful programming environments that are themselves more accessible to domain experts (see Chapters 6 and 12).

There is one more type of architecture to be mentioned here, although it is one that is only now moving from being a subject of research in the AI community toward being a tool for engineering application. **Blackboard architectures** represent an approach to problem solving in which an assembly of knowledge sources are permitted to respond *opportunistically* as the solution develops. The knowledge sources actually represent a decomposition of the knowledge base according to some hierarchical or functional scheme so that each knowledge source represents one aspect (or level or perspective) of the problem being solved. Further, each source only comes into play when its level or perspective can provide some useful input to the solution as it is being developed. The notion of the blackboard comes into play because the solution is developed thereon and the sources are "reading" that blackboard to see if they have an opportunity to apply their specific knowledge. The blackboard idea was originally developed in the HEARSAY system for speech understanding [Erman 1980]. A nice overview of this architecture can be found in [Nii 1986]. We shall touch on this architecture again when we discuss the notion of using interacting KBESs to solve problems in a cooperative fashion in Chapter 8.

1.5 KNOWLEDGE-BASED SYSTEMS IN ENGINEERING

We now complete our introduction to the book by listing some of the recent work on applying knowledge-based systems to engineering and by providing pointers to related work. Applications can be found in all the engineering disciplines, and they are all relatively new. (Recall that the technology is itself young and that the propagation speed from computer science to engineering has been relatively slow.) Note that in outlining these developments we shall not include those research efforts where the focus was the development and application of new representation techniques to what are, in serious engineering terms, "toy" problems. Thus, for example, while early work in qualitative physics used electronic circuits as a domain (see Chapter 7), the intent was not to solve an engineering problem but to illustrate a new AI approach.

A listing of some of the applications to engineering by task type should include the following:

Diagnosis   SPERIL-I and SPERIL-II for diagnosing possible causes of structural failure [Ishizuka 1981; Ogawa 1984]

DELTA for diagnosing malfunctions in electric locomotives [Bonissone 1983]

SACON for advising on how to use a large finite element package [Bennett 1984]

Interpretation PROSPECTOR for interpreting geological surface data to evaluate potential mineral deposits [Campbell 1982]

CONPHYDE for prediction of physical properties in chemical engineering processing [Banares-Alcantara 1983]

Dipmeter Advisor for interpreting boring log results [Smith 1984]

CONE for interpreting soil samples [Mullarkey 1985]

Monitoring   PLATFORM for monitoring the status of an ongoing construction project and forecasting durations of remaining activities [Levitt 1985]

Planning   ISIS for planning work flow in a job shop scheduling environment [Fox 1987]

PLANEX for planning in construction [Zozaya-Gorostiza 1989]

Design   HI-RISE for the preliminary design of high-rise buildings [Maher 1984a]

PRIDE for the mechanical design of paper-handling subsystems in copier machines [Mittal 1986a]

This list is representative; however, it is certainly not exhaustive. It is meant to illustrate the variety of engineering tasks to which KBES techniques can be usefully applied. We should note in this regard that as the technology has become more familiar, the sophistication of the applications has increased dramatically. The earliest systems were invariably rule-based (see Chapter 5), but increasingly, engineers and other system developers are using frames and object-oriented programming techniques (see Chapter 6) and more general representation languages and programming environments (see Chapter 4).

We shall describe several engineering KBESs in much greater detail in the applications part of the book (Part III), and the reader is encouraged to read the literature for information on past and more current applications. Extensive bibliographies of KBES engineering applications can be found in [Dym 1985b; Maher 1987a; Waterman 1986]. Among the leading journals in this area are *Artificial Intelligence for Engineering Design, Analysis and Manufacturing*, published by Academic Press; *Artificial Intelligence for Engineering*, published by Computational Mechanics Ltd.; and *IEEE Computer* and *IEEE Expert*, published by the Computer Society of the Institute of Electrical and Electronics Engineers.

PART

I

CONCEPTUAL UNDERPINNINGS

In this part of the book we shall introduce two ways of looking at problems that depart sharply from the traditional applied mathematics models that we employ in the engineering sciences. In particular, the focus of this section is on the formulation of problems, on their representation when standard approaches such as differential equations do not provide an adequate means for stating (and solving) a problem. Thus, the concern of this section can be seen as representation for problem solving.

In Chapter 2 we look at the concept of searching for solutions within a space that contains not only a solution to the problem under consideration, but also definitions of initial and final problem states; partial, incomplete, or wrong solutions; and other relevant information about the problem, such as the relations between states and the operators that are used to move from state to state. Clearly, in a large, complex problem encompassing many variables, choices, and decision points, the number of states that need to be examined and evaluated can be prohibitively large. Thus, in this discussion, we will need to examine two kinds of search. First we describe exhaustive search algorithms that are used to generate and examine every conceivable state in a search space. Then we examine guided or directed search, in which knowledge about the problem domain is used to guide the search and to make more informed choices during the search.

In Chapter 3 we introduce formal logic systems. These are mathematically precise languages that allow one to deduce logically consistent new facts from a given database of facts by the application of logical inferences. As we shall also see, however, an almost infinite number of possible deductions could be made from a database of any significant size. Hence, deduction must usually be guided by the kinds of directed search strategy described in Chapter 2 so as to find solutions to nontrivial problems efficiently.

We close Part I with Chapter 4, where we describe the ways in which the construction of highly stylized programming languages facilitates computer-based reasoning. The principal features of the two languages most used in knowledge-based programming, Lisp and Prolog, are outlined.

Chapter 2

PROBLEM FORMULATION AND SEARCH

2.1 INTRODUCTION

In this chapter we shall introduce the concept of searching for solutions within a search space. A search space, often called a problem space, is an imaginary space that contains not only a solution to the problem under consideration, but also definitions of initial and final states; partial, incomplete, or wrong solutions; and other relevant information about the problem, such as the relations between states and the operators that are used to move from state to state. In order to make this more concrete, we need to talk about representation. Moreover, we need to discuss representation in two contexts: representation for problem solving and representation for computing. The latter case, representation for computing, is dealt with in detail in Chapter 4, where we discuss programming languages, and in Part II, under the rubric of implementation techniques (that is, in a discussion of methods of representing domain knowledge so as to allow us to do computation with that knowledge).

For the present, however, we are concerned with ways of representing problems so that they can be readily solved, or at least so that the structure and the important and relevant features of a problem appear when and where they can be best exploited. One may wonder why this needs to be discussed here. After all, can't we simply write down and solve—even if "only" numerically—the appropriate equations for the problem and be done with it? Well, as might already be clear from Chapter 1, the answer to that question is "No!" This is because we are interested in formulating and solving problems for which our more conventional mathematical models are inadequate, either for stating these problems or, as a consequence, for solving them. Examples of such problems will follow very soon in this chapter and in the remainder of the book. It is important to keep in mind that we are *not* dismissing mathematical approaches to problem solving, especially those approaches of the mechanistic, deterministic variety that form the basis of much of how we think about the physical world that is the central concern of engineering. What we *are* saying is that these models can be augmented by other kinds of problem-solving approaches that will enable us to do even better engineering.

The organization of this chapter parallels the foregoing discussion in that we begin by examining different ways of stating or representing problems. We cite here two classic examples from the AI literature on problem formulation and introduce some of the ideas and nomenclature of problem solving and of state space search. Then we present the relatively straightforward exhaustive search algorithms that are used to generate and examine every conceivable state in a search space. Clearly, the number of states that need to be examined and evaluated can be prohibitively large in a large, complex problem that encompasses many variables, choices, and decision points. AI researchers call this phenomenon the **combinatorial explosion**. This phenomenon requires special search techniques in which we use knowledge about the problem domain to guide the search and to make more informed choices during the search. Next we discuss these techniques for directed search, and then we look at how exhaustive and guided search techniques can be combined to exploit their respective advantages in domains where such combinations offer useful leverage. Finally, we consider how knowledge-based systems can be seen as tools for implementing guided or directed search.

2.2 FORMULATION AND REPRESENTATION OF PROBLEMS

2.2.1 Missionaries and Cannibals

We begin by focusing on problem statement and formulation, that is, on how we describe what we are looking for and under what conditions. We will introduce along the way some of the ideas and terminology of search. We will do this by looking at some classic examples taken from the literature on problem solving, remembering that these examples are intended to highlight "new" ways of representing problems so that, in turn, we can introduce new ways of looking for solutions. Consider the **missionaries-and-cannibals** (M & C) problem, which can be stated as follows:

> Three missionaries and three cannibals seek to cross a river. A boat is available which will hold two people and which can be navigated by any combination of missionaries and cannibals involving one or two people. If the missionaries on either bank of the river, or en route in the river, are outnumbered at

any time by cannibals, the cannibals will indulge in their anthropophagic tendencies and do away with the missionaries. Find a schedule of crossings that will permit all the missionaries and cannibals to cross the river safely. (After [Amarel 1968])

In this problem we have a clearly defined **initial state**, six people on one side of a river, and a clearly defined **goal state**, all six having moved safely to the other side of the river. The objective is the determination of a safe path between the initial state and the goal state. What we also have is a wordy problem statement that perhaps raises more questions than it answers. For example, do we need to worry about the width of the river? Food supplies? Carry-on luggage restrictions? More important, how do we identify and enumerate any safe configurations that may exist between the initial and goal states? And, assuming that a safe passage can be found for the three missionaries and the three cannibals of this problem, can we extrapolate that solution to more extended cases—for example, five missionaries and five cannibals with a boat that seats three?

The solution presented here will make explicit the answers to the above questions, and it is extensible to higher-order cases. In order to clearly delineate the intermediate states between the initial and goal states, we construct a set of **nodes**, each of which represents a possible arrangement of the three missionaries and the three cannibals arrayed on both sides of the river (see Figure 2-1). The dashed line in each node, or box, represents the river. Inasmuch as there are six people who can each be in one of two places, it would appear that there are some 64 possible arrangements. However, a little thought suggests that we really need to consider only what happens on one riverbank—the left bank, say—because each arrangement on that bank has a unique complement on the other bank. Thus, if we adopt the notation of representing a state on the left bank as (#M, #C, +/−), where the sign indicates the presence or absence of the boat, it is clear that only 32 independent states can be identified (see Figure 2-2).

Many of these states can be excluded from further consideration. States (3, 3, −) and (0, 0, +), for example, are untenable because the boat cannot end up on a bank without any people. The exclusion of these states is an instance of making clear and explicit a **constraint** that had heretofore been implicit, a matter of common sense that was not mentioned in the problem statement. Further, in view of the explicit constraint that the number of cannibals can never exceed the number of missionaries, many of the remaining configurations can also be deleted. Note that when we are applying this constraint, we must remember to exclude those arrangements

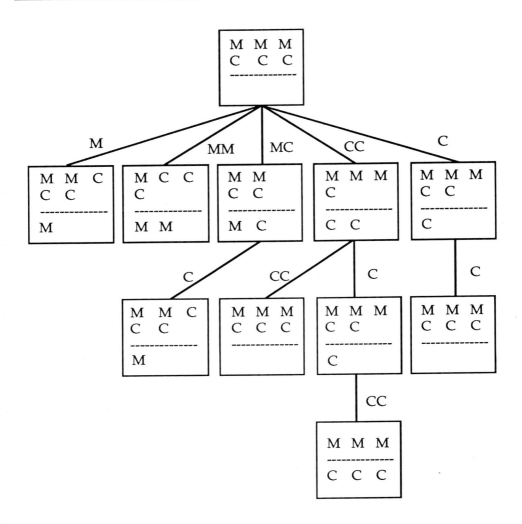

Figure 2-1 A node-and-link representation of the missionaries-and-cannibals problem. The dashed line in each box (node) represents the river, and the links are annotated with the types of moves leading from one node to the next.

that themselves look safe but whose complements violate the constraint. Thus, not only are the states (2, 3, +/−), (1, 3, +/−), and (1, 2, +/−) not allowable, but the complements of (2, 1, +/−), (2, 0, +/−), and (1, 0, +/−)

(3, 3, +)	(2, 3, +)	(1, 3, +)	(0, 3, +)
(3, 3, –)	(2, 3, –)	(1, 3, –)	(0, 3, –)
(3, 2, +)	(2, 2, +)	(1, 2, +)	(0, 2, +)
(3, 2, –)	(2, 2, –)	(1, 2, –)	(0, 2, –)
(3, 1, +)	(2, 1, +)	(1, 1, +)	(0, 1, +)
(3, 1, –)	(2, 1, –)	(1, 1, –)	(0, 1, –)
(3, 0, +)	(2, 0, +)	(1, 0, +)	(0, 0, +)
(3, 0, –)	(2, 0, –)	(1, 0, –)	(0, 0, –)

Figure 2-2 A tabular listing or representation of the 32 independent states in the missionaries-and-cannibals problem. The numbers in each pair of parentheses represent the number of missionaries and the number of cannibals, respectively; the sign (+/–) indicates the presence or absence of the boat.

require that those six states also be deleted from the list of acceptable arrangements. Then, after all the constraints have been applied, there are only 18 safe states left to consider. Now we must figure out how to move between the remaining states.

The transitions between the various states are represented by **links**, also called **directed arcs**, which connect the states or nodes. A few of the nodes and links are shown in Figure 2-3, arranged here in the form of a **tree**. The initial state appears in the tree as the **root node**, and we see that this node is **expanded** into five states (some of which we already know to be inadmissible). Node expansion occurs here through the simple expedient of making all the moves that can be made in one boat trip from the initial state of the root node. The possible moves are five, as the boat can be taken by either a cannibal or a missionary, by two of each, or in one trip by one of each. The resulting states, the **child nodes** of the tree, are shown in the second layer of the tree. This process can then be continued, with each of the five nodes being expanded, and their children expanded in turn, and

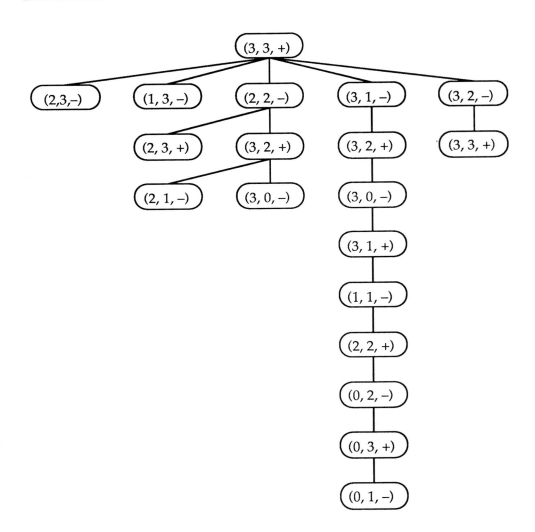

Figure 2-3 A partial search tree for the missionaries-and-cannibals problem, showing several layers of development. Note the generation of multiple copies of some nodes, as well as nodes representing inadmissible states.

so on, until a state identifiable as a goal state—the state $(0, 0, -)$—is reached. Once the goal state is found, the search can be concluded, the path back to the initial state can be retraced and printed, and success can be announced.

search [Nilsson 1980]. However, whereas breadth-first search produces this solution after expanding 26 nodes, the heuristic solution requires that only 6 nodes be expanded! The use of this simple heuristic thus produces a clear win.

And why do we call it a heuristic? Simply put, because it works! That is to say, we often have good reasons—based on experience or grounded in first principles—for choosing a heuristic, but what makes a heuristic a good heuristic is the fact that it works.

2.2.3 Search and Engineering Problems

It is clear from the foregoing that many interesting problems can be formulated as search problems and that a variety of "nonstandard" (i.e., other than classical applied mathematics) representation techniques can usefully employed in this process. What may be less clear, however, is the relationship of search to real engineering problems (especially in view of the focus above on problems that are classics of the AI literature). Thus, this is an appropriate point at which to make that connection more evident. Recall that in Chapter 1 we discussed Amarel's spectrum of problem solving [Amarel 1978]. Here we illustrate how some engineering examples of the various classes of problems [Dym 1985a] can be cast as search problems (after [Stefik 1990]).

Diagnosis. Find the sets of possible causes, consistent with domain knowledge, that explain the observed symptoms in a failed structural system.

Diagnosis/selection. Identify an analysis strategy and the corresponding tool(s) for analyzing a structure under certain constraints on time, cost, and degree of accuracy required of the answer.

Interpretation. Locate the source and determine the magnitude of an earthquake from ground motion data recorded at several remote seismometers.

Monitoring. Identify the states that require action, as well as the actions to be taken during the processing of polymers in a chemical plant.

Planning. Find the sequence of steps required to ensure that construction equipment of the appropriate type and capacity arrives on-site at the right time.

Design. Identify in terms of their type, dimensions, materials, and locations the set of devices that are required to move paper through a copying machine.

Lest it be thought that these are "made-up" textbook examples, let it be noted that each of these problems is representative of specific applications of knowledge-based systems to engineering domains and problems. (More on this in our discussion of applications in Chapters 11 and 12!) For now, however, we are content to make the point that the ideas of search can play a useful role in the formulation and representation of engineering problems. In particular, we shall see that the notions of search are central to the exploration of the knowledge-based systems that are the primary focus of this book. Thus, it is clearly worthwhile for us to discuss state space search in greater detail.

2.3 STATE SPACE SEARCH

2.3.1 Search Trees and Graphs

We seek now to generalize and learn from our two sample problems so that we can apply similar techniques and ideas to problems that are more interesting and significant to us as engineers. To do this well, we need to establish a common vocabulary, as free as possible from ambiguity, so that we can easily share ideas. The definitions we present are culled from and consistent with those found in the standard reference works on AI which are listed at the end of the book. We also note that the fundamental definitions are spread across Sections 2.3.1 through 2.3.4 as we define (1) trees and graphs as ways of representing the search space; (2) directions for conducting the search of a given tree (or graph); (3) problem characteristics; and (4) problem-solving strategies as mechanisms for traversing a search tree (or graph). The selection of a strategy is a decision that depends on the domain, the nature of the problem, and the available data. The selection of a search direction can be made independent of the choice of strategy, but it is strongly linked to the shape of the tree that will be generated as the search unfolds.

The first definition we offer is a formalization of one stated at the beginning of this chapter. A **search space**, also called a **problem space**, is a space within which is contained the set of states of the problem being considered, the **operators** or moves that describe transitions between states, and the specifications of the initial state from which the solution process begins and the goal state which defines the end of the search for a solution. The various states in the space are also often referred to as **nodes**, especially where a search tree or graph is used to organize the search space. If each node or state in the space represents or describes an actual configuration of the evolving solution, then the problem space is called a **state space**. In the M & C problem, for example, the nodes were initially represented by the boxes illustrated in Figure 2-1, that is, the various configurations into which the problem's six people could be organized. The operators were represented by the links between the nodes, as these links indicated the possible moves that individual or paired missionaries and cannibals could make between states. In our search for the solution, the representation of the nodes was rather different, as can be seen in Figure 2-3.

The search of the state space can be thought of as the traversal of a search tree in which each state of the problem is represented by a node and the nodes are, again, connected by links or directed arcs.   These arcs incorporate (via operators) the relationships between the states they connect. (See Figure 2-3 for an example of a search tree.) The initial state is the root node of the tree. As any given node is expanded, it is termed a **parent node**; its successors are called variously children or successor nodes or descendant nodes. A node that has no successors or children is called a **tip node** or **leaf node**. (Note that in terms of these definitions, the root node has no parent.) Thus, the process of expanding a node is the process of generating its successors. A node is said to be **open** until it is expanded; afterward, it is said to be **closed**. Also, in keeping with the analogy of trees, we often speak of the **branches** of a search tree when we wish to refer to any nodes and links stemming from a particular node of the tree.

A search tree is a special case of a **search graph**. In a tree, as we have seen, nodes are very often repeated; that is, duplicates or copies of nodes appear as the tree unfolds. This is due to the fact that each node in a tree has only one parent. An alternative expansion of the search would be one where we seek to establish whether or not a newly created node already exists. If this node has been generated earlier in the search, we don't have to expand it again. Rather, we can just display a link from this new copy's parent back to the first version of the copy (see Figure 2-6). In this case we see that a given node may have several parents, and that the root node itself may have parents if copies of it appear later in the search.

A significant computational issue arises as to whether it is worth checking each new node to see if it is a copy of a node previously generated, or whether it might be as well to simply expand each node as if it were totally new and thus ignore any redundancy in the computation. That is, in any given search, we must calculate the tradeoff between the cost of checking a node for redundancy and the cost of generating redundant branches of the search tree.

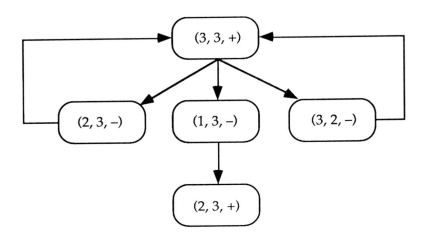

Figure 2-6 A partial search graph for the M & C problem.

2.3.2 Data- and Goal-Driven Reasoning

Having defined a tree as a representation for a problem, we must decide how to traverse it, which is in part a question of deciding on a search direction. That is, we could search forward from the initial state(s), backward from the goal state(s), or perhaps forward and backward at the same time. The choice depends largely on the characteristics of the tree and the structure of the data. However, there are two basic strategies for making moves up or down a tree, and they are functions more of the tree topology or shape than of the other dimensions of a problem.

In the search of a tree, movement occurs because some condition or set of conditions triggers an operator. The operators can be viewed as **condition-action** statements which define actions to be taken if certain conditions are met. (We shall see in Chapter 5 that search operators are quite often expressed in terms of rules or if-then statements.) In the first of the two basic styles of moving through a search space, we match the problem data against the condition statements of the available operator(s), find those operator(s) that are applicable, and then take the actions dictated by those operators(s). This is **data-driven reasoning**, or **forward reasoning**.

In the other style we first examine the action statements of the operators to see which of them have as their consequences the goals we wish to achieve. For those operators which have the desired outcomes, we examine the condition statements to see what facts are required to enable their invocation. If the relevant facts are not available to trigger these operators, we take the establishment of these facts as subgoals, and we search recursively in this fashion. This is **goal-driven reasoning**, or **backward reasoning**.

How do we decide on a direction for searching or traversing a tree? The principal determinants of this decision are the shape of the tree, as expressed in its branching factor, and the relative number of initial states. The **branching factor** is the average number of child nodes that can be reached from a node as a tree is traversed. And, as a general principle, one should try to move through a tree in the direction of the lowest branching factor. If the branching factor is roughly the same in either direction, then the choice would depend on how the number of initial states relates to the number of goal states, and we should work in the direction toward which the relative number is greatest. Let us illustrate these principles with a few elementary examples [Rich 1983].

Consider first how we would identify a route for driving from home or office to some facility in an area that we do not know well. Would we be better off to construct a chain forward from our familiar starting place or to work backward from our destination? Intuition and experience indicate that we should work backward from the intended destination, as we generally do when we pore over a map seeking a direction. Why do we do this? Clearly, the branching factor would be pretty much the same in either direction, barring a pathological number of detours or one-way streets. However, it is also true that there are many more places that look familiar as we near our home or office. Thus, as we work backward from our destination, there are that many more places that can be treated as subgoals that bring us closer to the goal state.

Another example occurs in the domain of axiomatic theorem proving. In particular, in what direction should we search to establish a particular theorem from a given set of axioms? In this instance, inasmuch as it is likely that any number of theorems could be deduced from a given set of axioms, we are better off searching backward from the theorem we would like to prove, treating that as a goal to be achieved, because the branching factor is clearly lower in this direction.

It is also worth pointing out that backward reasoning is possible only if there is an *explicit statement* of *the* goal state—or of very few possible goal states. This suggests that problems with a large number of goal states would not be amenable to backward reasoning, as in chess, for example, where the number of checkmates is very large. Moreover, and perhaps more important, for those problems where we have only an *implicitly* defined goal, where the solution is specified by **constraints**—conditions that must be met—it is impossible to reason backward.

There are situations in which a **bidirectional search** can be undertaken— that is, where we could reason forward from the data and backward from the goal(s) at the same time. Ideally, this would be quite efficient and we would achieve a solution as the two searches intersect. However, it is also conceivable that the two searches could slip right past each other as they both work to narrow their respective paths.

2.3.3 Problem Characteristics

A few thoughts on characterizing problems are appropriate here, in an- ticipation of our outline of strategies for solving problems. This discussion is at a different level of abstraction than our discussion in Chapter 1 of Amarel's spectrum of problem types, and it is particularly relevant to our discussion of state space search. We may think of problems as being of one of three types: pathfinding problems, two-player games, and constraint satisfaction problems [Korf 1988].

Problems such as the 8-puzzle and the M & C problem epitomize the notion of pathfinding, in which the desired outcome is the specification of a set of moves from an initial state to a goal state. Theorem proving is yet another example. Engineering is filled with pathfinding problems, and in terms of Amarel's spectrum, there are examples from the derivative end of the spectrum to the formative.

Two-player games include chess, checkers, and other board games [Luce 1957]. Attempts to formulate these problems as search problems so as to render them computable have long been a part of AI research. They are also important in many aspects of operations research and economics, but they are not of direct interest to us in our present concerns.

Constraint satisfaction problems are very important both in search and in engineering applications. The objective in such problems is the estab- lishment of a goal state that can be described only implicitly at the start of the search. That is, we can describe features or characteristics of the desired solution, but we cannot state explicitly what the solution must be. In engineering design, especially, such problems abound.

Again, we want to reinforce the notion that the problem characteristics just mentioned are rather naive descriptions of problem solving. They represent descriptions at a level that gives no guidance about how to find paths or satisfy constraints. Thus, we still need both strategies for achieving these objectives and algorithms (or rules or operators) to tell us how to expand the nodes in a search tree so that the search can proceed.

2.3.4 Strategies for Solving Problems

Although we are striving for an unambiguous terminology, we should note that there are alternative ways of defining search. For example, a **search system** could be defined as having a database, a set of operators for manipulating the database, and a control strategy for applying the operators [Barr 1981]. This definition is not terribly different from that presented in Section 2.3.1, but it does make explicit the notion that the operators will be applied in accordance with some strategy for solving the problem at hand. This is important, for as we observed with our two puzzle problems, strategies of problem solving were being applied as the solutions were being sought through search. Recall that we referred to the generate-and-test strategy in the M & C problem, while in the 8-puzzle we introduced the idea of guided or heuristic search. Strategies for and ideas about solving problems are intimately tied to notions of search. Thus, it is useful to initiate here a discussion of some strategies for solving problems. At the same time, these definitions and descriptions are less abstract than the search problem characteristics described in Section 2.3.3, and they are more specific—at a lower level of abstraction—than the tasks of Amarel's spectrum presented in Chapter 1. Each of the strategies represents an approach to using search to find paths or satisfy constraints, and each can typically be used in classification tasks or in formation tasks.

Perhaps the most basic control strategy is generate-and-test, the strategy we applied to the M & C problem. In this strategy, we simply generate all the possible states in a systematic manner and then test each one to see if it is a goal state. No domain knowledge is applied here; we need only be careful that we generate every possible state so that we don't ignore any possible solutions. Ideally, in fact, the generator should be complete and nonredundant so that it generates every possible state, but only once. In addition to the generator, we need a tester that can evaluate each state generated to see if it is a goal state. Generate-and-test works well in domains where the number of possible states is relatively small so that the search performance is not degraded by the combinatorial explosion.

In its basic implementation, generate-and-test is an example of **blind search**, where no knowledge is applied to aid the search process. However, it can be extended to **directed** (or **guided**) **search** by applying domain knowledge to **prune** branches of the search tree to eliminate those branches which are unlikely to lead to a solution. This technique, hierarchical generate-and test [Stefik 1990], will be discussed further in Section 2.4.5.

Another basic strategy is that of **decomposition**, or **problem reduction**. Here we attempt to divide the problem into subproblems, each of which is presumably easier to solve. A familiar example is the process of breaking up complex integrals into ordered collections of simpler ones by using various algebraic and trigonometric identities. Decomposition is often useful in problems where the goals of a search can be subdivided: for example, where travel between two cities might be seen as achieving the subgoals of getting to the airport, catching a flight, landing at the destination airport, finding a taxi, and so on. In a mechanical design problem whose ultimate goal is the creation of plans for a certain part, subgoals could include defining the geometry, checking stress and deflection values, ascertaining manufacturability, and so on. The process of subdividing goals is often called **goal reduction** or, in more colloquial terms, "divide and conquer."

Still another strategy for solving problems is that called **match**, in which we compare a current state to a goal state and produce a description of the difference between the two states. This difference can then be used to drive the search by becoming the basis for choosing the next operator(s) to be applied to the current state. Match can thus be seen as an instance of bidirectional search. This strategy also clearly falls into the category of guided search, as we have to use domain knowledge to assess the values of the differences between states. There are several versions of implementing match, including simple and **hierarchical** match and **means-ends analysis** [Stefik 1990; Newell 1963]. Means-ends analysis also makes use of subgoals as it chooses operators to achieve subgoals along the path to attaining the overall goal of the search.

2.3.5 Stopping Criteria; Satisficing and Optimizing

We wish to note a distinction that is often extremely important in establishing an approach to a problem. We accept as routine the fact that many engineering problems have but a single solution. This happy result occurs, of course, because our linear mathematical models, which imply uniqueness of solution, work very well as descriptors of significant physical processes. It is also true, however, that even in cases where more than one solution can be found, we are often willing to accept without preference any one of the solutions rather than continue to search for other solutions. In the M & C problem, for example, we sought any safe path between the initial and goal states. In such a case, wherein any one of several solutions is considered acceptable, we say that we are **satisficing** because we are satisfied with a solution even if it may be other than optimal [Simon 1981].

The most obvious way to achieve a satisficing solution is to conduct an exhaustive search, stopping after any single solution is found. A more refined search would collect and order several solutions from an exhaustive search, assuming that there are several, and then choose among them. In the limit, of course, we could find all the solutions and select from among them the "best" solution according to some appropriate criteria. For example, we could have posed a different version of the M & C problem and sought the shortest safe path across the river, that is, the path with the smallest number of moves or transitions between states. In this instance, we are obviously **optimizing**—we are searching for the optimum solution.

Optimization is an important part of engineering, and it is a field in which significant advances have been made in recent decades [Gero 1985]. Nonetheless, it is also a field in which the focus has been much more on achieving better algorithmic results than on integrating notions of knowledge-guided search. Therefore, it is a topic that is currently more closely associated with the field of operations research than with our present concerns. As a result, beyond some brief discussion in Section 2.5, we shall not delve much into optimization in this book.

2.4 EXHAUSTIVE SEARCH

Sections 2.4 and 2.5 are devoted to descriptions of search algorithms and, to a lesser extent, some problem-solving strategies that make use of the algorithms. Thus, it is useful to point out again the relationships between the algorithms and the strategies. We noted earlier that the algorithms are used to develop information about the problem being solved and its intermediate states, while the strategies define how the information is to be used to reach a solution. This dichotomy can also be stated in terms of a classic AI paradigm that was originally spelled out for rule-based search [Nilsson 1980]. The facts and details of a problem represent the **declarative knowledge** of the domain. The algorithms that are concerned with the manipulation of that knowledge in the search process represent **procedural knowledge**. And, finally, we use the term **control knowledge** to describe the invocation of one or more strategies to solve a problem. Or, as Nilsson [1980] put it, the control knowledge consists of that "variety of processes, strategies and structures used to coordinate the entire problem-solving process." We might say, therefore, that this section will be concerned with representations of procedural and control knowledge for blind, uninformed search.

2.4.1 Weak Methods

The algorithms and strategies for exhaustive search—that is, those methods for straightforwardly expanding every single node in a search tree—are sometimes called the **weak methods** because, although they are very general, they lack the power associated with knowledge-guided search [Barr 1981]. Thus, their very generality implies a certain weakness. (These approaches are also referred to as **syntactic search** to reflect the fact that there is an emphasis on form or grammar, without the meaning or semantics implied by knowledge-guided search [Barr 1981].) We shall present in this section several algorithms for exhaustive search (plus two problem-solving strategies) in a form sometimes referred to as "structured English" ([Winston 1984a]; see also [Barr 1981; Charniak 1985; Nilsson 1980; Stefik 1990]). These structured statements mask many of the details necessary for their implementation—for example, "testing" a node also implies removing that node from its queue or stack—and we suggest that the reader work out all the steps necessary for implementation.

2.4.2 Breadth-First Search

As we observed in our discussion of the 8-puzzle (see Figure 2-5), **breadth-first search** attacks the search tree layer by layer—one layer at a time. That is, all the nodes at a given depth are examined to see if they might be solutions before any of them are expanded. In other words, breadth-first search pushes uniformly into the search tree [Winston 1984a]; breadth-first search examines all the children of one generation before moving on to the next [Stefik 1990].

Breadth-first search is probably most effectively used when most of the solutions are at relatively shallow depths in the tree. Further, it ought to be reasonably clear that once breadth-first search finds a solution node, the length of the path from the root node to the solution node is as short as possible, or in this sense optimum [Korf 1988]. A structured English algorithm for satisficing breadth-first search is as follows.

To implement a **breadth-first** search:

1.   Form a one-element queue consisting of the root node.

2.   Cycle through Steps a–c until the queue is empty.

   a.   Test the first queue element to see if it is a solution.

   b.   Exit with success if the tested element is a solution.

   c.   If the first element is not a solution, add its children to the *back* of the queue.

3.   Exit with failure if no solution is found.

When the solutions lie very far down in a tree, breadth-first search requires expensive processing of a large number of layers before getting down to those where the solution(s) might be found. Since an entire level of the tree must be saved to generate the next level, and since the computer memory required is proportional to the number of nodes saved, it is quite possible that the available memory can be exhausted rather quickly. The memory requirements are in fact proportional to the average branching factor raised to the power of the tree depth. Breadth-first search is thus a less than ideal choice because of this storage problem. As noted by Korf [1988], "breadth-first search tends to run out of space before we run out of patience."

2.4.3 Depth-First Search

In **depth-first search** we proceed from the root node by shooting straight down into the tree along any path. By convention the initial path is usually taken along the leftmost unexplored branch of a node—although this is not a requirement. We stop when we find a solution or when that branch terminates. In the latter case, we backtrack up the tree until we find the nearest ancestor node with untried children, from which node we plunge back down again. Thus, in contrast to breadth-first search's traversal across levels to visit "sibling" nodes, in depth-first search we visit child nodes first.

The structure of the depth-first algorithm is very much the same as that for breadth-first search, save only the crucial substitutions (in Step 2c) of *stack* for *queue* and *top* for *back*. (Most of the algorithms presented here have a very similar appearance and the differences between them are often rather subtle.) The algorithm is as follows.

To implement a **depth-first** search:

1. Form a one-element stack consisting of the root node.

2. Cycle through Steps a–c until the stack is empty.

    a. Test the top element of the stack to see if it is a solution.

    b. Exit with success if the tested element is a solution.

    c. If the first element is not a solution, add its children to the *top* of the stack.

3. Exit with failure if no solution is found.

The principal advantage of depth-first search is that its memory requirements are linearly proportional to the tree depth. This is because the algorithm needs to store only those nodes on the path from the root node to the current node. Thus, although the amount of time required—the **time complexity**—is the same for both depth-first search and breadth-first search [Stefik 1990], the smaller space requirements make depth-first search the preferred choice of these two algorithms.

The problem with depth-first search is that the search can go on indefinitely if there is no natural termination point. In order to avoid this, a **cutoff depth** is often used to limit the depth to which search can proceed. However, it is hard to make an a priori estimate of what the cutoff depth should be. If it is too small, the solution will never be reached. If the cutoff depth is large enough, one or more solutions may be found, but there is no guarantee of optimality as there is with breadth-first search.

2.4.4 Depth-First Iterative-Deepening Search

Depth-first iterative-deepening (DFID) search is an exhaustive search technique that is designed to deal with with the problem of assigning a cutoff depth for a depth-first search [Korf 1988; Stefik 1990]. In particular, the idea is that a cutoff depth is assigned *dynamically* as the search proceeds.

Thus, we start with a very small value (e.g., 1) and then increase it incrementally until the solution is found. The search begins anew at the root node each time the cutoff depth is incremented, and although this may appear wasteful, we shall see that DFID produces optimal solutions in a reasonable time. A skeletal version—as before, we leave the details for the reader—of this algorithm is as follows.

To implement a **depth-first iterative-deepening** search:

1. Form a one-element stack consisting of the root node.

2. Cycle through Steps a–c while incrementing by 1 the levels of the tree, until the stack is empty.

    a. Test the top element of the stack to see if it is a solution.

    b. Exit with success if the tested element is a solution.

    c. If the first element is not a solution, add *its children only* to the *top* of the stack and return to the root node.

3. Exit with failure if no solution is found.

The DFID search idea was first used in a program devised for time-constrained chess in which the idea was to search iteratively for moves during the time that was available between an opponent's moves. Thus, a move was sought and, if there was time remaining, the search was extended recursively by additional levels as time allowed. As it turns out, when extended to pathfinding searches or other single-player games, DFID produces optimal solutions just as breadth-first search does.

As noted, this algorithm provides for a sequence of depth-first searches over an ever deepening tree. The solutions are optimal—again, in the sense of being the shortest path from root node to solution node—because, by the very nature of the search process, it is impossible for a shorter solution to have been found, just as in breadth-first search. And although it seems wasteful to generate all the nodes over and over (see Figure 2-7), it should be noted that DFID is doing repetitive depth-first search, so that the memory required is linearly proportional to the depth at which the solution is found. Further, although the details are beyond the scope of the present discussion, it is possible to demonstrate that the time complexity of DFID is the same as that for both breadth-first and depth-first search and that "this algorithm is the best one can do under the assumptions of brute-force search" [Korf 1988].

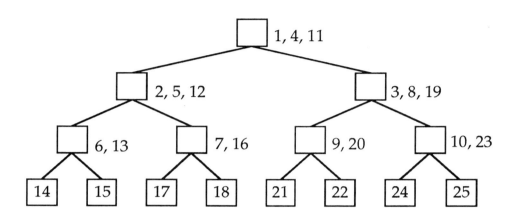

Figure 2-7 A depth-first iterative-deepening search (after [Korf 1988]).

2.4.5 Generate-and-Test

We now present an algorithm for the problem-solving strategy called generate-and-test, a control strategy that, again, uses no domain knowledge. It is a very general strategy, one that does not have even the specificity of the three exhaustive search algorithms we have presented. Moreover, it can be used with any one of the search algorithms given, with the chosen algorithm playing the role of the generator of the candidate solutions. The generating and testing roles are strictly separate in this blind formulation: everything known about generating candidates is contained in the generator, and everything known about assessing solutions is contained in the tester.

The separation imposed here, between generating solutions and testing them, can be remarkably inefficient. This is because the generator needs to put together complete solutions before they can be tested. Stefik [1990] points out that even for the conceptually simple case of opening a safe whose combination consists of five numbers between 1 and 100, there are

10 billion possible combinations that have to be considered. Generating that many combinations clearly constitutes a combinatorial explosion that would overwhelm any straightforward computational exploration of this problem. As an algorithm, this strategy takes the following form.

To implement a **generate-and-test** search:

    1.   Cycle through Step 1 until the generator is empty.

        a.   Get a candidate solution from the generator.

        b.   Test the candidate to see if it is a solution.

        c.   Exit with success if the tested candidate is a solution.

    2.   Exit with failure if no solution is found.

Hierarchical generate-and-test is a modification of generate-and-test that is designed to overcome this drawback. The idea is to use information to test partial solutions so that, hopefully, entire subtrees can be pruned or ruled out from further search. Hierarchical generate-and-test assumes that the information is there to be applied, that partial solutions can be generated, and that the pruning of subtrees can be done correctly [Stefik 1990]. (This is somewhat different than pruning by the effective application of constraints, as we saw in the reduction of the number of allowable states in the M & C problem of Section 2.2.1.) The information used in this process is likely to be domain knowledge; we discuss this method further in Section 2.4.6.

2.4.6 Constraint Satisfaction

As we observed in the discussion on backward reasoning, it is often the case that we do not know precisely what form our solution is to take. Rather, we know only a set of constraints or conditions that the goal state must satisfy. A variation of generate-and-test that is designed to solve these sorts of problems is a strategy called **constraint satisfaction**. The algorithm for simple constraint satisfaction makes it clear that it is a variant of generate-and-test, which means that it suffers from all of the drawbacks of that method.Constraint satisfaction problems occur frequently in engineering, particularly in design problems whose principal focus is the specification of a new device in terms of functional and behavioral attributes and constraints. That is, we are often faced with the problem of creating an artifact whose purpose is relatively clear and from which we expect certain conditions to be maintained or not violated, although we are not able to specify a priori an explicit form for the device. Solving such problems does not, in and of itself, require a new methodology. We could simply generate various designs and test them to see if our objectives have been achieved and our constraints not violated. Indeed, we have already noted that the constraint satisfaction algorithm is remarkably like that of the generate-and-test algorithm. So why the fuss?

To implement a simple **constraint satisfaction** search:

    1.   Cycle through Step 1 until the generator is empty.

        a.   Generate the next set of possible values for the variables.

        b.   Test the set of variables to see if all constraints are satisfied.

        c.   Exit with success if all constraints are satisfied, as a solution has thus been found.

    2.   Exit with failure if no solution is found.

The simplicity of the statement of this algorithm hides the fact that the key idea of constraint satisfaction is an emphasis on the representation and manipulation of the constraints. The constraint satisfaction terminology is meant to imply a focus on how the constraints are brought into the problem, as opposed to our simply thinking of them as being incorporated in the tester in some unspecified way. Again, we refer back to the use of constraints in the M & C problem, wherein we found that common sense dictated a reduction in the number of allowable states. This in turn is reflective of the idea of using the constraints in the generator, rather than in the tester, to make the generator "more knowledgeable." The constraints themselves can be organized as a network whose structure can help guide the process of selecting interacting variables [Stefik 1990].

Constraint satisfaction has proved to be useful in many applications, one of the earliest and most notable being in the interpretation of line drawings (see the extended discussion of Waltz's work in [Winston 1984a]). The idea of constraint satisfaction is also found in the classical mathematical technique of relaxation and in the underlying mathematics of today's widely popular spreadsheets.   We shall see in our discussions of applications that constraint satisfaction is applicable to many problems in engineering design.   Also, when combined with logic as a representation scheme, constraint satisfaction produces the idea of **truth maintenance systems** which enforce consistency as a design or other solution process unfolds [Sussman 1975a].

Another aspect of the use of constraint satisfaction is **backtracking**, the undoing of steps already done in some way that contributes to search efficiency.   The most obvious backtracking scheme is the most naive and inefficient one, that is, to go back to the root node and start again.   More informed approaches would test against constraints as the variables of that constraint are **instantiated**, or given specific values.   Here, instead of waiting until all the variables are known in a candidate solution, we examine groups of variables along the way as soon as we can check against one or more of the constraints.   This is analogous to moving some of the testing to the generator in generate-and-test [Stefik 1990], and it makes for a more efficient search.   We shall see in the applications two principal styles of backtracking.   In **chronological backtracking** we undo the most recent decision made that leads to a constraint violation.   In **dependency-directed backtracking** we keep track of the links between variable values and constraints, and we undo and recalculate those variables that lead to failure. As a matter of terminology, these refined methods of backtracking are often lumped together under the name **hierarchical backtracking** [Stefik 1990].

2.5 DIRECTED SEARCH

This section describes search algorithms for guided or directed search. Thus, the focus is on incorporating domain knowledge within the procedural knowledge of a search in order to make it more efficient.

2.5.1 Strong Methods; Heuristic Search

We have previously introduced the idea that very general search methods that do not make use of domain knowledge are considered weak methods simply because they do not exploit such knowledge. Now we introduce **strong methods**, which are more powerful because they incorporate different degrees and kinds of what is called heuristic knowledge. We should note that there is a tradeoff here between generality and power in the sense that the weak methods are essentially universally applicable, even if often inefficient or even inadequate because of combinatorial issues. The strong methods, however, may be less universal in their applicability, and the domain knowledge or heuristics used in a given problem may even be totally inapplicable in another domain or task.

We also need to say a few words about the meaning of the word *heuristic*. In terms of general usage, we use the word *heuristic* to mean a rule of thumb or a piece of advice that is usually based on prior experience and is not always guaranteed to work. In search we speak of a **heuristic evaluation function** as a more specific measure of the (conceptual) distance between a given state and the goal state. In our discussion of the 8-puzzle, for example, we introduced a heuristic function that provided a measure of the distance between any given configuration of the tiles and the goal state (see Section 2.2.2). In that case, the measure of the distance was the number of tiles that were not in their final places.

There are two important considerations in choosing heuristic evaluation functions. The first and most obvious is that such a function should provide a useful and realistic estimate of the merit of a particular state. Second, the evaluation function should not, in general, require a great deal of computation in its application. If an evaluation function is computationally complex, it may not be worth the added time or storage. That is, it may be more efficient to do an exhaustive search rather than spend resources on evaluation as the search is in process.

2.5.2 Hill-Climbing

Hill-climbing is the name we give to a variation of depth-first search in which a heuristic evaluation function is used to estimate the distance remaining to be traversed from a given node to the goal node. In some searches, this conceptual distance can indeed be a measure of geographic distance between two points. For example, in classic operations research (OR) problems, such as that of the traveling salesman trying to minimize the total travel distance through a network of cities, a good heuristic measure would be the Euclidean distance (also called the airline distance, or the "as the crow flies" distance) between a given city or node and the goal [Hillier 1980]. This is a good heuristic because it is easy to calculate and it provides a reasonable estimate of the actual travel distance.

The algorithm for hill-climbing is, not surprisingly, very much like that for depth-first search. The difference is in Step 2c, where we apply our heuristic.

To implement a **hill-climbing** search:

1.   Form a one-element stack consisting of the root node.

2.   Cycle through Steps a–c until the stack is empty.

   a.   Test the top element of the stack to see if it is a solution.

   b.   Exit with success if the tested element is a solution.

   c.   If the first element is not a solution, sort the first element's children by the estimated remaining distance to the goal, and then add the children to the *top* of the stack.

3.   Exit with failure if no solution is found.

Hill-climbing is very similar to what we do in parameter optimization—for example, in how we might adjust a thermostat without markings to change the temperature in a room [Winston 1984a]. What happens is that we move the control in the direction we intend the temperature to change and by an amount that is based on some intuitive sense of how much we need to move the control to get the temperature to where we want it to be. The farther we are away from our desired goal, the larger will be our initial adjustment. Then, as we near the goal temperature, we fine-tune our prior adjustments. In this case, of course, we are dealing with a continuous system whose control-response behavior is similar to how we look for maxima and minima in calculus.

Hill-climbing's drawback is one that might be expected of an approach based on feedback while adjusting parameters. And its very name, intended to be suggestive of a naive climber attacking the most evident, steepest path at some point on a mountain trail [Luger 1989], also suggests its limitations. The problem is that the search thus conducted is responsive to the local situation rather than to a more global view of the search space. That is, there are situations where the search could be "stuck" along a path that produces result that appear optimal within a neighborhood of the path, whereas better results may be obtainable in other neighborhoods within the search space. Three such neighborhood problems occur frequently enough to be worth noting here [Rich 1983; Winston 1984a]. Their names are also meant to be geographically suggestive.

In the **foothill** problem, even though a better result may be in some sense visible (e.g., a not-too-distant peak), one is prevented from getting there by intervening foothills or similar anomalies of the search space. In other instances, the search may be stuck on a **plateau**, unable to move to other, higher plateaus without some major change in the evaluation metric. (A helpful analogy here is to the plateaus atop the buttes of Monument Valley, astride the Utah-Arizona border, often used as a backdrop for automobile advertising.) Finally, in the **ridge** problem, we are stuck in a part of the search space that is higher than surrounding areas, but which cannot be traversed in any direction by single moves. (The obvious analogy here is being stuck on the knifelike edge of a ridge line.) The point is that hill-climbing is very much a *local* method that is not terribly well suited for exploring rough search terrains.

2.5.3 Best-First Search

In **best-first search** the sorting is done over the *entire* queue of nodes already expanded in the search. That is, in best-first search we move forward from the best node that has been expanded so far, regardless of when we expanded it or where it might be on the parts of the tree that have already been developed. Thus, best-first search combines features of both depth-first search (which it does locally from each node that is currently identified as "the best" node) and breadth-first search (in that it must retain in memory all the prior nodes and the values of their evaluation functions in order to select the node that is currently best). Winston [1984a] notes an interesting analogy to teams of cooperating mountain climbers looking for the highest point on a mountain. They monitor each other's progress, and by radio contact they continually readjust the focus of the search according to the progress of each team.

We note that both hill-climbing and best-first search operate with an evaluation function that measures or estimates the distance remaining to the goal. In neither case do we inquire as to the distance traveled or the cost incurred to get to the current state, or to the goal state for that matter. In Sections 2.5.4 and 2.5.5 we explore these aspects of search and see how they affect the optimality of the solutions found with each. The best-first algorithm is similar to the hill-climbing algorithm, with a corresponding change in Step 2c.

To implement a **best-first** search:

1.   Form a one-element stack consisting of the root node.

2.   Cycle through Steps a–c until the stack is empty.

    a.   Test the top element of the stack to see if it is a solution.

    b.   Exit with success if the tested element is a solution.

    c.   If the first element is not a solution, add its children to the stack, and *sort the entire stack* by the estimated remaining distance to the goal.

3.   Exit with failure if no solution is found.

2.5.4 Branch-and-Bound Search

Let us now consider how we might conduct a guided search where the cost of doing the search is important and, in fact, where we want to minimize the cost—or some measure of distance—of getting from the initial state to the goal state. It is obviously desirable to keep track of the costs, then, and to make decisions using heuristics that reflect the desire to keep the total cost as low as possible. How do we do this?

As we traverse a tree we develop many incomplete paths that compete for attention. In **branch-and-bound search**, we expand by one level the node at the end of the *shortest* path from the initial state, thus creating as many new incomplete paths as there are branches to that node. Then we sort *all* the paths generated thus far, the old ones along with the newly developed ones, and expand the node at the end of the shortest path of this list. We repeat this process until we find a path to the destination. Further, since we have always extended the path that was shortest, we should find that our resulting path is optimal, that is, that its cost is minimal [Hillier 1980].

The process just described is not entirely foolproof, as the last step may be just long enough to make its corresponding solution costlier than that of one of the incomplete paths. That is, we might need to add only a very small step to one of the incomplete paths to make it shorter than the solution just found. We can avoid this possibility by improving our stopping condition, and this really is at the heart of branch-and-bound search. We terminate the search only when the shortest incomplete path is longer than the shortest complete path. The corresponding algorithm is given in [Winston 1984a].

To implement a **branch-and-bound** search:

1. Form a one-element stack consisting of a zero-length path from the root node to nowhere.

2. Cycle through Steps a–c until the stack is empty.

   a. Test the first path to see if it leads to the goal.

   b. Exit with success if the tested path leads to the goal.

   c. If the first path does not lead to the goal:

      1. Remove the first path from the stack.

      2. Form new paths from the removed path by expanding one level.

      3. Add the new paths to the stack.

      4. Sort the entire stack in increasing order of path length so far, least cost on top.

3. Exit with failure if no solution is found.

2.5.5 The A* Algorithm

Our final algorithm, the **A* procedure**, represents a twofold improvement of branch-and-bound. First we include a heuristic to estimate the distance from a given node to the goal node. Adding this to the distance traveled—or cost incurred—to reach the node, we obtain an estimate of the total length of the path currently being explored. Then we work on those paths that, at any given point in the search, have the shortest estimated path length. Further, it can be shown that if we consistently *underestimate* the distance to the goal, we cannot help but find the shortest or least costly path [Nilsson 1980]. This follows simply because once all incomplete path distance estimates are longer than a completed path, it is impossible for there to be a real path that is shorter. We need only be sure that the estimates of the distance traveled are truly underestimates. The path estimate is in Step 2c4 of the A* algorithm [Winston 1984a].

To implement an **A*** search:

1. Form a one-element stack consisting of a zero-length path from the root node to nowhere.

2. Cycle through Steps a–c until the stack is empty.

   a. Test the first path to see if it leads to the goal.

   b. Exit with success if the tested path leads to the goal.

   c. If the first path does not lead to the goal:

      1. Remove the first path from the stack.

      2. Form new paths from the removed path by expanding one level.

      3. Add the new paths to the stack.

      4. Sort the entire stack by the *sum* (cost incurred so far + underestimate of the cost remaining), least cost on top.

      5. If there are multiple paths to a node, retain only the path with the lowest cost to that node.

3. Exit with failure if no solution is found.

The second improvement is a reflection of the **dynamic programming** principle, which effectively turns the search tree into a search graph [Winston 1984a]. In particular, when examining an intermediate node that can be reached by several different paths as the tree unfolds, we retain only the shortest path to that node (from the root node) and discard all others. Again, it ought to be fairly clear that when looking for the shortest path through an intermediate node, all paths other than the shortest path from the root node to that intermediate node must produce final results that cannot be optimal. Thus, they can be ignored. The application of the dynamic programming principle occurs in Step 2c5 of the A* algorithm.

2.6 SUMMARY

We have presented in this chapter an overview of the concepts of search as they might be used to formulate and solve problems. Our main concern was to provide a different perspective on how engineering problems might be formulated, thus laying the groundwork for seeing later how the problem-solving process can be made computable. We focused on state space representation of problems, and then we described both algorithms and strategies for searching trees and graphs. While our exposition was not intended to be comprehensive, it provided the basic vocabulary, themes, and techniques.

It is also worth noting that search has been developed within the field of operations research as well as within AI. Indeed, there are debates that verge on being theological wars about which discipline is responsible for bringing forth the various search schemes, and certainly there have been major contributions to search as applied to discrete numerical models of systems [Hillier 1980]. Our own view is that there is much to learn from both disciplines, but that in fact AI has exploited broader notions of knowledge representation and reasoning than has operations research. As noted elsewhere, operations research works within a limited range of representation schemes and tends to " . . . [be] highly numerate, and to avoid symbolic and recursive processing" [Grant 1986]. The other kinds of representation are the focus of much of this book, so now we shall move on to representation for computing.

Chapter 3

DEDUCTION WITH FORMAL LOGIC

Formal logic systems are mathematically precise languages that allow us to deduce logically consistent new facts from a given database of facts by the application of logical inferences. There are, however, an almost infinite number of possible deductions that could be made from a database of facts of any significant size; hence, deduction must usually be guided by the kinds of directed search strategies described in Chapter 2 if we are to find solutions to nontrivial problems efficiently. Knowledge-based systems thus employ both deduction and search in varying degrees.

In spite of the fact that most applications of knowledge-based systems require both kinds of reasoning, the proponents of deduction and those who tend to stress heuristic search are engaged in a vigorous ongoing debate about the relative elegance and power of their concepts. AI practitioners who stress the use of deduction in representation and reasoning are often referrred to as "neats," while those who stress the importance of heuristic search techniques in problem solving are termed "scruffies." In this chapter we talk about the "neat" underpinnings of KBESs.

3.1 INTRODUCTION

Systems of formal logic provide rigorous means to define and manipulate symbols representing declarative knowledge. For this reason, philosophers have been developing and using systems of formal logic since classical Greek times to erect and challenge elaborate belief systems about fundamental questions of existence, knowledge, reasoning, religion, and ethics. Logicians (or *logicists*, as computer science logicians call themselves) create complex belief systems by assuming the truth of a few axioms and then deducing and proving many other implications from these axioms using the logic system as a mathematical inference tool. Similarly, they investigate the coherence of existing belief systems by formalizing the beliefs and relating them using logical rules of inference.

In contrast to philosophers, pure mathematicians interested in formal logic systems focus on defining and manipulating the **syntax** (or grammar) of a given logic system, rather than the **semantics** (or meaning) of the ideas that might be expressed using its syntax. It is important for engineering readers to realize that the semantics of the propositions, predicates, and arguments in logic formulas is typically of only passing interest to mathematicians. This is why many—but not all—mathematics textbooks on logic baffle or bore engineers, applied scientists, or others to whom the syntax of logic systems is viewed as a tool for manipulating the semantics in their domain of interest, rather than as an interesting end in itself. (See the Preface for a very brief review of the literature on formal logic systems and related topics.)

This chapter is not intended to serve as a complete or deep review of formal logic; this would require a separate book. Its aims are considerably more modest. The major part of this chapter provides an introduction to some important concepts of two widely used formal logic systems: propositional logic and first-order predicate logic. We go on to show how logic systems like these can be incorporated into programming languages that enable computers to carry out useful kinds of deduction. Note that we will make no judgements yet about the relative merits of neat versus scruffy approaches to knowledge representation. (See *Computational Intelligence* **3** (3) [1987] for one of the more insightful debates on this subject.) After explaining how humans and computers use formal logic systems to perform deduction, we will express our engineering point of view about the complementary nature of deduction and heuristic search in engineering knowledge-based systems.

3.2 FORMAL LOGIC SYSTEMS

Before plunging into a discussion of propositional and first-order predicate logic systems, we provide some overview comments about each and our reasons for covering them in this text.

Propositional logic (which is explained in Section 3.2.1) gives us a rigorous way to apply rules of inference in transforming expressions containing simple statements, or propositions, joined together by one or more connectives into new expressions. With propositional logic we can deduce the truth or falsity of an expression by knowing the truth values of, and connectives linking, each of the propositions contained in it. Propositional logic can also be used to provide formal proofs of theorems. This is done by using rules of inference to transform a set of expressions representing assumptions or axioms into an expresssion representing a theorem or conclusion, one inference step at a time.

Using propositional logic, we can solve the following little mystery from the facts contained in the first two lines. The solution appears in the third line.

IGOR KILLED THE SPY OR CHUCK KILLED THE SPY.
IGOR DID NOT KILL THE SPY.

THEREFORE CHUCK KILLED THE SPY.

First-order predicate logic (explained in Section 3.2.2) provides a richer representation of the meaning of natural language sentences by adding to the concepts of propositions and connectives contained in propositional logic the notions of functions, predicates, variables, and quantifiers. The fundamental unit of propositional calculus, the proposition, represents an entire declarative statement—for example, Socrates taught Plato. In predicate calculus, however, we are able to treat explicitly the components of propositions, such as the name *Socrates* and the relation *taught*.

These additional features of the language vastly improve its expressiveness and enable many more kinds of deduction to be carried out. In particular, we can employ predicate logic to deduce characteristics of a particular object from more general statements about the attributes of some or all objects in a set to which this object belongs. (And there are logicians who believe that higher-order logics are sufficiently expressive to represent virtually any idea that can be stated in a natural language.) By way of an example, the third line of the following well-known syllogism can be deduced from the first two lines by means of predicate logic.

ALL MEN ARE MORTAL.
SOCRATES IS A MAN.

THEREFORE SOCRATES IS MORTAL.

This turns out to be a useful kind of deduction for many engineering applications. Many other powerful kinds of deduction are possible in first-order predicate logic. We will illustrate the power of the language by describing some of them in Section 3.2.2.

Propositional logic (sometimes called sentential logic) contains many of the key ideas used in both formal logic systems, so it is appropriate to introduce it first. We can then cover predicate logic by adding the required concepts.

3.2.1 Propositional Logic

In **propositional logic**, one begins with a set of ideas, or **propositions**, which are true or false **expressions** in a natural language such as English. Following a set of conventions, propositions can be formalized as **well-formed formulas (WFFs)**. Using a small number of logical connectives we can then combine two or more WFFs into more complex WFFs. Finally, a small set of inference rules for manipulating WFFs and connectives in expressions allows us to deduce new expressions from existing ones, and to determine whether an expression is true or false from the truth value of its component propositions. This is the essence of propositional logic.

3.2.1.1 Propositions

Atomic propositions are simple statements, that is, propositions which cannot themselves be subdivided into simpler statements. (VALVE_27_IS_OPEN) is an atomic proposition. In contrast, the proposition

(EITHER JANE_IS_AN_ENGINEER OR JANE_IS_A_SCIENTIST)

can be broken down into two separate statements about Jane by using the connective OR, so it is a compound proposition.

Note that the words contained in propositions, for example, VALVE_27 or ENGINEER, represent and convey important meanings to human readers when viewed in their expanded natural language form. However, since whole propositions must evaluate to either true or false in propositional logic, they are treated as chunks with no internal syntax. They are usually represented using **sentence symbols**—the uppercase letters A through Z, or alternatively A_1 through A_n. The semantics of atomic propositions are thus opaque and unusable for purposes of deduction by the inference rules of the language. This is an important limitation of propositional logic that drastically restricts its expressive and deductive capabilities.

3.2.1.2 Connectives

Since atomic propositions must be simple statements, more complex ideas are created by combining propositions using connectives. Propositional logic usually uses five connectives, with parentheses to delimit their scope as in conventional algebra. Of these five connectives, only three are independent—AND, OR, and NOT—and the others can be derived from these three. However, all of the five are commonly used in logic texts, and so we will define them here.

Not. English-speaking readers who see the proposition (VALVE_27_IS_CLOSED) immediately know that valve 27 is not open. This is because we understand the meanings of the words *closed* and *open* and recognize them as mutually exclusive states of a valve. Recall, however, that the meanings of words in propositions are not understood for purposes of deduction in propositional logic systems.   Thus, a mathematician speaking only Greek or a computer programmed to perform propositional logic deductions would be unaware that *closed* means the same as *not open*.   Propositional logic can not even relate the two propositions by their common use of the word VALVE_27.   Thus, (VALVE_27_IS_CLOSED) would simply be treated as a second proposition whose truth value is unrelated, a priori, to the truth value of the proposition (VALVE_27_IS_OPEN).

If we want the system to reason in the intuitively correct way about states in which the valve is open or closed, we must describe the closed state of the valve by using the exact form of the original proposition, (VALVE_27_IS_OPEN); the **negation connective**, NOT; and parentheses to delimit the scope of the N O T connective, that is, (N O T (VALVE_27_IS_OPEN)). A computer can then **match** the proposition in this new expression with the original proposition—since they contain the identical string of characters, they can be recognized as being the same proposition.   It can then apply the negation connective, NOT, to the proposition in the second expression and use this knowledge in making its deductions about the state of the piping system.   That is, (NOT (VALVE_27_IS_OPEN)) is true only if (VALVE_27_IS_OPEN) is false, and it is false only if (VALVE_27_IS_OPEN) is true.

And. The AND connective, often called the conjunction symbol, is used to express the state in which both of the propositions or expressions which it connects are true. Thus the expression

((VALVE_27_IS_OPEN) AND (NOT (PIPE_363_IS_BLOCKED)))

is true only when both valve 27 is open and pipe 363 is clear. Otherwise it is false.

Or. The sentence "Sam likes windy or rainy weather" is ambiguous in English. Sam may or may not like weather which is both windy and rainy. In probability theory and set theory we distinguish clearly between inclusive and exclusive event probabilities (or set intersections), respectively. In propositional logic we use the OR connective, often called the **disjunction symbol**, only in the inclusive sense. Thus, the expression (A OR B) is true in propositional logic if at least one of A and B is true; it is false otherwise.

Implies. Knowing that the truth of one proposition depends upon the truth of another proposition or expression is an important form of deduction in engineering and many other domains. We use the IMPLIES connective (frequently written as the conditional symbol $\rightarrow$ or the hook symbol $\supset$) to convey this meaning.

We capture this idea in our true/false semantics by saying that (A $\rightarrow$ B) is false if A is true and B is false (preventing the inference) and true otherwise. Using this definition, we see that knowing that B is true tells us nothing about the truth of A. Nor does knowing that A is false imply that B is false.

In ((A AND B) $\rightarrow$ C), the previously defined AND connective tells us that the first expression is true if both A and B are true, and hence C is true. In natural English, we would express this by saying, "If both A and B are true, then C is true."

Bidirectional implication (IFF). The $\leftrightarrow$ symbol is used to indicate bidirectional implication. It corresponds to the natural language or algebraic connective IF AND ONLY IF. Thus, (A $\leftrightarrow$ B) means that A and B have the same truth value: both are true or both are false. In effect, (A $\leftrightarrow$ B) means that (A $\rightarrow$ B) and (B $\rightarrow$ A).

We can summarize these definitions of connectives by means of a **truth table** (Table 3-1), which shows the values of compound propositions employing each of the connectives for all true or false values of the component atomic propositions.

The first two columns of Table 3-1 show assumed truth values of two propositions, A and B. The next five columns show the values of compound propositions assembled from A and B using each of the five connectives described in this section.

Table 3-1 Truth table for propositional logic connectives

A	B	(not A)	(A and B)	(A or B)	(A → B)	(A ↔ B)
T	T	F	T	T	T	T
F	T	T	F	T	T	F
T	F		F	T	F	F
F	F		F	F	T	T

3.2.1.3 Inference Rules

Having defined the meanings of propositions and connectives in propositional logic, we can now show how **inference rules** are used to carry out deduction. Inference rules are used to manipulate gramatically correct expressions, or WFFs, in propositional logic. An expression is a WFF if and only if one of the following holds.

1. The expression consists only of a single, or atomic, proposition; or

2. A and B are WFFs, and the expression is one of the following: (NOT A), (NOT B), (A AND B), (A OR B), (A → B), or (A ↔ B).

Ten primitive rules of inference can be used to carry out deductions in propositional logic. Two primitive rules are used for each connective: an **in rule**, which defines the operation of deducing to a WFF containing that connective, and an **out rule**, which defines the operation of deducing from a WFF containing that connective. Other rules of inference can be derived from the ten primitive rules.

A complete presentation of the rules of propositional inference is beyond the scope of this chapter—see, for example, [Pospesel 1974] for a readable introduction—but we will illustrate them with some examples. First we show the two primitive rules for bidirectional inference.

↔ **In rule**   From (A → B) and (B → A), derive (A ↔ B)

↔ **Out rule**   From (A ↔ B), derive (A → B) and (B → A)

Similarly, the two primitive rules for the OR connective are

Or in rule   From (A) derive either (A or B) or (B or A)

Or out rule   From (A or B), (A → C), and (B → C), derive C

We can construct elaborate proofs of theorems using propositional logic. We do so by asserting a set of assumption WFFs, or premises, and a conclusion WFF that we wish to prove from these assumptions. We then use in and out rules of inference like the ones described above, or other inference rules that we have previously proved can be derived from them, to transform the assumption WFFs into new WFFs, eventually obtaining the conclusion WFF through this process of deduction.

Note that rules of inference in formal logic systems are merely syntactic transformation rules. There is no clear or simple way to predict which rule should be used next to proceed from a set of assumptions to a desired conclusion; experience, insight, and a fair measure of luck may be needed to prove a particular theorem. Because successful theorem proving combines rigor with intuition in this way, logicians derive great pleasure—and sometimes great fame—from discovering new, shorter, or more elegant proofs to interesting theorems.

From an engineering point of view, a particularly useful rule of inference from this system of logic is the **modus ponens rule**. The modus ponens rule is simply the → out rule. It can be stated as "From (A → B) and A, deduce B." Stated in English, the rule means, "If we know that A implies B, and we have determined that A is true, we can deduce that B is true." An equally important converse to this rule is **modus tollens**: From (A → B) and (NOT B), deduce (NOT A). In English, this rule for proof by negation means "If we know that A implies B and we observe that B is false, we can deduce that A is false." We illustrate these two inference rules with a simple English example.

Modus ponens. From "If Fred rescued the baby then Jane knows about it" and "Fred rescued the baby," deduce that "Jane knows about it."

Modus tollens. From "If Fred rescued Bob then Jane knows about it" and "Jane does not know about it," deduce that "Fred did not rescue Bob."

In Chapter 5 we will show how production rule systems that perform automated diagnosis or other engineering tasks can be constructed by creating a knowledge base containing a series of propositions of the form (A → B), truth values for some of the propositions, and an inference engine based upon modus ponens or modus tollens.

This concludes our rapid survey of propositional logic. Since the main virtue of this system of logic appears to be proving theorems, it does not serve our aims to develop the subject further here. First-order predicate logic, which we discuss next, adds a little complexity and a great deal of expressive power to propositional logic.

3.2.2 First-Order Predicate Logic

Recall that propositional logic treats propositions as "black boxes." From the point of view of the logic system, they are simply arbitrary sequences of characters which might or might not have any real meaning; they are typically represented as sentence symbols such as A or A_n. As we have seen above, this limits the kinds of meaning that can be formally conveyed and the kinds of deduction that can be carried out by the language.

In contrast, the expressiveness of natural languages derives in part from their use of specialized kinds of words, such as, verbs, nouns, and adjectives, which play particular roles in assigning meaning to sentences. For example, in English, the word *play* can have many meanings. The correct meaning of *play* in a particular sentence is inferred by a reader or listener from its context—its position in the sentence and the words surrounding it.

First- and higher-order predicate logic systems provide structure and hence local meaning to the black box propositions in propositional logic. **First-order predicate logic** builds upon the concepts already introduced in our discussion of propositional logic by introducing specific roles for elements of its sentences, along with a few additional inference rules for manipulating them, analogous to the ways we use parts of speech and grammatical rules in natural languages. The parts of speech that we must add to move up to a first-order predicate logic system include predicates, three kinds of terms, variables, and quantifiers.

We note again that the discussion presented here is intended only as an introduction to and illustration of the powers of expression and deduction that are afforded by the encoding and manipulation of knowledge about the semantics (meaning) of propositions. For greater depth, see [Charniak 1985; Enderton 1972; Genesereth 1985, 1987; Pospesel 1974, 1976; Richards 1989].

3.2.2.1 Predicates, Arguments, and Connectives

The basic building blocks of propositions in predicate logic are predicates and their arguments. A **predicate** asserts a fact—such as an action or a relationship—about one or more entities called **arguments**. In a rather rough analogy, a predicate can be viewed as corresponding to the verb, and its arguments as corresponding to the subject and object (if any), of a natural language sentence. Thus, the English sentence "Beam 12 supports column 86" might be represented by the predicate SUPPORTS with two arguments, BEAM_12 and COLUMN_86. In this case, the ordering of the arguments clearly makes a difference; this is often, but not always, true for predicates with multiple arguments. The sentence could be represented in predicate logic as

SUPPORTS (COLUMN_86 BEAM_12)

By writing the expression in this way, we are saying that the proposition evaluates to true for the given predicate with this pair of arguments—that is, it is true that column 86 supports beam 12. Each predicate has a unique meaning and a specified number of arguments whose order is usually semantically significant.

English uses an **infix** convention for active, transitive verbs: the verb is usually contained betweeen the subject or actor and the object acted upon (e.g., the column *supports* the beam). We also generally use infix notation for arithmetic expressions [e.g., $(4 + 5)$ or $(12 \times (6 - 4))$]. We will generally use **prefix** notation for predicates in this chapter, in which the predicate precedes all of its arguments. (We will use infix notation for the $\rightarrow$ operator in a few examples involving implications, where this aids clarity.) After one uses prefix notation for a short while, it becomes very natural. Its main advantage over the loose form of infix or postfix notation used for verbs in English or German, respectively, is that it avoids the kind of ambiguities of natural language that can be caused by, for example, reversing the order of subject and object in a passive English sentence.

The **arity** of a predicate defines the number of arguments that it takes. A predicate may have arity 1, as in FATHER_OF_MICHAEL (SAM); or 2, as in PARENTS_OF_MICHAEL (SAM, PAULINE); or the arity may be indefinite, as in MALFUNCTIONING_PARTS (SWITCH_23, CONDUCTOR_65, LOGIC_GATE_11, . . .).

If we use one or more particular objects as the argument(s) of a predicate, we have created a **singular statement**. (We will discuss universal statements, which describe attributes of entire classes of objects, later in this section.) The following are examples of singular statements.

English expression

Arguments	Predicate
Pipe 27	is obstructed
Column 13	has yielded
Beam 32	has not yielded
Column 13, beam 32	are connected

The same facts can be expressed in our prefix form of predicate logic as follows.

Predicate logic expression

OBSTRUCTED (PIPE_27)

YIELDED (COLUMN_13)

NOT (YIELDED (BEAM_32))

CONNECTED (COLUMN_13, BEAM_32)

This notation is reasonably concise, and it comes close enough to expressing the English meanings of the argument and predicate symbols that a reader would probably not need to consult a table of abbreviations to understand their meaning. Note, also, that predicates and their arguments are represented separately so that, unlike the case in propositional logic, the meaning of the predicates and arguments contained within a proposition can be exploited for deduction in a first-order predicate logic system.

The connectives we defined for propositional logic can also be used in predicate logic formulas. So we can express the fact that beam 32 has not yielded as NOT (YIELDED (BEAM_32)). The connectives AND, OR, IF, and IFF can likewise be used in predicate logic formulas to connect propositions containing predicates and terms.

In Chapter 4 we show how computers can be programmed to manipulate logic expressions. When we do such programming, it may be convenient to abbreviate predicates and arguments down to a single letter each. Since this textbook is intended for processing by humans, we ask our computer scanner readers to bear with our slightly more cumbersome, but decidedly more people-friendly word notation.

3.2.2.2 Terms

The arguments in predicate logic formulas are called **terms**. A term can take one of three forms: it can be a constant symbol, a variable, or a functional expression.

Constant symbols are used to represent arguments whose reference never changes. A constant could be a noun, adjective, adverb, phrase, or clause in a natural language. Thus the predicate COLOR_OF might have the arguments COAT_27 and BLUE. These two arguments are constant symbols.

Variables are used here in the same sense as in algebra. A variable represents an entity or attribute which can have different values in different contexts. Using our linguistic analogy, variables are akin to pronouns, which derive particular references from their context (e.g., *"He* is asleep," or *"I* saw *that"*). We will say more about variables when we discuss quantifiers in Section 3.2.2.3.

Functional expressions are used to specify terms by describing them rather than by naming them. For example, "the color of the sky" is a way of *describing* the color of an object, just as "dark blue" is a way of *naming* the color of the same object. So the sentence "John painted the wall the color of the sky" could be expressed in predicate logic form as

PAINTED (JOHN_1, WALL_8, COLOR_OF (SKY_2))

In this case the predicate PAINTED has three arguments; the first two are constant terms representing the actor and object acted upon, while the third is a functional expression to determine the color that John will use. As the color of SKY_2 changes, so does the meaning of this argument. The function COLOR_OF can be viewed as a kind of internal predicate which itself has an argument, in this case the constant term SKY_2. The color of wall 8 will now be described by the COLOR_OF some particular sky, designated SKY_2. The function COLOR_OF has arity 1 in this case; that is, it has only one argument.

Thus, a functional expression defines the way to obtain the value of an argument: by applying the function to the terms which are its local arguments. Functions can be nested to arbitrary levels of depth by using a second functional expression as the term in the first one, and so on (e.g., "the father of the husband of Jane").

The values of arguments in components of an engineering system are often specified as being functionally related to other subsystem attributes in this way. Although arithmetic or quantitative functions are frequently used (e.g., BEAM_DEPTH $\geq$ SPAN/30), qualitative functional relationships can be equally important. For example, we might believe that a bus should have a high-pressure fuel pump if it has a diesel engine. We can express this compatibility constraint in predicate logic syntax as follows.

IS_COMPATIBLE ((FUEL_TYPE (ENGINE_21))
      (DELIVERY_PRESSURE (FUEL_PUMP_57)))

In this example, IS_COMPATIBLE is a predicate of arity 2 which will evaluate to true or false. Its arguments are an engine type and fuel pump pressure. The functional expressions FUEL_TYPE (ENGINE_21) and DELIVERY_PRESSURE (FUEL_PUMP_57) are used to describe (rather than to name) the particular engine type and fuel pump pressure which should be checked for compatibility.

In first-order predicate logic, functions and predicates must have constant meaning. A language in which functions and predicates are variables is termed a second-order language. Since first-order predicate logic is expressive enough for most engineering applications, we will not discuss higher-order logics here.

We now introduce the notions of variables and quantifiers; we will have more to say about using functional expressions later.

3.2.2.3 Variables and Quantifiers

We constantly make deductions about the behavior or properties of an object by knowing that the object is a specific instance of a more general class of known objects. We also routinely make inferences (at least in a probabilistic sense) about the properties of entire classes of objects from sequences of observations about specific objects belonging to a given class. Both of these kinds of inference are notoriously prone to bias and error. Nevertheless, we depend heavily upon them for everyday decision making and problem solving in a world where we cannot devote the required resources to investigate and discover the properties of every object that we encounter anew. Quantifiers, used together with variables, give predicate logic the power to reason rigorously about classes of entities and the individual objects that belong to them.

Two quantifiers are used in predicate logic. The **universal quantifier** FOR_ALL is used to say that some formula is true for all values of one or more specified variables contained within the formula; and the **existential quantifier** FOR_SOME is used to say that a formula holds for at least one value of each of the one or more specified variables. We adopt the convention that variables are represented by lowercase letters, for example, x.

We will talk about universal quantification first. It is often desirable to assert some general facts about a system we are interested in modeling. For instance, if we were creating a model or belief system for reasoning about chemical process design, we might wish to express the general statement that all pipes are hollow. We can express this fact as follows, using our logic syntax.

FOR_ALL x (PIPE (x) → HOLLOW (x))

In order to express the general statement that pipes are hollow, we had to transform the natural English sentence into the pseudo-English form "For all possible values of x, if x is a pipe, then x is hollow." This may seem cumbersome, but it turns out to be necessary for the rigor that we want such formal languages to possess.

Alternatively, we might wish to express the statement that there exists at least one object with certain attributes. We might, say, want to assert the fact that there are some titanium pipes in the piping system we are currently designing. Again, we will need to use a somewhat more complex form than that of the original English statement to express this rigorously. This fact can be translated into our pseudo-English form as "There exists at least one entity which is a pipe and whose material is titanium."

FOR_SOME x (PIPE (x) AND MATERIAL (x, TITANIUM))

Note that x is a variable, and we used it in this formula where we could have used a constant term as the argument (e.g., PIPE_034). As we will shortly see, quantifiers and variables are needed for many nontrivial kinds of deduction.

3.2.2.4 Rules of Inference for First-Order Predicate Logic

In Section 3.2.1 we developed ten inference rules for moving into or out of expressions containing the five connectives: NOT, AND, OR, →, and ↔. These primitive inference rules for propositional connectives, and rules derived from them, apply when manipulating propositions in predicate logic. In addition, we need a set of rules for dealing with variables and quantifiers. Pospesel [1976] proposes three additional rules as the basis for first-order predicate logic deduction.

The **universal quantifier out rule** is quite straightforward and intuitive. It merely states that "what is true for *every* individual is true for *any named* individual" [Pospesel 1976]. For example, if we know that all things made of copper are conductors, then we can deduce that wire 26, which is made of copper, is a conductor. Or, in predicate logic form, from

FOR_ALL x (MATERIAL (x, COPPER) → CONDUCTOR (x))

we can deduce that

MATERIAL (WIRE_26, COPPER) → CONDUCTOR (WIRE_26)

Using this rule, we can convert a complex expression involving quantification into a simpler conditional or other expression to which inference rules of propositional logic, such as modus ponens, can be applied.

The **existential quantifier out rule** permits us to derive an instance of an existential quantification from it, provided that certain conditions hold. A rigorous discussion of these conditions is beyond the scope of this chapter, but the essence of the rule is that there is some individual for which the existential quantification holds, and the instance of the existentially quantified variable in the simplified expression can represent one of these individuals. For example, if we know that some gauges are out of calibration, we can state that GAUGE_A is OUT_OF_CALIBRATION, where GAUGE_A serves as the name of the gauge or gauges which are out of calibration. Stated in predicate logic symbols, this rule enables us to deduce that the following proposition is true for some instance, GAUGE_A, of the variable x.

GAUGE (GAUGE_A) AND OUT_OF_CALIBRATION (GAUGE_A)

This statement is true if the conditions of the following rule are met.

FOR_SOME x (GAUGE (x) AND OUT_OF_CALIBRATION (x))

For this rule to be valid, the instance GAUGE_A should not appear—as indeed it does not—in the assumptions or conclusion of the theorem being proved, nor should it have appeared in any previous line of the proof. It is a term made up on the spot in the course of applying the rule. Also, like the universal quantifier out rule, the current rule is valuable for carrying out proofs since it allows us to transform a complex WFF into a proposition whose connectives can be manipulated by the rules of propositional logic. However, the universal quantifier out rule allowed us to make specific deductions about a particular entity from a universal quantification, whereas this rule just inserts a more restricted variable to represent the identity of one or more instances that exist. The former is thus likely to be of greater practical value for reasoning about engineering systems.

The **quantifier exchange rule** is also quite intuitive from natural language. It permits us to deal with the negation of a universal or existential quantification by switching from one to the other and transposing the negation symbol with the quantifier. So we can use this rule to transform a statement like "It is not true that all gauges are functioning" to a statement that says "Some gauges are not functioning." In predicate logic syntax,

NOT (FOR_ALL x (GAUGE (x) → FUNCTIONING (x)))

becomes

FOR_SOME x (NOT (GAUGE (x) → FUNCTIONING (x)))

The second instance of the rule converts a negated existential quantification which states "It is not true that some gauges are functioning" to a universally quantified negated sentence that states "All gauges are not functioning." That is,

NOT (FOR_SOME x (GAUGE (x) → FUNCTIONING (x)))

becomes

FOR_ALL x (NOT (GAUGE (x) → FUNCTIONING (x)))

In either case, once we have transformed the quantifier to a non-negated form, we can apply one of the two previously described quantifier inference rules to it.

Besides their value in proving theorems, these rules for manipulating quantifiers can be used to transform expressions involving quantifiers into simpler expressions, termed **Horn clauses**, which are used for logic programming in computer languages like Prolog. Writing expressions in Horn clause form facilitates the use of a powerful form of deduction called resolution.

3.2.3   Unification and Resolution

Resolution is a powerful process of logical inference somewhat analogous to solving a set of equations in algebra. We will use a simple example from [Jain 1990] to explain both resolution and a closely related logical operation called unification.

Let us begin with a beam, P, whose structural design we wish to check. From our knowledge of the structural behavior of beams, we can say that the critical behavior that governs the design of beam P can be either FLEXURE or SHEAR. Let us further suppose that we have determined from some high-level heuristics that SHEAR is not the critical behavior for beam P. From these two statements we can infer that FLEXURE must be the critical behavior for beam P. Employing predicate calculus notation, we can write the following expressions.

From

CRIT_BEHAV (P, FLEXURE) OR CRIT_BEHAV (P, SHEAR)   (1)

and

NOT CRIT_BEHAV (P, SHEAR)   (2)

we should be able to infer

CRIT_BEHAV (P, FLEXURE)   (3)

The **resolution principle** permits us to do precisely this. However, before we can exercise the resolution principle, the statements above have to be converted into **clausal form**. In clausal form, facts are represented by means of clauses, where a clause contains one or more literals separated by commas. A clause represents a disjunction of the literals it contains. Thus the clause

(CRIT_BEHAV (P, FLEXURE), CRIT_BEHAV (P, SHEAR))   (4)

is equivalent to statement (1). The detailed process for converting any predicate calculus expression into equivalent clause(s) can be found in [Genesereth 1987]. Here we will use the end results of the process without explicitly carrying out the conversion. The equivalent clause for statement (2) is the following.

(NOT CRIT_BEHAV (P, SHEAR))   (5)

According to the resolution principle, if there exist positive and negative instances of the same literal in two different clauses, we can obtain a new clause by joining together the two clauses—but omitting the literal in question. Intuitively, resolution involves canceling out the positive and negative instances of the literal with one other. Thus, clauses (4) and (5) above can be resolved to yield

(CRIT_BEHAV (P, FLEXURE))   (6)

which is equivalent to statement (3) and is the desired result.

Extending the above example, assume that our knowledge of structural analysis tells us that statement (1) can be generalized to hold true not only for beam P, but for any beam in a certain structure. We can express the more general statement as

FOR_ALL x (CRIT_BEHAV (x, FLEXURE)
          OR CRIT_BEHAV (x, SHEAR))   (7)

Intuitively, we should be able to infer statement (3) from statements (7) and (2) above. Moreover, consider the case of a different beam, Q, which has a very short span and for which we have ruled out the possibility of FLEXURE being the critical behavior. Reasoning along similar lines, from statement (7) and

NOT CRIT_BEHAV (Q, FLEXURE)   (8)

we should be able to infer

CRIT_BEHAV (Q, SHEAR)   (9)

It is thus apparent that we need some mechanism whereby we can substitute P, Q, and so on in place of x in statement (7). The mechanism for doing this is **unification**, which permits us to substitute specific instances— or even other variables—in place of a given variable in a statement, so that literals in two clauses can become identical and "resolve" each other out. The clausal forms of statements (7), (5), and (8) are

(CRIT_BEHAV (x, FLEXURE), CRIT_BEHAV (x, SHEAR))   (10)

(NOT CRIT_BEHAV (P, SHEAR))   (11)

(NOT CRIT_BEHAV (Q, FLEXURE))   (12)

Now, if we substitute P for x in clause (10), CRIT_BEHAV (x, SHEAR) and CRIT_BEHAV (P, SHEAR) will unify. This allows us to resolve clauses (10) and (11), yielding

(CRIT_BEHAV (P, FLEXURE))   (13)

which is the expected result.

Similarly, with the substitution of Q in place of x in clause (10) we can unify the literal CRIT_BEHAV (x, FLEXURE) with CRIT_BEHAV (Q, FLEXURE). We can then resolve this clause with clause (12) to yield the new—and intuitively correct—result

(CRIT_BEHAV (Q, SHEAR))   (14)

This example, although simple, illustrates the operations of unification and resolution. The generality of unification and resolution and their ability to match inferences made by other predicate logic rules of inference (e.g., modus ponens) make them extremely useful in performing deduction. Logic programming languages such as Prolog (discussed in Chapter 4) employ unification and resolution extensively to perform deductive reasoning with computers. There are variations and extensions (e.g., factorization) to the basic concepts presented here. A more complete mathematical treatment of resolution and unification can be found in [Genesereth 1987].

3.2.4 Interpretation in Logic Systems

For a logician, the exercise of developing or extending formal logic systems can be a delightful and worthwhile end in itself. Engineers are more likely to encode facts in formal logic for the purpose of modeling or representing the behavior of some engineering system. The logic system can then be used as a simulator of the real or hypothetical engineering system and exercised to aid in analysis, design, or diagnosis of the engineering system.

The semantics of a language define its meaning in some domain. An **interpretation** provides a semantic mapping of elements in a language to corresponding elements in a domain or system that the language is being used to represent. Each constant, function, or predicate symbol is assigned a value in the domain—say, the electrical circuit—which the logic system is intended to represent.

Engineers will have no trouble with this view of interpretation. We have been building both physical and mathematical models of engineering systems for centuries, in which elements of the model—variables and functions in a mathematical model, or physical elements and their analogical behavior in a physical model—represent components, concepts, and behaviors of the engineering system whose behavior we wish to understand or predict. Note, however, that logicians call the engineering system a **model** of the formal logic system only if sound deductions produced by the formal logic system are true in the model. Engineers are accustomed to viewing things the other way around!

3.3 HOW DEDUCTION CAN BE USED BY ENGINEERS

We have now completed our rapid overview of propositional and predicate logic symbols and rules. The intention of this coverage was not to provide the reader with a watered-down substitute for a full-blown course in logic, but rather to impart a feeling for how formal logic systems can be used to represent facts about the world and to carry out several kinds of deductions, including the following.

1. Deduce from a set or knowledge base of assumed facts additional facts which may help in finding a solution to a problem, or

2. Test whether a given new fact is logically consistent with facts already in a knowledge base.

The facts that formal logic systems have been employed to generate or test to date have most often been steps in proofs of theorems, wherein philosophers or mathematicians wished to show that a given conclusion could be derived from an initial set of assumptions using logical rules of inference, step by step. However, most engineering readers are undoubtedly more interested in exploring the ways in which formal logic systems can be used to deduce or test facts that might aid in the solution of engineering problems.

First, engineers are interested in the behavior of complex mechanical, electrical, chemical, cybernetic, and other systems. Where such systems involve continuous numerical relationships among variables, differential and integral calculus have provided powerful modeling paradigms. More recently, applied mathematicians and computer scientists have further extended the power of continuous mathematical models by developing finite element models and other numerical solution methods to provide approximate solutions for systems of equations that were tedious or impossible to solve in closed form. Meanwhile, desktop workstations have become ever more powerful and inexpensive. As a result, engineering simulation and analysis systems that only large engineering firms could afford are now well within the budgetary possibilities of individual engineering practitioners or students.

However, in spite of the striking advances in our ability to model continuous phenomena, some engineering systems are simply not adequately modeled using continuous mathematics alone. For such systems, logic-based approaches, as well as approaches using the representation techniques presented in Chapters 5 through 8, offer exciting new opportunities to extend the engineer's toolbox. A few examples serve to illustrate this.

❑ Digital electronic circuits exhibit a switching behavior that is categorized by discontinuous, binary states rather than continuous relationships. Modeling circuit behavior for simulation, diagnosis, and testing purposes was an early area of application for logic-based systems and continues to be an active research area [Genesereth 1987].

❑ Engineering design involves finding values for parameters that will satisfy constraints. Codes or experience-based handbooks often express these constraints in binary or discrete form, so that design knowledge is often more effectively modeled as logical statements than as continuous mathematical equations. For example, a structural code may state, "If a beam is simply supported, its depth shall be greater than one-thirtieth of its clear span." Inequalities of this kind are either satisfied or not satisfied, so propositions containing them will evaluate to true or false. The logic-based design interpreter discussed in Chapter 4 exploits this characteristic of engineering design [Chan 1987].

❑   Many separate disciplines are involved in most contemporary kinds of engineering work. The constraints that must be satisfied across disciplines can often best be formalized as logical expressions. Knowing the choice of catalyst for a chemical reaction will allow one to deduce the desired reaction temperature and pressure. These values will, in turn, permit deduction of the best material for fabrication of the reactor vessel and its allowable stresses, and so on. Relationships or constraints of this kind can be conveniently represented in formal logic systems, permitting allowable downstream values of related design components to be deduced using logical inference.

Our discussion so far has dealt primarily with the form of logical inference known as deduction—that is, inferring specific instances from more general statements. However, logic systems also support two other kinds of inference: abduction and induction. Both are useful, although somewhat more problematic than deduction.

Abduction is like reverse modus ponens: From B and A → B, abduce A. With abduction, we want to explain the cause of some observed symptom B by proposing possible causes, using the modus ponens inference rule in the backward direction. Note that this is not a robust form of inference. Although A implies B, the reverse is not true. Let us assume in this case that C, D, and E can also imply B, and, if the implications are based upon some notion of causality, any one of them could be the cause of the observed symptom B.

Abduction can, however, help us to construct a list of plausible causes of B which we can then investigate further. This is the essence of diagnosis, in which a physician or mechanic attempts to explain the malfunctioning of a human or mechanical system by generating and then testing plausible underlying causes of the malfunction. This kind of problem-solving behavior is widely employed in every branch of engineering.

Induction involves inferring a plausible general statement from a set of specific facts. Recall that the universal quantifier out rule allows us to deduce that any specific instance of a globally quantified formula is true. Induction is tantamount to using the universal quantifier out rule backwards. Like abduction, induction is not a robust or sound form of inference. If one or several trees lose their leaves in October, it is not necessarily true that all trees lose their leaves in October.

Like abduction, induction suggests inferences—in this case general statements about a world of interest—which, although not provably correct, are plausible. We can temporarily suspend doubt, assume that an inferred general statement is correct, and then deduce from it a set of logically consistent specific facts whose validity can be independently tested. Induction is thus a kind of learning by generalization. The process of observing some facts about the world, inducing a plausible general statement from these facts, deducing new facts that should hold if the general statement is correct, and investigating whether the deduced facts are true, is nothing other than the *scientific method*—the approach used by natural and social scientists to extend the frontiers of human knowledge.

3.4 SUMMARY

In this chapter we explained how systems of logic permit us to deduce new and consistent facts from a given knowledge base of facts using rules of inference and to test the validity of new facts against a known set of assumed or axiomatic facts. A practical difficulty in doing this, however, is in knowing which deductions to make in order to generate facts that will extend a fact base in the direction of a desired solution or proof.

For example, a knowledge base might contain the fact (in the form of a universal quantifier) that all San Francisco telephone numbers have the area code 415; and the knowledge base might also contain a series of singular facts in which we assert the names of all San Francisco telephone subscribers. Using this knowledge base, we could apply the universal quantifier out rule once for each named subscriber and deduce that his or her telephone number had the area code 415. Even with the power of current computers, this would be a costly and rather pointless exercise. The universal quantifier out rule only needs to be applied to the specific subscribers whose complete telephone numbers are needed at a given stage of problem solving, but logic systems alone provide no guidance about when to make the needed deductions.

Mathematical logicians are not especially concerned with questions of efficiency, but developers of computer programming languages must be. Logic programming languages, if they are to be useful in solving significant engineering problems, must provide "meta inference rules" or other ways to guide deduction—in effect, making deduction a form of directed search. The Prolog computer language, discussed in Chapter 4, uses depth-first backward search as a way to guide its process of deduction; and the inference procedures used with production rules, frames, and semantic nets, discussed in subsequent chapters, can all be viewed as specialized kinds of deduction guided by some form of directed search.

Viewed from this perspective, deduction and search can be seen as complementary rather than competing paradigms for representing and reasoning with knowledge—they are the yin and yang of knowledge-based systems. As unabashedly pragmatic engineers, we leave to the neats and scruffies their ongoing jihad about the one true religion as we go on to explore paradigms that engineers can use to implement knowledge-based systems.

Chapter 4

LANGUAGES FOR
SYMBOLIC COMPUTATION

In Chapters 2 and 3 we described systems of logic that enable people to make valid deductions from an initial knowledge base of facts, along with search strategies to help them determine which deductions to make next. Such inference and search processes are at the core of what most people usually think of as "intelligent" behavior. If we were able to program computers to perform logical inference operations guided by appropriate search strategies, we could therefore claim to have implemented a form of "artificial intelligence." Considerable progress has been made in this area since the idea was first seriously entertained by George Boole around 1850 and more recently by scientists like Alan Turing, Claude Shannon, Alan Newell, Herbert Simon, John McCarthy, Marvin Minsky, and others in the 1950s. Computer scientists have developed a number of specialized languages to facilitate such logic programming; we shall describe two of them in this chapter.

4.1 INTRODUCTION

Computer languages for logic programming must have structures for storing and retrieving known and deduced facts in a fact base or knowledge base, and they must have functions or procedures for deducing new facts. In principle, we can do these things with procedural languages like Fortran or Pascal. However, operations like list processing, which are useful for performing logical inferences, are inefficient and difficult to implement in procedural languages. Thus the need for specialized languages.

In this chapter we discuss the features of two commonly used programming languages designed specifically for manipulating logical expressions. We start by describing Lisp, one of the the oldest and the most widely used of these languages. We will show that Lisp is an extremely flexible language with built-in capabilities for defining and manipulating sequences of symbols that can represent objects, classes of objects, and predicates. We then discuss Prolog, a higher-level language—often implemented on top of Lisp—which contains several built-in kinds of deduction and search as primitive functions. Finally, we talk about KBES shells: even higher-level languages for developing knowledge-based systems which are often, but not always, built on top of languages like Prolog and Lisp. These higher-level languages incorporate capabilities for search and deduction, as well as user and program interfaces, and constitute programming environments that are akin to "power tools" for knowledge engineering [Sheil 1983].

We note that our presentation is not a substitute for serious study of these languages. Rather, it is intended to highlight how they differ from conventional programming languages and to illustrate some of the ways that their unique characteristics empower them to manipulate logical expressions. More detailed coverage is provided in an excellent chapter on Lisp in [Charniak 1985]. There are several good introductions to Lisp, including [Anderson 1987; Tatar 1987; Touretzky 1984; Winston 1984b]. The definitive reference on Prolog is [Clocksin 1984]. Sterling [1986] gives a clear and rigorous introduction to Prolog.

4.2 LISP

Lisp was developed by John McCarthy in the late 1950s as a specialized language for artificial intelligence applications. Lisp is an acronym for List Processor. Procedural languages like Pascal or C have primitive operators to perform algebraic computations with formulas containing integer or real number symbols. In addition to these, the Lisp language also has a set of primitive operators that enable it conveniently to carry out several kinds of deductions with sentences (lists) containing words (arbitrary strings of characters) representing predicates and their arguments. In this section we provide an overview of the structure and philosophy of the language and some examples of these higher-level functions.

4.2.1 Atoms and Lists in Lisp

Lisp programs contain expressions which are lists of atoms enclosed by parentheses. An **atom**, represented by an unbroken string of characters, is the smallest symbol that can be manipulated in Lisp. For example, the following strings are each atoms: PUMP_21, BEAM_27, and X. A **list** is simply zero or more atoms, separated from each other by one or more spaces and enclosed by parentheses. Thus ( ), (PUMP_21 BEAM_27 X), and (MBM @%_@!) are all lists. The parentheses are used for **scoping**, just as in algebra, although they tend to proliferate in Lisp. (In fact, Lisp aficionados often regard the acronym as standing for lots of insipid parentheses.)

The components of a Lisp expression are a predicate and its arguments, contained in a list. Lisp does not distinguish between predicates and arguments in the way that it stores them. The argument of a predicate in Lisp is often another expression containing one or more predicates and their arguments. (Note the similarity between Lisp and predicate logic expressions. The expressions used to illustrate our discussion of predicate logic in Chapter 3 are all valid Lisp expressions.)

4.2.2   Evaluation of Expressions in Lisp

The basic operation of a Lisp program is much like that of a pocket calculator [Touretzky 1984]. The READ, EVAL, PRINT loop in Lisp reads an expression entered at the top-level prompt, evaluates the expression, and prints the result. Expressions nested within other expressions are enclosed by parentheses and are evaluated from the inside outward. The empty list is called NIL and is used to signify the opposite of true. Each expression evaluates to NIL, that is, false, or to a value other than NIL, corresponding to true.

4.2.3   Defining Functions in Lisp

Since Lisp is an interpretive language, functions can be defined at any time and then called from within the environment. Lisp has a function, DEFUN, to do this. Its form is

```
(DEFUN NAME_OF_FUNCTION (ARGUMENTS)
    (FUNCTION_DEFINITION))
```

Thus the function to compute the maximum midspan moment of a simply supported beam might be defined as follows.

```
(DEFUN  SS_BEAM_MOMENT (LOAD  SPAN_LENGTH)
    (/ ( * (LOAD (EXPT SPAN_LENGTH 2)) 8)))
```

Evaluating the expressions in parentheses from the inside out, this function raises SPAN_LENGTH to the exponent 2 (using the primitive Lisp function EXPT), multiplies it by LOAD (using the * Lisp function), and then divides this value by 8 (using the / Lisp function).

Having defined this function in a Lisp environment, we can then call it at any time through the READ, EVAL, PRINT loop to compute a beam's moment by typing the function name and a set of values for the two arguments.

(SS_BEAM_MOMENT 3000 8.3) returns 25833.75

Moreover, if this is a function we wish to use again in the future, we can save it and list it in an initiation file (which Lisp reads when loading) as one of the functions to be loaded in the future along with the basic Lisp environment. A user can thus customize her or his Lisp environment in a very straightforward way. We will return to this point later.

4.2.4   List Processing in Lisp

One feature of Lisp that makes it attractive for logic programming is its ability to do search or deduction with strings of characters as its elementary or atomic chunks. This feature stems from Lisp's built-in **primitives** or primitive functions for manipulating arbitrary strings of characters—that is, words—and lists of such strings. Examples of these follow.

CAR (JOHN PETER MICHAEL) returns JOHN, the first atom from the list.

CDR (JOHN PETER MICHAEL) returns (PETER MICHAEL), the remainder of the list after the CAR has been extracted.

CONS (ELAINE (JOHN PETER MICHAEL)) adds the atom to the beginning of the list and returns (ELAINE JOHN PETER MICHAEL).

These functions are useful for parsing sentences to extract their meaning, or for generating natural language explanations of reasoning by assembling sentences from words or phrases.

4.2.5   Defining Classes and Their Properties

Lisp has a primitive function for assigning properties and values to objects or object classes. This function, PUTPROP, uses the syntax (PUTPROP SYMBOL VALUE ATTRIBUTE).

(PUTPROP 'INLET_VALVES 'STAINLESS_STEEL 'MATERIAL) sets the property MATERIAL of the object class INLET_VALVES to the value STAINLESS_STEEL.

(The quotes that appear before the SYMBOL VALUE ATTRIBUTE triple are required in some versions of Lisp to indicate that what follows should be read literally and not evaluated.) The values of property attributes thus defined can be retrieved using the GET function.

(GET 'INLET_VALVES 'MATERIAL) returns STAINLESS_STEEL

Moreover, using Lisp, it is easy for attributes and their values to be inherited by instances of the object classes. A simplistic way to do this is the following.

(SETQ VALVE_14 'INLET_VALVES)

This creates a pointer from VALVE_14 to the symbol INLET_VALVES and its property list, making VALVE_14 an "instance" of the class INLET_VALVES.

(GET VALVE_14 'MATERIAL) now returns STAINLESS_STEEL

Because Lisp provides these primitives for creating and retrieving property lists as part of its basic repertoire, and because it is so easy to customize a Lisp enviroment, some advanced Lisp programmers developed more powerful ways to manipulate objects and classes as extensions to the core Lisp functions. The Common Lisp Object System (CLOS) is an evolving standard for Lisp object systems [Bobrow 1988]. In Section 6.3 we discuss how such object-oriented programming languages can be used in KBESs.

4.2.6 Conditional Statements

The COND function in Lisp tests premises and fires conclusions contingently. It is valuable for implementing flow of control logic structures akin to IF-THEN-ELSE rules. The form of the COND statement is given in [Charniak 1985].

```
(COND   (TEST₁ ACTION₁)
        (TEST₂ ACTION₂)

        . . .
        (TESTₙ ACTIONₙ))
```

The COND statement evaluates the predicate in $TEST_1$. If $TEST_1$ evaluates to true, Lisp returns the value of $ACTION_1$ and ends execution of the function. If the first test evaluates to false, Lisp proceeds to evaluate $TEST_2$

and, if it evaluates to true, returns the value of ACTION₂, stopping execution. If all tests fail, Lisp returns NIL as the value of the function.

4.2.7 Recursion in Lisp

Recursion is the process in which a function calls itself as a subfunction. It is naturally and easily performed in Lisp. Recursion is useful in many ways for AI applications, for example, in searching through trees at progressively deeper levels, as described in Chapter 2. Such recursion can be made to operate both on numbers and on lists. For example, a recursive function that adds all the integers between zero and any terminating integer N is contained in the following definition of the function SUMALL, adapted from [Anderson 1987]. It uses the COND function defined above and the Lisp function-defining statement DEFUN.

```
(DEFUN SUMALL (N)
      (COND ((ZEROP N) 0)
            (T (+ N (SUMALL (– N 1))))))
```

This formula recognizes that the sum of the integers between 0 and N is equal to N plus the sum of the integers between 0 and N–1, and so on, recursively. A list recursion formula would look very much the same except that we recognize that the sum of all the atoms on a list is the sum of the first atom plus the CDR of the list [Anderson 1987].

```
(DEFUN LIST_SUM (LIS)
      (COND ((NULL LIS) 0)
            (T (+ (CAR LIS) (LIST_SUM (CDR LIS))))))
```

Note that in both of these simple examples, we need to be sure that we have exactly the same number of closing ("insipid") parentheses as we do opening parentheses.

4.2.8 Variables and Dynamic Memory Management in Lisp

In Lisp, variables are defined as needed within expressions. If a variable occurs both inside and outside of a given expression, its value outside of the expression is unchanged by the values it may take on inside the expression. Lisp can therefore assign memory addresses for variables dynamically, thus relieving the programmer of the need to declare variables with unique names and fixed array sizes. When no longer needed, the assigned memory space is reclaimed for reuse as Lisp carries out a process called **garbage collection**.

Dynamic memory allocation can be a real productivity aid to Lisp programmers. This is especially true for rapid prototyping and refinement, a style of software development eschewed by classical software engineers as being sloppy because of its emphasis on rapid and informal experimentation. The disadvantage of dynamic memory allocation is the need in many Lisp environments to stop program execution for significant periods—several minutes is not unusual—to do garbage collection when the environments run out of memory space. This is obviously a fatal drawback for applications like patient or equipment monitoring in which real-time program execution is important. However, more recently developed Lisp environments which run on traditional engineering workstations can perform continuous garbage collection in the background.

4.2.9   Summary and Discussion of Lisp Features

Lisp is in many ways as much a programming environment as it is a language. Lisp provides a built-in set of primitive functions for operations that are useful in symbolic computation (e.g., string handling, conditional evaluation, property definition, and recursion), along with the numerical primitives provided by many procedural languages. Additional functions can be easily defined at any point within a program and can then be called immediately in subsequent lines of code. If newly defined functions are saved and loaded together with a basic Lisp environment, the environment has, in effect, been customized.

Because of features like the ones we have described, Lisp is an attractive language for implementing formal logic systems, such as predicate logic, in which we use word symbols that are close to natural language words to represent predicates, terms, and quantifiers. Lisp is also useful for creating qualitative models of engineering systems containing objects with properties and relationships. These features distinguish Lisp from procedural languages like Fortran or Pascal, which were designed primarily for computation with numerical variables. This is why some of the most powerful artificial intelligence programming environments are implemented in Lisp (see Chapter 12).

Many excellent Lisp compilers now exist so that developed Lisp code can be compiled to produce run-time systems whose efficiency is comparable to compiled C or Pascal code. However, Lisp is inherently an interpretive language. Thus, debugging can be done with uncompiled Lisp code or, in some environments, with a mixture of compiled code for the part of a program that has already been debugged and uncompiled code for the part currently being developed. The interpretive nature of Lisp, its dynamic memory allocation capability, and the superb graphics, window-oriented error tracing, and debugging facilities of many Lisp environments make it an extremely flexible and productive programming tool for building applications that employ logical as well as numerical symbol processing. Since Lisp is both a language and a customizable environment, many versions or dialects of Lisp quickly sprouted from McCarthy's original version of Lisp. Thankfully, in the last few years there has been significant movement toward a standard version of Lisp which is called Common Lisp. The definitive reference on Common Lisp is [Steele 1984].

Some of the earliest knowledge-based systems were implemented in languages like Pascal and Fortran and even lowly Basic, and knowledge-processing systems are still sometimes implemented in procedural languages like C. There are several reasons for this. First, many KBES developers were already familiar with procedural languages and thus used them. Second, powerful Lisp environments for workstations or personal computers only became available during the mid-1980s. Third, in some hardware/operating system configurations, Lisp programs could not easily call or be called from external functions implemented in other languages. And fourth, the need for Lisp programs to stop execution while doing garbage collection made early Lisp environments unsuitable for some real-time applications.

Most of the shortcomings of earlier Lisp environments have been addressed by Lisp software developers in the current versions of their software. Moreover, many universities are beginning to teach introductory computer programming courses using Lisp (and Prolog, which we describe next). Thus, it is reasonable to assume that Lisp will retain or even enhance its position as the AI programming language of choice during the 1990s.

This "instant" review of the features of Lisp barely skims the surface of a powerful and expressive language that has become the underlying programming language for the majority of high-level AI development environments and many AI applications developed to date. We now review features of the Prolog language.

4.3 PROLOG

Prolog was developed as an alternative language for artificial intelligence programming by Alain Colmerauer and his colleagues in Marseilles during the early 1970s. It was based upon ideas proposed by C. Green, P. Hayes, R. Kowalski, and others. (See [Genesereth 1987] for a brief history of AI languages.) Like Lisp, it spawned many dialects. The definitive standard for Prolog today is arguably Edinburgh Prolog [Clocksin 1984]. It has been widely used in Europe, Japan, and Australia for AI applications, but less so in the United States. Prolog is a higher-level language than Lisp in that it has some kinds of deduction and search already built in.

4.3.1   The Architecture and Philosophy of Prolog

Prolog can be viewed simply as a theorem prover implemented in the form of "a language interpreter which we program by giving it axioms" [Charniak 1985]. Viewed in this way, Prolog is the ultimate vehicle for declarative programming: all we need to do is provide Prolog with a set of statements or axioms describing some system about which we wish to reason, and it deduces the desired additional facts—the solution to our problem—using its built-in powers of deduction. Actually Prolog is both more and less than this. We shall try to demonstrate this in the following brief discussion (which follows [Sterling 1986]).

We explained in Chapter 3 how deduction permits us to answer two kinds of questions about systems: (1) whether a statement is true for a given interpretation of the statement's symbols, and (2) whether a new statement is a valid deduction from a given set of statements or axioms. The Prolog language facilitates the development of computer programs that can answer both kinds of questions.

A Prolog program is simply a set of logical statements—comprising facts, queries, and rules—written in a precise syntax. Given such a set of axioms, a Prolog interpreter either verifies whether a given additional fact is true or it deduces new facts which are valid logical consequents of the axioms provided.

4.3.2   Facts, Variables, and Queries in Prolog

The Prolog program for an engineering application typically contains a database of **facts** or axioms to describe the properties of and relationships among a set of objects in a system we wish to model. These facts can be used to describe properties, as in LENGTH_IN_MM (SCREW_95, 16.25)., or relations, for example, CONNECTED_TO (VALVE_17, PIPE_32). and CONNECTED_TO (VALVE_17, PIPE_34). Note that Prolog uses commas to delimit atoms in lists, and it uses a period to delimit facts.

It is easy to **query** the database of facts in a Prolog program. We simply ask a question of the form CONNECTED_TO (VALVE_17, PIPE_32)?, and Prolog will answer YES. If Prolog does not find the fact in its database and has no way (e.g., no relevant rule to use) to attempt to deduce the answer to the query, it will answer NO.

Prolog uses **logical variables** (written in uppercase letters) to enable more powerful kinds of questioning through existential queries. **Existential queries** are queries containing one or more logical variables. This is intuitive from our earlier discussion of predicate logic. We are asking whether there exists an instance of the variable X which makes the query true in our database of facts. The answer to this form of query is thus the instance or instances of X that can be found in the database, or NO if none can be found.

Thus, instead of guessing at the length of a screw and asking if this guess is correct, we could use the variable X in the following query to find the unknown length of screw number 95: LENGTH_IN_MM (SCREW_95, X)? This would return X = 16.25. Similarly, the query CONNECTED_TO (VALVE_17, X)? would return (X = PIPE_32), (X = PIPE_34).

Variables can also be used in facts within Prolog. Thus, from a universal fact of the form likes (X, FREEDOM_FROM_PAIN). we can deduce the instance of the fact LIKES (JOHN_WILKINS, FREEDOM_FROM_PAIN). by substituting JOHN_WILKINS for X.

Prolog gets more interesting when we try to answer an existential query by employing a universal fact. It does this by searching for a fact which is an instance of both the existential query and the universal fact. If one is found, the answer is that common instance. If not, the answer is NO.

4.3.3 Rules in Prolog

A rule in Prolog states that a goal is implied by the conjunction of a set of goals. It is expressed in the following form.

GOAL_0 ← GOAL_1, GOAL_2, GOAL_3, GOAL_4 . . . . . . GOAL_N.

This rule means that GOAL_0 is true only if all of the goals on the right-hand side of the implication are true. GOAL_0 is termed the **head** of the rule and the conjunction of GOAL_1 through GOAL_N is termed the **body**. (A fact as we have defined it above is simply a rule with no body.)

In Prolog, rules—along with queries and facts—are called **clauses**. As we explained in Chapter 3, such clauses are restricted to be Horn clauses. A

Horn clause is either a simple sentence or **literal**; its negation; or a set of literals, representing their disjunction, in which at most one simple literal is positive. It takes some practice to express engineering or other concepts in Horn clause form, but any predicate logic sentence can be converted into a set of Horn clauses that is equivalent to the original sentence, following procedures outlined in standard logic texts such as [Genesereth 1987; Richards 1989]. The payoff for following the rigor of Horn clause notation is the ability to employ a powerful deductive language that can be applied automatically to the declarative knowledge thus expressed.

Prolog will answer a query about the truth of GOAL_0 by setting up each of the goals in its body as subgoals, and by checking whether each one is true in the database of facts and rules that constitute the program. If one of these goals occurs in the head of another rule in the program, it will set up the goals in the body of the second rule as subgoals at the next-lower level, and so on. Thus, Prolog automatically performs backward chaining on rules expressed in this form, employing a depth-first search procedure in which the ordering of clauses in the body of successive rules governs the order of deepening search. This embedded, depth-first backward-chaining mechanism in Prolog is one reason why we view it as a higher-level language than Lisp.

If the goals in a rule are **ground facts**—that is, they contain no variables— then the solution process merely chains backward through rules from a goal in the body of one rule to the matching head of another until no further rules can be used to generate subgoals. It then searches the database for facts that match these leaf goals in the tree.

If goal clauses contain variables, Prolog can perform unification and resolution (see Section 3.2.3). These more complex forms of deduction are required to compute valid substitutions—if any legal ones exist—for matching variables in a set of clauses (see [Genesereth 1987; Nilsson 1980]). In effect, Prolog solves a set of logical equations by finding particular values for the variables in the goal clauses that resolve the system of logical equations. Moreover, Prolog can backtrack out of dead-end searches and try other, potentially more fruitful branches of a search tree in performing these more complex kinds of deduction. Using facts, queries, and rules, a Prolog program is able to perform many of the operations used in relational databases. (See [Sterling 1986] for an explanation of how Prolog implements unions, intersections, joins, and other relational operations on data.) And, like Lisp, Prolog supports recursion.

4.3.4 Illustration: A Prolog System to Support Design

We now briefly describe an example to illustrate the power of Prolog for engineering applications. Chan [1987] presents a general design interpreter that exploits many of Prolog's high-level logic manipulation capabilities. The design interpreter was used to automate the design of truss bridges. As its input, the program takes a set of structural constraints that must be satisfied by the bridge. It then uses Prolog as a "design interpreter" in two ways.

❑   **To propagate constraints**—that is, to find legal values (which may still be specified in terms of the values of other variables) for currently unknown variables in a constraint; and

❑   **To check constraints**—that is, to verify that constraints are still satisfied, when all of their variables have been bound to particular values in the solution process.

Notice that these two kinds of constraint manipulations correspond to the two kinds of deduction that formal logic systems help us to do: finding consistent new facts from a database of given facts, and checking the validity of proposed new facts against a database of existing facts.

This design interpreter subdivides the design task into a series of modules (associated with steps in the design process or with clusters of components). Each module encloses a group of tightly mutually constrained variables, which are first resolved using only local constraints (i.e., constraints with other design variables contained in the same module). Once local constraints have been propagated and resolved, the system propagates, and attempts to resolve, interface constraints (those dealing with variable values in other modules) in a second pass. The flow of control in this program is achieved using heuristics encoded as Prolog rules.

The system produces a design for the bridge, in the form of a set of values or **bindings** for each of the design variables—member sizes, in this case— that satisfies the given constraints. In the course of finding solutions, the program exploits Prolog's ability to backtrack out of dead ends—solution paths which lead to values of design variables that violate one or more constraints. (Chan [1987] presents more detail on this system and provides a good introduction to the use of constraints in logic programming.)

4.3.5   Summary of Prolog's Features

We have tried to explain and illustrate how Prolog acts as an interpreter of logic systems and how its interpretation features can be harnessed for deduction in engineering systems. The embedded mechanisms for answering queries, backward chaining through related rules, unification and resolution, and backtracking make Prolog a higher-level language than Lisp.

Facts about engineering systems can be represented in Horn clause notation, and engineering tasks can be specified using rules as heuristics to guide a search for legal solutions or for constraints that can be propagated and checked to generate and test legal designs. Prolog thus provides a powerful and flexible language for implementing search and deduction and can therefore be employed for automating engineering tasks ranging across the classification-formation continuum (see Chapter 1).

4.4   HIGHER-LEVEL LANGUAGES FOR COMPUTER REASONING

We have shown in Section 4.3 how Prolog provides a higher-level logic programming environment than Lisp by implementing embedded capabilities for both deduction and search. A complete application requires more than this, however. In particular, applications designed to be used by humans need user interfaces, and applications designed to work with external applications and their databases need software interfaces. Moreover, there are many kinds of search or program control strategies besides depth-first backward chaining that a knowledge engineer may wish to employ in a KBES. Prolog and particularly Lisp are flexible enough languages in which to build arbitrary interfaces or search strategies for a given application, but building them can be a time-consuming and tedious programming job, often requiring more than 50 percent of total system development effort (see Chapter 12).

Early consultation-style expert systems such as MYCIN [Buchanan 1984] used depth-first backward chaining as their only search strategy. And they typically accessed their "data" by posing a series of queries to the user for input at the keyboard. Since many of these early consultation systems used the same search techniques and had similar user interface requirements, it became apparent to the developers of MYCIN that they could develop a higher-level language yet—a so-called expert system **shell**—into which knowledge could be inserted by engineers, doctors, technicians, and others in a form even closer to natural language than Lisp or Prolog. The developers of MYCIN thus abstracted the inference mechanism and user interface components of MYCIN to create EMYCIN, or Essential MYCIN, as the first such shell. Interestingly, the first application of EMYCIN to a different domain was SACON, a KBES that helped structural engineers use a complex suite of finite element analysis packages (see [Bennett 1978, 1984] and Chapter 5). Other shells proliferated rapidly after the success of EMYCIN and became available on microcomputers in the early 1980s.

It should be pointed out that not all expert system shells are implemented in AI languages like Lisp or Prolog. For example, two personal computer–based KBES shells were both implemented primarily in Pascal: Insight 2+, a production rule shell in the style of MYCIN [Level 5 1987], and the Deciding Factor, derived from the PROSPECTOR inference net expert system [Campbell 1985; Duda 1979].

What both Prolog and the aforementioned rule-based shells lack, however, is the representation flexibility offered by frame-based and object-oriented knowledge representation schemes. We shall discuss these representation schemes in detail in Chapter 6. It is worth noting that the most powerful and flexible tools for programming KBES applications—often called AI development environments—provide a variety of representation schemes (e.g., rules and frames) and several inference styles (e.g., forward chaining and backward chaining). These features, combined with the flexibility of Lisp environments, powerful bit-mapped graphics, and tools for building external program interfaces, produce truly powerful **general-purpose representation languages** [Dym 1987]. We shall discuss these general-purpose languages—often called **environments** or **tools**, so as to distinguish them from the less powerful shells—in greater detail in Chapter 12.

In subsequent chapters, we will allude to a number of these KBES shells or environments that can be used by engineers as "power tools" for building knowledge-based systems. In most cases, however, we will pay a price in using a higher-level tool because there is invariably some attendant loss of flexibility. The user of a particular shell typically surrenders some degree of control over the inference scheme and the design of the system's user interface. Thus, the user must try to fit the problem into a somewhat restricted—and potentially unsuitable—architecture for representation and reasoning.

However, the good news is that, for many classes of engineering applications (e.g., diagnosis, evaluation, monitoring, or configuration), there now exist high-level KBES shells and tools whose representation and reasoning paradigms match the requirements of the applications rather well. If a suitable shell or environment can be found in which to implement a given application, it can significantly enhance both the productivity and quality of the knowledge engineering process.

4.5   SUMMARY

In this chapter we have introduced and briefly described the two programming languages most often used in AI programming, Lisp and Prolog. We have provided an overview, introductory concepts, and a starting vocabulary to launch readers into texts on programming in these languages. We have also begun to describe the higher-level programming environments sometimes called general-purpose representation languages.

While both Lisp and Prolog have their advocates as the "best" AI language, this really is not the issue. In choosing a language the main point is that it must support the paradigms that will be useful for the application at hand [Bobrow 1985b]. Indeed, perhaps the most cogent observation on the language issue—one that we shall make repeatedly in the broader context of integrated engineering environments—is that multiple paradigms are most often what is needed for serious AI applications [Bobrow 1986a]. Hence we do not take sides here in this artificial war. Rather we emphasize that there are choices to be made and that the user/chooser must be aware of both the choices and the metrics for choosing among them. We have already mentioned some of these metrics and issues in this chapter and we shall do so again (see especially Chapter 12).

Part II of this book presents the most important paradigms currently available for representing and reasoning about engineering knowledge. As we introduce these higher-level representation paradigms, we will build upon the basic ideas introduced in this chapter to explain how they are implemented in computers, and we will provide guidelines for using them to build engineering KBES applications.

PART

II

IMPLEMENTATION TECHNIQUES

We now turn to the process of implementing our new approaches to solving problem on computers. Thus, we focus on how we can represent the knowledge of our problem domains so that it can be applied in computer-based search and logic. And, therefore, we devote this part of the book to representation for computing.

We begin in Chapter 5 with rule-based approaches to computer-aided reasoning. Here we wish to use some of the structure of mathematical logic to express problem-solving knowledge in terms of rules that represent the plausible reasoning exhibited by human experts. We shall also find that rules alone do not have enough expressive power for describing the complex objects and multifaceted concepts that are typical of serious engineering problems, particularly those in the domains of planning and design.

Therefore, in Chapter 6 we introduce semantic nets, frames, and object-oriented programming techniques—knowledge representation and reasoning paradigms that can represent and reason with broader and deeper kinds of knowledge about engineering systems than can rules alone. We then go on to show how these paradigms can be integrated with production rules to create powerful hybrid knowledge-processing environments with the power to address a wide range of engineering applications.

Chapter 7 is devoted to a discussion of advanced topics in representation. Here we survey several topics that are rather more advanced than the fundamentals we have stressed so far. The particular ideas we shall outline include qualitative reasoning, also called qualitative physics; belief revision systems, also known as truth maintenance systems, and the creation of "multiple worlds"; and reasoning about space and time.

In Chapter 8 we introduce some emerging ideas that have the potential to meet the challenges imposed by engineering tasks. After discussing the special requirements of the engineering workplace, we present a methodology and architecture for engineering applications that integrates KBES environments with computer-aided design and drafting (CADD) systems and their databases. We then go on to discuss two KBES architectures that can support concurrent or simultaneous engineering, that is, environments which facilitate the interaction of multiple experts—both humans and KBESs—to solve complex problems. These are blackboard architectures and a more decentralized approach called cooperative distributed problem solving

Chapter 5

RULE-BASED REPRESENTATION

In this chapter we concern ourselves with the implementation of rule-based approaches to computer-aided reasoning. We need to be clear, however, that such implementation involves more than programming elementary logic statements. Our focus, in fact, will be on ways that we can use some of the structure of logic to express problem-solving knowledge in terms of rules. We shall see that there is much power in the representation of reasoning with rules, as might be expected from our discussion of logic in Chapter 3. In particular, we shall see that we can account for patterns of *plausible inference* in addition to the precise mathematics of logic [Buchanan 1983b; Hayes-RothF 1985]. We shall also find that rules alone are not enough for the formulation and solution of complex engineering problems, principally because they do not allow sufficient *expressive power* for describing complex objects and multifaceted concepts.

5.1 LOGIC AND PLAUSIBLE INFERENCE

We begin by observing that human experts often express their own expertise in terms of **situation-action rules,** which are statements to the effect that in such-and-such a *situation,* one should take the (following) specified *action* [Brownston 1985; Buchanan 1984]. To make up an example from the domain of structural mechanics, consider the following rule.

IF   A STRUCTURE IS THIN (SAY IN THE Z DIMENSION);

AND   THE LOADING ON THE STRUCTURE IS IN THE Z DIRECTION;

AND   THERE IS NO OTHER SIGNIFICANT LOADING;

THEN   ELEMENTARY PLATE (BENDING) THEORY CAN BE USED TO DESCRIBE THE STRUCTURE'S BEHAVIOR.

This rule indicates that in a certain situation—where we have a thin planar structure whose loading is largely normal to its plane—the appropriate action to be taken is that the elementary bending theory of plates should be used to model the structure's behavior. Note that this rule is not precise; that is, it contains descriptors that are not readily quantifiable. For example, precisely what do we mean when we refer to a dimension of a structure as being considerably smaller than its other dimensions? And what is meant by an absence of substantial loading in the plane of the structure?

To an expert in mechanics or structures, however, this rule is certainly plausible because it is consistent with the development of plate theory as a subset of the theory of elasticity [Shames 1985]. While the rule is plausible, it is not ironclad. There are further conditions (and possibly exceptions) that would need to be considered before we could say something that is absolutely definitive.

What does this have to do with logic? And why do we care? The connection with logic is that the situation-action rule just given bears a marked resemblance to the style of inference called modus ponens (see Chapter 3).

Given   A and A → B

deduce B

The rule of modus ponens is one of strict inference, of a deduction that must follow, and it assumes that the propositions A and A → B are themselves either facts or axioms or have been established by rigorous logic from axioms and/or known facts. Our rule on plate theory, however, is more suggestive than precise. Thus, while there is a resemblance of form, and while the analogy with strict logic is useful for representing rules in a computable form, we are more interested here in dealing with rules that are plausible even though they may not be quite as rigorous as logic statements.

Which brings us to the second question. We care because, as we have already noted, it turns out that much of the style of problem solving that experts apply in their given domains looks like a concatenation of plausible rules [Buchanan 1984; Hayes-RothF 1985; Newell 1963]. The rules themselves have their origins in a variety of sources. Some are **heuristics** that are based on experience, on what is known to work from prior trials. Other rules reflect **compiled knowledge** and are based on a compilation of or extraction from the first principles of a particular domain. Still other rules are **causal** in nature; that is, they describe very specific cause-and-effect relationships. Thus, rules can represent several different kinds of knowledge, are typically suggestive rather than axiomatic, and can be used to express or represent knowledge about a specific problem or domain.

5.2 FORWARD AND BACKWARD CHAINING

In our discussion of tree search, we talked about the fact that motion occurs because some condition or set of conditions triggers an operator (see Section 2.3.2). These search operators are quite often defined in terms of rules in which the IF clauses, the left-hand sides of the rules, define the situation(s) that must obtain before the rule can be applied or **fired**. The right-hand sides of the rules, the THEN statements, define a set of actions to be taken in a given situation, that is, if the data for the problem at hand **match** the situation data given in the left-hand side of the rule. The left-hand sides of rules are sometimes also called the rule **antecedents** and the right-hand sides **consequents**.

Now, there are two basic styles of using rules to define a direction of movement through a search space or in otherwise representing a problem-solving process. These two styles follow from the fact that modus ponens can be used in two different ways. In the first, we could treat A as data and regard the implication A → B as the relevant operator or rule. In this style we would match the problem data against the antecedents of all the available rules, find the set of applicable rule(s), select the particular rule(s) to be fired, and then take the actions dictated by the consequents of the fired rule(s). From this straightforward application of modus ponens, we would then naturally conclude B. This kind of reasoning is **data-driven reasoning** or **forward chaining**.

The second style of reasoning follows from the fact that we can write a rule in which the consequent appears first without changing the meaning of the rule in the slightest. That is, instead of writing

IF   A

THEN   B

we could instead write an equivalent formulation as

B

IF   A

This inversion of the original rule suggests that we examine consequences or goals before we worry about whether the data are available to support the indicated conclusion. Thus, in this second style we start by examining the right-hand sides of rules to see which rules have as their consequences the problem goals we wish to achieve. For those rules which have the desired outcomes, B in the above simple case, we examine the antecedents, A here, to see what facts are required to enable these rules to be fired. If the relevant facts are not available to trigger these rules, we take as subgoals the establishment of the relevant facts, and the search proceeds recursively in this fashion. This is **goal-driven reasoning** or **backward chaining**. B is thus regarded as the goal to be achieved and A is the data to be verified or perhaps established as a subgoal in the search process.

Let us look at a simple example of rule chaining in the domain of structural analysis (see Table 5-1). Here the rules are meant to provide advice on choosing a means of analyzing a structures problem depending on the availability of various tools—which depends in turn on location. The means available for doing the calculation are three in number: doing a finite element method (FEM) analysis; performing a back-of-the-envelope calculation; and deriving and applying an exact formula. There are three consequents that do not appear *as predicates* in any other rule in this set. They are

DO_FEM_ANALYSIS, GET_ENVELOPE_ESTIMATE, and
GET_EXACT_FORMULA

These predicates are, in fact, the three **hypotheses** that can be tested with this set of rules. We would do this by chaining backward from one of the hypotheses.

We can also identify six **terminal predicates**, that is, predicates that do not appear *as consequents* in any other rule in this set [Walters 1988]. They are

WANT_NUMBER, WANT_FORMULA, HAVE_COMPUTER,
HAVE_NO_COMPUTER, HAVE_MATH_BOOKS and OUT_IN_FIELD

These could be regarded as the set of all the possible facts which could possibly be used to establish all the hypotheses. As we shall see with two simple examples, we do not need to establish all the facts all the time.

Suppose we wished to test the hypothesis that the calculation would be done with an FEM package. The backward chaining of the rules would proceed as follows.

Table 5-1 Rules for choosing among analysis strategies depending on available tools and location

1.	IF	WANT_NUMBER			
	AND	HAVE_COMPUTER	THEN	USE_COMPUTER	
2.	IF	USE_COMPUTER	THEN	DO_FEM_ANALYSIS	
3.	IF	WANT_NUMBER			
	AND	HAVE_NO_COMPUTER	THEN	DO_HAND_CALCULATION	
4.	IF	DO_HAND_CALCULATION	THEN	GET_ENVELOPE_ESTIMATE	
5.	IF	WANT_FORMULA			
	AND	HAVE_MATH_BOOKS	THEN	DO_EXACT_ANALYSIS	
6.	IF	DO_EXACT_ANALYSIS	THEN	GET_EXACT_FORMULA	
7.	IF	WANT_FORMULA			
	AND	OUT_IN_FIELD	THEN	DO_HAND_CALCULATION	

Rule 2 requires the establishment of USE_COMPUTER

Rule 1 requires the establishment of WANT_NUMBER and HAVE_COMPUTER

Thus we now have arrived at a point where we can simply ask whether these two terminal predicates are given as true facts for the situation being analyzed. If they are, the hypothesis is established.

A forward-chaining process would begin with some given facts which must match some of the entries in the list of terminal predicates. We note two things immediately. One is that we need a "complete" set of facts in order to execute the rules. The other is that there is a potential for conflict in the order of execution of the rules in a set of rules. The first point is evident in the following case. Suppose we want to use a formula. It is clear that we cannot execute either Rule 5 or Rule 7 without additional facts. The second point becomes evident if we happen to have our math books with us out in the field. Then we have two rules that are potentially applicable. That is, both Rule 5 and Rule 7 could be executed, and we would have to find a way to choose between them. This is the problem of conflict resolution in rule execution; we treat it in greater detail in Section 5.3.4.

To keep the discussion simple, we consider now only that we want a formula to apply to our structural problem out in the field (and that our math books are safely elsewhere!). Then, with the two given facts being terminal predicates, we see that

Rule 7 requires the establishment of DO_HAND_CALCULATION

Rule 4 requires the establishment of GET_ENVELOPE_ESTIMATE

And so, if we perform a back-of-the-envelope estimate, we are done in this very simple example. However, even with this simple set of rules we have had to wonder about the kind and number of hypotheses that could be established, the number of facts that are needed to establish conclusions, and the possibility that we might be able to fire more than one rule at any time. This suggests that the ordering and management of the rules in a large production rule system is a nontrivial task.

As we have noted before, it is possible to do bidirectional search, that is, reason forward from the data and backward from the goal(s) at the same time (see Section 2.3.2). In principle this could be very efficient, but it could also lead to inefficiency or missed solutions if the data-driven and goal-driven paths miss each other. It is also true that in the representation of a complex problem-solving process, there could be occasion to decompose the problem into subproblems which might require separate and different inference styles. For example, in Chapter 10, in our discussion of knowledge-based systems for design, we shall describe the PRIDE system, in which there are both goal-driven and data-driven subproblems [Mittal 1986a].

Notwithstanding these remarks, we focus on the fact that there is really only one way to execute or fire a rule, and there are a set of mechanical issues that need to be addressed whatever the direction of the search. These issues, which form the core material of this chapter, include the specification of the syntax or grammar for writing rules; the organization of rules, perhaps into sets of rules; and the architecture of rule-based inference engines. In the latter category we deal with the questions of how an inference engine recognizes that a rule is applicable and what actions it takes to incorporate the consequences of firing an applicable rule. One important issue that we will address only briefly is the process of *matching* a rule antecedent or consequent to the appropriate data or goal(s). This is a highly technical problem of **pattern matching** that can only be addressed within the context of a particular rule syntax and the language in which the inference engine is written. Inasmuch as KBES shells typically specify a rule syntax as part of their environment, it is not something that we need be concerned about here (as long as we are content that a chosen shell offers the flexibility of syntax required for our particular application).

5.3 WRITING AND ORGANIZING RULES

5.3.1   Rule Syntax

In this section we examine the process of *writing* rules. We do so using the English-like constructs that we have already employed in our discussions of logic (Chapter 3) and Lisp (Chapter 4). And as illustrations we shall take examples from the SACON system [Bennett 1978, 1984] and its logical predecessors, the MYCIN and EMYCIN systems [Buchanan 1983b].

Rules specify actions to be taken in certain situations. The question before us now is, How do we actually write rules as computable elements that adequately represent the knowledge involved in whatever reasoning we are trying to simulate? The notion of the rule as a computable element is not meant to convey a specific computer language. Rather, it is a reminder that a rule is fired only when some of the problem data match the conditions for the application of that rule found in the rule antecedent, following which some prescribed action is taken—which will in turn change some aspect of the problem data. (We will say more about the data changes in the discussion on architecture in Section 5.4.) This means that there needs to be a match also of the *form* in which the data is stored with the way the conditions and actions are stated in a rule. Thus, our discussion of **rule syntax** or rule grammar must encompass not only the construction of the rule itself, but also the structure of the rule's antecedents and consequents.

The basic structure of a rule is familiar; that is, it consists of antecedents, the left-hand sides, and consequents, the right-hand sides. The structure of the antecedents and consequents parallels the structure described in our discussion of logic in Chapter 3; that is, they are made up of **clauses**. The structure of each clause then parallels the structure of logic statements. The simplest kind of clause structure, analogous to formulas from propositional calculus, is composed simply of strings of characters whose meaning is supplied by the user because the computer has no sense of what the string means. A good example, although perhaps a shade too simple, is the example of modus ponens given in Section 5.2. Consider the following rule:

IF A

THEN B

The symbols A and B in this rule could be single characters or they could be strings of any length. And, as we've just stated, their meanings are imposed or read into them by the user.

A more complex clause structure consists of an ordered listing of a verblike element called the **predicate** and the clause's subjects or objects, which are the **arguments** of the predicate. As in the discussion of logic in Chapter 3, and of first-order predicate logic in particular here, we shall use the prefix notation for listing predicates and arguments. To make up the antecedents and consequents, clauses are combined with **Boolean operators**, such as AND, OR, ELSE, or NOT, and with **relational operators**, such as EQUAL TO (=), LESS THAN (<), GREATER THAN (>), and so on [Brownston 1985]. Again, all of this is a straightforward extension of our discussion of predicate logic. Our example rule on plate structures might then look something like the following for a plate in the (X, Y) plane.

IF   SMALLER   (DIMEN_Z DIMEN_X DIMEN_Y)

AND   PARALLEL_TO (LOADING DIMEN_Z)

AND   GREATER (LOADING_Z LOADING_X LOADING_Y)

THEN   PLATE_BEHAVIOR (BENDING)

We see here that the antecedent contains three clauses, two of which are preceded by the Boolean operator **AND**. The clauses themselves have been written in prefix form by introducing the predicates SMALLER, PARALLEL_TO, and GREATER, with an assumed ordering—here relatively obvious—of how the arguments are applied by these predicates. Thus, for example, the first clause states that

DIMEN_Z < DIMEN_X, and DIMEN_Z < DIMEN_Y

The single clause in the consequent can be viewed as the predicate PLATE_BEHAVIOR operating on the argument BENDING, or it may simply be viewed as a truth statement. That is, it could be written as [Buchanan 1984]

(PLATE_BEHAVIOR BENDING TRUE)

Note that the last version of the rule makes use of the notion of organizing information in a list; this is one of the building blocks of the Lisp language (see Chapter 4). A more compact version of this rule can be written using parentheses to order the lists and by adopting the convention that the first item in any specific list is the predicate for the remaining items in the list.

IF   (AND   (SMALLER DIMEN_Z DIMEN_X DIMEN_Y)

                  (PARALLEL_TO LOADING DIMEN_Z)

                  (GREATER LOADING_Z LOADING_X LOADING_Y))

THEN   (PLATE_BEHAVIOR BENDING)

We see that organizing rules this way—using prefix notation for the predicates and organizing both predicates and arguments in lists—avoids the ambiguity found in different natural languages such as English and German because of the location of verbs. It also begins to look like something that is computable in a formal sense.

We should also point out that our choice of predicates and of arguments is somewhat arbitrary. For example, the third antecedent clause might well have been written as

(NEGLIGIBLE LOADING_X LOADING_Y)

It would seem that the practical effect of this version of the third clause of our example rule would produce the same effect as would the version given above in terms of the predicate GREATER; that is, we would neglect LOADING_X and LOADING_Y. Note, however, that here there must be another rule that has already been invoked in the background for us to be sure that the two loading components are in fact negligible. In a similar vein, we also see that the second antecedent clause refers to the argument LOADING, while in the third clause the loading has been decomposed into the components LOADING_X, LOADING_Y, and LOADING_Z. How did this happen? And where and why did this happen?

The specifics pertaining to this simple example are not important. What is important is that there is a connection between the rule syntax and the organization of the rules and data in the knowledge base. And, in fact, the use of more complex constructions in clauses will reflect also the use of similar data structures both in rules and in the frame-based representation scheme that we shall describe in Chapter 6. Thus, we now turn to a discussion of the organization of rules in a rule-based system, while noting that to some extent we will still be dealing with issues of rule syntax.

5.3.2 Organization of Rule-Based Knowledge Bases

As noted, we would like to have our rule syntax be responsive to different ways of organizing knowledge about the domain under consideration. This is because rules are used to represent chunks of knowledge in a highly modular fashion (see the discussion in Section 5.4.2 on the attributes of rule-based systems). Thus, it is in our interest to make the syntax reasonably flexible so that we can express these knowledge "bytes" in a manner appropriate to our domain. As an example, we turn here to a brief examination of the SACON system, whose representation scheme, as we have already noted, is a specialization of that used in the MYCIN system [Bennett 1978; Buchanan 1984]. SACON was designed to be a "front end" to the MARC finite element code, enabling the user to identify with efficiency and accuracy the portions of MARC that must be exercised in order to perform a numerical analysis of a particular structure.

Our description of the organization of the SACON knowledge base starts with the representation of facts as **associative triples**, that is, as ordered listings consisting of the name of an object, a specific attribute of that object, and the value of the attribute.

<OBJECT ATTRIBUTE VALUE>

For example, the triple

<SUBSTRUCTURE_1 SS_STRESS FATIGUE>

is equivalent to the statement "Fatigue dominates the state of stress in the part of the structure identified as SUBSTRUCTURE_1." (Actually, the representation of facts in MYCIN also includes certainty factors that are used to assess the effects of uncertainty; they are not used in SACON. We shall discuss these certainty factors in greater detail in Section 5.5.)

We now extend SACON's representation scheme to give it greater power in terms of its ability to represent the domain in question. We do this by organizing the objects in SACON into a **context tree** which describes the structure and loading and their respective components for the particular problem at hand. A generic context tree from SACON is shown in Figure 5.1. This tree is instantiated during a SACON run as the user enters the facts about the problem that is to be analyzed. Thus, the contexts or nodes of the context tree are representations of the objects that describe the physical structure and its loading. The objects' attributes are, in turn, parameters that are appropriate to the context to which they are attached.

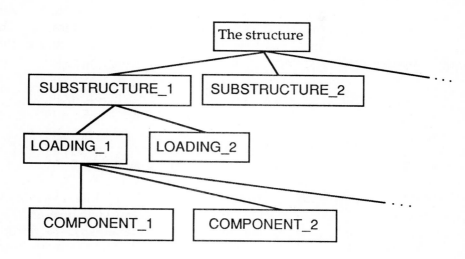

Figure 5-1   Part of a generic SACON context tree (after [Bennett 1978]).

SACON's rule syntax uses the data structure that defines the objects in the context tree. In particular, a rule clause is made up of a predicate and an associative triple, that is,

<PREDICATE> <OBJECT ATTRIBUTE VALUE>

or, in Lisp-like notation,

(PREDICATE OBJECT ATTRIBUTE VALUE)

Then, and this is perhaps the crucial point for the organization of this particular knowledge base, the rules are invoked within a particular context—for a particular object—by including within their syntax a free variable, CNTXT, that gets bound to the object under consideration. So a typical rule clause appears as

(PREDICATE CNTXT ATTRIBUTE VALUE)

Consider the following rule from SACON, given in [Bennett 1978].

IF   (AND (SAME CNTXT MATERIAL LIST_OF_METALS)

              (BETWEEN CNTXT ERROR 5 30)

              (GREATER CNTXT ND_STRESS 0.7))

THEN   (CONCLUDE CNTXT SS_NONLINEARITY MATERIAL)

This rule states that for the object under consideration, that is, for whatever object of the context tree to which the variable CNTXT is currently bound, the stress state of that object is one of nonlinear material behavior if (1) the object is made of metal, (2) the tolerable analysis error is between 5 and 30 percent, and (3) the dimensionless stress is greater than 0.7.

The SACON knowledge base is structured around the hierarchical context tree of the objects of the domain, that is, the physical structure and the loading on that structure. And the rule syntax is designed so as to provide easy access to the domain knowledge as it mimics the data structure that defines the objects in the context tree. But the rules themselves are not ordered in any particular fashion. This is because there really are not that many rules (there are 170 in SACON). However, it is worth noting that each rule represents a single chunk of domain knowledge, which does make the system quite modular (see Section 5.4.2).

There is no single prescription for organizing a knowledge base in a rule-based system. There are techniques other than the context tree of MYCIN and SACON. The choice will depend upon the complexity and structure of the task being encapsulated, the control strategy employed in replicating the task, the availability of suitable software tools, and the skills and preferences of the knowledge engineer(s). As we continue the discussion in Section 5.3.3 and again in Chapters 10 through 12, we shall see particularly how the task structure and the control strategy might affect the choice of rule organization, but it is worth noting that the power of the software will come into play. For example, in the simplest of PC-based shells, what is typically available is a straightforward listing of all the rules, each of which has a very simple—and limiting—syntax. The rules are then examined in a linear fashion to see if a match is available to trigger the firing of a rule. Other PC-based shells contain more sophisticated syntactic structures, and some incorporate a rough equivalent of metarules to help organize the knowledge base (see Section 5.3.3). In the more sophisticated shells and general-purpose representation environments (see Chapter 4), there are many other options available, and the choices will be influenced by technical considerations, such as representation, and by considerations such as cost and portability (these issues are addressed in Chapter 12).

5.3.3   Rule Sets and Metarules

One way of organizing a large set of rules is to decompose it somehow, perhaps by task decomposition or by relevancy to particular objects or subjects. This becomes very important when the number of rules becomes so large that an exhaustive search of all the rules to find the applicable one(s) is no longer feasible. For example, the XCON system for configuring VAX computers contains more than 10,000 rules [Barker 1989]. The overall configuration task is broken down so as to create intermediate task results, and the rules are similarly decomposed into identifiable subgroup schemas which facilitate the modification of the rule base. (This is particularly important for the ongoing support of a large, dynamic system such as XCON, as there are many developers working to maintain it at any given time.) Further, within XCON there are some rule sequences whose firing orders are prescribed in an algorithmic fashion at development time, because this is appropriate to the specific subtasks. There are also rule sequences whose control is much more open-ended because of local variations in the decision process.

In the PRIDE system, design rules are organized into groups with specified design subtasks; within each of these groups are nested rules that represent methods for performing specific designs [Mittal 1986a]. What enables this particular decomposition to work efficiently is that PRIDE was built on top of a general-purpose representation environment called LOOPS [Bobrow 1983] which includes not only rule-based representation, but also frame-based representation (see Chapter 6). This additional capability facilitates the grouping of rules, and of other kinds of information and data, by using a framework for describing objects—including rules—and their attributes. Inasmuch as we have not as yet discussed frame-based representation in any detail, we shall defer examples of this kind of rule grouping until our discussion of the PRIDE system in Chapter 10.

We can use the context tree to organize the rules more directly, as was done in the MYCIN system that preceded SACON [Buchanan 1984]. The basic idea is that individual contexts or nodes in the tree are identified as being of a particular context type. The context types may thus be instantiated more than once during a consultation run. For example, with reference to the infectious diseases that are the domain of the MYCIN system, we could identify CURCULS as the context type of current cultures from which organisms are isolated, with CULTURE_1 being the first culture taken, CULTURE_2 a later culture, and so on. There is also a context type PRIORCULS that denotes cultures previously obtained. All rules that would apply to either of these two context types are gathered together in the category CULRULES. Each of the rules in the category CULRULES becomes available whenever the user creates a node that is a statement about a prior culture or a current culture. Each of MYCIN's 200 rules belongs to one, and only one, of twelve categories.

MYCIN also contains **metarules**, that is, rules about rules, or rules about how to use the knowledge encapsulated in the object rules [Buchanan 1984]. For example, one metarule from MYCIN states, "If the patient has had a bowel tumor, then in concluding about organism identity, rules that mention the gastrointestinal tract are more likely to be useful." We can see that this rule provides guidance about object rules that ought to be invoked during a consultation. The motivation for considering the use of metarules is similar to that for organizing the rules into sets or categories. We often do not have the resources to perform exhaustive search, particularly for large searches. Further, it might also be the case that specific object rules are applicable in more than one situation and we may want to be able to call on that knowledge in different circumstances. Thus, the metarules serve as pointers to specific knowledge that may be invoked in several situations.

5.3.4 Rule Selection and Conflict Resolution

The actual firing of a rule is the result of a control process that can be divided into two phases. In the **recognize** phase, a single rule is selected for execution. In the **act** phase, the prescribed action of the rule is taken. However, notwithstanding our ability to effectively group our rules into sets or classes, it is still possible that more than one rule could be recognized as potentially applicable. That is, there may be more than one rule whose antecedent conditions are satisfied. If more than one rule is recognized, we need a means of selecting which of the applicable rules should be fired. We need to define some type of **conflict resolution** strategy (as part of recognition) whereby we can resolve any conflict about which rule(s) to fire and in what order. Of course, the simplest possible means of conflict resolution might be to fire the very first rule recognized as applicable. While this makes conflict resolution trivial, it still leaves open the questions of where to look and how to select from a rule set on the next iteration through that set.

The set of rules that are potentially applicable at any point in a consultation is called the **conflict set**. A number of criteria for selecting a rule from the conflict set have been proposed, among which are the following [Brownston 1985; Buchanan 1984].

Rule ordering   Priorities are assigned in advance to all rules. Fire the applicable rule having the highest priority.

Data ordering   Priorities are assigned in advance to all data. Fire the applicable rule that matches the data having the highest priority.

Generality ordering   Fire the most specific rule.

Recency ordering   Fire the most recently executed rule or the one that matches the data most recently added or modified; in the first case we must guard against the possibility of firing the same rule again and again.

Of course, metarules also can play a role in selecting rules from a conflict set, as we noted above with our example drawn from MYCIN. Also, the rules can be arranged in advance in an algorithmic fashion, as we have seen in XCON, or a **rule precedence network** can be established in order to lay out a network of priorities or preferences for rule selection for any and all runs of the system being built. These are all choices to be made by the system designer, and they will be influenced by the task complexity and structure as well as the tools available.

5.4 ARCHITECTURE OF A RULE-BASED SYSTEM

5.4.1 Organization of a Rule-Based System

The basic components of a rule-based system are illustrated in Figure 5-2. They include the following:

Knowledge base   The core rules and data that make up the domain knowledge

Working memory   The dynamic memory containing the data entered by the user about the particular problem at hand as well as updates produced by the execution of rules

Rule selector   The device that selects the rule to be executed,
                       invoking if necessary the system's conflict resolution
                       mechanism

Rule interpreter   The device that acts to change the working memory
                       in accordance with the rule's consequent

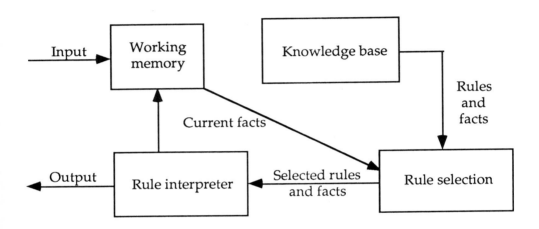

Figure 5-2 The basic components of a rule-based system (after [Hayes-RothF 1985]).

These components follow logically from our prior discussions of knowledge
base organization and rule selection and execution. They make somewhat
more concrete the recognize-act cycle that is at the heart of a rule-based
system. However, underlying the workings of a rule-based system is one
very important piece of computing which we have mentioned only in
passing. This is the operation called **matching**, by which the rule selector
sorts through and recognizes those rules that are potentially applicable.
Typically, the matching algorithm in a shell or representation language is
hidden from the user, and so we may not be aware of its presence—or of
the different kinds of algorithms that are available. However, inasmuch as
the choice of a particular matching algorithm can seriously influence the
efficiency of a rule-based system, some comments are in order.

In the simplest terms, a matching algorithm could check each clause in each
rule against every piece of data in working memory, at every cycle of rule

application.   This is simply unoptimized pattern matching—it is *pattern matching* because the idea is to match the pattern of the data structures in each rule clause—and is guaranteed to work [Brownston 1985].   It is also fairly evident that this equivalent of exhaustive search is terribly inefficient for all but the smallest of rule-based systems.   One matching algorithm that was defined for efficiency within a large rule-based system is the **Rete match algorithm** [Brownston 1985; Forgy 1979, 1982].   This algorithm compiles the features of the clauses that must be checked (these features are typically values of object attributes) and stores them in a tree network.   This tree structure is both automatic and hidden from the user.   At the same time, a separate small program tracks the values of these features and updates them as the working memory is updated.   This combination—of the network and the side program—then means that only working memory data that is changing needs to be tracked and propagated.   The common data structure imposed by the features used in the network and the side program means that additional efficiency is gained, as there does not have to be continual recomputation based on the declarative data structures used in the original rule syntax.   See [Brownston 1985; Forgy 1979; Forgy 1982] for further details on the Rete algorithm within OPS5, and see [Sedgewick 1983] for a discussion of other matching algorithms.

5.4.2   Attributes of a Rule-Based System

Rule-based systems are often described in terms of certain attributes that are commonly linked to them.   Some of these are, we believe, quite important from an applications view.   Buchanan's treatise [1984] presents an extensive compilation of such attributes; a shorter listing is given in [Hayes-RothF 1985].   Our presentation stresses some of the most important *positive* qualities of rule-based systems.

The attribute that is perhaps most often connected with rule-based systems is **modularity**, the notion that the knowledge base is composed of individual chunks or bytes of knowledge.   Thus it is possible to add (or delete) knowledge from the system without having to rewrite pieces of the code and without having to revise the control structure.   It is this attribute that has given currency to the idea that the fundamental distinction of knowledge-based systems is the *separation of knowledge from control*.   One of the benefits of modularity is ease of programming.   Another is that such systems are **extensible**; that is, they are easily extended to incorporate new knowledge.   Still another is that the addition or deletion of specific rules should, in general, not seriously impinge on the ability of such a system to produce plausible behavior.

The principal drawback of modularity is that its very nature makes the operation of a rule-based system relatively opaque. It is much harder to follow the actual behavior flow here than in a conventional procedural program. This is because the rules do not interact with each other directly. Instead, they are selected and fired by the control structure in what amounts to a rather indirect channel of interaction. As a practical matter, this means that large knowledge bases containing many, many rules are hard to organize and maintain. It is one of the reasons that one of the most successful KBESs, the XCON system, requires a very large maintenance team [Barker 1989].

Another attribute that distinguishes rule-based systems is **transparency**, the quality of being able to explain the reasoning, the chain of rules that produced the system's output. If the rules are truly modular (and independent), and the contexts for their firing are accurately stated, then a plausible and useful chain of reasoning can be uncovered. It is worth remembering, however, that transparency refers to the ability of a KBES to retrace the reasoning path; it should not to be confused with the opacity of program behavior that was mentioned above. We shall deal with explanation more extensively in Chapter 6.

5.5 REPRESENTATION OF UNCERTAINTY

In our discussion of the SACON rules in Section 5.3.2 we noted that the representation of objects included certainty factors to assess the effects of uncertainty in reasoning about these objects. In this section we shall identify the sources of uncertainty, describe some of the different ways in which uncertainty is accounted for within the context of rule-based representation, and illustrate the approach taken to incorporating uncertainty in the EMYCIN system [Buchanan 1983b, 1984]. The main point that emerges in incorporating uncertainty is that the choice of an underlying model for *assessing and combining probabilities* is more important than how the uncertainty is reflected in rule syntax or structure [Cohen 1985].

Also, as we shall see in Section 5.5.2, part of our problem in representing uncertainty arises because of the fact that there are two approaches to the mathematical definition of probability [Parsaye 1988]. In the classical mathematical definition, probability is assessed on the basis of the *frequency of occurrence* of an outcome in a series of identical experiments or trials, as in the standard experiment of tossing a fair coin. The other definition, the **Bayesian definition**, is that probability reflects the *degree of belief* that one holds in a fact, outcome, or hypothesis. This is an important distinction for our purposes because KBESs are built in part to express expertise in domains where it is not possible to simply repeat experiments to assess a frequency distribution. Indeed, expertise is often reflective of some accumulated experience that suggests that some facts or situations or causal relationships are more likely than others. The origins of these beliefs are less important to us now than the simple fact that they exist and are reflective, in some sense, of the reality experienced by an expert.

5.5.1   Sources of Uncertainty

Uncertainty arises from several different sources, including the reliability of information, the completeness of information, the aggregation or combination of information from multiple sources, and the inherent imprecision of the representation language in which information is stated [Bonissone 1987]. Information may not be reliable because we are unable to obtain it with sufficient precision or because we are unable to sharply define the idea or concept behind the information. In the first instance we are recognizing the inherent *randomness* that we experience, for example, in making measurements of events in experiments, in which case the event itself is clearly defined but we may not have complete assurance of precisely measuring that event. In the second case we are acknowledging a certain *fuzziness* in our description of a class of events in addition to the uncertainty of our knowledge about whether the event in question belongs in that class [Zadeh 1975]. For example, there is some ambiguity in defining a structure as a thin plate or as a thick plate or even as a three-dimensional structure. We may know precisely which mathematical model to apply once we have decided which kind of structure we are dealing with, but we may not be certain about how to make that decision. (Cohen [1985] cites an example that may be more interesting—that is, when is a beer a *cold* beer?)

Oftentimes our information is incomplete, in which case we need a way to assess the significance of what we don't know. For such cases it turns out that symbolic, non-numerical characterizations are more useful than numerical ones (see, for example, [Doyle 1983]).

The issue of combining or aggregating information and its attendant uncertainty is a crucial aspect of reasoning with uncertainty. This is because the only formal, logically correct approaches available for combining uncertainty measures assume that the probabilities being aggregated have certain attributes, such as statistical independence, which may, in practice, be difficult or impossible to ascertain. Further, without the mathematical precision inherent in the theory of probability, we may unknowingly generate estimates of confidence levels that are contradictory or inflated in value. We shall have more to say about combining uncertainty measures in what follows.

Finally, as we noted at the beginning of this chapter, the rule-based representation that we are describing does not have the formal structure of mathematical logic. Indeed, while we are trying to represent suggestive or plausible reasoning—as opposed to rigorous mathematical logic—we are at the same time surrendering our ability to derive exact interpretations of the meaning of the rules employed [Bonissone 1987].

5.5.2 Probability Theory and Measures of Uncertainty

In probability theory we assign for every assertion a number in the closed interval [0, 1] which defines either the relative frequency with which that assertion occurs in a large number of trials, as in the classical mathematical definition, or the degree of belief that we have in that assertion, as in the Bayesian approach. In particular, we say that $P(A) = 1$ if the assertion A is true, and $P(A) = 0$ if it is false. In the classical case we would call these **objective probabilities**, while in the Bayesian case we call them **subjective probabilities** [Buchanan 1983b]. Since, as we have already noted, we will be concerned almost exclusively with subjective probability, we shall assume the adjective to be understood in the present discussion (which draws heavily upon [Buchanan 1983b]).

Now, let $P(A)$ reflect our initial or prior belief that A is true. What really interests us, from the viewpoint of rule-based reasoning, is the *conditional* probability $P(A|B)$ that reflects a revised belief in A that is conditioned upon knowing that B is true. Thus, consider that B is an *effect* due to the *cause* A, as reflected in the implication rule $B \rightarrow A$. Then $P(A|B)$ reflects the inference drawn from the effect B that the cause A is present. In medical diagnosis, for example, if the effect B is a symptom, then the cause A is a disease, and $P(A|B)$ reflects our belief that the disease A is the cause of the symptom B. Or, in a more homespun example, the effect B of our car not starting might be taken as indicating the presence of the cause A of a dead battery.

It turns out in practice that the expert finds it easiest to estimate $P(B|A)$, the conditional probability that B is present if A is observed or known. That is, we know the car won't start if the battery is dead, and we find it easier to attach symptoms to a specified disease. The question is, then, if we can get $P(B|A)$ from the experts, as well as the prior probability $P(A)$, can we compute the conditional probability $P(A|B)$ for use in inferential reasoning? The answer is affirmative and is expressed in **Bayes' rule**.

$$P(A|B) = \frac{P(A) * P(B|A)}{P(B)}$$

The probability $P(B)$ really doesn't matter much in this formula because it is always a constant that could be normalized away or calculated by imposing the requirement that $P(A|B) + P(\sim A|B) = 1$, where $\sim A$ is the negation of A. This rule is also often written in terms of a hypothesis H whose confirmation is sought on the basis of evidence e (see [Pearl 1987]).

$$P(H|e) = \frac{P(H) * P(e|H)}{P(e)}$$

In the classical case where objective probabilities are used, the above formulas represent identities that derive from conditional probabilities. When subjective probabilities are used above, as is our interest, the results may be viewed as a standard way of revising our beliefs as we acquire evidence, a view that the mathematical probabilists find unacceptable. However, as it allows us to calculate a conditional probability that we would otherwise find difficult to obtain, and to do so in terms of probabilities that we can either observe ($P(A)$), estimate ($P(A|B)$), or calculate ($P(B)$), it is of substantial use in our endeavor to represent plausible reasoning [Pearl 1987].

Now, application of the Bayesian rule can be cast in terms of the prior probability $P(A)$ and the **likelihood ratio** L. Thus

$$L = \frac{P(B|A)}{P(B|\sim A)}$$

where $P(B|\sim A)$ is the conditional probability of observing the effect B in the absence of the effect A. We may think of the likelihood ratio as expressing the *sufficiency* of the rule B $\rightarrow$ A [Parsaye 1988]. That is, a high value of the ratio L implies that the evidence e is sufficient to confirm the hypothesis. Conversely, the logarithm of the likelihood ratio L can be interpreted as the *weight* of belief that we would assign to that rule. Thus, if the weight is negative the probability of A decreases, while the probability increases if the logarithm of L is positive.

We are faced now with the problem of extending this result to cases where there are multiple effects and where the evidence for these effects is itself uncertain, and it is here that we begin to see problems. The extension of

Bayes' rule to multiple effects B_i can be accomplished by viewing B as the conjunction B_1 & B_2 & $\cdots$ & B_n. The likelihood ratio then becomes

$$L = \frac{P(B_1 \text{ \& } B_2 \text{ \& } \cdots \text{ \& } B_n | A)}{P(B_1 \text{ \& } B_2 \text{ \& } \cdots \text{ \& } B_n | {\sim}A)}$$

We begin to get into deep water here because in order to compute the conditional belief for multiple effects, we would have to ask the experts to estimate the joint probability $P(B_1 \text{ \& } B_2 \text{ \& } \cdots \text{ \& } B_n | A)$, which is a difficult, if not impossible task. That is, we would need weights not only for the individual effects B_i as they are connected to the cause A, but also for the pairs B_i & B_j, for the triples B_i & B_j & B_k, and so on. One simplification we can invoke is the assumption that the effects are disjoint, or independent, for which case it follows that

$$L = \frac{P(B_1 | A)}{P(B_1 | {\sim}A)} * \frac{P(B_2 | A)}{P(B_2 | {\sim}A)} * \cdots * \frac{P(B_n | A)}{P(B_n | {\sim}A)}$$

Even with this assumption, we still need large amounts of statistical data that simply may not be available. And the assumption of independence is hard to justify in practice because it may well disguise complexity inherent to the domain for which the rules are written. One example cited by Buchanan [1983b] arises when there are two strongly interacting effects such that individually

$B_1 \rightarrow A$ with weight L1 and $B_2 \rightarrow A$ with weight L2

but where the presence of both effects simultaneously rules out A. In this instance the fix is to add a rule such that

B_1 & $B_2 \rightarrow A$ with weight $- \infty$

Note that by doing this we are moving away from accepting probability as a model or paradigm for dealing with uncertainty and are beginning instead to view it as a way to reflect and process the knowledge we wish to capture in a rule-based system. We should also observe that we have not dealt with the uncertainty that may be inherent in the evidence or the effects, the B_i, but we shall defer consideration of this aspect until we deal with the EMYCIN approach to uncertainty (see Section 5.5.3).There are several other methods of dealing with uncertainty in KBESs, and we shall now outline some of them very briefly [Bonissone 1987; Buchanan 1983b; Cohen 1985, 1987b]. One, of course, is the EMYCIN approach, in which certainty factors are introduced in such a way as to facilitate both the estimation of prior probabilities and the combination of evidence, both done in the context just mentioned of thinking of ways that we can manipulate uncertainty for our own representation purposes. We shall expand on the EMYCIN approach in Section 5.5.3.

Another approach is **possibility theory,** which is in turn based on the ideas of **fuzzy set theory** [Zadeh 1975]. As we have commented earlier, we are acknowledging in this approach a certain fuzziness in the description of a class of events as well as in the uncertainty of our knowledge about whether the event in question belongs in that class. The intent here is to allow subjective quantification of the imprecise or vague terminology that enters into so much of our descriptive vocabulary. With regard to the prior discussion of the thinness of a plate, we might let P(h) represent the class of all plates of any thickness (h), and let TP represent the fuzzy subset of the thin plates belonging to that class. Then we define a membership function μ that measures the strength of our belief that any one plate belongs to the class TP. We could then stipulate that for the plates of thickness h_1, h_2, h_3, and h_4, $\mu TP(h_1) = 1.0$, $\mu TP(h_2) = 1.0$, $\mu TP(h_3) = 0.9$, and $\mu TP(h_4) = 0.2$. If the variable x can assume values in the class B, the statement of the possibility that x is a thin plate would be represented as $\mu TP(x)$.

Possibility theory focuses not on how the possibility distributions are obtained but on how one might do numerical calculations to obtain the possibility values for fuzzy variables. This parallels the application of probabilities within the theory of random variables (see, for example, [Papoulis 1965] or [Elishakoff 1983]). Some examples of the predicates that might be useful in rule-based applications are given in [Buchanan 1983b]. While this approach promises a great deal of utility for KBES applications, there has not been much so far. A discussion of potential applications in engineering can be found in [Chang 1988].

The last approach we describe here is the **Dempster-Shafer theory of evidence** [Buchanan 1983b; Cohen 1985]. The basic ideas underlying the Dempster-Shafer technique relate to the fact that we often do not know individual prior probabilities; as a consequence, any assignment of a prior probability is arbitrary. However, we often do know something about a class of objects or events such that we can assess a strength of belief to that class. Dempster-Shafer offers a calculus for assigning and manipulating weights to sets and subsets of elements as a reasoning process goes on. There have been more recent developments in the combining functions—

those functions used to combine probabilities and uncertainty assessments—that are used to combine weights in Dempster-Shafer [Cohen 1987b].

Further elaboration of the ideas outlined above can be found in [Bonissone 1987; Buchanan 1984; Cohen 1985] as well as in the other references cited.

5.5.3 Certainty Factors in EMYCIN

We again turn back to the MYCIN/EMYCIN system, here to illustrate the use of certainty factors in the representation of reasoning in a KBES. We noted in Section 5.3.2 that the rule syntax there did include such factors. The representation of uncertainty is most evident in the inclusion of a certainty factor (CF) that is attached to each associative triple to indicate a degree of belief in the value in that triple. Thus we would have

<OBJECT ATTRIBUTE VALUE CF>

For example, the triple

<SUBSTRUCTURE_1 SS_STRESS FATIGUE 0.7>

is equivalent to the statement "Fatigue dominates the state of stress in the part of the structure identified as SUBSTRUCTURE_1 with strength 0.7." The questions of most interest to us are, What do the certainty factors mean? and How are they used and combined?

The certainty factors in EMYCIN derive from a more heuristic approach than the use of uncertainty in MYCIN, an approach which recognizes a point we made before, namely, that we are interested in developing a calculus for manipulating estimates of prior probabilities [Buchanan 1983b]. In this approach we associate with every assertion A a certainty measure $C(A)$ such that $C(A) = 1$ if A is true, $C(A) = -1$ if $C(A)$ is false, and $C(A) = 0$ if we have no information about the assertion A. Then we associate a similar certainty factor CF with every rule. Note that we are not defining probability measures here, nor are we adopting the probability measure as being a number within the closed interval [0, 1].

Of particular note is that the definition $C(A)$ admits an estimate for the case when we have no information about the assertion, that is, when $C(A) = 0$. This allows us to deal with one of the problems outlined above: the difficulty of obtaining meaningful prior estimates from the experts when they may believe that there is not enough information to warrant assigning the analog of a prior probability. Buchanan [1983b] also notes that, stated as they are given above, the certainty factors can be seen as heuristics that not only offer assessments of strength; they also may be indicative of the importance or usefulness of a particular assertion. That is, whether or not the CF is an accurate measure of something like a prior probability, it can be interpreted as reflecting the expert's assessment of the importance of the assertion.

Initially, the certainty factors attached to all assertions are set to their null values. When an assertion B is found to be true and there is a rule such that $B \rightarrow A$ with a certainty factor CF, then the certainty of A is changed to the value specified in the rule.

We now turn to the EMYCIN formula for combining evidence. Consider the following situation. An assertion A has a current certainty CA which could be zero or could have taken on a nonzero value as a result of the prior firing of a rule with that certainty. We find that B is true and that there is an untried rule $B \rightarrow A$ that has a certainty factor CF. We now wish to calculate the change in C(A) to C(A|B); that is, we wish to revise our belief in the hypothesis because of the emergence of some evidence. The EMYCIN formulas for calculating this revision are taken from [Buchanan 1983b].

For CA and CF > 0, $C(A|B) = CA + CF - CA * CF$

For CA and CF < 0, $C(A|B) = CA + CF + CA * CF$

Otherwise, $$C(A|B) = \frac{(CA + CF)}{[1 - \min(|CA|, |CF|)]}$$

These are nice, easy formulas to apply. The result C(A|B) is symmetric in the variables CA and CF, so it can be applied in either order to two pieces of evidence. In fact, we can combine the conclusions of a series of rules simply by applying the formula sequentially. Further, as a number, C(A|B) is always somewhere between −1 and +1. In fact, C(A|B) = −1 if either CA or CF is −1, and C(A|B) = +1 if either CA or CF is +1. The only caveat that needs to be borne in mind is that these formulas do not represent a "truth," but an attempt to quantify subjective reasoning.

As a simple illustration of the application of these formulas, let us suppose that three rules are applied in response to various effects that suggest a structure is a plate (as in the first example given at the beginning of this chapter). Let us further suppose that these rules have certainty factors of

0.8, 0.5, and –0.3, respectively. Applying the first of the EMYCIN formulas to the first two certainty factors, in either order, yields an intermediate certainty factor of 0.9, representing additional confirmation for the conclusion that the structure is a plate because of the combination of two certainty factors. Now, when the third factor is applied through the last of the formulas, we find that the final certainty factor is $6/7 = 0.86$, a slight discounting of our intermediate result. It is easy enough to show that if the certainty factors were applied in the order 0.5, –0.3, and 0.8, exactly the same result is produced.

Finally, we turn to the issue of including the uncertainty that may be attached to pieces of evidence. We want to recognize that the strength we attach to the conclusion of a rule will be lessened if the evidence for that rule is itself uncertain. In EMYCIN a simple calculation is performed to achieve this; namely, the certainty factor for the rule is multiplied by the (positive) certainty of the evidence. Should the uncertainty in the evidence be negative, the rule is considered inadmissible and so is not invoked. If the absence of the evidence, say B, is considered important, EMYCIN would reflect that by adding a rule (and corresponding certainty factor) of the form ~B $\rightarrow$ A [Buchanan 1983b]. In the application of this weighting of the evidence, EMYCIN also employs the heuristic that a rule will not be employed if the certainty attached to the evidence for that rule is less than 0.2. The reason for this is straightforward: if the evidence is that marginal, then there probably is not much use in spending the resources required to fire this rule.

5.6 INFERENCE NETS FOR REASONING WITH UNCERTAINTY

We now introduce a variant of production rules for modeling knowledge in domains where both the evidence and the inferences drawn are uncertain. An **inference net** is an inverted tree in which the degree of belief in the validity of a hypothesis or top-level goal is computed by weighing and combining degrees of belief in a series of contributory subgoals, that is, by combining the evidence that supports the hypothesis.

Evidence can be combined in different ways to compute the degree of belief in a hypothesis. In some cases, all pieces of evidence are needed to confirm a hypothesis; this corresponds to a logical AND. In other cases, a hypothesis could be confirmed by any one of its supporting pieces of evidence; this corresponds to a logical OR. Moreover, any of the pieces of evidence for the top-level hypothesis can itself be viewed as a hypothesis, with lower-level evidence used to compute its degree of belief and so on, recursively, generating an inverted tree or inference net.

Each hypothesis or evidence node in an inference net is called an **idea** or a **factor**. Inference nets for industrial applications developed to date have from two to ten pieces of evidence supporting any given hypothesis, about five levels of hypotheses, and—typically—from 50 to about 500 factors.

We may also view an inference net as a graphic way of representing a hierarchical set of production rules involving uncertainty. And, in fact, it is possible to transform an inference net into such a set of rules. However, the inference net paradigm imposes a discipline which is not afforded by production rules. A large rule set can easily end up containing rules with premises and conclusions that no longer chain together, duplicate premises but different consequents, or other logical inconsistencies. The knowledge in an inference net is much easier to manage because it must be organized hierarchically. Moreover, KBES shells that use inference nets help a user conceptualize the knowledge base by allowing hypothesis nodes to be expanded individually (much like an outlining facility in a word processor). As an added bonus, natural language explanations are especially easy to generate with inference nets since the ideas are all complete sentences and can be parsed together into elegant justifications for a hypothesis.

The PROSPECTOR KBES, which evaluates geological prospects as potential mineral deposits, is probably the best-known application of inference nets to date [Campbell 1982]. This system was successfully used to discover a large, previously unknown molybdenum deposit and did much to arouse commercial interest in AI during the late 1970s. PROSPECTOR employed logical AND and OR combinations of evidence and used Bayesian inference to propagate uncertainty in both evidence and inference links [Duda 1979].

The experts whose knowledge was being modeled in PROSPECTOR were thus required to provide prior probabilities for all factors, as well as likelihood factors of sufficiency and necessity for all inference links. As we might anticipate from remarks in Section 5.5.3, this turned out to be extremely awkward from a knowledge engineering point of view. This in turn led to the development of a simplified form of PROSPECTOR's uncertainty propagation [Campbell 1985]. (A similar approach for rating and weighting evidence in an inference net was taken in the Syntel system for applications in the insurance and financial services sector [Duda 1987]).

In this simplified Bayesian approach, all factors are assigned an initial or prior degree of belief of zero and users are asked to assess their degree of belief in evidence ideas at the leaf nodes of the net on a scale from –5 to +5 [Campbell 1985]. Here –5 represents positively false, +5 represents positively true, and 0 represents "unknown." Each inference link between evidence and a hypothesis is assigned two weights: one for a positive degree of belief, that is, an expressed degree of belief between 0 and +5, and another for a negative degree of belief. Each piece of evidence then passes up the product of its degree of belief and its corresponding positive or negative weight to the hypothesis it supports. Each hypothesis is assigned a way to combine the degrees of belief passed up by all of its supporting evidence.

❑   ALL logic gives the hypothesis a degree of belief corresponding to the weighted sum of the degrees of belief passed up by all of its pieces of supporting evidence;

❑   BEST assigns the hypothesis the highest degree of belief passed up by any of its pieces of supporting evidence (like the logical OR); and

❑   WORST assigns the hypothesis the lowest degree of belief passed up by any of its pieces of supporting evidence (like the logical AND).

Assigning different weights for evidence, positive versus negative, provides us with a simplified way to incorporate Bayesian prior probabilities of each piece of evidence for a given hypothesis. If the prior probability of a piece of evidence is high, then a positive degree of belief by the user is expected and adds little belief to the hypothesis, so the link is assigned a low positive weight. However, a user's negative belief in the evidence is regarded as surprising and should thus be weighted more heavily. The converse would obtain when we have evidence with a low prior probability. This approach to dealing with uncertainty thus combines elements of Bayesian (subjective) probability with the belief scales of MYCIN [Buchanan 1983b].

A number of systems have been implemented using these successors to PROSPECTOR, from which we may infer that experts are more easily able to articulate their knowledge about combining uncertain evidence and inference in these simplified formats, while preserving the flavor of Bayesian inference and the organizational strengths of the inference net paradigm.

Inference nets are especially well suited for building KBES applications involving the evaluation of a hypothesis along a single dimension. For example, consider the following list.

❑   How likely is it that this site contains a molybdenum deposit?

❑   How safe do I expect this construction company to be?

❑   How well does this analysis approach fit my problem requirements?

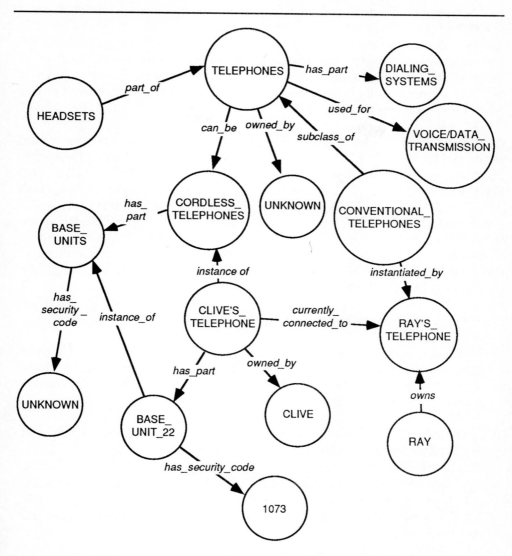

Figure 6-1 A semantic net showing some facts that hold for telephones.

arcs in different parts of the semantic net to illustrate the notion of inverse links.

AI researchers refer to such taxonomic hierarchies as **abstraction hierarchies** since an object or concept closer to the root of the hierarchy, typically positioned higher up or toward the left of the diagram by convention, is a more general or abstract entity than its subtypes or instances. For a hierarchy properly defined in this way, much of what is known about an entity at any level in the hierarchy will typically hold for any more specific subtypes or instances positioned below it in the hierarchy. We will see later in the chapter that this turns out to be a very important notion. Figure 6-2 highlights two abstraction hierarchies contained in our telephones example of Figure 6-1.

In Figure 6-2, the nodes and arcs defining the abstraction hierarchies rooted in the classes TELEPHONES and BASE_UNITS have been highlighted with bold circles and arrows. Thus, CORDLESS_TELEPHONES and CONVENTIONAL_TELEPHONES are two subclasses of the class TELEPHONES, CLIVE'S_TELEPHONE is a particular instance of the subclass CORDLESS_TELEPHONES, and RAY'S_TELEPHONE is an instance of the subclass CONVENTIONAL_TELEPHONES. Since CLIVE'S_TELEPHONE and RAY'S_TELEPHONE are unique instances of the type TELEPHONES, the abstraction hierarchy cannot be meaningfully extended below this level.

Note that we use a number of conventions in drawing semantic nets.

❑ Class and subclass names are plural, while instance names are singular and/or have unique numbers as suffixes. In our experience, these conventions are very helpful for thinking clearly about abstraction hierarchies and avoiding errors in constructing them.

❑ Arrow labels are infix operators. That is, relationships should be read as a triple: source node label–arrow label–target node label. Thus, CONVENTIONAL_TELEPHONES [are a] *subclass_of* TELEPHONES, and TELEPHONES *can_be* CORDLESS_TELEPHONES. This appears to us to be a more natural convention than the opposite (target node label–arrow label–source node label), which is used in some AI textbooks.

6.1.2 Properties of Entities

The abstraction attributes of an entity—that is, its superclasses, subclasses, or instances—are just one kind of property that can be shown in a semantic net. Semantic nets can be used to show arbitrary properties or attributes of classes or instances of objects. In terms of predicate logic, the arc labeled with the property or attribute name serves as the predicate while the labeled nodes at the beginning and end of an arc represent its arguments.

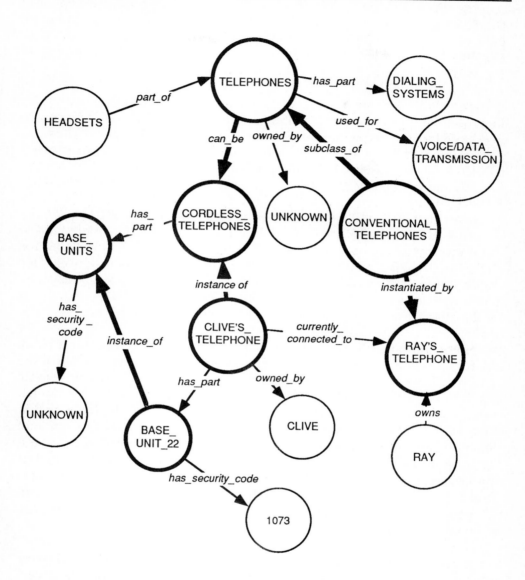

Figure 6-2 Abstraction hierarchies. The semantic net of Figure 6-1 with the separate abstraction hierarchies for the classes TELEPHONES and BASE_UNITS highlighted. A single semantic net may contain several linked or independent abstraction hierarchies.

Any relationship that can be expressed in first-order predicate logic can thus be represented graphically in a semantic net [Hayes 1977]. In Figure 6-3, we have highlighted with shaded arrows the attribute links used to convey descriptive knowledge about objects in the abstraction hierarchy of Figure 6-2.

Figure 6-3 illustrates why abstraction hierarchies are so useful for knowledge representation. Attributes of the class TELEPHONES can be used to describe the properties of its subclasses and instances. Thus, the attributes *used_for* and *owned_by* are **inherited by** the subclasses CORDLESS_TELEPHONES and CONVENTIONAL_TELEPHONES and by their instances, CLIVE'S_TELEPHONE and RAY'S_TELEPHONE. Subclasses also inherit the values of attributes from their superclasses but can override these with locally defined values. In the case of *used_for*, the value VOICE/DATA_TRANSMISSION applies to conventional telephones, but a more restricted value, VOICE_TRANSMISSION, is substituted for CORDLESS_TELEPHONES and is then inherited by its instance. This transmission and specialization of properties between classes, subclasses, and instances is often viewed as the **inheritance** of attributes, for which reason abstraction hierarchies are also called **inheritance lattices**.

In some situations, the value of an attribute is undetermined for a class, although we know that instances of the class will have known values for the attribute. The attribute *owned_by* is an example of this type of generic attribute of TELEPHONES, whose discrete values serve to distinguish instances of the class from one another. LICENSE_PLATE_NUMBER is often used to identify instances of automobiles and is another example of this type of attribute. We know that all instances will have a value for the attribute, so we define the attribute at the highest class level for which it applies, assign it the value UNKNOWN at the class level, and inherit it as a placeholder for local values down the abstraction hierarchy. We can subsequently provide a local value of the attribute for a given class instance at the time we create that instance.

There are other attributes of entities which are meaningful at a class or subclass level but which cannot be usefully applied to instances. *Average_weight* is an example of an attribute that might convey useful information about TELEPHONES or CORDLESS_TELEPHONES, but it would not be particularly useful for describing RAY'S_TELEPHONE or CLIVE'S_TELEPHONE.

Relationships among objects that are part of the same abstraction hierarchy are another kind of attribute that can be shown in a semantic net. For

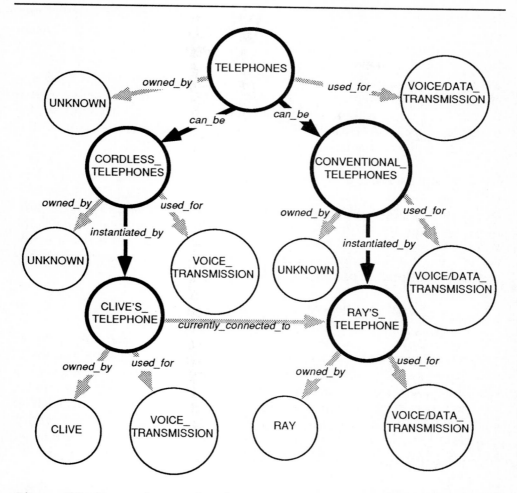

Figure 6-3 Semantic net showing property links (shaded arrows) and abstraction links (solid arrows).

example, the *currently_connected_to* relationship between RAY'S_ TELEPHONE and CLIVE'S_TELEPHONE provides useful information about the telephones in our example.   The *connected_to* predicate is a useful one for modeling circuit topology in KBESs that reason about electrical systems or about piping topology in process plant models.

The *connected_to* relationship is symmetric, so ambiguity in its meaning is unlikely.   In predicate logic parlance, the order of its arguments is unimportant.   However, other relationships that might be used in a semantic net are like transitive verbs—they have a distinct subject and object, so the order of the arguments is semantically important and depends on the definition of the predicate (e.g., whether it represents an active or a passive verb). The predicates SUPPORTED_BY or SUPPORTS in a structural frame, or the predicates PRECEDED_BY and PRECEDES in a critical path network diagram, are transitive and directional. Using a terse or imprecise form of the predicate in either of the two examples above, for example, LOAD_PATH or PREDECESSOR, is likely to cause errors in the building of inheritance lattices.

Relationships among a set of objects may be even more complex than subject-predicate-object, as in BENJAMIN *throws* YELLOW_BEACH_ BALL *belonging_to* JOANNA *to* ZOE. Representing these more complex kinds of relationships in semantic nets can become confusing, especially when node and arc labels are abbreviated. And since semantic nets for any realistically complex system quickly get cluttered, their developers are constantly tempted to use terse labels.

6.1.3 Subsystem/Component Hierarchies

Semantic nets can also be used to represent the hierarchical subsystem/component breakdown of an engineering system—usually a physical system of some kind, such as an aircraft, a process plant, or a building. This type of graph, frequently termed a **part-of hierarchy,** can be used to represent the generic part-of hierarchy of a class of systems such as BOILERS, or it can be used to represent the unique part-of hierarchy associated with one particular system of a given type, such as PORT_ORFORD_PAPER_PLANT_LIQUOR_RECOVERY_BOILER_5.

Figure 6-4 shows a semantic net containing two linked hierarchies: an abstraction hierarchy of steel structural elements, and a part-of hierarchy for a few components of a particular building's structural system. Our inability to show more than a very few parts within the page-size format of this book points out an oft-repeated limitation of semantic nets: they rapidly become large and cluttered. This is not necessarily a problem in performing computations on semantic nets with powerful computers, but it poses a practical problem for the process of building a knowledge base if the nets become so large and cluttered that neither experts, programmers, nor users can view and edit them easily.

The part-of hierarchy for an instance of an engineered product may correspond very closely to the generic part-of hierarchy of its parent product type, or it may be nonstandard due to the addition or deletion of

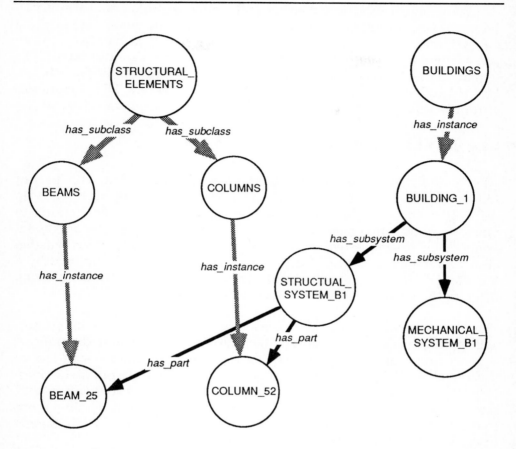

Figure 6-4 Semantic net showing two abstraction hierarchies (linked by shaded arrows) and a part-of hierarchy (linked by solid arrows).

components. We will show in Chapter 8 that if the part-of hierarchies for typical instances of a type of engineered system are essentially similar to one another—that is, if we are dealing with a semicustom type of product—then the knowledge-based representation and reasoning techniques described in this chapter can be readily employed to automate parts of the design process for such products.

Note that only a few attributes of a system or subsystem (e.g., its geometric envelope, or the layer of the graphics model in which it should be stored) will usually apply to its subsystems and components. However, many interesting properties of an engineering subsystem or part, especially those dealing with its behavior, can be naturally inherited from a true abstraction hierarchy in which higher-level entities represent more general types of the subsystem or part. In Figure 6-4, for example, it is natural to store knowledge about the kinds of attributes that beams should have (e.g., length, depth, section modulus, and material specification) in the subclass BEAMS and to allow an instance of BEAMS such as BEAM_25 to inherit the attributes needed to reason about its behavior in the structural system.

6.1.4 A Cautionary Word

Abstraction hierarchies are often erroneously confounded with part-of hierarchies by novice knowledge engineers. At best, this leads to difficulties in the knowledge acquisition process; at worst, it leads to mistakes in the implementation of the system. Moreover, computational methods for reasoning with class structures have no way to detect whether class hierarchies or part-of hierarchies have been properly defined by a knowledge engineer. Thus, remembering and maintaining the distinctions between these two types of semantic nets is quite important.

The use of the conventions we have suggested—plural names for classes, and ending in specific numbers (like automatically generated names in some programming languages) to represent instances—can be of considerable help in defining logically correct class and part-of hierarchies. (Try sketching an abstraction hierarchy that violates these conventions and see if it looks and feels like it is incorrect!) Even while using these conventions, however, novices and (even) expert developers of KBES must pay careful attention to this aspect of knowledge engineering.

The payoff for carefully defining class structures and part-of hierarchies is the opportunity to exploit inheritance for a variety of purposes in engineering applications. Abstraction hierarchies and generic part-of hierarchies can be used to complement one another in extremely powerful ways for reasoning about tasks like design, as we will show in Chapter 8.

6.1.5 Computer Reasoning with Semantic Nets

We have shown that semantic nets can be used to represent a wide variety of knowledge about the world, and we have drawn a parallel between semantic nets and first-order predicate logic. In fact, this parallel is so close that many AI texts use semantic nets to explain predicate logic. We have explained in Chapters 3 and 4 how computer languages like Lisp can be used to perform deduction in predicate logic. It is thus possible—some would even say easy—to perform automated reasoning over semantic nets. For example, inheritance of class properties to subclasses or instances is done by applying the universal quantifier out rule: "What is true for all instances of a class is true for any of its members."

There are, however, some practical difficulties in performing computer reasoning with completely general semantic nets, which have prompted knowledge engineers to use more specialized kinds of semantic net representations for automated reasoning.

First, computer languages cannot tolerate the ambiguity of natural languages, so it is necessary to have a well-defined set of predicates and arguments to reason about a domain. Finding a minimum set of mutually exclusive and collectively exhaustive predicates to rigorously represent all of the possible concepts and relationships that can be communicated more loosely via natural language is still an active area of AI research (sometimes referred to as **conceptual dependency theory** [Schank 1972]). A complete or nearly complete set of such predicates is arguably a prerequisite for automating commonsense reasoning in a broad variety of domains and is the subject of several research efforts [Lenat 1986].

Second, we have mentioned that semantic nets for realistic problems become complex, large, and cluttered. Displaying such nets on sheets of newsprint on a wall can serve adequately for initial brainstorming, but they are difficult to view and edit on computer workstations with current levels of screen resolution in the range of 1 million pixels. (By comparison, text like this printed on a laser printer has a density of 300 dots per inch in both dimensions and thus has a resolution exceeding 6 million "pixels.") The expressiveness and clarity of hand-drawn semantic nets for representing a variety of kinds of concepts and attributes graphically for small illustrative problems thus turns into a disadvantage. It just becomes overwhelming when we attempt to build semantic nets for realistic problems on a computer.

For these reasons, computer scientists have developed paradigms that employ some of the key ideas derived from semantic nets and predicate logic for representation and reasoning in complex domains. Frame-based representation and object-oriented programming are two such paradigms which can be viewed as specializations—that is, *subclasses*—of semantic nets, with additional capabilities and features. For further details about semantic nets, Woods [1975] provides a rigorous treatment of their theoretical foundations and Sowa [1984] presents a broad review of how people and computers represent and reason with knowledge about the world.

6.2 FRAME-BASED REPRESENTATION

We have shown that a class of objects is represented in a semantic net by defining at the class level those attributes that apply both to the class itself and to all of its subclasses and instances. More specific subclasses or instances are then represented by adding the attributes that specialize or differentiate them from other subclasses or instances of the class. Yet, because semantic nets attempt to represent all relationships among objects graphically, they become cluttered and unmanageable. **Frame-based representation** was invented to manage the information overload inherent in large semantic nets without sacrificing their rich expressive power [Minsky 1975; Bobrow 1977; Fikes 1985; Brachman 1985].

Frame-based representation retains the fundamental notions of abstraction hierarchies and inheritance of properties from superclasses, but it packages the descriptive attributes associated with each class or instance into more compact local data structures variously called **frames** (the term we will use), **schemas**, or **units**. By representing abstraction hierarchies graphically, and permitting the other attributes of each class or object to be expanded and viewed only as needed for inspection and modification, frame-based representation provides a two-level user interface that makes possible the construction and manipulation of realistically large knowledge bases.

6.2.1 Information-Hiding in Frame Hierarchies

A frame hierarchy is nothing more than an abstraction hierarchy of objects or concepts, and it can thus be drawn as a semantic net. Early frame-based systems provided only textual interfaces for defining and editing frames, but now even some PC-based frame systems support graphic display and editing of frame hierarchies. Figure 6-5 shows this kind of high-level graphic view of some frames describing a building and its components.

Note that each object in this frame abstraction hierarchy is represented by a single node. In addition to the class and instance relationships used to generate an abstraction hierarchy, objects in a frame system typically have a number of descriptive properties (e.g., color, size, strength, temperature, pressure, and pH), which either have been inherited from superclasses or have been defined locally. All of these other attributes can be used in frame-

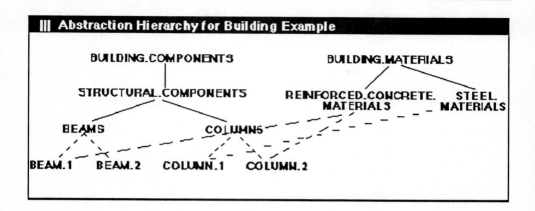

Figure 6-5 Abstraction hierarchies in a frame system.   Abstraction hierarchies like this are the default output for displaying a knowledge base in most frame-based systems.   They provide a way for the knowledge engineer or user to obtain an overview of the contents of a knowledge base. (Source: Screen image reproduced from a knowledge base developed using the KEE environment.)

based reasoning, too; however, they are *hidden* at this level of representation. **Information-hiding** is thus a deliberate device employed to help us comprehend large knowledge bases [Pascoe 1986]. This device also permits the modular style of programming termed **object-oriented programming** (see Section 6.3).

AI programming tools for frame-based reasoning may provide special facilities to graph relationships other than abstraction among objects in a frame hierarchy. The load path in a structural system and the precedence diagram of activities in a project are examples of the types of specialized graphs depicting specific object relationships that might be useful for customized explanation or debugging purposes in the structural engineering and project management domains, respectively (see Section 6.5). However, only abstraction relationships are normally graphed in the process of creating and editing frames.

6.2.2   The Internal Structure of a Frame

Frames represent objects as lists of **attribute-value pairs**. Attributes of frames are called **slots**. The metaphor used here is of a prototypical object (the superclass) that contains a number of slots to describe the attributes that it and its subclasses or instances need to have. These slots may be filled with known values or they may be empty. (Empty slots in a frame system have the value **UNKNOWN**.) The prototypical object with its slots serves as a template for all of its subclasses and instances. Descendant objects inherit the slots defined in the prototypical object, either filled with a known value or empty so that a locally defined value can be placed in the slot.

The first slot in an object is usually the name of the object. The **SUBCLASS_OF** and **INSTANCE_OF** slots of each object, typically listed next, are used to locate it in all of the abstraction hierarchies to which it belongs. (The redundant inverse abstraction links **HAS_SUBCLASS_OF** and **INSTANTIATED_BY** are typically also used to speed up computation when searching through frame hierarchies.) Additional attributes are then added at any level of the abstraction hierarchy to define (1) interesting properties of the class or object represented by the frame, for example, its capacity, color, or temperature; or (2) relationships that the class or object might have with other classes or objects in the hierarchy, for example, **UPSTREAM_OF** or **CONNECTED_TO**.

6.2.3   Inheritance of Attributes in Frame-Based Systems

Figure 6-6 shows the **BEAM.1** object from Figure 6-5, expanded to show its internal attributes. As expected, we see that this object is a member of the classes **REINFORCED.CONCRETE.MATERIALS** and **BEAMS** and has no subclasses or instances. We can see that BEAM.1 has inherited several attributes from its superclasses. Some examples of attributes that BEAM.1 has inherited from different superclasses are

❑   The **DEPTH** slot from its parent class **BEAMS**;

❑   The **PERCENTAGE.OF.REINFORCEMENT** slot from its other parent class, **REINFORCED.CONCRETE.MATERIALS**.

❑   The **HORIZONTAL.LOAD** slot from its grandparent class, **STRUCTURAL.COMPONENTS**; and

❑   The **PURCHASING.LEAD.TIME** slot from its great-grandparent class, **BUILDING.COMPONENTS**.

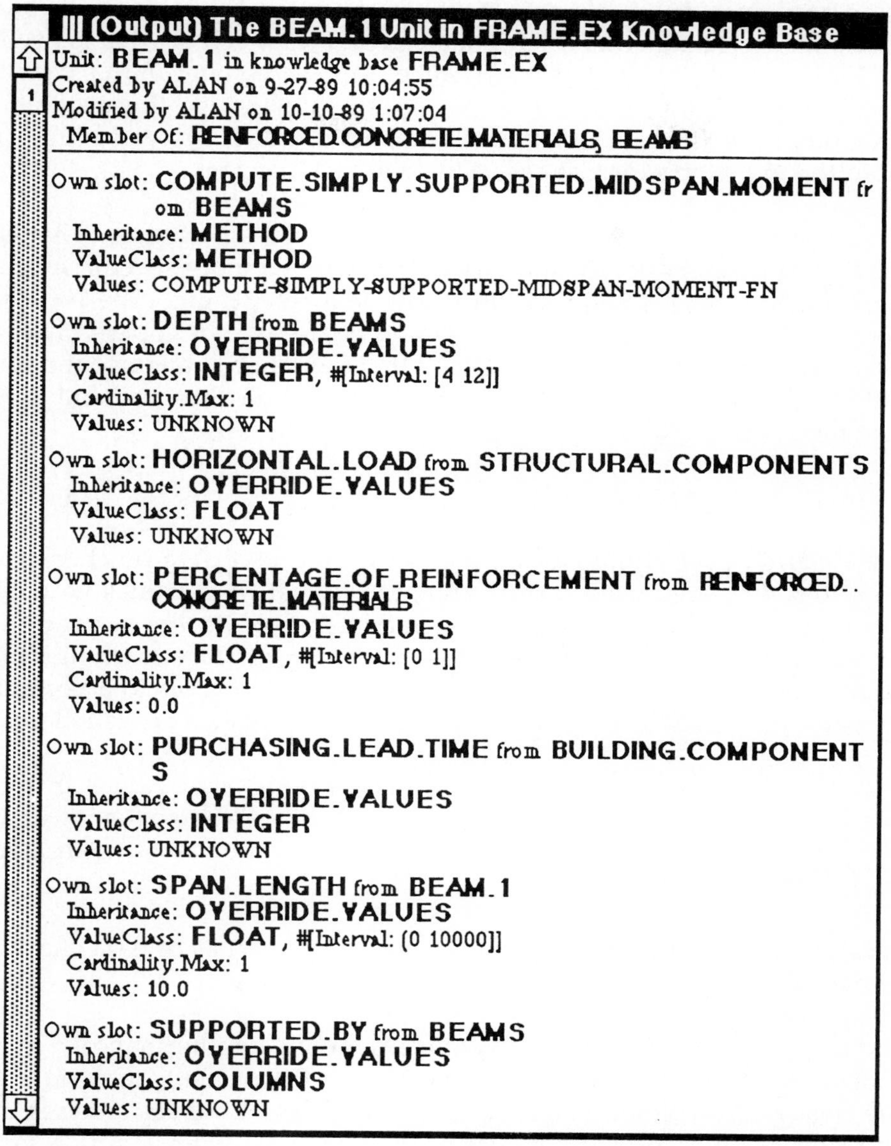

||| (Output) The BEAM.1 Unit in FRAME.EX Knowledge Base

Unit: **BEAM.1** in knowledge base **FRAME.EX**
Created by ALAN on 9-27-89 10:04:55
Modified by ALAN on 10-10-89 1:07:04
Member Of: **REINFORCED.CONCRETE.MATERIALS, BEAMS**

Own slot: **COMPUTE.SIMPLY.SUPPORTED.MIDSPAN.MOMENT** fr
  om **BEAMS**
Inheritance: **METHOD**
ValueClass: **METHOD**
Values: COMPUTE-SIMPLY-SUPPORTED-MIDSPAN-MOMENT-FN

Own slot: **DEPTH** from **BEAMS**
Inheritance: **OVERRIDE.VALUES**
ValueClass: **INTEGER**, #[Interval: [4 12]]
Cardinality.Max: 1
Values: UNKNOWN

Own slot: **HORIZONTAL.LOAD** from **STRUCTURAL.COMPONENTS**
Inheritance: **OVERRIDE.VALUES**
ValueClass: **FLOAT**
Values: UNKNOWN

Own slot: **PERCENTAGE.OF.REINFORCEMENT** from **REINFORCED..
      CONCRETE.MATERIALS**
Inheritance: **OVERRIDE.VALUES**
ValueClass: **FLOAT**, #[Interval: [0 1]]
Cardinality.Max: 1
Values: 0.0

Own slot: **PURCHASING.LEAD.TIME** from **BUILDING.COMPONENT
      S**
Inheritance: **OVERRIDE.VALUES**
ValueClass: **INTEGER**
Values: UNKNOWN

Own slot: **SPAN.LENGTH** from **BEAM.1**
Inheritance: **OVERRIDE.VALUES**
ValueClass: **FLOAT**, #[Interval: (0 10000]]
Cardinality.Max: 1
Values: 10.0

Own slot: **SUPPORTED.BY** from **BEAMS**
Inheritance: **OVERRIDE.VALUES**
ValueClass: **COLUMNS**
Values: UNKNOWN

Figure 6-6 The BEAM.1 frame, including its attributes and values. (Source: Screen image reproduced from an example knowledge base developed using the KEE environment.)

The inheritance of attributes and values from more than one parent class is termed **multiple inheritance**. Multiple inheritance allows us to build intersecting abstraction hierarchies that can deduce much of what is needed to be known in each frame by inheritance. As we see later in this chapter, the added power of inheritance can drastically reduce the number of rules—when compared with pure production rule systems—that are needed to model the expertise associated with a given task.

Some AI programming environments allow upward inheritance. That is, a general class can inherit attributes and values from a more specific subclass or instance—corresponding to induction in formal logic. We have not encountered situations in which this would be useful, but apparently some developers have. We noted in Chapter 3 that induction is an unsound form of inference. Therefore, upward inheritance should be used only with strong motivation, and then with considerable caution.

6.2.4   Facets: Attributes of Slots

In real-world applications, it is highly desirable that data be checked to ensure that they are of the correct type, to see that their values lie within some acceptable range, or to initiate some inference process or procedure whenever data in a given slot are accessed or changed. Most current frame-based systems permit the developer to add "facets" to slots to accomplish these and other kinds of functions. Some examples of such facets follow.

The **cardinality facet** is used to constrain the number of values that can reside in a slot. Minimum and maximum cardinalities define the lower and upper bounds of the *number* of separate values (not the values themselves) that a slot can contain.

The **value class facet** permits us to implement two types of data checking automatically: data type and data range.

Value class and cardinality facets complement one another handily, as we demonstrate in the following examples (from Figure 6-6). Consider the value class and cardinality facets of the slot SPAN.LENGTH. We see that they collectively restrict the slot from having more than a single value (Cardinality.Max is 1); they restrict its value type to be a real (FLOAT) number, with a value between 0 and 10,000 units. Similarly, the facets of the slot SUPPORTED.BY allow the slot to have an arbitrary number of values (since no cardinality facets are specified), and the term COLUMNS in the ValueClass facet restricts the value type of the slot to be any of the frames in the class COLUMNS. Thus, value class facets can be used to check for data types and legal values of both properties and relationships.

These kinds of data checking are extremely useful in developing a KBES. The price to be paid for this is slower processing speed as data checks are performed each time a slot value is changed. To deal with the efficiency versus power tradeoff, the KEE programming environment allows for "compact units" in which these data-checking facets are suppressed to speed up system performance once a system has been debugged. Ongoing research on object-oriented databases addresses the same tradeoff [Stonebraker 1986].

Special facets called **demons** (sometimes called **active values**) can be used to initiate some desired behavior any time that the value of a slot is either accessed or changed. Demons that fire just before or after a slot value is changed serve several purposes. A demon might perform a more elaborate type of filtering or analysis of data than value class or cardinality facets can do *before* a new value is entered into a slot. Alternatively, active values can be used to create animated graphic displays of a knowledge base by firing a method or process which redisplays an image such as a dial gauge or a histogram with the new slot value *immediately after* a slot value is changed.

Demons that fire when a slot value is *accessed* can likewise be useful in a KBES. In particular, we will show in Section 6.3.2 how demons can be used to fire methods, to initiate forward- or backward-chaining inference in a set of production rules, or to compute a slot value that is being accessed by a rule or procedure.

6.2.5   Inheritance of Behavior by Subclasses

We are now ready to introduce the notion of object-oriented programming (see Section 6.3). Frames in an abstraction hierarchy inherit attributes—and sometimes values for those attributes—from their superclasses. Thus far we have talked about attributes as static properties of the frames—e.g., color, length, and so on. But why should objects inherit only data defining their states? Objects could also inherit behavior—that is, descriptions of how they change state—from more general superclasses. For instance, if we have an equation that predicts the maximum bending moment for beams with concentrated midspan loads and simply supported ends, why not have BEAM.1 and other instances of beams inherit this behavior? A method to do this was defined in our frame example and has been inherited as the first slot in Figure 6-6. Note that this slot has been inherited from the

BEAMS frame; its value class is METHOD; and its value is the function COMPUTE.SIMPLY.SUPPORTED.MIDSPAN.MOMENT.FN.

This idea, which is implemented in frame systems, is one of the essential elements of object-oriented programming. Along with data that define their states, objects also inherit a series of procedures, usually called **methods**, which tell them how to change their states. Methods in frame-based systems are written so that they can be executed by objects lower in the abstraction hierarchy, referencing local slot values for their arguments. We will discuss this in more detail in Section 6.3.1.

It may appear at first glance that there is massively redundant storage of both data and methods in a large frame-based system. In fact this is not the case. Lower-level objects simply have pointers to the superclass where the attribute and its value (data or procedure) were first defined, so that frame-based systems use memory relatively efficiently.

6.3 OBJECT-ORIENTED PROGRAMMING

Object-oriented programming (OOP) is a relatively new style of programming that has its roots in the SIMULA simulation language written in Algol that first implemented this style of programming [Dahl 1966]. The more recently developed Smalltalk language implemented essentially all of the features now considered to make up an OOP language (including graphics), and it has recently been ported to a wide range of personal computers [Goldberg 1983; Kaehler 1986]. OOP is being increasingly used to develop both KBES and procedural applications. We will describe some of the key features of OOP as used in knowledge-based systems.

6.3.1 Syntax of Methods in OOP

We want to describe the behavior of a class of objects by writing a generic method at the class level in a frame hierarchy and then allow members of the class to execute the method, referencing local values as its arguments. To do this, we use a variable argument SELF with each method and bind it dynamically—at run time—to the name of the frame from within which the method was fired. The special argument SELF in object-oriented programming has been termed a **pseudovariable** [Pascoe 1986].

Thus, the familiar $wL^2/8$ formula to compute the bending moment of a simply supported beam with a concentrated midspan load was encoded as an OOP method of the BEAMS object in that object's slot,

COMPUTE.SIMPLY.SUPPORTED.MIDSPAN.MOMENT. This method, shown below, is inherited by all beams. The method uses the GetValue function to retrieve the needed arguments from the VERTICAL.LOAD and SPAN.LENGTH slots of the particular beam object from within which it is fired; and it uses PutValue to place the value returned by the method into the MIDSPAN.BENDING.MOMENT slot of this beam.

```
((PutValue 'MIDSPAN.BENDING.MOMENT of SELF)
    (* (GetValue 'VERTICAL.LOAD of SELF)
        (/ (EXPT (GetValue 'SPAN.LENGTH of SELF) 2) 8)))
```

The reference to SELF in the above method means that any time the method is fired, it will find the values of its arguments by reading the slot values in the slots VERTICAL.LOAD and SPAN.LENGTH of the beam frame SELF from within which the method was fired, rather than by reading the arguments from these slots of the superclass frame BEAMS in which the method was originally defined. Thus, we have a way to define a generic method at the highest level of abstraction to which it applies and to then point to and execute it within any frame lower in the abstraction hierarchy. The method will then generate appropriate behavior (in the context of local values for its arguments) for an entire class of objects.

Some object-oriented programming languages also provide the capability to read values from slots of frames that are related to SELF in the abstraction hierarchy (e.g., INSTANCES_OF_SELF, PARENTS_OF_SELF, or SIBLINGS_OF_SELF). This provides for rapid development of methods that require data sharing among objects in a frame hierarchy.

6.3.2   Control in OOP Languages

To explain how control is implemented in object-oriented programs we need to introduce the concept of **message passing**. A method executes or fires when the slot in the frame containing the method is sent a message to execute. (A message must specify a particular slot in the frame, since a single frame may contain methods in several of its slots). The message itself might also carry one or more arguments needed by the method to which it was sent. These would not reference SELF.

In AI programming environments where object-oriented programming is mixed with rule and frame-based representation, a sequence of message passing could be initiated when either a rule or a method sends a message to a slot of some frame to fire its method. The method fires, reads its arguments locally, generates any "side effects" (which can include sending messages to other slots to fire their methods), and then returns a value to the slot that initiated the message. This may result in messages being sent to other methods to fire, and so on.

Many people find the notion of message passing and method firing confusing and anarchistic when compared to structured programming in languages like Pascal. The paradigm has been informally described as follows: "Message passing in OOP is like having one or more fireworks in a box of fireworks start exploding, igniting other fireworks in the box, and finally burning out, without any apparent control." Where the behavior of the system being modeled involves significant interdependence between the behaviors of its components, OOP techniques may lead to confusing systems which rapidly become difficult to debug. This is exacerbated by the fact that many OOP languages lack the capability to produce traces of messages being sent or of the values returned by methods. Advanced users of such languages often resort to writing their own trace programs in order to debug the behavior of complex systems that they are developing.

In fact, when used appropriately, object-oriented programming can be a very powerful and modular programming approach that provides significant benefits in programmer productivity and transparency of program code. OOP is especially appropriate for problems where groups of similar objects must reason more or less independently about their behavior and communicate the results of their computations to other objects. However, the style and philosophy of OOP are quite different from those of more conventional, procedural programming languages. An example will serve to illustrate this.

The STRUCTURAL.COMPONENTS frame in Figure 6-5 might have a method in a slot called COMPUTE.SYSTEM.WEIGHT for computing the weight of the entire structural system. When this method is fired, it begins by sending messages to the COMPUTE.MY.WEIGHT slot in each of its instance frames—that is, each of the leaf nodes of the abstraction hierarchy below it—to compute that element's weight. The computations of each element's weight would be carried out by the COMPUTE.MY.WEIGHT.FN function defined and stored in the COMPUTE.MY.WEIGHT slot of the STRUCTURAL.COMPONENTS frame and inherited by its members.

This method would fire for each structural element in turn and return the value of its weight to be appended to a list of weights in the ELEMENTS'.WEIGHT slot of STRUCTURAL.COMPONENTS. The method would wait for a value to be returned from each of its members and would then sum the list of member weights in its ELEMENTS'.WEIGHT slot to produce a total weight for the structural system.

Note two aspects of this example. First, the task of computing each element's weight has been delegated to the elements themselves; this illustrates the notion of modularity and distributed problem solving. Second, the procedure can easily be made a little more sophisticated. For example, RECTANGULAR.CONCRETE.BEAMS could compute their weights using an inherited method defined in the CONCRETE.BEAMS frame, referencing their own locally defined dimensions and the constant unit weight of reinforced concrete, whose value might be inherited from the CONCRETE.STRUCTURAL.ELEMENTS frame. Steel columns and beams, on the other hand, could compute their weights in a different way using a method stored in the STEEL.STRUCTURAL.ELEMENTS frame which references a database of structural steel shapes to read a given element's lineal weight. The message COMPUTE.MY.WEIGHT that is sent to each element can thus be interpreted appropriately by different kinds of structural elements, each of which has been specialized by methods and data to respond appropriately to the message from its own perspective.

It is a trivial extension from this example to imagine an OOP model of a space shuttle computing not only its total weight but also its center of gravity in three dimensions as parts are added or modified. And it requires only a modest leap of the intellect to imagine how OOP techniques are being used to have semiconductor or automobile parts in a factory plan the steps and sequences of their required processing, then send messages to all of the machines in the factory to find which ones have the capability to perform the machining action that they require next and which are currently free. In fact, such applications are now in routine use in a number of manufacturing settings, and their use is proliferating. Chapter 11 describes some planning applications of knowledge-based systems in which OOP is the core methodology.

Note also that although OOP has the feel of distributed processing (see Chapter 8), this is only a software metaphor at the present time. Virtually all OOP programming environments have been implemented on standard sequential processing computer hardware platforms. Nevertheless, modularity, information-hiding, abstraction, and message sending are all important innovations that can be powerful tools in the hands of knowledgeable programmers unfettered by the restrictions imposed by conventional procedural programming languages.

6.3.3 Programming Languages for OOP

We explained in Chapter 4 why a language like Lisp facilitates storing and accessing the state and behavior of an object in an integrated way. Unlike conventional engineering programming languages such as Fortran, Lisp does not distinguish between the ways that it stores data and programs; both are stored within a Lisp program as atoms in lists. Thus, in Lisp, the inheritance of methods is no different from the inheritance of data.

Inasmuch as implementing OOP is relatively straightforward in Lisp, OOP extensions to Lisp began to proliferate rapidly once the concepts became widely known in the AI community. Flavors (now offered by several vendors) was an early variant of a Lisp-based object language that gained a substantial following. As is also the case for Lisp, a standard for OOP in Lisp is now emerging. It is called the Common Lisp Object System, or CLOS [Bobrow 1988].

The object-oriented programming paradigm is also gaining in popularity outside the AI community. As a result, a number of procedural languages such as C and Pascal have been extended to create higher-level OOP languages, for example, C++ and Objective C, with features that facilitate the definition of class hierarchies and with functions to implement the inheritance of properties and methods. For serious KBES applications, however, the high-level OOP languages used thus far have been primarily Lisp-based.

AI development environments such as Xerox's LOOPS, IntelliCorp's KEE, and Inference's ART are even higher-level OOP languages built in Lisp. To the set of functions found in OOP languages such as Flavors or CLOS, they add more capabilities for frame editing and graphic browsing (as in Figure 6-5), along with built-in inference engines and truth maintenance (see Chapter 7). More recently, a number of high-level OOP environments have been developed in traditional programming languages such as C. We discuss the approaches used for integrating the various representation and reasoning paradigms within some of these tools next.

For readers who wish to venture deeper into the subject of OOP, an easily accessible review of the conceptual underpinnings of OOP languages, including examples of programs implemented in OOP style, is found in the series of articles by Whyte [1986].

6.4   INTEGRATING RULES, FRAMES, AND PROCEDURES

As we have noted before, KBES technology grew out of the recognition that production rules are a natural and intuitive way for representing heuristic knowledge. Indeed, much of the early work in domains such as medicine, law, and business—as well as engineering—focused on rule-based systems. And it is also true that much of the early KBES work was on derivation or classification tasks, for which heuristic rules seem a natural representation (see our discussion of Amarel's spectrum in Chapter 1). It turns out that for formation or synthesis tasks such as planning and design, rule-based representations are not enough—indeed, they are not adequate even for large, complex derivation tasks. Thus, we can now look forward to solving harder and more interesting problems by integrating rules, frames, and OOP. Besides the advantages of integrated paradigms for representation and reasoning, we shall see in Section 6.5 how these representations can be combined to produce explanations.

In engineering, many aspects of computing are still best handled by procedures (many of which seem almost rule-like in their structure) and algorithms which are embodied in numerically based programs. Given our interest in expanding engineering computing to include qualitative as well as quantitative knowledge, we want the power to use numbers, rules, nets, frames, and OOP approaches to express knowledge of varying types (see the taxonomy of engineering knowledge in Section 7.1.1). Thus, the ideal engineering programming environment would support all of these representations in an integrated, convenient, and inexpensive package.

We shall explore the integration of algorithmic and graphics packages with KBES environments in Sections 8.1 and 8.2. For now we focus on the integration of rules, frames, and OOP. There are several commercial software packages available that run on a variety of platforms and support the following facilities.

❑   Frame-based representation, including graphic browsing and editing capabilities;

❑   The capability to attach arbitrary procedures or methods written in the underlying language of the frame system (usually Lisp) to slots, to inherit these methods in the frame hierarchy, and to send messages to them; and

❑   An inference engine that supports both forward and backward chaining with a rule syntax that allows rules to reference slot values of objects in the frame hierarchy.

We will build on the introduction to computer-based reasoning in Chapter 4 to describe how these AI paradigms can be integrated in a single computing environment. However, we shall avoid any discussion of current, commercially available AI programming environments. First of all, any attempt to provide a complete review of the features, strengths, and weaknesses of such products in a textbook such as this would be dated even before it got to press. More important, we believe that any attempt or perceived attempt to evaluate particular products would be inconsistent with—and orthogonal to—our desire to accurately present the underlying concepts employed in integrated AI environments.

To integrate rules with frames we simply need to use a rule syntax in which rule premises and conclusions have the following form.

The SLOT_NAME of FRAME_NAME is VALUE

When the system is trying to establish whether a premise expressed in this form is true, it retrieves the value of the named slot in the named frame and compares the value found there to the value specified in the rule clause. Furthermore, most systems allow rules to include some predicates from the underlying programming language (e.g., EQUAL, NOT_EQUAL, PLUS, MINUS, GREATER_THAN) so that simple arithmetic or Boolean operations can be performed within a rule clause as it is being evaluated. If all of a rule's premises are satisfied, the conclusion of the rule uses the same syntax to place a value in the slot of some object; this new value can then be retrieved by premises of another rule, and so on. Moreover, in most of these environments, rules can have side effects in their conclusions, such as sending messages to procedures to fire.

For instance, consider the following rule, which contains both natural language clauses and infix syntax for mathematical operators.

IF   ((the pH of EFFLUENT) − (the pH of FEEDSTOCK) > 2.0)

THEN   (the ACIDITY_GAIN of process is EXCESSIVE)

AND   (SEND_MESSAGE ((OPEN BUFFER_SOLUTION_VALVE) 20))

This rule would retrieve the value in the slot pH of the objects EFFLUENT and FEEDSTOCK, perform the arithmetic and the Boolean inequality check, and evaluate to TRUE or FALSE. Since the rule has only one premise, if it evaluates to TRUE the conclusion places the value EXCESSIVE in the ACIDITY_GAIN slot of the object EFFLUENT and sends a message to the method in the slot OPEN of the frame BUFFER_SOLUTION_VALVE, together with the argument 20 (meaning here 20 degrees of rotation). The message in the slot OPEN would then fire from within the frame BUFFER_SOLUTION_VALVE. This method would fire and, as an important side effect, would actuate the appropriate relays to open the buffer solution valve (SELF) by 20 degrees.

This type of rule syntax for integrating rules with frames and procedures is common to most integrated rule-frame systems. However, the ways in which rules are stored and the approaches used to control the firing of rules can differ substantially. We describe three ways in which rules can be accessed and stored in frame-based systems in Sections 6.4.1 through 6.4.3.

6.4.1   Production Rules as Slot Values of Rule Frames

One approach to integrating the representations—the approach used by IntelliCorp's KEE system—is to take the OOP paradigm completely to heart and regard rules simply as special kinds of frames. To create a set of rules that are intended to chain together, either forward or backward, the user would simply create and name a class of rules, for example, POWER_SUPPLY_DIAGNOSTIC_RULES. This named class of rules is then typically made a subclass of a (hidden) system-level rule class from which it then literally inherits the inference engine as a method. Any number of rules that belong to this class can then be encoded by creating instances of the named rule class, writing the rule in the system's natural language rule syntax, and then storing the natural language version of the rule as the value of a slot in the rule frame corresponding to its external form.

Rules in a given rule class will attempt to chain forward or backward only with other rules in their rule class. This provides a modular way to organize chunks of related knowledge and helps to limit the amount of search done by the inference engine, since it only looks at rules in a single rule class at one time.

Another desirable feature of rule integration is the ability to use abstraction hierarchy predicates, for example, IN_CLASS, to limit the frames whose values will be retrieved in an attempt to match a rule premise. Thus the premise of a rule in KEE's quasi-English syntax might be

```
((IF        (?ACTIVITY is IN_CLASS CONCRETE_ACTIVITIES)
  AND       (the COMPLETION_STATUS of ?ACTIVITY is COMPLETED)
  AND       (>  (the ACTUAL_DURATION of ?ACTIVITY)
                (the PLANNED_DURATION of ?ACTIVITY)))
 (THEN    (the EMPLOYMENT_STATUS of SUPERVISOR
                              is UNEMPLOYED)))
```

KEE treats an argument whose first character is a question mark—like ?ACTIVITY—as a variable. (Other AI programming environments have similar ways to tag variables in rule clauses.) It therefore uses the first clause of the premise to define the scope of the rule. It applies the remaining premises of this rule for all of the legal values of this variable; that is, it attempts to satisfy the remaining rule premises for each of the activities that is an instance of the class CONCRETE_ACTIVITIES. A rule of broader scope might use the argument ALL_PROJECT_ACTIVITIES for the predicate IN_CLASS; in contrast, a rule with the argument CONCRETE_SLIPFORM_ACTIVITIES for IN_CLASS would have a narrower scope than the original rule.

Besides following the OOP spirit closely, this way of integrating rules into a frame-based knowledge base facilitates the organization of a set of rules according to the kinds of tasks that they perform. The secondary organization of the scope of rules according to the objects that they reference is obtained by making use of the ?VARIABLE IN_CLASS CLASSNAME construct illustrated in the example above. Thus, it encourages developers to think primarily about kinds of reasoning tasks— rather than about kinds of objects involved—when developing a set of rules. For many developers, especially those accustomed to structured programming languages where subroutines or procedures perform specific tasks, this is a natural and intuitive way to work.

6.4.2 Attribute Values Point to Rules

An alternative approach to implementing rules is found in the Rule-Based Frame System (RBFS), in which the slots of objects can contain known values or rules to derive the slots' values [Kellett 1989]. When a slot value containing a rule is accessed, the rule in the slot is fired. This rule may reference other slots in its own frame or slots in other frames of the knowledge base. If a slot referenced by the first rule contains a rule as its value, it fires its rule to compute a slot value to send to the first rule, and so on, chaining between the rules in different frames in this way.

This style of rule-frame integration tends to lead developers to organize a system's reasoning behavior around a set of objects—typically subsystems or components in configuration or planning KBES applications—and all of their possible interactions, rather than around a set of tasks that might be performed on the objects in a system. This approach and the one we will describe next lend themselves especially well to reasoning about design configuration problems where objects are often defined in terms of attributes of other objects.

6.4.3   Attribute Values Obtained by Rules or Procedures

With sophisticated general-purpose representation tools, it is possible to create a hybrid system which uses both rules and procedures to compute and propagate slot values on demand. Using "when accessed" and "when changed" facets, or demons, on the desired slots, a knowledge engineer can set up a KBES to trigger either rule inference or method firing when values are accessed or changed by the user, an external program, a rule, or a method within the frame system.

Hybrid programming environments with rules, frames, and procedures can be used to develop intelligent design systems that provide the following kinds of assistance to a user.

❏   Perform subsystem- or system-level analyses when appropriate (e.g., initiate a structural analysis when a newly added element is assigned a value for one of its dimensions that is significantly different from an assumed or default value);

❏   Carry out consistency checks on new or modified components of a design, in terms of the defined or default values of other components, at the time they are defined;

❏   Highlight inconsistencies with previously defined components, and suggest ways to reconfigure the design.

This style of rule integration can be implemented in a variety of ways—for example, with rules or methods that are fired when local slot values are changed, and whose conclusions reset the values of all other attributes that are constrained by the new local value. Moreover, slot values for design objects can be retrieved from CADD or relational databases. There are now several high-level engineering design automation languages (e.g., Design++, ICAD, and Concept Modeler) which take the concept of intelligent configuration several steps further, as we show in later chapters.

6.5 EXPLANATION IN A KBES

We claimed in Chapter 1 that one of the hallmark characteristics of KBES applications was their ability to provide clear explanations of their reasoning processes and knowledge, both to system builders for debugging purposes and to end users for clarification or training purposes. In this section we review the kinds of explanations that can be generated automatically by integrated AI environments, and we explain the mechanisms used to generate such explanations.

6.5.1 Frame Hierarchies

Most AI development environments provide graphic displays of frame hierarchies. These are intended primarily for display of abstraction hierarchies and for access to the internals of frames. Figures 6-5 and 6-6 illustrate this two-level explanation capability for knowledge contained in frames. Without such tools it becomes very difficult to manage the development of a complex KBES application, although text-only frame-based systems continue to be used by some developers.

Some AI programming environments can also generate graphs of relationships other than abstraction among the frames in a knowledge base. For instance, KEE provides the function (SLOTGRAPH 'FRAME_NAME 'SLOT_NAME) which allows a user to generate a graph using a named frame to define the root of the graph and a named slot of the frame (containing other frame names as its legal values) to define the relationship.

Thus, (SLOTGRAPH 'CIRCUIT_BREAKER_27 'DOWNSTREAM) would generate a graph rooted in CIRCUIT_BREAKER_27 showing all of the downstream electrical components and their topology. This might be helpful for doing a quick visual spot check of the adequacy of the circuit breaker for all of its downstream loads. The precedence network of a project's activities, the load path of a structure's horizontal and vertical loadings, and the piping topology of a process loop are other examples of relationships that can be explained graphically using a slotgraph or equivalent capability.

6.5.2 Rule Traces

Many production rule KBES shells can produce traces of the rules that they fire, in order. This simple explanation or debugging device is analogous to the line number traces produced by programming languages like Basic; it is the minimal explanation facility that might be expected of a commercial KBES shell.

6.5.3   Automatic Explanation (Transparency of Reasoning)

The syntax of production rule systems, in which premise and conclusion clauses are near–natural language sentences, makes it easy for KBES shells to generate near–natural language explanations of why a question is being posed or how a conclusion was reached, simply by stringing together with a few connectives the appropriate clauses and the names of any arguments contained in arithmetic formulas within rule clauses.

Recall the example rule set from Table 5-1 of Chapter 5. Consider that the system is chaining backward from Rule 2 to Rule 1. In response to a "Why?" question from a user, the production rule shell might generate the following response. (Clauses or arguments taken from rule premises or conclusions are shown in italics.)

> We are attempting to determine whether to *DO_FEM_ANALYSIS.*

> In order to do so, we need to know whether you can *USE_COMPUTER.*

> We are attempting to determine whether to *USE_COMPUTER.*

> In order to do so, we need to know whether you *WANT_NUMBER.*

> In order to do so, we need to know whether you *HAVE_COMPUTER.*

> Please affirm that you *WANT_NUMBER.*

> Please affirm that you *HAVE_COMPUTER.*

Similar kinds of explanations can be generated to explain how a conclusion was reached. If a KBES shell includes a facility for uncertain reasoning, certainty factors can be parsed into both kinds of explanations.Expert system shells whose reasoning schemes are based on inference nets provide similar natural language explanations. They do this by parsing together ideas and user-supplied or deduced beliefs with a few connectives. For instance, consider that a user of the SafeQual system for prequalifying construction contractors (described in Chapter 9) is being asked to provide the contractor's in-state EMR (a measure of its worker's compensation insurance losses).   Asking "Why?" produces the following textual explanation of the inference process.

> Overall hypothesis: *This contractor's safety record and practices are acceptable.*

> Current hypothesis: *The Experience Modification Rating is acceptable.*

> → *The contractor's in-state EMR is acceptable.*
  The contractor's interstate EMR is acceptable.
  The contractor's average EMR for states worked in is acceptable.

> Current idea: Range of responses to continue: –4.5 to 5.0

As in the previous example, the natural language clauses or ideas are shown in italics and the plain text is generated by the KBES shell—the Deciding Factor, in this case—in parsing together its explanation. The arrow marks the idea currently being evaluated.

After reviewing this explanation, the user provides a value of 205 for the contractor's EMR—that is, insurance losses are 2.05 times the expected losses. This answer corresponds to positively false or –5 for this question, which is outside the range of permissible answers shown at the bottom of the previous explanation screen. The system thus informs the user that the top-level hypothesis, *This contractor's safety record and practices are acceptable,* has become totally negative (-5.0). Asking "Why?" produces the following explanation.

> Whether *this contractor's safety record and practices are acceptable* has become totally negative (–5.0) because the following idea is out of range.

> There is a totally negative (–5.0) evaluation that *the contractor's in-state EMR is acceptable.*

Ideas not evaluated:

> There is no evaluation of whether *the contractor's interstate EMR is acceptable.*

> There is no evaluation of whether *the contractor's average EMR for states worked in is acceptable.*

6.5.4   Rule Graphs

Integrated AI environments which have the capability to graph frame hierarchies often also have the capability to graph rules. A graph of a set of rules which chain together provides an excellent vehicle for understanding the structure of the rule set (for debugging) and for understanding how answers to previous questions led to a given conclusion. Figure 6-7 shows a rule graph produced by Neuron Data's Nexpert Object system. Checks indicate rule premises or conclusions that have been found to be true; inverse checks indicate false premises or hypotheses; and question marks indicate that premises or hypotheses whose truth is unknown. Links going off the screen to the left chain back to the conclusions of other rules. For a rule system of even moderate complexity, browsing the rule network is a very powerful way to understand or debug rules, compared to reading through a long list of randomly ordered production rules in a text editor or tracing through natural language textual explanations.

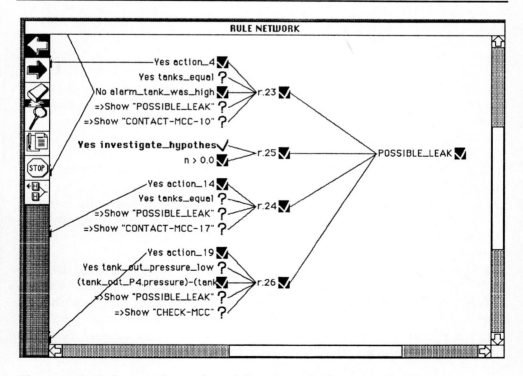

Figure 6-7 Rule graph produced by the rule browser in Neuron Data's Nexpert Object System.

Inference net systems can produce graphs showing the ideas (evidence) supporting each hypothesis in the net, typically together with the logical connective for combining the evidence at that node, prior probabilities of each idea, and likelihood-of-sufficiency/necessity coefficients or positive and negative weights of evidence on each link. In the same way that looking at a rule graph provides a graphic overview of how a set of production rules chain together, browsing around the nodes in an inference net allows a user of an inference net system to understand the structure of the knowledge (in debugging or training mode) and the accumulation of evidence for hypotheses (in consultation mode).

6.5.5 Knowledge-Based Interactive Graphics

A tight integration between underlying data representation and graphics was implemented in early object-oriented programming languages such as Smalltalk. It also has been the basis for the current generation of icon- and object-oriented windowing computer systems initially found only in very expensive Lisp-based workstations and more recently popularized by the Apple Macintosh computers. This style of user interface is rapidly becoming the standard user interface for all personal computers and workstations—with attendant litigation about who owns the ideas. AI development environments like LOOPS (developed at the Xerox Palo Alto Research Center) and KEE, whose features have been described in this chapter, were among the first computer systems to integrate bit-mapped graphics with the frame data structures used to support symbolic reasoning.

The symbolic reasoning capabilities of KBESs have been the primary focus of our discussions up to this point. However, we believe that tight integration of bit-mapped graphics with the underlying data used in problem solving is an important contribution of AI programming environments to the tools available for engineering computation.

Current AI development environments go far beyond allowing users to point and click on icons to open and copy files. "Active image" demon-driven graphics for display and data entry in KBES applications provide a high-level programming environment for rapidly prototyping and refining lively and powerful user interfaces to enrich KBES applications. Two-way interactive graphics can play a vital role in explaining the reasoning processes and conclusions of a KBES to its developers and to its end users and in facilitating data entry by users.

Two-way interactive graphics, linked to a knowledge representation and reasoning system, has been called "knowledge-based interactive graphics" [Levitt 1987b]. Knowledge-based interactive graphics allow an engineer to collaborate with a KBES in a synergistic manner that exploits both human cognitive strengths such as spatial reasoning and analogy and the abilities of computers to perform data storage and retrieval, computation and display. We will describe some KBES applications that exploit the notion of knowledge-based interactive graphics in Chapters 9 and 11.

6.6 SUMMARY

We have described three knowledge representation formalisms in this chapter: semantic nets, frames, and object-oriented programming. These formalisms can be integrated with production rules and interfaced to traditional engineering design tools such as CADD systems and algorithmic and simulation programs. Such integration facilitates implementation of the high-level approaches to representation and reasoning that we shall see in Chapter 7. At the same time, tool integration permits the development of powerful KBES applications in engineering—as we shall see in extenso in the applications discussions in Chapters 9 through 11—across Amarel's spectrum of problem types.

Chapter 7

ADVANCED TOPICS IN REPRESENTATION

In this chapter we survey several topics that are rather more advanced than the fundamentals we have stressed so far. These are ideas about representation that are beginning to find their way into engineering applications, and they offer a great deal of promise because of their power. The particular ideas we shall outline include qualitative reasoning, also called qualitative physics; belief revision systems, also known as truth maintenance systems, and the creation of "multiple worlds"; and reasoning about space and time. Note that this survey will only scratch the surface of these topics, which we cannot treat in detail here. However, we will introduce the vocabulary in brief discussions of the key ideas, and we will provide references to the salient literature by citing some of the original research papers as well as review and tutorial articles.

7.1 QUALITATIVE REASONING

At the beginning of this book (see Chapter 1 and the early part of Chapter 2) and in various other places (in Chapter 8, for example), we stressed the view that much of what we are concerned about when we talk of different representation schemes is the development of different kinds of models that can be used to describe different engineering tasks. We are quite familiar with the analytical formulas and numerical models that we consistently use to formulate and solve particular problems. However, much of what we know cannot be represented in these terms, or is perhaps represented so implicitly or indirectly as to hinder its application or render obscure our understanding. It would be of more than casual interest, therefore, to find some representation technique to bridge the gaps between the analytical formulas and all the other things we know about our respective (engineering) domains. To make such a discussion useful, it would be helpful to put it into a context, and in particular, into a **taxonomy,** or ordering, of the kinds of knowledge that we do employ.

7.1.1   A Taxonomy of Engineering Knowledge

In order to keep this discussion from becoming too abstract, we will exhibit this rough taxonomy of engineering knowledge for a particular domain, that of structural mechanics. This is the branch of engineering that is concerned with modeling structural behavior; it is founded upon that fundamental branch of physics called mechanics. It is a domain in which the knowledge can be usefully cast and applied in many forms and at many levels. The kinds of knowledge include first principles (e.g., conservation of momentum, equilibrium); phenomenological models, which can be either mathematical or qualitative (e.g., mass-stiffness-frequency relations, force-deflection relations); analytical models, both exact and approximate; numerical representations (e.g., finite element codes); and heuristics (or rules) that are based both on compiled knowledge and practical experience [Dym 1991a]. We elaborate these categories below, keeping in mind the intended focus on structural mechanics.

First principles. These are the basic physical laws upon which stand both the field of mechanics as a branch of physics and the discipline of engineering mechanics. Examples include Newton's laws of motion, conservation of momentum, and conservation of mass. Note that these principles, while expressible in mathematical terms, are also representations of concepts that we can reason about in qualitative or symbolic terms. For example, while we might often write Newton's law of motion for a particle as

$$F = m * \frac{d^2x}{dt^2}$$

we could also write it as

$$Force = mass * (acceleration)$$

which symbolic version we could now encode in one of the representation schemes discussed in earlier chapters so that we could reason about it qualitatively. Further, it is at this level, too, that we can incorporate other kinds of reasoning—for example, **causal reasoning**, in which we can relate cause and effect at a *conceptual level*, as in the statement that an unbalanced force produces a nonzero acceleration. Thus, instead of calculating force magnitudes, we can reason in *qualitative* terms about their presence and any resulting effects. We shall have more to say about this when we discuss qualitative reasoning.

Phenomenological models. These are models often based on experimental results or on compiled high-level extrapolations of the fundamental laws. Examples of such models include pressure-volume relations, stress-strain laws, and generalized force-deflection and mass-stiffness-frequency relations. These phenomenological models can be expressed in analytical terms, either as formulas or in some numerical model, but they are often also amenable to representation in qualitative terms. Again, these formulations permit—and even encourage—causal reasoning, and they are particularly helpful in modeling the *behavior of devices*, a major concern of qualitative reasoning [de Kleer 1987a].

Analytical models. These are models, both exact and approximate, used to represent specific "cases" or subsets of the more general first principles and phenomenological models. For example, in modeling elastic continua, we would apply special-case models to analyze the behavior of beams, columns, plate structures, and shells. The case-specific models could be very general in terms of the kinds of behavior they admit; for example, they might incorporate time-dependent (dynamic) effects, stability and buckling, and nonlinear constitutive behavior.

Numerical representations. These are the numerical versions of the analytical models just described. Perhaps the best-known examples in structural mechanics are the finite element codes that are in widespread use in structural and mechanical engineering [Shames 1985]. Another increasingly important class of numerical models is the boundary element technique [Cruse 1988].

Heuristics. Inasmuch as heuristics or rules can be used to represent many different kinds of knowledge, this type of information transcends, in some sense, the entire hierarchy just outlined. For example, rules may be used to express various aspects of fundamental principles (as in SACON); compiled versions of both phenomenological and analytical models (again, as in SACON; see also [Chandrasekaran 1984]); preferences and assumptions about the use of numerical codes; experiential rules of thumb; and strategic knowledge about using any or all of the available tools in searching for an appropriate way to solve a given problem, subject to constraints about granularity, time requirements, cost, and so on [Dym 1989].

We should note here that this taxonomy is not monotonically hierarchical, especially in the representations that are used. Many of these different kinds of knowledge can be—and often are—expressed in different forms, depending on the problem at hand. Momentum considerations for particles (and structures), for example, can be written in several forms, depending on the type of information sought and the uses to which that knowledge will be put. Momentum, however, cannot be measured directly, but is calculated from velocity measurements; yet the most common form of motion detector (the accelerometer) measures acceleration. On the other hand, if we were modeling the dynamic behavior of a structure in order to deal with changes in structural form, information about the relative motion of components will be needed. This suggests that *multiple perspectives* may be important in structural mechanics problems as well as in more general engineering problems.

7.1.2 Qualitative Physics: Some Definitions

We come now to the heart of this discussion. We noted above that there are some representation ideas which could be very helpful in facilitating conceptual reasoning about first principles, equations, devices, and so on. The ideas stem in part from the recognition that humans respond to their environments by reasoning in qualitative terms about physical phenomena and devices. This has given rise to the study of *naive physics*, in which attempts are made to provide an experience-based calculus for causal qualitative reasoning [Hardt 1987]. This endeavor is also related to the study of the *commonsense reasoning* which we all employ in a matter-of-fact way to deal with the common knowledge that we have about the world and that stems from our routine experiences [DavisE 1987]. In fact, it is worth restating here a point made in Chapters 1 and 12: that one feature of expert systems is that they are typically designed to perform very narrow tasks in which commonsense reasoning does not come into play. Part of the agenda of the study of qualitative reasoning is the attempt to supply a means by which such reasoning can be incorporated in expert systems [de Kleer 1987a].

Qualitative physics is the symbolic representation of the physical *structure* of phenomena and devices that facilitates the qualitative description of the *behavior* found in these phenomena and devices. What makes qualitative physics useful, and where it sharply contrasts with our normal use of quantitative physical models, is the expression of behavioral aspects in qualitative terms. That is, some of the important aspects and concepts of the behavior of physical devices involve qualitative terms such as "state, cause, law, equilibrium . . . feedback, etc." [de Kleer 1987a]. These are concepts which cannot be stated in quantitative terms, but about which we reason whenever we are involved in describing or solving physical problems. And, in fact, they are concepts for which we have or can develop an intuitive feel which can be quite significant in problem solving.

It follows from this definition that the formalization of qualitative physics requires a calculus for dealing with statements that a structural quality or attribute exists and that it is increasing, is decreasing, or is not (or no longer) changing. Thus, we are seeking a symbolic representation of the quality of an attribute rather than of its numerical magnitude. Then we would construct **qualitative differential equations** to calculate the changes in the behavior of the device we are modeling. And, instead of calculating numerical values of variables as in the classical approach, we would calculate values in a **quantity space** that must perforce be limited to the values + (increasing), − (decreasing), or 0 (constancy).

We now present a brief illustration of how qualitative modeling proceeds by adapting the description of the behavior of a valve [de Kleer 1987a]. In so doing, we note that qualitative physics is a young field of research for which a uniform notation has not yet emerged [Bobrow 1985a]. Thus, our presentation is in the notation pioneered by de Kleer [1984, 1987a]. The qualitative value of the variable x is denoted by $[x]$ where $[x] = +$ if and only if (iff) $x > 0$; $[x] = -$ iff $x < 0$; and $[x] = 0$ iff $x = 0$. Addition and multiplication of variables can then be defined in a straightforward way.

$$\{ [x] = + \} + \{ [y] = + \} = +$$

and

$$\{ [x] = + \} * \{ [y] = - \} = -$$

Some of the addition operations, however, cannot be defined; for example,

$$\{ [x] = + \} + \{ [y] = - \} \text{ is undefined}$$

This lack of definition should be not surprising, because we are not writing down specific positive and negative numbers here; we are only relating values in the quantity space.

Qualitative equations are defined as **confluences** which relate qualitative variables or values. A confluence of qualitative values is satisfied if qualitative equality is satisfied exactly by virtue of the defintiions for multiplication and addition, or it is satisfied if the lack of an additive definition leaves one side of the confluence open. Thus, if $[x] = +$ and $[y] = -$ the confluence $[x] + [y] + [z] = 0$ is satisfied for any value of $[z]$. However, a set of values will contradict a confluence if both sides of it are calculated and the confluence cannot be calculated. With $[x]$ and $[y]$ as just given, then, the confluence $[x] = [y] = [z] = +$ is contradictory. We also point out that this definition means that a confluence need not be satisfied or contradicted if values have not been assigned to all the variables.

We now need some notation to describe rates of change, and for this we adapt some from the conventional calculus. In particular, we write $\partial x = +$ if we wish to say that $[dx/dt]$ is increasing with time (t). And, by extension, we would calculate and write the higher-order changes as

$$\partial^n x = [d^n x / dt^n]$$

The last definitional point we discuss here relates to the extension of the range of values that a variable can take. In many applications we would find that the quantity space consisting of $+$, $-$, and 0 is not sufficient to describe the phenomenon under consideration. For example, there may be a critical frequency ω_{crit} in our problem for which we need to distinguish between $\omega < \omega_{crit}$ and $\omega > \omega_{crit}$. In order to deal with this situation, a set or network of inequalities can be introduced to subdivide the real line beyond the binary division implied by the definition given above for the quantity space. This perforce introduces complications in the arithmetic, not the least of which are the corresponding definitions of derivatives of such variables.

7.1.3   Qualitative Physics: A Simple Model

We now describe a simple model for a valve in which we focus on the individual components of the device, each of which has its own specific model. (See [de Kleer 1987a] for an introduction to other kinds of modeling.) In this approach, the admissible behavior of a component is specified by a set of possible states and their corresponding specifications and confluences. For the valve, let A be the flow area, p the pressure drop across the valve, and Q the flow rate through the valve. Then the description of the valve being open is

$$\text{VALVE\_OPEN:} \quad [A = A_{max}], \quad [p] = 0, \quad \partial p = 0$$

This constituent model represents the facts that the maximum flow area obtains if the valve is fully open, there can be no pressure drop across an open valve, and the pressure cannot change across the valve as long as it stays open. On the other hand, if the valve is shut completely, we obtain

$$\text{VALVE\_CLOSED:} \quad [A = 0], \quad [Q] = 0, \quad \partial Q = 0$$

Here we are reflecting the facts that when the valve is closed the flow area is zero, there is no flow through the valve, and the rate of change of the flow rate must also vanish in this circumstance.

Finally, in the working state, we see that we have a qualitative differential equation represented in the last confluence. Here the valve acts like a fluid resistance such that $\partial p = \partial Q$ if $\partial A = 0$.

VALVE_WORKING: $[0 < A < A_{max}]$, $[p] = [Q]$, $\partial p + ([p] * \partial A) - \partial Q = 0$

Our model thus describes the device as a collection of states, each characterized by its own set of inequalities and sets of confluences. Admissible behavior, then, consists of a complete set of variable values that satisfies all of the confluences of all the component states. This model is, of course, not complete, for if we wanted to describe a piping system, we would have to write down the relevant laws—such as the conservation of mass and the conservation of energy—that govern the entire piping circuit. There are also corresponding compatibility conditions for which confluences must be written (e.g., the sum of the pressure drops along any different paths between two points must all be the same). For further details, see [Bobrow 1985a; de Kleer 1984, 1987a].

In constructing our qualitative differential equations or models we must be careful to adhere to the **no-function-in-structure principle** according to which we must ensure that the laws of any part of a device do not presume the functioning of the whole device [de Kleer 1987a]. The reason for this principle is the desire to separate behavior from structure so that behavior can be inferred from structure and solely from structure. We thus wish to make sure that we do not build into the qualitative model some aspects of expected behavior or function that could lead to erroneous conclusions. In fact, the whole point of qualitative physics is the determination of function *from* structure. (In Section 8.2 we discuss another approach to inferring system behavior from CADD data on component geometry, enriched by rules, to add component topology and behavior.)

7.2   BELIEF REVISION SYSTEMS

We now turn our attention to the question, How does a KBES adapt itself to changing circumstances? It is all too often the case that the problem-solving environments within which we operate are dynamic: facts change, assumptions are revised, new relationships and dependencies emerge, and so on. We should note, though, that for the present discussion we are really considering what—in engineering terms—is a *quasi-static* model, as we are not going to focus here on changes that occur because of time-dependent events such as in the monitoring of a time-varying process. Rather, we are interested in the question of what happens as a result of changes forced by the reasoning process itself, where time is not an explicit variable. For example, suppose that on the basis of some input data we assume a structure can be modeled using the classical bending theory of plates, subsequent to which we discover the presence of significant in-plane loading. Depending on where we are in the solution of the problem, we might have to revise estimates and their consequences, change models, seek additional data to confirm or disconfirm the latest information, and so on. In order to address these issues, it will be helpful to have available some definitions from the AI research literature.

Belief revision is the process of detecting and managing contradictory information in a reasoning process [Martins 1987]. The concern is thus one of updating information to detect emerging contradictions and then deciding what needs to be done to properly reflect the effects of the apparent contradictions as the solution to our problem unfolds. The intellectual roots of belief revision can be found in two strands of AI research, one related to the application of mathematical logic (see Chapter 3), the other related to notions of search (see Chapter 2).

The mathematical logic strand has to do with recognizing both change and the lack of change in the application of the formalism of mathematical logic. To borrow a simple example from Charniak [1985], let us suppose we are reasoning about the melting of ice cubes on a summer picnic table. We can postulate a set of rules or operators such that an ice cube will melt if the ambient temperature exceeds a certain value and that the table will get wet if an ice cube melts. Now we apply these operators to cube 1 and, if the data reflect a high enough value of the ambient temperature, we conclude that the table will indeed get wet. Now we consider cube 2 and ask whether it, too, will get the table wet. It seems a straightforward enough conclusion to reach, and it is certainly consistent with our commonsense experience, that cube 2 will melt and the table will be made wet again (or wetter). However, as a matter of logical reasoning, we cannot deduce this result because we cannot be sure that the ambient temperature remains *unchanged* by the melting of cube 1. The only way we can be sure of reaching a correct result—in the logical sense—is to include a statement to the effect that the ambient temperature is unchanged by the (prior) melting of cube 1. The **frame problem** of mathematical logic is, then, the problem of recognizing which operators are unchanged by results obtained as a solution unfolds. The frame problem is dealt with by including **frame**

axioms, which are logical statements to the effect that particular operators are left unchanged by later conclusions. In this problem the relevant frame axiom would be the logical expression of the fact that the melting of an ice cube does not change the ambient temperature.

The second root of belief revision harkens back to one aspect of our discussion of search (see Section 2.4.6). We raised the question, within the context of constraint satisfaction, of what to do when we reached a dead end in the search process. We noted that the approach taken is to *backtrack* to see if we can undo the step(s) that lead to the dead end. As with dead ends, so with contradictions. That is, we backtrack to undo the steps that have produced the present difficulty. The traditional approach has been to apply **chronological backtracking**, in which steps are undone starting from the most recent one made before the contradiction emerged [Winston 1984a]. The second approach, **dependency-directed backtracking**, aims at discovering the conditions or assumptions—typically reflecting some inconsistency in the knowledge base—that produced the contradiction, with the aim of eliminating the inconsistency. In fact, the goal of dependency-directed backtracking is twofold: we want to avoid processing a node in a problem when we have the knowledge to predict that a contradiction will occur, and we want to avoid rediscovering contradictions that have already been found [de Kleer 1987b]. It is this second approach, dependency-directed backtracking, that really lies at the heart of what is now called belief revision.

The earliest work in belief revision made explicit use of mathematical logic; indeed, the intent was to use the ideas of theorem proving to build rudimentary planning systems. The work was done on planning in the "blocks world" domain, in which the idea is to develop a sequence of steps—a plan—such that blocks on a plane can be picked up and put down, moved around, and arranged into stacks in which the blocks are placed in varying positions [Fikes 1971]. In this pioneering system, called STRIPS, each step consists of the application of an operator whose application is enabled by the satisfaction of one or more conditions, sometimes called preconditions. Similarly, the execution of a step produces as consequences further conditions that represent changes in the environment. Both sets of conditions are maintained in lists that are attached to the operator. STRIPS contains a knowledge base that represents the current state of the blocks world. At each step in the plan the knowledge base is updated by appropriate additions or deletions of the conditions attached to the operator that performs the step. The emergence of the frame problem seems self-evident, as with our ice cube example, in that there is room even in this simple domain for a lot of ambiguity if the preconditions are not carefully stated. For example, in order to pick up a block, we need to be sure that its top is clear, just as we need to have a clear space available when we want to put down a block. The frame axioms help us clearly state these requirements for action that might otherwise remain implicit. However, it turns out that the management of the lists of conditions in STRIPS is a major complication in two regards. The addition and deletion of lists has to be carefully monitored so that we do not develop infinite loops when we are modifying the knowledge base. We also need to be aware that deleting a condition or proposition from the knowledge base may not happen automatically unless it is explicitly linked to the action just being taken [Martins 1987].

The next major step in the development of belief revision dealt with the flaws just mentioned, and particularly the second one—that is, the lack of explicit tracking of conditions and propositions—by introducing a **dependency record** for each assertion or operator [Stallman 1977]. This work, which introduced the idea of dependency-directed backtracking, created a system called EL in the domain of electronic circuit analysis [Sussman 1975]. The EL system keeps a complete record—the dependency record—of all assertions and propositions developed, and it includes in this record a listing of the propositions and rules of inference that were used to derive the assertions in the dependency trace. Martins [1987] cites a simple example in which EL, in the absence of any specific data, might have to estimate the range of operating values for a circuit element. If a contradiction should subsequently emerge, EL would search the trace to find out which device produces this erroneous state. The significance of EL's approach is that it uncovers the flaw by looking for the assumption that is behind the error, rather than simply undoing the last choices in reverse chronological order. Once such a contradiction is uncovered, EL stores the assumptions leading to the contradiction (as a unit) and prevents them from being invoked again as problem solving proceeds.

We noted that the first work on dependency-directed backtracking was in the domain of circuit analysis [Stallman 1977]. The next step was the development of a **truth maintenance system (TMS)**, which is a domain-independent program or environment for belief revision programming [Doyle 1979]. The central feature of a TMS is a knowledge base of propositions or assertions, each of which is clearly identified as being believed or disbelieved. The propositions are one of two basic types of objects in TMS, the other being **justifications** that are the reasons for believing, or not believing, a particular assertion. The justifications are implemented mainly in lists that are subdivided according to whether any supporting propositions are believed (the **inlist**) or whether they are disbelieved (the **outlist**). Without going into great detail, it is worth pointing out that **assumptions** are propositions whose current justification consists of a nonempty outlist; that is, assumptions are based on the disbelief of other propositions.

This last point emerges as being important because the inspection of a TMS knowledge base for contradictary propositions can be done in two distinct ways [Martins 1987]. The propositions in the knowledge base of an *assumption-based* TMS contain data about the nonderived assertions or hypotheses from which they are derived. Each proposition in *justification-based* TMS contains information about the assertions that directly support it. In assumption-based systems, backtracking can be eliminated because all the assumptions beneath a contradiction are easily and directly identified, in large part because such systems update the current context rather than marking (or unmarking) a list of propositions.

The main point for us to consider here, however, is not the specifics of such a system. Rather, it is that assumption-based TMS is the basic idea behind the notion of maintaining "multiple worlds" as problem solving proceeds. That is, such a system operates by updating the current context while maintaining the contexts that preceded the current state. Such ideas are very useful in design, for example, because it becomes possible to maintain alternative designs for retrieval and evaluation. We shall see one such example in the discussion of the PRIDE system in Chapter 10. These ideas are also important when there are multiple problem-solving systems or agents working on pieces of a large problem (see Chapter 8). In an environment of interacting agents, each agent will perforce have to reason about the beliefs of fellow agents. Thus it will be very important that any single agent be able to distinguish its beliefs from those of the other agents.

7.3   SPATIAL AND TEMPORAL REASONING

We noted earlier that we take for granted our human ability to do common-sense reasoning, that is, to reason about the everyday mundane facts and events of our lives. As part and parcel of this talent, we reason about both time and space in very familiar fashions, taking for granted our ability to find our way around, to make maps and locate objects, to fill in our calendars, to infer things from the order of events, and so on. Nevertheless, as easy as these tasks seem to us in our daily pursuits, they are—just like commonsense reasoning—very difficult issues to model for reasoning and computation. So we shall devote this section to highlighting some of the important issues.

7.3.1 Spatial Reasoning

Reasoning about spatial issues can be seen as encompassing a good many ideas and processes, so it is well to be more precise about our present concerns. For example, much of operations research has been taken up by the formulation of search problems such as the traveling salesman problem, in which the goal is to minimize the cost of travel in a network of cities. Although distances on a map are involved here, space itself has been abstracted out of the problem and so it is not of great interest to us here. Likewise, the issues of computer-based or knowledge-based vision, which involve the automated interpretation of images, are also not of direct concern, although there is some overlap in the use of knowledge to interpret image data [Arbib 1987]. And, in a similar vein, we shall not concern ourselves with the cognitive and visualization processes that go on in the mind when we talk about events in space. What we are really interested in are the computational aspects of reasoning in symbolic terms about objects and their relationships to each other, a goal to which we can aspire without probing into the internal representations used by the mind [McDermottD 1987]. Thus, we shall focus on aspects of spatial reasoning that are likely to be important from an engineering viewpoint.

We start with **shape representation**, that is, how we describe the shapes of objects (and spaces).   There are three basic ideas here: part-whole, volumetric, and surface descriptions [McDermottD 1987]. In **part-whole representation**, objects are described in terms of the parts or pieces of which they are made up or assembled. The parts are arrayed in networks which, depending on the complexity of the domain, might be simple semantic nets or more complex inheritance lattices. From an engineering standpoint, a part-whole representation might also have functional connotations beyond the geometric description; that is, an object might have to include certain parts or components in order to accomplish some functionality. This sort of intermingling of spatial and functional reasoning can be found, for example, in the R1/XCON system which configures VAX computers by considering functional requirements and satisfying constraints about objects fitting into confined spaces, cable lengths, and so on [Barker 1989; McDermottJ 1981].

Another approach to shape representation is that of **volume description**, in which objects are represented in terms of constituent volumes which may often overlap and may not be clearly distinct from one another. The component volumes typically come from a library of primitives. Objects are then assembled by identifying particular dimensions, locations, and orientations for each component. For example, a disk with a central hole could be described a a short wide cylinder with a smaller parallel cylinder subtracted at the axis of revolution. Again, this kind of approach could be useful in functional terms, as in the **design with features** approach to the mechanical design of manufacturable objects [Cunningham 1988; Dixon 1987a, 1989]. Here the component volumes can be described as objects for mechanical design, having geometric features as well as material properties and other characteristics.

Another approach to shape description would characterize objects in terms of the shapes of their boundaries. Often this is a natural description for engineering work, particularly when the representations are numerically based, as in the use of splines in graphic design systems. The problem here is that these numerical descriptions do not lend themselves to reasoning. For example, the rooms of a building can be represented in an architectural design system in terms of the coordinates of the corners, which might in turn be related to some "absolute" set of coordinates for the building as a whole. This information could be useful for calculating distances to exits if we need to satisfy building code requirements about fire safety. However, if we want to reason about the safety of the room in terms of the type of wall or the openings in the wall, we would have to impose on the geometric description a more general representation such that we could reason about other attributes. This was done in the LSC Advisor, an architectural code-checking system which will be described in detail in Chapter 9 [Dym 1988]. Similarly, the SightPlan system reasons about rectangular objects in a two-dimensional space using a set of spatial primitives and a constraint engine to process all constraints ([Tommelein 1989a]; see Chapter 10 for details). Goel [1988] has proposed a general approach to combining geometric information with function and purpose.

There is related work stemming from research in qualitative physics (see Section 7.1) which, in its attempt to relate structure and function, does touch on some aspects of spatial reasoning. For example, the program NEWTON can infer that a block starting down from a roller coaster peak may not reach the next peak if its initial velocity is not high enough [de Kleer 1979], but the spatial representation used is not particularly general [McDermottD 1987]. The FROB program, however, reasons about the bouncing of a ball through a (geographic) region by restating a geometric map of the region as a qualitative map with properties that can be reasoned about as the ball bounces around [Forbus 1981].

Finally, on the topic of spatial reasoning, we mention that **route-finding** is an important aspect of robotics which may involve applications of KBESs as controllers of robots. If we exclude any robot that reasons from an image obtained by using an on-board vision system, then we must find ways to give our robot its own *internal* map of the environment in which it will operate. One interesting aspect of such work is the relative size of the robot as compared to the significant features of the space in which it moves. If the robot is in this sense small, then the principal issues are not unlike finding a route on a map. However, if the robot is large and there are objects of significant size scattered around the region, the robot may need to perform some intricate reasoning to move between and around the obstacles posed by the objects [McDermottD 1987].

7.3.2 Temporal Reasoning

Temporal reasoning, reasoning about time, is an interesting aspect of KBES development. Time is in some sense always there as a variable, although usually as an *implicit* variable that is assumed in the ordering of events in a reasoning process. It is implicit in a diagnostic system when we infer cause from effect, for example, or in a design system when we impose an ordering on operations in the design process. And, of course, it may be more explicit if, for example, we are using a KBES to monitor a process or series of events or to generate time-sequenced plans of action.

Time is important because things do change, and it is the response to change that we must manage in representing a problem-solving activity in a KBES [Shoham 1987]. Thus, there are two requirements we must try to satisfy if we are to successfully account for time in a KBES. We need first of all a way of stating what is true and what is false through the passage of time. And we need to define criteria for "admissible changes" of time.

In fact, we have seen in our discussion of belief revision in Section 7.2 that time is typically handled implicitly through frame axioms or the equivalent, as in the STRIPS planning system. We ought to recognize that there are serious modeling assumptions about—in AI parlance, strong commitments to—time in such logic-based models [Shoham 1987]. To begin with, time is discrete, and the possibility of describing a dynamic process, as we do quite ordinarily in mechanics, for example, is excluded. Also, the effect of an action is felt in the very next step of the solution process. At the same time, STRIPS and similar systems exclude concurrent actions, although later systems such as NONLIN permit them [Tate 1976]. Even though we can track the changes (or constancy) in some attributes with frame axioms, we may be deluged with frame axioms if we want to explore variations in several attributes. Further, we have no way to explicitly express things that are entirely unaffected by the actions being considered. Thus, as Shoham [1987] points out, picking up any one block in STRIPS doesn't change its color, doesn't affect any other block, doesn't change the president of the United States, and so on.

One response to these problems has been the incorporation of **histories** which allow some notion of time as a continuous variable, thus allowing the description of continuous process, such as the flow of water [Hayes 1984]. Then one can get a snapshot in time by slicing through the history of a process. Another approach, a variation on frame axioms, is the inclusion of **persistences** in the description of an event [McDermottD 1984], the notion being to delineate explicitly the time span over which an action is true. Thus, a consequence of a road repair is that the road is closed for five months, meaning that one can predict there will be no traffic on that road for that time. The prediction will be violated if an action is taken to double the size of the repair crew.

We should note that the work in qualitative physics does attempt to uncover the time sequence of events by working backward from the final state. Note that we are not describing simulation here. Rather, as in the roller coaster example of the NEWTON system (see Section 7.3.1), the system attempts to *envision* how the final state came to be by reasoning backward from the final state to uncover previous states in reverse chronological order [de Kleer 1979a].

Last, we note that time interval planning can be included rather explicitly as, for example, in project planning, where time spans do not appear as variables but as attributes of a process or action. Then one can reason about these actions and their corresponding time spans to plan a sequence of events. This has recently been done for construction planning [Levitt 1987b].

7.4 SUMMARY

This chapter has been devoted to a discussion of some more advanced topics in representation. They are advanced in the sense that they build on the basic representation schemes presented in Chapters 5 and 6. In some sense these advanced representation topics are elaborations of the "elementary" representations and, indeed, they build on and use the elementary representations of rules, nets, and frames. And these more sophisticated representation approaches have, for the most part, only recently found their way into some engineering applications research. Among the advanced topics we reviewed are qualitative physics, belief revision, and spatial and temporal reasoning.

Chapter 8

KBES ARCHITECTURES FOR ENGINEERING APPLICATIONS

We have now reviewed the principal implementation-level techniques for knowledge representation and reasoning, as well as some more advanced approaches. However, before we can routinely use knowledge-based systems to solve engineering problems, we require something beyond a description of the underlying representation tools; we need to develop an understanding of how the various representation techniques can be organized in a KBES designed to solve engineering problems. This brings us into the realm of KBES architectures for engineering applications.

In both Chapters 1 and 5 we have outlined the basic elements of KBES architectures. Now we extend these ideas in several ways. In Section 8.1 we discuss the special requirements of the engineering workplace for KBES architectures. In Section 8.2 we discuss some emerging solutions that might have the potential to meet these needs. In particular, we present a methodology and an architecture for developing engineering applications that integrate rule/frame/OOP KBES environments with computer-aided design and drafting (CADD) systems and their databases. We then go on to discuss two alternative KBES architectures that can support **concurrent** or **simultaneous engineering**, that is, environments which facilitate the interaction of multiple experts—both humans and KBESs—to solve complex problems. In Section 8.3 we describe blackboard architectures, a hierarchical approach to modeling concurrent problem solving. In Sections 8.4 and 8.5 we present the ideas behind cooperative distributed problem solving, a more decentralized approach to this problem.

8.1 ARCHITECTURAL REQUIREMENTS OF ENGINEERING KBESs

Engineering work involves collaboration among specialist engineers from many disciplines, each of whom may have invested substantial human and financial resources in developing and learning to use their own set of computer tools. The computer tools used have historically been primarily analysis and drafting tools which were valuable to engineers within a particular discipline and at a given stage of the product life cycle. However, engineers were generally unable to share data with people in other disciplines or across stages in the product life cycle. The tools were, therefore, local "islands of automation."

Further, the various engineering disciplines often develop designs in parallel, coordinating their decisions through a series of design reviews— more or less structured—in which inconsistencies can be detected and corrected. Expensive design changes and retrofits during manufacturing are the results of failure of the coordination process. Since frequent, large design review meetings are expensive and error-prone, great reliance is placed in this process on the knowledge of experienced design team leaders to control the timing and sequence of key design decisions. These design team leaders are also reponsible for resolving conflicts specialists in different disciplines may have over space, weight, power supply, heat balance, and other kinds of interface parameters.

As we pointed out in Chapter 1, many engineering tasks are still best supported by procedural computer tools. Thus, KBES applications will augment, rather than replace, a wide range of currently used computer tools. Moreover, the increasing complexity of engineered products in most sectors means that engineers will likely continue to be trained, certified, and employed within specialty disciplines. To be truly useful—rather than just intriguing—to engineers, KBES tools and techniques must therefore be well integrated into the current and future working environments of engineers within each of the multiple disciplines that contribute to an engineered product. This raises two kinds of challenges for the architectures within which KBES engineering tools will be developed and deployed.

❑   KBES architectures must facilitate interfaces with drafting, analysis, simulation, and other computer tools used by each discipline; and

❑   KBES architectures must recognize and support the inherent interdisciplinary nature and concurrent problem-solving style associated with engineering product life cycles.

As engineers begin to design at CAD workstations rather than on paper, there are new opportunities for automated data sharing and coordination in real time. The use of KBES techniques to automate and integrate the engineering tasks associated with planning, designing, and manufacturing semiconductors, automobiles, aircraft, buildings, process plants, and other engineered systems is an active area of research at many leading universities and research laboratories worldwide [Howard 1989b].

8.2 AN ARCHITECTURE FOR MODEL-BASED REASONING

We wish to describe here some methodological ideas for building KBESs for engineering applications. These ideas are philosophically grounded in our discussions of modeling (see Section 1.2) and of the organization of engineering knowledge (see Sections 1.2 and 7.1). The methodology is abstracted from experience with a growing number of engineering applications. In particular, we can define an approach for modeling available knowledge about an engineering system that is intuitive and efficient to implement and which permits multiple kinds of reasoning about the system. This approach, which is becoming known as **model-based reasoning (MBR)**, employs the representation and reasoning techniques described in Chapters 5 and 6, including rules, frames, and object-oriented programming. We shall also see that MBR encompasses some of the notions of qualitative reasoning about structure and function that were outlined in Chapter 7. MBR represents an emerging methodology for extending the reach of KBES techniques from classification problems, such as diagnosis (for which they are already well established), to problems that involve the formation of solutions from primitive elements, that is, design and planning.

The early KBES applications in medicine, chemistry, engineering, and other domains typically used production rules to model *heuristic* knowledge about systems or objects. In these applications, the premises of production rules referenced possible states of the system or object in terms of patterns of their attributes. These KBESs did heuristic inference by matching patterns corresponding to particular system or object states. In so doing, they associated *plausible hypotheses* about possible malfunctions (or other kinds of conclusions) directly with observed system states. Thus, while the patterns of attribute values corresponding to interesting system states in heuristic rules were often quite complex—involving conjunctions, disjunctions, and negations of groups of patterns—the conclusion drawn by any given rule was more typically *associative* than causal. Any causal connections between a pattern of "symptoms" and a suggested failure mode was unknown, or at most implicit, in the rule. Hence the structure, function, and behavior of the system or domain and its components were represented only implicitly—if at all—in heuristic KBESs [Clancey 1985].

By way of contrast, KBESs developed in the spirit of model-based reasoning are intended to be models in the usual engineering sense (cf. Section 1.2). They explicitly model the behavior of components—either quantitatively or qualitatively—and propagate effects among topologically linked objects representing system components or subsystems in a manner that models *causality* in the system as it is understood by the modeler. In the course of their reasoning, therefore, such KBESs will generate descriptions of intermediate and final states of the modeled system (in terms of patterns of system or component attribute values) that can be checked to validate the descriptive power of the model. Thus, KBESs developed in the MBR style represent structure, function, and behavior explicitly and deduce the states of the modeled system by qualitative or quantitative simulation of component behavior [Kunz 1989b].

Moreover, as engineers begin to develop their designs on line, much of the data needed to support MBR for configuration, diagnosis, simulation, and planning tasks can be extracted from CADD databases rather than being entered at the keyboard in response to prompts, as in the early diagnostic systems, which used the consultation metaphor. The architecture and methodology that we describe in this section use many of the AI-based techniques we have discussed to interact with CADD, database, and algorithmic software currently used by engineers for design and analysis.

8.2.1 Obtaining Component Descriptions from CADD Databases

Selection, refinement, and topological mapping of system components are the principal tasks of design synthesis for most engineering disciplines. In particular, CADD systems have become extremely useful not just for drafting but also for the synthesis tasks of component selection and topological mapping. This transition from computer-aided drafting to computer-aided design and drafting could occur once CAD systems evolved to a point where they could represent physical features and components as their primitives rather than graphic elements such as points, lines, and arcs. As a result of this advance in CADD system capability, which occurred in the 1980s, engineers can productively design products ranging from semiconductors and cameras to space shuttles and power plants by synthesizing engineering designs on workstation screens rather than drawing them on paper.

Further, for all but the most unique products, designers at CADD workstations can now extract components from a company, vendor, or industry database of standard components, stored in an appropriate CADD format, and insert them into a particular synthesis. A series of components that has been selected, resized, or adapted in some other way, as well as appropriately connected to other components in the model, defines a unique **instance** of a product.

For products designed in this way, the component records or "blocks" in the CADD database contain—or point to records in an external database which contains—several kinds of descriptive information that can be used by a KBES to support design, manufacturing, and operation of the product.

❑ **Component geometry** is described in sufficient detail to draw components at the scale used in the CADD system in which the design is being performed. Geometry can also be used to compute attributes such as surface area, volume, mass, and center of mass for components.

❑ **Topological information** about the components of a product is provided only implicitly in purely graphic CADD systems by the user at the time that components are situated in a model. Historically, this (implicit) topological information had to be interpreted manually from geometric representations (on screens or on paper) and used as needed by analysts or manufacturing engineers who required it later in the process. For complex three-dimensional products, scale models or full-scale mock-ups were often used to help engineers evaluate the manufacturing or operating concerns associated with geometry and topology. Spatial reasoning techniques can interpret a purely geometric model to infer topology for simple cases like office building structural frames (see Section 7.3), but they tend to bog down when required to interpret more irregular topologies. Consequently, high-level designer interfaces have recently been developed for a number of CADD systems to facilitate the capture of explicit topological data about product components as they are inserted into a design. These interfaces typically require a minimum of additional input by the designer. The explicit topological information thus stored in the CADD database can then be used to support several kinds of reasoning using standard KBES techniques [Ito 1989].

❑ **Physical properties** of components' materials are defined for use by structural, heat flow, chemical, or other analysis programs.

❑ **Technical specifications** are given for manufacturing, assembly, testing, or operation of the component in the engineered system.

❑ **Administrative information** needed in the manufacturing process is included (e.g., vendor name, contract number, or payment provisions).

Several AI programming tools now run concurrently on the same workstations that are used for CADD or can easily access CADD data over networks. Thus, they can readily extract these types of product information from a CADD database (or an attached relational database) and can automatically create a frame representation of the product that incorporates these data.

Typically, each component is represented in a single frame at the level of detail at which the engineer wishes to reason about the engineered system. A single component frame can thus be used to represent a subassembly consisting of hundreds of separate parts or an individual keyway, hole, or washer in a product. The frames in such a product model can represent geometric, physical, and administrative attributes of a product's components together with their topological structure. All of this information about the structure of a product and the local values of its component attributes is then available in a representation easily accessible to KBESs for several kinds of engineering tasks.

Up to this point, we have not really enriched the data available in the CADD system; we have just reorganized it into frames. Sections 8.2.2 and 8.2.3 show how we can exploit the power of production rules and inheritance to enrich the data, transforming a database of component data into a knowledge base of an engineered product.

8.2.2 How Components Can Inherit Behavior

The specific components which make up an engineering system can be viewed as instances of more general classes of components. Some component attributes and their values—especially those describing component behavior—can be defined at the most generic class level to which components belong (e.g., in a class called AUTOMOBILE_ COMPONENTS). Additional attributes and their values representing descriptive properties or behavior of more specific subclasses of components (e.g., FUEL_SUPPLY_SYSTEM_COMPONENTS or IGNITION_SYSTEM_COMPONENTS) can then be added at each level of specificity and inherited down the abstraction hierarchy to particular instances of each type of component.

The key to inheriting component behavior is that objects retrieved from the CADD system must be correctly associated with the component abstraction hierarchy. That is, they must automatically be made instances of the correct subclasses. The importance of strict naming conventions for components becomes obvious at this point. If all beams are labeled BEAM_XX in the

CADD system database, then they can be attached automatically as instances of the subclass BEAMS in the abstraction hierarchy, whence they can inherit beam bending formulas, deflection limits, and so on. (Recall that Lisp handles strings effortlessly, so that simple methods or rules to identify and attach instances to an abstraction hierarchy are easy to write in Lisp.)

Once a component has been correctly placed in its primary class (e.g., BEAM_23 has been made an instance of BEAMS), it is easy to generate other links that can provide more specific behavior using additional rules or procedures which reason about attributes of the component (e.g., its material type). The following rule shows how easy this is to do.

```
((IF      (?BEAM IS IN CLASS BEAMS)

 AND      (THE MATERIAL_TYPE OF ?BEAM IS CONCRETE))

 (THEN    (?BEAM IS IN CLASS CONCRETE_COMPONENTS)))
```

This rule would search over all instances of BEAMS and would add the subclass parent CONCRETE_COMPONENTS to any instances of the class BEAMS whose material type is concrete, causing them to inherit additional behavior from the subclass CONCRETE_COMPONENTS. Thus, by firing a set of rules of this type on the frames generated from a CADD model of a product, we are able to automatically add knowledge about component behavior to a knowledge base containing information about component geometry, topology, and material type.

8.2.3   How Components Can Deduce Their Function

A KBES can deduce a substantial amount of knowledge about the roles that individual components (such as beams, valves, shafts, or switches) play in the functioning of a product by reasoning about the part-of hierarchy for the product and the topological links among its components. Thus, by noting that a beam is PART_OF a liquid nitrogen supply subsystem and is CONNECTED_TO the liquid nitrogen pump platform, we might conclude that its role or function in the product is to provide structural support for the pump. This allows the beam to reference the weight of the pump in computing its size.

Similarly, an electrical connector that was PART_OF the liquid nitrogen supply system and was UPSTREAM_OF the pump (in terms of electrical circuit topology) could reference the pump's starting horsepower to determine its needed current carrying capacity, and so on.

Again, strict naming conventions are extremely important to ensure that components are properly attached to their part-of and abstraction hierarchies so that component function can be correctly deduced. Knowledge of component function provides significant leverage in performing tasks like design, simulation, or diagnosis.

The RATAS building product model developed in Finland was one of the first systems to exploit this capability in the building domain [Bjork 1987]. We will illustrate the use of linked abstraction hierarchies and part-of hierarchies to infer component behavior and function in describing the Intelligent Boiler Design System in Chapter 10 [Riitahuhta 1988] and the OARPLAN system in Chapter 11 [Darwiche 1989].

8.2.4 Generating System Behavior in MBR

MBR can be used to predict the behavior of the modeled system by simulation. Inherited methods give components the correct behavior in the context of local descriptive data. The topological information stored with each component allows such a model to deal with interactions among its components (e.g., current flow between connected components of an electronic circuit, fluid flow through a piping system, load paths through a structure, or the propagation of vibration through an airframe).

The simulation of system behavior can be quantitative, as in conventional engineering analysis programs, which use mathematical formulas or numerical algorithms to model system behavior. And while such simulation packages have traditionally been written in conventional procedural programming styles, we may also anticipate that OOP styles will be used in the future. For example, the case has already been made that an OOP approach may offer substantial advantages for finite element modeling [Baugh 1989].

Alternatively, product simulations in model-based reasoning can be purely qualitative, thereby exploiting the unique strength of AI representation and reasoning techniques. Thus, for tasks such as product configuration and diagnosis, the qualitative modeling techniques described in Chapter 7 are often perfectly adequate for simulation while at the same time offering the advantage of being able to explain their conclusions. However, qualitative simulation will not always produce definitive results; often, two or more opposing qualitative effects must be quantified in order to determine which dominates. Thus, we can develop KBESs which move through a natural progression from purely qualitative simulation through simple quantitative simulation (e.g., a back-of-the-envelope approximation) to detailed numerical modeling. This corresponds closely to the way experienced engineers work. We use detailed numerical analysis in very focused ways to resolve specific design questions whose answers may not be clear from qualitative or simple quantitative analysis.

We summarize the four basic points of the model-based reasoning approach to engineering KBESs as follows (see also Figure 8-1).

1. Components needed for a product are retrieved from a library of standard components and attached to their primary parents in a component abstraction hierarchy based upon standard naming conventions. Rules or procedures that reference additional attributes of named components then generate multiple abstraction links for components. This provides components with knowledge about arbitrarily complex behaviors by inheritance from multiple subclass parents.

2. Product structure is represented by a part-of hierarchy for its components and by topological links—either explicitly provided by the product designer as components are added to a design in the synthesis stage, or automatically deduced by spatial reasoning techniques.

3. Component function is deduced by reasoning about links in a generic part-of hierarchy and by component topological relationships.

4. Product behavior is deduced by simulation—qualitative, quantitative, or both—of the product, using inherited component behaviors and local attribute values to generate component behavior. Again, topological links capture interactions among components and subsystems.

One of the principal advantages of this approach to engineering KBESs is the extensive use of generic component libraries represented as frames, whose attributes and behavior can be inherited by instances of the components in engineered products or systems. This provides two important results. First, it drastically reduces the number of new rules that need to be employed in a given MBR engineering application. As a company develops new products which incorporate generic components, much of the system behavior is already captured in the inherited behavior of the components. The volume of new rules to be encoded in order to define configuration or diagnosis knowledge for new products will thus increase linearly—or more slowly, if new products share configuration or

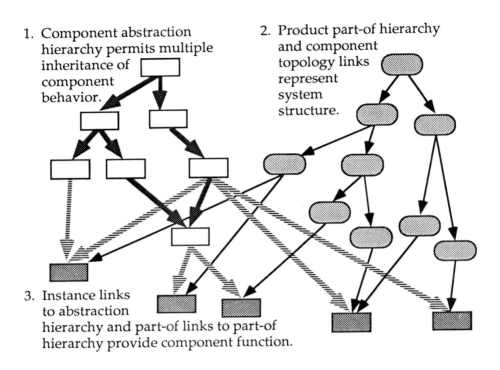

1. Component abstraction hierarchy permits multiple inheritance of component behavior.

2. Product part-of hierarchy and component topology links represent system structure.

3. Instance links to abstraction hierarchy and part-of links to part-of hierarchy provide component function.

4. Qualitative or quantitative simulation uses component behavior and topological links to generate emergent system behavior.

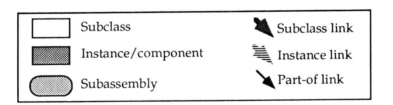

Figure 8-1 The elements of model-based reasoning. Component data are inserted into a design model from CADD or database component libraries. The inference processes shown in this figure flesh out a KBES product model using rules, frames, and OOP, and permit the model to be used for a variety of engineering applications.

diagnostic knowledge with past products—rather than exponentially, as would be the case with a rule-based system.

Second, as we explained in Chapter 6, frame-based inheritance is a much easier form of deduction to program and maintain than rule-based inference. Thus, MBR systems implemented in this way are far easier for an organization to develop and maintain than corporate knowledge bases consisting only of production rules.

8.2.5   Engineering Applications of MBR

The MBR approach to KBES development is model-based in that it explicitly represents product and component structure and function. For this reason, a model-based KBES is inherently more flexible than one based on heuristics alone, and it can typically support several kinds of reasoning about an engineered product with the addition of just a few rules or methods. We briefly review some important classes of applications for MBR here, and we will see further examples in the applications discussions in Chapters 9 through 11, which will illustrate the concepts in greater detail.

❑   **Synthesis.** A model-based KBES can be used to automate the synthesis process for many kinds of semicustom products. The KBES—instead of the user—synthesizes a design by selecting, modifying, and then connecting components into a product model. In this style of synthesis, we use MBR to transform a formation task into a series of well-structured selection tasks, making extensive use of inheritance and OOP techniques. In particular, we use rules or demons to populate the leaf nodes of a generic part-of product hierarchy with the appropriate number of properly configured component instances.

❑   **Diagnosis.** Model-based systems such as we have described can also provide excellent support for automated diagnosis of faults in engineered systems. A set of system failure modes can be established as goals to be investigated by firing a set of production rules or demons which propagate failure conditions and effects forward and backward along topological links. Since we model all components of a system (at whatever level of analysis we wish to conduct), along with their behavior and their topology, intermediate values of other component properties can be deduced, then checked manually or by automated sensors linked to the KBES to confirm or disconfirm a line of reasoning. In at least one case, an MBR approach to qualitative simulation was successfully used to develop diagnostic "experience" for a system that had never before been built—the CO_2 recycling system for a space station [Malin 1985].

Thus, engineering KBESs that carry out model-based reasoning can be implemented using KBES and CADD systems together to transform a database of information about a product's components into a knowledge base of component properties and behavior, and then to perform various kinds of reasoning with this rich knowledge base.

This type of approach has been applied in the LSC Advisor for architectural code checking [Dym 1988] and in the Guardian system for monitoring and control of intensive care patients [Hayes-RothB 1989], both of which are discussed in Chapter 9. Other MBR applications include a description of a high-level MBR language for automating boiler design [Riitahuhta 1988] and the OARPLAN system that encodes product topological data using a high-level CADD interface [Darwiche 1989] and imports it into a KBES via a generic, object-oriented product model to automate construction planning for buildings [Ito 1989]. These systems are discussed in Chapters 10 and 11.

We now turn to the second challenge that engineering problems pose for KBES architectures: how to model concurrent design and management decision making by teams of specialists acting in parallel. We discuss the "blackboard" approach for addressing this challenge first.

8.3 BLACKBOARD ARCHITECTURES

Blackboard architectures for KBESs evolved out of the HEARSAY project on speech recognition at Carnegie Mellon University [Lesser 1975; Erman 1980] and the HASP project on sonar data interpretation at Stanford University [Nii 1982]. Reasoning at multiple levels of abstraction, where each level of reasoning helps to resolve uncertainties at other levels, was needed for both speech understanding (phonemes, words, sentences) and sonar ship identification (vibrations, sources, platforms). The blackboard architecture is an attempt to organize such multilevel or multidisciplinary kinds of knowledge into a single KBES. Recently, attempts have been made to use blackboard architectures developed for integrating knowledge at multiple levels of abstraction in domains such as concurrent engineering, which involves multiple sources of expertise at the same level of abstraction.

The blackboard metaphor for integrated computer-based reasoning with multiple sources of expertise was abstracted from HEARSAY and adapted in HASP and other subsequent applications, and it is now incorporated into a number of general-purpose blackboard programming environments akin to the ones discussed in Chapters 4 and 6. We set the stage for this section with a discussion of how the decision making of specialist designers is coordinated in human organizations. Then we show that KBES blackboard architectures incorporate some of the same kinds of coordination devices to manage concurrent reasoning by their separate knowledge sources. We illustrate the details of blackboard architectures by describing how representation, reasoning, and control are implemented in the BB1 blackboard system [Hayes-RothB 1985]. We conclude with an evaluation of the suitability of blackboard systems for modeling concurrent engineering tasks.

8.3.1   A Human Organizational Analogy

Most KBES applications developed to date represent knowledge in a well-specified part of a single narrow domain (e.g., diagnosis of bacterial meningitis, evaluation of molybdenum ore deposits). This distinguishes the strong or knowledge-intensive methods that KBESs use for problem solving from weak or domain-independent methods such as mathematical optimization techniques (see Sections 2.4 and 2.5). The latter rely on extensive search and computation in solving problems, but they are potentially applicable across a broader range of problem domains. It has been observed that outside of a KBES's scope of intended application, its capability degrades rapidly and ungracefully. In the words of E. A. Feigenbaum, one of the pioneers of KBES technology, the KBES falls off the edge of its "knowledge mesa" [Lenat 1987]. Since KBES applications have usually represented and reasoned with knowledge that is highly specialized, it might seem like an impossible task to model the many kinds of expertise used by diverse engineering specialists within a single KBES.

This problem is, of course, not unique to computers. Humans also tend to pursue their training and experience within focused areas of knowledge to achieve high levels of problem-solving capability. And they, too, can fall off their own knowledge mesas when they attempt to be "experts" in unfamiliar domains. Engineering organizations—like most other industrial, military, or even philanthropic organizations—therefore assemble teams of specialists who collectively have the needed expertise to plan, design, manufacture, and operate an engineered product.

The means that are used to coordinate such engineering project teams include the usual repertoire of coordination devices used by any organization: rules and standards, direct supervision, hierarchical planning, and face-to-face meetings [Logcher 1979; Thompson 1967]. These coordination techniques are used successively, in the order that they are listed, as the interdependence among specialists' tasks and their degree of novelty or uncertainty increase. Much of the work of engineers is high in both interdependence and uncertainty. Thus, engineering organizations tend to rely heavily on face-to-face meetings among specialists to share information and coordinate decisions.

The blackboard architecture described in this section is a KBES architecture which incorporates some of the same four means for coordination of its disparate knowledge sources as do human engineering organizations. We will see that a blackboard architecture

❑   Accommodates the need for specialization of expertise by organizing chunks of related but distinct knowledge into separate modules termed **knowledge sources**—analogous to rule sets in the integrated rule/frame/OOP environments discussed in Chapter 6;

❑   Incorporates the information sharing—but not the negotiation—that occurs in face-to-face meetings by allowing knowledge sources to communicate directly with one another by writing to and reading from a common data structure called a blackboard; and

❑   Approximates hierarchical planning and direct supervision by having one or more control modules that form a solution strategy against which it can evaluate and implement recommendations from each knowledge source as problem solving proceeds.

Several general-purpose blackboard architectures with these three basic features—but varying in the details of their implementation—have been abstracted from applications that used the blackboard style of reasoning. The evolution of these blackboard architectures for problem solving through a series of applications is thoroughly reviewed by Nii [1986, 1989]. (An alternative, more decentralized architecture for multiagent problem solving, cooperative distributed problem solving (CDPS), is described in Section 8.4. It relies almost entirely on the "face-to-face meeting" mode of coordination.) To ground our discussion of blackboard architectures, we will next discuss how representation, reasoning, and control are implemented in one blackboard system.

The **BB1** blackboard architecture is a general-purpose blackboard architecture originally developed to support opportunistic planning [Hayes-RothB 1985]. BB1 grew out of the Opportunistic Planning Model (OPM) system developed at Rand Corporation [Hayes-RothB 1979]. It was strongly influenced by developments in the HEARSAY projects [Lesser 1975; Erman 1980] in terms of agendas for knowledge sources (see Section 8.3.2), the concept of an abstract blackboard architecture, and the idea of control as a problem-solving process to be carried out in a blackboard framework.

BB1 was subsequently employed for several other classes of problems, including intensive care patient monitoring and control (see the outline of the Guardian system in Chapter 9 [Hayes-RothB 1989]); construction site layout (see our discussion of SightPlan in Chapter 10 [Tommelein 1989a]); case-based reasoning about structural design [Wang 1989]; and project planning (we describe the OARPLAN system in Chapter 11 [Darwiche 1989]). Using BB1 as our exemplar of blackboard architectures thus has the advantage of laying the groundwork for the subsequent discussions of these applications. BB1 is implemented in Common Lisp and has been widely distributed and used in many research efforts besides those mentioned here. Our discussion of BB1 is adapted from [Tommlein 1989a].

8.3.2 The Blackboard Metaphor in BB1

The BB1 architecture emulates a "structured meeting." Imagine a meeting situation in which a number of participants—here called knowledge sources (KSs)—are faced with a problem that is described on the blackboard (BB). None of the KSs can solve the entire problem on its own, but each of them may be able to contribute problem-solving steps that, when combined in a reasonable sequence, lead to a solution. By looking at the BB, KSs know when it is appropriate for them to focus their attention, and they know when it is proper to propose to take action. The KSs can only communicate with each other indirectly, by making changes on the blackboard. In each step toward the solution, one—and only one—KS gets to execute its proposed action—that is, is allowed to make changes to the BB. In reaction to such changes on the BB, other KSs may now focus their attention or propose to take action. It is the moderator in the meeting—here called the **scheduler**—which, at each cycle, evaluates each of the contributions that KSs propose and which selects one of these proposed actions for execution. Thus, as embodied in the scheduler, the problem-solving style of BB1 is *hierarchical*, in its distribution of KSs at different levels of abstraction and in its assignment of authority for control to the scheduler; *incremental*, as it only does one piece of the puzzle at a time; and *opportunistic*, in adjusting its strategy for picking the most appropriate KS to call on at any stage in the problem-solving process.

8.3.3   Representation in a Blackboard System

All concepts (objects, constraints, events, etc.) in a BB1 knowledge base are represented by frames that can have any kind of user-defined attributes or links to other objects and that can inherit attributes over specific links (not just abstraction links).   Concepts in a BB1 knowledge base thus form a conceptual graph defined by all of the relationships existing between them, including—but not limited to—the abstraction relationships [Sowa 1984].

For clarity and flexibility, the semantic net or **conceptual graph** of concepts in a BB1 knowledge base is layered.   Concepts specific to a particular application domain are grouped in what is termed a blackboard (BB), itself part of a knowledge base (KB).   System-level concepts applicable to many domains are layered into higher-level blackboards that form part of the overall conceptual graph for a knowledge base.   A BB1 knowledge base thus contains several blackboards, including system- and application-level BBs, a problem BB containing the description of the current problem, and a solution BB on which the evolving solution to the problem is stored.

8.3.4   Reasoning in a Blackboard System

Knowledge sources in BB1 are responsible for reasoning.   KSs are similar in structure to **situation-action rules** and reside on the knowledge sources' blackboard.   KSs contain the knowledge that BB1 will apply to make its inferences from the current state of the problem and solution BBs.   These KSs are not designed to "chain" together as in traditional rule-based systems; rather, they are independent entities whose antecedent can become true on the basis of facts stated on any of the BBs and whose consequent— upon execution—posts new facts onto the frames in any of the BBs.   Thus, KSs need not be "aware" of each other's presence.   KSs, as all other concepts in BB1's conceptual graph, are represented by means of frames.

The antecedent of a KS in BB1 distinguishes among three different conditions: trigger conditions, preconditions, and obviation conditions. **Trigger conditions** state when the KS becomes applicable.   **Preconditions** state when the KS is executable.   When these are satisfied, a knowledge source will propose its consequent or conclusion as a **knowledge source activation record (KSAR)** to the BB1 scheduler.   Since the conditions of KSs are stated in terms of concept types, the KS makes use of context variables (as discussed in Section 5.3.2) to specify which of the examples in the particular domain of application apply.   When more than one example of the concept type is applicable, multiple KSARs are generated, one for each example. Finally, **obviation conditions** state when the KSAR is no longer applicable.

Two types of knowledge sources are distinguished in BB1: domain knowledge sources and control knowledge sources. **Domain knowledge sources** are application-dependent and are specific to the problem-solving method that is used. **Control knowledge sources** contain so-called meta-knowledge, which allows the BB1 scheduler to assign priorities on KSARs. For example, control KSs express strategic information on the desirability of domain actions, as well as on the desirability of control actions. The control knowledge sources allow a BB1 application to alter its strategy *dynamically* and select its actions *opportunistically*.

8.3.5   Control in a Blackboard Architecture

The BB1 scheduler goes through the execution cycle displayed in Table 8-1. A cycle starts with the execution of one action. The action causes events. Each of the events of the current cycle is used to try to trigger any of the KSs that implement the system. For each KS that is triggered, the scheduler instantiates multiple KSARs, binding context variables to the appropriate objects in the context of the run. All of the KSARs—whether just generated or existing from previous cycles—have their preconditions and obviation conditions checked. If the preconditions are found to be true and the obviation conditions are found to be false, the KSAR is then put on the list of executable KSARs on the agenda. The scheduler then rates each of these executable KSARs and proposes the one with highest rating for execution (we describe the rating criteria below). To the best of the system's knowledge—which is the strategy knowledge at that cycle—the highest-rated KSAR is the best action to take. Thus, execution of the preferred action ends this cycle, and the next cycle can start.

The consequent of a KS tells BB1 what changes to make to BBs when the KS in question is executed. Although multiple KSARs may compete for execution at any time, the BB1 scheduler embodies an incremental problem solver, so it picks only one at a time to execute. Control KSs make changes to the control data BB, on which they can post or modify one of three things: a strategy, a focus, or a heuristic. **Strategies** provide high-level statements of what needs to be done to solve the problem. **Focuses** (or foci) do the same, but they describe the preferred steps in more detail. Foci are used by the scheduler to determine *which* of the executable KSARs is most desirable at that cycle. **Heuristics**, which implement foci, prescribe which function should be used by the scheduler to compute this desirability.

Table 8-1 Structure of an execution cycle in BB1 ([Levitt 1989])

Action	Explanation
Execute	Execute the action selected in the preceding cycle.
Trigger	Use the generated events to trigger KSs in the system; generate KSARs.
Check	Check pre- and obviation conditions of each KSAR.
Rate, select, and confirm	Rate all executable KSARs; select the one with the highest rating for execution and ask the user to confirm this selection.

We have noted that there can be multiple executable KSARs at any cycle. This is a desirable situation because a central design feature of the blackboard architecture is that the scheduler can decide which of the competing proposed actions to execute. The scheduler makes this decision by assessing how well the action of each of the executable KSARs matches the actions prescribed by the current control strategy. This match is expressed by a numerical rating which by convention ranges from 0 (no match) to 100 (perfect match). On the basis of this rating, the scheduler ranks the KSARs and proposes the one with the highest rating for execution; the absolute value of the rating is therefore not important. In case of a tie, when the rating values do not allow the scheduler to discriminate between KSARs, the default choice is **last in, first out (LIFO)**: the KSAR that became executable most recently is proposed for execution.

When a noun and/or a verb in the KSAR's action sentence are of the same type as those of the focus sentence, a rating value of 100 is assigned; otherwise, a value of 0 is assigned. If modifiers precede a noun or verb in the focus, then the modifying function (the value of an attribute of a modifier) is applied to the matching noun or verb in the KSAR's action, and a value between 0 and 100 is returned. (See the SightPlan example in Chapter 10 for an illustration of how BB1 rates competing KSARs.)

8.3.6 Suitability of Blackboard Architectures for Engineering KBESs

The applications developed so far in BB1 or other blackboard architectures such as GBB [Corkill 1986a, 1986b] and DICE [Sriram 1989] are only prototypes, and it is thus too early to evaluate the quality of solutions produced by blackboard systems for concurrent engineering. However, on the basis of our description of concurrent engineering in Section 8.1, we can evaluate the extent to which a blackboard approach captures that process.

We stated that concurrent engineering, as practised by humans for routine or standard kinds of engineering tasks, usually involves truly parallel reasoning by separate specialists (the knowledge sources in the blackboard analogy) with only periodic coordination of decision making through design reviews and somewhat less emphasis on hierarchical coordination of decision making at each step of problem solving. The BB1 blackboard architecture thus models only loosely the way that human organizations perform routine concurrent engineering. It appears to correspond better to the ways humans perform novel tasks with a high degree of interdependency, for which parallel reasoning is likely to produce many inconsistencies.

A blackboard architecture is inherently a sequential and opportunistic model of problem solving. A prerequisite for this type of architecture is the ability to specify the knowledge used for control. One or more problem-solving strategies involving task decomposition and the sequenced solution of partial problems are needed to guide problem solving in a blackboard system. Thus, it is not clear that a BB1 type of architecture is entirely appropriate for modeling a full range of concurrent engineering activities.

If good interfaces can be developed for human users of blackboard KBESs, then the human can function as another knowledge source in the system, perhaps with a higher priority than the system's internal knowledge sources. The SightView interface for the SightPlan system described in Chapter 10 [Levitt 1989b] suggests intriguing opportunities for KBESs that exploit the knowledge-based interactive graphics described in Chapter 6. Such an interface also combines and manages the input of multiple experts—of both the flesh-and-blood and silicon varieties—while exploiting the strengths of both humans and computers in problem solving [Levitt 1987b, 1989b; Mittal 1986a].

Note that departing from human problem-solving approaches may not be a disadvantage for a KBES—computers have very different strengths and weaknesses in problem solving than humans, so that a system for machine reasoning in this domain should probably not be restricted to just emulating the problem-solving styles of humans. This question is explored in some depth by Tommelein [1989b] and in our discussion of PRIDE in Chapter 10 [Mittal 1986a]. In terms of an analogy with the concurrent engineering process used by teams of designers, the cooperative distributed problem-solving KBES approach described next may be a better fit.

8.4   COOPERATIVE DISTRIBUTED PROBLEM SOLVING (CDPS)

We now turn to **cooperative distributed problem solving (CDPS)**, the idea of distributing a computation or a task over an assembly or network of processors or agents that, together, solve a complex problem or achieve some overarching goal. In brief, what we will be talking about here is the organization of many KBESs in a network designed to solve some large problem. Each KBES within the network works on a piece of the larger problem, hopefully in cooperation with all the other KBESs in the network. Thus, in another view that will be further elaborated, we are trying to describe the decomposition of the problem-solving process. In that decomposition we must confront the issues of how we represent the decomposition of a search and of how we maintain control of the solution process so as to ensure a coherent outcome. CDPS is a rapidly developing set of ideas that, we suggest, is a suitable architecture for concurrent engineering.

We make two comparisons here. The first is that CDPS is not distributed processing, which is often viewed as a hardware issue [Stankovic 1984]. In distributed hardware processing, each of the processors in a network is strongly coupled to a central processor with which it communicates directly. Here it is useful to begin to look at the issues from a software perspective: the individual processors typically have complete autonomy and do their work in a predetermined and prescribed manner, in which they may share (or compete for) data and communication resources. However, the processors do not communicate about goals or their tasks which are, again, preset by the system designer. (In fact, from a global perspective we might say that these nodes really have no autonomy rather than complete autonomy, since from a top-level view their activities are entirely predetermined.)

The assignment of task autonomy just described reflects the fact that the problems solved in distributed processing are decomposable into separate tasks that require little interaction and can therefore be done in parallel. Thus, the individual nodes need have little knowledge of the tasks performed by or within the network, other than their own. Further, these individual task agents will not function outside the context provided by the designer of the network. This is not a model that is particularly useful for the complex engineering organizations that we have outlined in Sections 8.1 and 8.2. In such organizations, the tasks are generally not decomposable into highly compartmentalized, independent subtasks that can be done in parallel. As a result, the distributed processing model is not useful for describing concurrent engineering.

The second comparison is with the blackboard architectures that we discussed. In some ways CDPS resembles a blackboard system, but we will be going beyond the ideas of knowledge sources operating within a particular hierarchy structure and controlled by a centralized scheduler. In fact, a very simple model of CDPS would replace each KS in a blackboard with a powerful KBES free to operate at all levels in the hierarchy. Moreover, it would give each KBES in the network the autonomy to do its problem solving, based on its own knowledge and resources, without waiting to be ordered into action by a scheduler. These elementary ideas seem much more consistent with how a complex engineering task would be done in a very complex organizational setting.

In this survey, therefore, we focus on CDPS in which, broadly speaking, the work is done through a network of loosely coupled, semiautonomous problem-solving processing elements or nodes. In a CDPS network, each node is capable of sophisticated problem solving and cooperative interaction with other nodes to solve a single problem. Each node may itself be a complex problem-solving system that can modify its behavior as circumstances change and can plan its own communication and cooperation strategies with other nodes. Our discussion begins with an overview of applications of and motivations for CDPS. We then outline some of the major research issues, highlight the principal approaches currently being taken to CDPS architectures, and mention some engineering applications. In organizing our brief survey we have drawn heavily on the work of Durfee [1986, 1989]; Lesser [1985, 1987]; and Rosenschein [1985].

8.4.1   Motivations and Applications

CDPS is an important area for several reasons. First, hardware technology has advanced to the point where the construction of large distributed problem-solving networks is both possible and economically feasible. Although the first networks may consist of only a small number of nodes, CDPS networks will eventually contain hundreds or thousands of nodes. And while exciting hardware possibilities draw nearer, the problem-solving technology required for their effective utilization lags behind.

Second, there are applications that are inherently distributed, many spatially, some temporally, and some functionally. A distributed architecture that matches the application distribution offers many advantages over a centralized approach. Concurrent engineering is clearly an application that could be enhanced through the use of CDPS techniques.

Third, understanding the *cooperative* aspects of CDPS is an important goal in its own right. Whether we are talking about social, managerial, biological, or mechanical systems, we know more about competition within them than we do about cooperation. Thus, in the same way that the development of AI systems has helped our understanding of problem solving and intelligence in linguistics, psychology, and philosophy, we may find that the development of CDPS networks will serve to validate theories in sociology, management, organizational theory, and biology. That is, research that views CDPS as *cooperative* problem solving could have a salutary impact on our understanding of cooperative behavior between independent agents. The top-level goals of such a research approach have been nicely summarized: (1) To use parallelism to speed up task completion; (2) to expand what is achievable by resource allocation and sharing; (3) to increase reliability by (selective) redundancy; and (4) to reduce the interference between tasks by avoiding harmful interactions [Durfee 1986]. These generic goals can then be elaborated as sets of goals for the individual agents—or KBESs—in a CDPS network.

There are four general application areas that seem well suited for CDPS approaches.

Distributed interpretation. Distributed interpretation applications require the integration and analysis of distributed data to generate a (potentially distributed) model of the data. Application domains include network fault diagnosis and distributed sensor networks. The distributions here are more often than not spatial.

Distributed planning and control. Distributed planning and control applications involve developing and coordinating the actions of a number of distributed effector nodes to perform some desired task. Application domains include distributed air traffic control, control of groups of cooperating robots, remotely piloted vehicles, distributed process control in manufacturing, and resource allocation in transportation and delivery systems. Distributed planning and control applications often require distributed interpretation for determining and monitoring node actions.

Coordination networks. Coordination network applications involve the coordination of a number of individuals in the performance of some task. Application domains include intelligent command and control systems, multiuser project coordination, and cooperative environments where work is shared among workstations. Concurrent engineering clearly can be viewed through the prism of network coordination, as it is that very coordination of the engineering process that we described in Section 8.3.

Cooperative interaction among KBESs. Cooperative interaction mechanisms would allow multiple KBESs to work together toward solving a common problem; this would be would be one means of applying expert system technology to larger problem domains. One example is the integration of a number of specialized medical diagnosis systems. Another is the negotiation between the expert systems of two corporations about details of price and delivery time on a major purchase. Again, this kind of application is central to engineering practice in general, to the integration of KBES and conventional tools that we described in Section 8.2, and to concurrent engineering.

The earliest work in CDPS was in three application domains: distributed sensor networks, distributed air traffic control, and distributed robot systems. (There have been periodic workshops on CDPS and on the more general idea of distributed artificial intelligence. A summary of the most recent such workshop and a listing of previous workshop reports appear in [Sridharan 1987].) In each of these applications we need to perform the (distributed) tasks of interpretation and of planning and control. By planning we mean not only determining what actions to take, such as changing the course of an airplane, but also deciding how to use the network resources to effectively carry out the various tasks. These application domains are also characterized by a natural *spatial distribution* of sensors and effectors and by the fact that both the local interpretation of sensory data and the planning of effector actions are *interdependent* in time and space. For example, in a distributed sensor network that tracks vehicle movements, our detection of a vehicle in one area would imply that we will shortly sense a vehicle of similar type and velocity in an adjacent area. Similarly, a plan for guiding one airplane must be coordinated with the plans for other nearby airplanes in order to avoid collision. Interdependence also arises from redundancy in sensory data. Often different nodes sense the same event because of overlaps in sensor *range* or because different *types* of sensors pick up the same event in different ways. The interdependencies among subproblems and the exploitation of redundant and corroborative views require that nodes cooperate in order to interpret and plan effectively. Such cooperation leads us to view network problem solving in terms of solving a single problem rather than as seeking solutions to a collection of independent subproblems.

8.4.2 Characteristics of CDPS Systems

We now describe some of the characteristics of CDPS systems [Lesser 1985]. In so doing, we will relate these characteristics to some of the now familiar dimensions of KBESs. As we do this characterization, it is well to remember that what we are in effect doing is discussing aspects of decomposing large problems into smaller ones—subproblems—whose individual solutions may or may not interact. If there is no interaction, we are at the extreme of the distributed (hardware) processing described earlier.

We begin our characterization of CDPS by looking at search, and we do so in part because it is also a good vehicle for examining some aspects of parallelism in CDPS. In goal-directed search, for example, the search proceeds through a decomposition of the primary goal into a tree of sub-goals, with operators being defined either to perform the decompositions or to directly solve the subgoals. Control is exerted by defining the choices about which goals or subgoals we should expand as the search progresses. If the decomposition at any level is such as to allow a goal to be described as an AND node, then each subgoal can be viewed as independent of the other leafs of this node and it can thus be solved in parallel. Similarly, when multiple search paths emanate from an OR node, each path may then be pursued concurrently.

In this description of parallelism in search, it is possible to decompose a search into subgoals or paths that *seem* to be independent. It is implicit that there needs to be little or no sharing of knowledge between parallel sub-goals, and that such sharing as does occur can be entirely **asynchronous**. That is, there is no need for any temporal synchronization or coordination among the individual search operators as the decomposition occurs. Thus, in this context, both the goal operators and their control can be implemented as parallel algorithms.

The second dimension that enters into our characterization of CDPS is **granularity**, that is, the fineness or level of detail at which the agents in a CDPS network operate. The notion of granularity is akin to scaling; it is the question of what level of detail is appropriate for a particular functional description of an object or a search. (Recall the apocryphal tale of the blind men and the elephant!) In the present discussion the granularity issue becomes a question of deciding at what level to decompose the structure of a network of processors and the task it is meant to solve. And, of course, the decomposition question is at the same time one of deciding on the appropriate level of description of an organization or a network of agents. For example, a group of autonomous (or nearly so) cooperating experts would be a model of large grain size. At the other extreme, the connectionist model of parallel computing is of very fine grain size [Hillis 1985]. In between are systems where the agents have varying degrees of autonomy and of knowledge of the relationship of their own tasks to other agents' tasks and the overall task; these are of medium grain size.

The notion of granularity of a network can be usefully elaborated in several other dimensions. For example, the notion of granularity is strongly linked to the strength of the coupling between processors or nodes in a network, the complexity of control required for the individual nodes, the degree of dynamic interaction between nodes that is allowed, and the relative number of processors in the network. Other dimensions that might be considered include the nature of the interactions between nodes and the resources allocated (or potentially available) to the individual processors. Shared access to physical or informational resources is the main reason for interaction among tasks. In CDPS networks we design the problem-solving procedures to be explicitly aware of the distribution of the network components and to make informed interaction decisions based on that information. In terms of information and communication the processors are free to communicate with each other.

It is worth pointing out that the research and paradigms of distributed processing do not, typically, address directly the issues of cooperative interactions of tasks to solve a single problem. Therefore, we need to be somewhat careful in making analogies between CDPS and concurrent engineering.

8.5   ARCHITECTURAL CONSIDERATIONS IN CDPS

In this section we will focus on just a few aspects of CDPS systems, in particular those that contrast with features that seem to be implicitly accepted as part of the current standalone, "first-generation" KBES technology. We will at the same time try to do this within the context of engineering concerns. Let us consider, for example, the integration of different kinds of expertise in the process of conceiving, designing, analyzing, and producing a product. As a thought exercise, we will consider how we might use both current KBES techniques and CDPS ideas to enhance this endeavor.

The application of current KBES technology to design and manufacturing is, at this level, straightforward enough. That is, the current approach would be to build individual KBESs that represent current knowledge on design, manufacturing, assembly, and so on, each of which would be used by specialists in the various areas to help them do their tasks—as well as to train neophytes or propagate techniques and standards. The major challenges in the development of such individual KBESs now are identifying experts and eliciting their expertise, identifying appropriate hardware platforms and software environments, and integrating the KBESs with existing hardware and software (see Chapter 12 for more detail). We noted in Section 8.2 an emerging prospect for integration of the entire conceive/design/analyze/produce cycle in the paradigms for the integration of CADD, database, and KBES environments. The questions we address in this section pertain to the characteristics that we would like a CDPS system to have in order to support concurrent engineering applications.

Design of individual agents. If we were to imagine a CDPS network whose nodes are independent KBESs or agents, the logical questions to ask would be, Could we use existing KBESs in such a network? and Can CDPS networks can be built up from assemblages of existing expert systems, themselves built within the framework of existing technology—that is, with existing shells or tools? Inasmuch as virtually all of today's expert systems run under "closed world" assumptions in which the individual systems do not communicate with other experts once they have started work on a particular problem, the answer to these basic questions is probably no. The individual agents in a CDPS network will have to be able to accept asynchronous data, which may well change their own individual goals, and they will have to respond to requests for results, perhaps while they are still in the process of solving some other problem. Expert systems as currently designed do not lend themselves to this kind of adaptive behavior. Thus, a major issue is the understanding of the design constraints that CDPS requires of the individual agents in a network.

Task decomposition. If we accept the fact that we cannot simply organize existing KBESs into a network, perhaps we should start by recognizing that decomposing the larger task or problem into "node-sized" pieces will be the first step toward a CDPS approach. There are several dimensions to task decomposition.

> **Functional versus spatial decomposition.** In a functional decomposition each agent is an "expert" at some part of the basic problem-solving process. Problem solving then proceeds by appropriate routing of subproblems to the corresponding expert as that expertise is required. In spatial decomposition, each node possesses all the problem-solving expertise and applies all of that expertise to the portion of the overall problem that is "nearby"

spatially.   Each agent is thus an expert at what is happening in its own (spatial) neighborhood.   Concurrent engineering would probably exploit decomposition along a mixture of functional and spatial lines, incorporating different functions such as analysis and design, but also having design done at concept, at redesign, and for manufacturing.

Hierarchical versus heterarchical structure. The node interaction structure is another important dimension of task decomposition. Hierarchical structures work well when there is a need to concentrate either control or results at one point in the network, but they are then sensitive to the loss of a high-level node in the hierarchy. Heterarchical structures may be more robust, and thus less sensitive to the loss of nodes, but they can exhibit increased communication and control problems.   It is not obvious whether concurrent engineering in general requires an approach that is either hierarchical, heterarchical, or some combination of hierarchical and heterarchical substructures. What can be fairly said, however, is that complex engineering tasks are often decomposed by technical discipline area, to accomodate the organizational structure of the institution.   This results in a set of work groups whose structure is much more heterarchical than hierarchical.

Redundant versus disjoint activities. Redundant activities consume network resources, while efficiency considerations suggest that redundant activities should be minimized.   However, a lack of (certain) redundant activities can leave the network open to severely degraded performance if a crucial activity is lost to node failure.   A more robust approach would have critical activities performed redundantly as insurance against node failure.

Organizational structure. The issue here is the organization of the network of agents in a distributed problem solver, and particularly questions of how the agents are controlled and how they will interact with other agents in the network.   Researchers in CDPS have explored a variety of approaches, several of which can be stated in terms of paradigms of organizational behavior: total cooperation among agents, analogies depending on master-slave control, and economic or bartering models of agent interaction.   As we noted earlier, complex engineering projects are undertaken within heterarchical organizational structures.   We should not be surprised, therefore, to see this reflected in the design of a KBES complex for concurrent engineering.

Dealing with incomplete, inconsistent information. Communication delays often make it impractical for a network to be structured so that each agent has all the relevant information needed for its local computation and control decisions. Another way of stating this problem is that the spatial decomposition of information among the nodes is ill suited to a functionally distributed solution. Each node may possess enough information to perform a *portion* of each function but not enough information to *completely* perform any function. Thus, a major issue in CDPS is the design of a network to cooperatively deal with possibly incomplete and inconsistent data and control information. In engineering we would reflect this concern by exploiting probabilistic methods where appropriate, and in the KBES components of an engineering environment, we would no doubt make use of our ability to reason with uncertainty (recall Section 5.5).

Communication and computation. Here we deal with the choices an agent or node might face in the need for additional information about the activities of other agents in the network. One choice is to question neighboring nodes in search of the information. The other option is for the agent compute the data it needs, assuming that the node in question has sufficient computational resources and enough of a model of other agent's activities. The selection of one of these choices depends on the relative costs of the two choices, upon limitations in both the processing time and the bandwidth of the communication channels, and upon the expectations that an agent has about responses from other agents. (And note the fairly obvious analogy to the dilemma facing a design specialist who doesn't have all the specifications or constraints about interacting neighboring subsystems.) There is an almost universal—if unstated—assumption in CDPS that communication is more expensive than computation. Hence, the agents are only loosely coupled and so have a lot of autonomy. To the extent that we change this assumption by increasing interagent communication, we approach the connectionism characteristic of distributed processing. A related question is the metalevel one about the amount of resources that should be devoted to allowing individual nodes to make these decisions (as opposed to having them made for them).

Resource tradeoffs. Akin to the need to balance communication and computation is the need to distribute resources effectively through a network of agents. Rosenschein [1985] draws an analogy to deciding where to locate formatting software in distributed systems, where file development and processing occur at locations distinct from where files are printed. Considerations must include the availability of formatting software at various sites, load balances, the sizes of unformatted and formatted files, costs of file transmission, and so on. In CDPS, plans for distributing resources over networks must be formulated and themselves distributed over the subject networks.

Synchronization. We should probably expect that a network of somewhat autonomous agents will exhibit asynchronous behavior. That is, there is no obvious guarantee that information transfer will be timely or that agents will not interfere with one another. One way to reduce interference is through the use of centrally formulated plans that contain the primitives needed to synchronize agents, while another approach depends on modifying individual plans to ensure that they do not conflict or interfere. In a concurrent engineering environment, the former is more likely to be attractive, as it would better reflect the sequential nature of product engineering—although within tasks (e.g., a design phase), asynchronous behavior may dominate.

Reliability and redundancy. One advantage of distributing computation over a network of agents—as opposed to having it in a single controlling node—is an increase in reliability. However, this must be weighed against the costs of having redundant expertise distributed over the network. There are no formal or universal guides for the evaluation of the appropriate balance between the gain in reliability and the expense of redundancy. Rather, we must leave it to the intuitions of individual system designers, from whose collective experience may emerge a more uniform approach.

Knowledge acquisition and disposition. We close this thought example with a look at the process of acquiring the knowledge that will be encapsulated in a KBES (see Chapter 12 for a discussion of the process of building such a system). In the current technological climate we would first plan to build individual systems for each of the major phases of the product's development, which means identifying and interviewing one or more experts for each phase. One issue that comes up immediately is that of dealing with conflicting advice or expertise from different experts. The current approach would be to use the knowledge acquisition phase to sort out these conflicts and let the particular KBES reflect the consensus [Mittal 1986a]. One prospective CDPS approach would be to encapsulate differences of expertise into different KBESs, letting such differences be sorted out during the running of the CDPS network rather than in the acquisition phase [Mayer 1988]. The idea of resolving conflict during performance of a task has two levels: one is to resolve issues of conflicting expertise within any one phase; the other is to let a CDPS network sort out conflicting requirements, for example, between design and manufacturing.

This completes our overview of some of the architectural issues involved in CDPS as they might be applied in a concurrent engineering context. We have obviously only scratched the surface of this new and exciting research area. Further details and implementations, as well as pointers to a growing body of literature, can be found in [Durfee 1986, 1989; Huhns 1987; Lesser 1987; Rosenschein 1985]. A compendium of readings in the broader context of distributed artificial intelligence can be found in [Bond 1988]. One engineering application has been reported by Mayer [1988].

8.6 SUMMARY

This chapter has been devoted to a discussion of two key architectural issues arising out of the need to apply the basic representation schemes presented in Chapters 5 and 6 to real-world engineering tasks: (1) integration of KBESs with CADD and other existing engineering software tools, and (2) modeling multiple kinds of expertise in integrated KBESs.

We have argued that model-based reasoning provides the beginnings of a structured methodology for building knowledge-based engineering systems to support analysis, design, and diagnosis. In the MBR approach, the structure and function of products and their components are modeled explicitly. We demonstrated how the AI techniques of production rules, frames, and OOP can be integrated with traditional engineering CADD, database, and analysis software to perform model-based reasoning in ways that leverage the advantages of each. Part III of this book illustrates the use of model-based reasoning techniques alongside other approaches for classification, design, and planning engineering tasks.

We also went into some detail about two kinds of architectures to model concurrent engineering. First, we discussed blackboard architectures as a model of concurrent engineering that implements an incremental and opportunistic style of problem solving by multiple experts, with strict hierarchical control at each step of problem execution. While noting that this style of problem solving departs from the way that concurrent engineering is practised by humans, we pointed out the potential of such systems to involve a human user or users as additional knowledge sources to be integrated with multiple knowledge sources contained in a KBES application. Several prototype blackboard KBES applications have already been developed in engineering domains and are described in Part III. And active research is under way on a number of others. Thus, we should be able to begin assessing the utility of blackboard architectures for engineering KBES during the early 1990s.

Next, we discussed a body of research on cooperative distributed problem solving (CDPS), a fairly new research area where there are few concrete examples and little empirical data. However, there is much promise for

Chapter 9

KNOWLEDGE-BASED SYSTEMS FOR CLASSIFICATION

In Chapter 1 we set out a taxonomy of problem types ranging from those involving derivation or classification to the more difficult problems involving formation or synthesis of solutions. Classification problems were the first to be addressed successfully using KBES techniques and still constitute the overwhelming majority of KBES applications to date. We therefore begin this section on applications of KBESs in engineering with a discussion of classification KBES applications.

In this chapter and Chapters 10 and 11 (on design and planning applications of KBESs), we will discuss characteristics of each problem type and the resulting issues to be addressed in developing KBES solution aids for that class of problem. We will then introduce approaches that can be used to address these issues by presenting the architecture, representation, and reasoning strategies employed in some example KBES applications of each kind.

9.1 CHARACTERISTICS OF CLASSIFICATION PROBLEMS

Classification problems commonly encountered in engineering include

❑ **Selection.** Choose the most appropriate analysis methodology, tool, chemical process catalyst, tunneling method, weld test procedure, and so on, from a finite set of alternatives known to be candidate solutions.

❑ **Diagnosis.** Find the underlying cause or causes of a system failure or malfunction that has been indicated by the appearance of one or more failure symptoms. Most diagnosis systems also select a repair or remediation strategy to correct the cause of the failure or malfunction.

❑ **Evaluation.** Assign a binary (pass/fail) or continuous (how good?) value to one or more dimensions of the performance of an engineered system. This task also includes what might be called **diagnostic evaluation**, in which information is provided about failures—and perhaps remedies—before performance values are assigned.

❑ **Interpretation.** Classify an event (e.g., an earthquake), a substance (e.g., an unknown soil type), or some other entity in terms of several categories of interest (e.g., magnitude and epicenter for the earthquake, or cohesion and moisture content for the soil type) from raw and potentially noisy data.

❑ **Prediction.** Select the most likely future values from among a known set of possible values for some important attributes of a system.

❑ **Monitoring and control.** This is a hybrid of the above problem types, in which we sample data from an ongoing process, interpret that data to identify potential failures or malfunctions, diagnose the cause of malfunctions, and select appropriate repair or remediation strategies for the identified and diagnosed problems.

All of these types of problems involve choosing one or more "solutions" from a predefined and finite set of possible solutions for the problem—even continuous evaluation involves choosing a point or interval on a defined scale for each dimension of interest. Humans solving such problems search through candidate solutions at some level of abstraction, identify plausible solutions, and then seek to confirm and refine them by more detailed kinds of testing.

What distinguishes expert human problem solvers from novices in performing classification tasks is the experts' ability to use associative heuristics—that is, associations that they have previously observed to exist between patterns of data and inferences that can be drawn from the data at several levels of abstraction. These multilevel heuristic associations that experts can make between data and candidate solutions or solution strategies allow them to reduce the range of potential solutions rapidly. Novices, who lack the necessary experience base from which to identify high-level problems and candidate solutions heuristically, must solve classification problems by exhaustive search, relying on first principles. For many real-world applications, exhaustive search for solutions from first principles is unacceptably slow and costly.

Knowledge-based systems aimed at solving classification problems are therefore usually designed to work in one of two ways.

❑   Emulate the problem-solving strategy of experts by using heuristics and multilevel reasoning, or

❑   Harness the power and speed of computers to perform more exhaustive searches, using algorithms or rules based on first principles to evaluate candidate solutions.

We will present and discuss examples of KBESs that use one or both of these kinds of approaches for solving classification problems in this chapter.

9.2 DIAGNOSIS

Some of the most important early KBES applications were developed to aid in medical diagnosis [Buchanan 1984]. Each one was built by an extensive process of knowledge acquisition, involving multiple iterations of prototyping, testing, and refinement. These applications typically involved teams of five to ten researchers for two to five years and cost millions of dollars to develop. Two improvements since these early systems were developed have made it possible to implement significant diagnostic systems with just a few person-months of effort.

First, the software tools for implementing diagnostic KBESs—along with other kinds—have improved greatly. The experience from MYCIN and many subsequent diagnostic systems has been encapsulated into a variety of elegant and powerful expert system shells for diagnosis, costing from $100 to about $10,000 and running on personal computers or workstations. Such systems have built-in inference engines for forward and backward chaining of production rules at the low end and have frames, interactive graphics, and OOP for model-based reasoning at the high end. These software "power tools" have certainly helped to speed the process of implementing KBESs for diagnosis. Second, and perhaps of even more importance, has been the identification of a generic structure for the knowledge in a diagnosis KBES. We discuss the latter development next.

9.2.1 The Inference Structure of Diagnostic Knowledge

William Clancey analyzed a number of diagnostic KBES applications in medicine and engineering and saw that they had in common a consistent inference structure, that is, a consistent pattern of representation and reasoning [Clancey 1985]. All the diagnostic systems studied across several domains, including medicine and engineering, employed a generic inference structure that he termed **heuristic classification**. This knowledge structure has the general form illustrated in Figure 9-1.

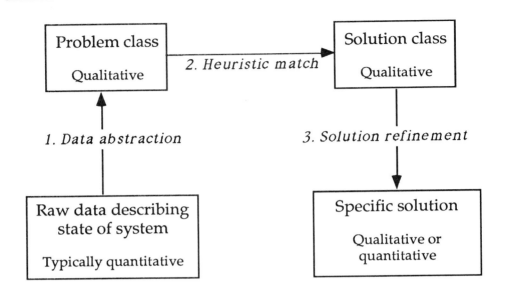

Figure 9-1 The inference structure of heuristic classification diagnosis systems (after [Clancey 1985]).

According to this analysis, diagnosis and prescription involve three kinds of knowledge processing.

❏   Diagnostic systems begin by trying to abstract from a set of symptoms (often described in quantitative terms) to a set of problem subclasses and then broad problem classes. Step 1 in diagnosis is thus a type of **data abstraction,** in which specific data patterns are classified as belonging to particular problem subclasses or classes.

❏   In Step 2 of diagnosis, heuristics are used to match the problem class with one or more generic solution strategies (often with stated degrees of belief or certainty) for that class of problem.

❏   Step 3 of diagnosis and prescription involves refining the heuristically matched generic solution strategy by using available data about the state of the system—the patient, machine, or process plant.

This analysis of the inference structure of diagnosis systems is an extremely important contribution. A clear description of the generic structure of the knowledge in a class of KBESs can be thought of as a **knowledge**

engineering methodology. This methodology for diagnosis systems provides a very useful guide for developing and maintaining diagnosis KBESs [Clancey 1985].

9.2.2   Examples of KBESs for Diagnosis

The literature contains numerous descriptions of KBES applications to engineering diagnosis problems. For example, see [DavisR 1984] and [Lambert 1988] on electronic circuit diagnosis using model-based reasoning, [El Ayeb 1988] on process plant diagnosis using heuristic and causal reasoning, and [Hajek 1988] on highway pavement diagnosis using heuristic reasoning and computer-based vision.

In addition to their widespread use for diagnosis of biological or electro-mechanical systems, KBESs have been used for diagnosis of organizational and behavioral systems. The HOWSAFE system, for example, diagnoses weaknesses in the management policies and practices of construction companies that could negatively affect the safety of their workers [Levitt 1986].

9.2.3   Recapitulation of KBESs for Diagnosis

Most diagnostic systems developed to date have been implemented using production rules alone, organized in the style identified in [Clancey 1985]. As we discussed in Chapter 5, using production rules with a context mechanism or some other way to guide search over components or subsystems has proved to be quite effective for solving monotonic medical and engineering diagnosis problems—that is, diagnosis problems where the data describing the state of the system being diagnosed do not change over the duration of a diagnostic session.

In more complex diagnosis and prescription systems, however, we may want to gat⸽ ⸽r data continuously from sensors connected to an operational system, to reason about changes over time in the state of the system, and to model the system causally rather than relying solely on heuristics. Accordingly, newer systems for diagnosis are tending toward the use of qualitative physiscs and model-based reasoning approaches for knowledge representation and reasoning. The Guardian system, described in Section 9.6, samples data continuously and reasons both heuristically and causally about changes in an intensive care patient's condition over time. Such systems can benefit from the added power of frame-based representation, OOP, blackboard control architectures, temporal reasoning strategies, and model-based reasoning (described in Chapters 6, 7, and 8).

Of all of the problem types to which KBES technology can be applied, diagnosis is probably the most mature area of application. Incorporating analog or digital sensor hookups and nonmonotonic, real-time reasoning about dynamic processes into diagnostic systems can pose significant practical and conceptual challenges for knowledge engineers. Nevertheless, even these challenges are being addressed by current systems; building a diagnostic KBES is nowadays generally straightforward and can be largely accomplished with off-the-shelf hardware and software tools.

9.3 DIAGNOSTIC EVALUATION: THE LSC ADVISOR

Evaluation is a classification task in which we want to classify a system in the correct interval along one or more dimensions of performance. The scale of performance along which we wish to evaluate the system's performance could be binary (e.g., pass or fail); it could contain a finite number of qualitative values (e.g., excellent, fair, good, poor, unacceptable); it could contain a finite number of integer or interval values; or it could contain an infinite number of real number values in some range. For example, we described in Chapter 5 how the PROSPECTOR inference net KBES evaluates the likelihood that a given prospect contains a certain type of mineral deposit, using real numbers ranging between –5 and +5 [Campbell 1985].

Evaluation also often involves diagnosis when we require an assessment of a number of failures and their potential consequences before assigning a performance value. In this section we present the first of two descriptions of KBES evaluation applications. The LSC Advisor is a prototype KBES designed to review an architectural design for high-level conformance with the Life Safety Code of the National Fire Protection Association [Lathrop 1985]. In Section 9.5 we will briefly discuss the SafeQual system for evaluating the expected safety of a prospective construction contractor.

9.3.1 The LSC Advisor: Binary Evaluation against Safety Codes

The Life Safety Code (LSC) is a document of hundreds of pages whose purpose is "to establish minimum requirements that will provide a reasonable degree of safety from fire in buildings and structures." The **LSC Advisor** focuses on those aspects of the code that relate specifically to egress and fire protection features and equipment [Dym 1988]. Egress requirements specify the type and number of exits and the maximum distances from points in the building to the nearest exit. Fire protection features include, for example, the specification of minimum fire resistance ratings for walls and doors, depending on their location and use.

Requirements for fire protection equipment include rules for specifying the number and locations of fire extinguishers and exit signs. The egress and fire protection requirements were chosen for encapsulation in the prototype because they are central to the LSC and because violations in those areas are among the most expensive to remedy. The LSC Advisor addresses these code requirements as they are relevant to new health care facilities, although they include many—if not most—of the requirements that would be applicable to all types of buildings.

9.3.2   Origins of the LSC Advisor

Our discussion of the LSC Advisor is drawn from [Dym 1988], which includes an extensive discussion of the motivations for building the system as well as much greater detail on the system itself. Suffice it here to say that it is both good design practice and economically sensible to consider a building's conformance with the LSC early in the design process. And since many architects are not familiar with all the details of the LSC, an automated computer system which could expedite design review could be of serious economic interest. Further, since a complete conformance review of a design of a complex facility such as a hospital is very time-intensive, automating this process—even to the extent of reducing it to an overnight batch process—could produce savings of time (and money), as well as ensuring that code checking is done comprehensively, consistently, and without error.

The review process itself, during which the architect works through the floor plans in a conventional order, has three basic procedures that are repeatedly applied to different areas of the building and to different aspects of the design.

❑   **Identification** of the parts of the building,

❑   **Selection** of applicable provisions of the LSC, and

❑   **Application** of those provisions to a particular situation.

For example, an element of the design might be identified as a mechanical shaft forming a vertical opening in the floor of an area of patient bedrooms in a hospital. The expert will then select as applicable a paragraph of the LSC specifying enclosure of such openings by walls with a two-hour fire rating. Finally, the expert will apply that paragraph of the code to this particular mechanical shaft by checking the fire ratings of all the walls enclosing the shaft.

Generally, the occupancies—or size and type—of different parts of the building are determined first, because the safety requirements vary with the intended use. The next major area of concern is the division of the building into fire zones which are separated from one another by walls serving as fire barriers. Then egress routes from the building are identified and their type, number, width, and length are checked against requirements. Other areas of concern include the enclosure of hazardous areas with fire barriers, the containment of smoke with smoke barriers, and the use of appropriate finishes on corridor walls. As noted above, the prototype LSC Advisor is mainly concerned with egress routes and fire protection features, but these are neccessarily related to questions regarding occupancy, the presence of particular equipment such as sprinklers and exit signs, and the type of construction.

9.3.3 Architecture of the LSC Advisor

The LSC Advisor is intended to function in concert with an architectural CADD system. After a building design has been developed within the CADD system, the LSC Advisor assists the architect in making sure that the floor plans are consistent with some of the more important fire safety regulations. The primary input to the LSC Advisor is a file obtained from the CADD system which serves as a knowledge base that describes a single floor of a building. The primary output from the system is a list of aspects of this floor plan which do not conform to requirements of the LSC.

The processing performed by the LSC Advisor can be divided into two main phases.

❑   **A precalculation phase** which makes extensive use of algorithms written in Lisp and rules fired in a forward-chaining strategy, and

❑   **A code application phase** which uses rules only so that the reasoning of the LSC will be transparent to the user.

In the precalculation phase, measurements are made on the floor plan and certain implicit relationships among floor plan objects are made explicit. For example, travel paths from rooms to exits are determined and their lengths are measured. The creation of links between fire zones and the rooms they contain is an example of making explicit a relationship which at the start of processing was only implicit in the coordinates of the objects involved (see Section 9.3.4). The results of the precalculation phase are stored in memory as additional frames, slots, and slot values in the same knowledge base that holds the original input data.

In the code application phase, the rule interpreter is instructed to apply *all* appropriate rules to the facts which have been accumulated in the floor plan knowledge base. Most of the rules correspond directly to a requirement stated in a paragraph of the LSC. Where a problem is found, the rule consequent places a string describing the problem in a special slot of the object involved. For example, the string FIRE RATING OF 1.5 HOURS TOO LOW, SHOULD BE > 2 HOURS might be attached to a frame representing a wall. These strings form the basis of the list which is the output at the end of the code-checking process.

We already noted that the LSC review process can be thought of as having three distinct aspects: identification of building elements, selection of applicable requirements, and application of selected requirements. It is important to understand how these three activities have been addressed in the design of the LSC Advisor.

For the most part, the identification problem has been left up to the user of the CADD system which acts as the front end to the LSC Advisor. The CADD system user must explicitly identify the floor plan's different elements, that is, the rooms, doors, and walls. This is accomplished partly by using specialized drawing functions provided by the CADD system and partly by following certain conventions with regard to the use of symbols and the organization of the floor plan into layered drawings. The user must also select room labels from a special list so that occupancy can be properly determined. This allows automatic translation of the CADD database into the frame-based floor plan representation that the LSC Advisor can analyze.

The process of selecting applicable requirements from the LSC is handled mainly by putting the necessary clauses into the antecedents of the rules that represent the LSC requirements. It is also handled implicitly in that the knowledge representation facilitates the handling of objects as groups. This is done by representing all objects of the same type as instances of a class. For example, all rooms are instances of the class ROOMS, all doors are instances of the class DOORS, and so on. The application of requirements to particular building elements is accomplished by the insertion of appropriate clauses in rule antecedents.

Many aspects of the application of LSC requirements are implemented through algorithmic procedures in the precalculation phase. For example, travel distances are measured in the precalculation phase. However, the determination of the required travel distance and the comparisons of the actual distances to those specific requirements are performed by rules in the code application phase.

The precalculation phase also contributes to the process of identifying building elements when it makes explicit certain relationships that are only implicit in the original input data. An example is the determination that a particular door provides a means of egress from a particular space. This fact is determined by a geometric procedure—written in Lisp—and made available to the rule interpreter through the frame system.

The prototype LSC Advisor contains some 100 rules and can complete egress and fire protection analysis of a representative floor plan—composed of some 2000 objects—in about an hour on a Texas Instruments (TI) Explorer I (or on a Sun 3/160). This performance was obtained by integrating a rule-processing system with a frame system, since a common data structure allowed the sharing of data among both rule-based and algorithmic procedures. The integration of rules, frames, and algorithmic procedures in the prototype LSC Advisor was implemented in Intellicorp's Knowledge Engineering Environment (KEE).

9.3.4 Representing Provisions of the Life Safety Code

We have noted that many of the LSC requirements are represented in the LSC Advisor as rules. Paragraph by paragraph, the text of the LSC was translated as directly as possible into the language recognized by the rule proccessor. Paragraph 6-2.2.5 [Lathrop 1985] will serve as an example of the translation of text into a rule. It reads

> Every opening in a fire barrier shall be protected to limit the spread of fire and restrict the movement of smoke from one side of the fire barrier to the other. The fire protection rating for opening protectives shall be as follows: (a) 2-hour fire barrier—1 and 1/2 hour fire protection rating; (b) 1-hour fire barrier—1 hour fire protection rating when used for vertical openings or 3/4 hour fire protection when used for other than vertical openings.

A Lisp-like translation of Part a is shown in Figure 9-2. The first clause focuses attention on fire zone objects in the knowledge base. The second clause further focuses attention to those fire zones which have required enclosure ratings of 2 hours. The next three clauses retrieve data about the walls of the fire zones and the doors (?OPENINGs) within these walls. The sixth (and last) clause compares the fire resistance of the doors with the minimum legal rating of 1.5 hours. The value of the slot REQUIRED_ENCLOSURE_RATING will have been determined by the previous firing of other rules. The doors are in violation of this paragraph if their fire rating is less than 1.5 hours.

```
((IF:     (AND   (?ZONE IS IN CLASS FIRE_ZONES)

                 (THE REQUIRED_ENCLOSURE_RATING OF ?ZONE IS 2)

                 (THE BOUNDARY OF ?ZONE IS ?WALL)

                 (THE WALL_TYPE OF ?WALL IS INTERIOR)

                 (AN OPENING OF ?WALL IS ?OPENING)

                 (LISP (< (THE  RATING OF ?OPENING)  1.5))))

  (THEN: (AND   (A LSC_PROBLEM OF ?ZONE IS
                 "FIRE RATING OF WALL OPENING TOO LOW:
                 ?OPENING")

                 (A LSC_PROBLEM OF ?OPENING IS
                 "FIRE RATING SHOULD BE 1.5 HOURS.
                 ACTUAL RATING: ?RATING"))))
```

Figure 9-2 A Lisp-like translation of the rule in Paragraph 6-2.2.5 of the LSC (after [Dym 1988]).

9.3.5 Representing and Reasoning about a Floor Plan

The floor plan representation developed for the LSC Advisor was intended to facilitate description of all the objects in a typical floor plan or blueprint, enable reasoning about these objects in the context of analyzing and applying the LSC, and provide an economical and efficient implementation for these descriptive and reasoning tasks. Inasmuch as the typical objects in a floor plan (e.g., fire zones, rooms, doors, walls) are fairly abstract, a rule-based approach would not by itself provide an adequate representation because, as we have stated repeatedly, rules alone are inadequate for describing objects with a large number of often complex attributes.

The LSC Advisor **inheritance lattice** (or **abstraction hierarchy**) is displayed in Figure 9-3. The class frames are organized into a single hierarchy of subclasses of the class of FLOOR_PLAN_OBJECTS. Thus, WALLS, ROOMS, CORRIDORS, and EXIT_SIGNS are examples of subclasses of FLOOR_PLAN_OBJECTS. Subclasses have all the slots of their superclasses, as well as additional slots which are applicable to them but not to other subclasses of the superclass. The slot LSC_PROBLEM is the only one which *all* the objects have in common; it is defined in the class FLOOR_PLAN_OBJECTS. NODES, one of the immediate subclasses of FLOOR_PLAN_OBJECTS, defines a COORDS slot for storing a single (x, y) location. The subclasses of NODES include CORNERS and EXIT_SIGNS.

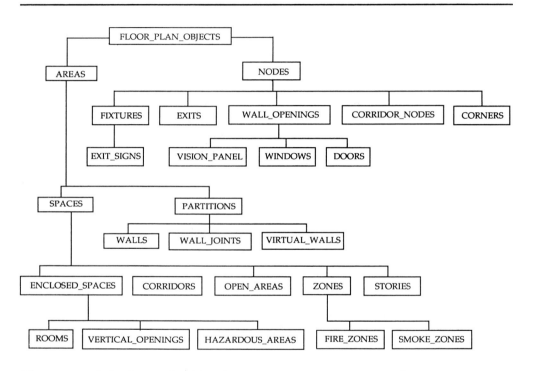

Figure 9-3 Inheritance lattice of LSC Advisor classes (after [Dym 1988]).

The superclass SPACES is used to organize building stories, fire zones, smoke zones, rooms, and corridors. All members of the class SPACES have the same general attributes: DOORS, NET_AREA, GROSS_AREA, BOUNDARY_WALLS, and a REQUIRED_ENCLOSURE_RATING. Rooms are then defined in this representation as having all the attributes of spaces, as well as those attributes that are specific to rooms alone (e.g., INROOM_TRAVEL_DISTANCE, NUMBER_OF_REQUIRED_EXITS).

One significant advantage of this hierarchical abstraction of the different types of objects in a floor plan is that general operations can be defined on a superclass. These operations will then work correctly on any object that is an instance of one of its subclasses. For example, a generic Lisp function that requires access to a COORDS slot can be defined for the superclass NODES; it will then work equally well, and without modification, for instances of CORNERS and EXIT_SIGNS. The attachment of a Lisp function to a slot of a superclass and its activation by message passing is an example of method inheritance in the tradition of object-oriented programming [Bobrow 1986a]. Additionally, many of the same economies can be derived when the operations are defined separately from the objects, either as Lisp source files or in the form of rules.

The rule we displayed in Figure 9-2 contains an implicit example of how a frame representation enables reasoning about symbols or objects. That rule is concerned with the fire resistance rating of a door in a wall intended to serve as a fire barrier. Given that a floor plan may contain several thousand objects, we want its representation to facilitate rapid and efficient identification of the door(s) in question. How does this happen? The process begins with the identification of all instances, or specific cases, of fire zones which are direct descendants of the class FIRE_ZONES (Figure 9-4). This could be a list of objects with between two and five entries. As the class FIRE_ZONES is itself a subclass of the class SPACES, it has a slot for the attribute BOUNDARY which lists all the walls that make up the boundary of the fire zone. This list of walls, with anywhere from 4 to 30 entries, is used first to eliminate exterior walls by excluding those with the value EXTERIOR in their WALL_TYPE slot (Figure 9-5). Now, the class WALLS contains the slot WALL_OPENING, which holds all the DOORS in a given wall, so it is possible to identify all of the specific doors to which Paragraph 6-2.2.5 applies. The RATING slot of each door so identified can now be examined and the relevant rule applied.

9.3.6   Travel Distance Algorithms

One of the novel aspects of the LSC Advisor is its combination of complex geometric calculations and algorithms with an accessible high-level approach to knowledge representation [Dym 1988]. The most interesting (and complex) of these algorithms are those which, in the precalculation phase, measure travel distances between points in the building and the building's exits. These algorithms are needed because the LSC sets maximum limits, referred to as corridor travel distances, on the travel distances from the doors of rooms to the nearest exit. Maximum limits are also set on the distance from the furthest point in a room to the nearest door leading into a corridor and on the sum of the in-room and corridor travel distances.

Slot	Values
CORNER	(# [Unit : CRNR_99 BUILDINGS] # [Unit : CRNR_104 BUILDINGS] # [Unit : CRNR_94 BUILDINGS] # [Unit : CRNR_32 BUILDINGS])
EXTERIOR_NODES	(# [Unit : CRNR_97 BUILDINGS] # [Unit : CRNR_102 BUILDINGS] # [Unit : CRNR_92 BUILDINGS] # [Unit : CRNR_37 BUILDINGS])
GROSS_AREA	(2408.0)
OCCUPANT_LOAD	(6200.0)
SUBSPACES	(ROOM_180 ROOM_151 ROOM_152)
ZONE_CORRIDORS	(CORRIDOR_1 CORRIDOR_2)
ZONE_DOORS	(DOOR_79 DOOR_86 DOOR_89 . . .)
ZONE_EXITS	(DOOR_79 DOOR_86)
ZONE_EXIT_SIGNS	(EXIT_SIGN_1 EXIT_SIGN_3 . . .)
REQ'D_ENCLOSURE_RATING	1.5
NET_AREA	(1956.0)
LSC_PROBLEM	NIL

Figure 9-4 Frame representation of an instance of the class FIRE_ZONES [Dym 1988].

The LSC also specifies that corridor travel distances be measured along corridor centerlines, so tracing these centerlines becomes a significant activity in the travel distance algorithm. This requires identifying and defining corridors, which is nontrivial for those of irregular shape. The details are beyond our current scope (see [Dym 1988]), but the algorithm entails constructing a connected graph of points along the edge of the

Slot	Values
CORNER	(# [Unit : CRNR_113 BUILDINGS] # [Unit : CRNR_112 BUILDINGS] # [Unit : CRNR_139 BUILDINGS] # [Unit : CRNR_138 BUILDINGS])
WALL_TYPE	INTERIOR
RATING	2.0
LSC_PROBLEM	NIL
WALL_OPENING	(DOOR_153)

Figure 9-5 Frame representation of an instance of the class WALLS (after Dym [1988]).

corridor that are visible from one another and then performing a carefully optimized depth-first search of the connected graph to identify the shortest path between each pair of wall midpoints. Once all the corridor centerlines have been formed, another connected graph is formed of nodes representing the building's exits, the doors for each room, and points along the centerlines of the corridors. A shortest-path algorithm determines the shortest distance from each room's doors to the nearest exit. In much the same way as was done for corridors, each room is then examined to see if any points in it are too far from its doors. Rooms with multiple doors require special handling. All the results are stored in appropriate frame slots where they are available for evaluation by the various rules. Again, see [Dym 1988] for the details.

9.3.7   Control Issues in the LSC Advisor

The LSC review process is largely amenable to implementation as a series of steps that follow one another in an order determined by a standard protocol. The precalculation phase consists of a set of Lisp algorithms and some 34 precalculation rules derived from the LSC. These precalculation rules do not themselves flag code violations. They work together with the algorithms to refine the raw CADD data, providing higher-level information about the floor plan representation which is needed by the code application rules. The code application phase has also been implemented using a set of rules. The collection of some 36 rules in this phase are then fired with a forward-chaining strategy to identify and flag code violations. This partitioning of phases, algorithms, and rules has produced a prototype system with good performance.

The LSC review process is really an exhaustive search for any possible problems in the building design. All objects on the floor plan must be checked—that is, they must be evaluated as meeting or violating every applicable building code requirement. This is quite a different situation from a typical diagnostic task, in which search is guided by a few symptoms or complaints. The need for exhaustive search also explains why the goal-directed processing of a backward-chaining strategy, which was tried first, did not pay off. A goal-directed search through a knowledge base is useful when a single or best result is desired. In this case, however, all violations, however minor, must be found.

The earliest version of the system also made extensive use of demons to do much of the processing that is now done in the precalculation phase. When a value of a slot was needed to determine whether a particular rule should fire, a Lisp function was activated by a demon to calculate the slot value for the particular object in question. Switching to a strategy in which all slot values were precalculated for all objects before the rule system was started up contributed to a reduction of the overall processing time. Since nearly all the slot values for all the objects in the floor plan—of which there are some 2000—need to be calculated before the evaluation is complete, the "on demand only" nature of demons provides no leverage in this situation. By precomputing all values efficiently, the cost of demon processing was avoided altogether. Efficiency was also gained by processing objects in groups rather than individually.

9.3.8   A Unifying Database

The floor plan information represented in the LSC Advisor goes well beyond the purely geometric data that is the province of the typical blueprint. Typically, detailed information on construction materials, wall finishes, and product names for prefabricated items must be obtained by reference to other documents, either detailed drawings or materials lists. However, since information from all these sources is needed for detailed LSC review, a representation which could unify these diverse types of information had to be developed.

Unifying these diverse data with a single representation takes a significant step beyond the capabilities of most CADD systems used by architects today, in which there are no unified databases for materials and floor plans (although, as described in Section 8.1, CADD systems of the 1990s will have these capabilities). In the original version of the CADD system within which the LSC Advisor was built, there were unique identifiers in the materials or finishes databases and individual records for objects such as doors and rooms. Floor plans, however, were generated by use of a drawing program which maintained a separate database of lines, arcs, and text strings. This graphic database contained no explicit indication as to which lines were meant to be understood as representing the two sides of the same doorway, for example. The architect (subconsciously) deduced this information on the basis of spatial reasoning, guided by general knowledge about how to interpret blueprints of buildings. Conversely, while materials and finishes databases may contain some dimensional information, they typically contain no information about the positions of objects relative to one another. Therefore, as input to the LSC Advisor, a floor plan representation was specified in which geometric information is explicitly related to high-level objects such as walls and doors, requiring that the architectural CADD system provide such a unified description of the building.

The LSC advisor is an early example of a KBES that reads data from a graphic CAD system; classifies and upgrades the geometric data with other kinds of data (e.g., about material properties); puts the resulting information about building components or elements into a frame system; and then performs reasoning about the building elements, using procedures, rules, and frames in ways that exploit the strengths of each. The result is a tabulation of all elements evaluated as violating the LSC code, with the possibility to generate a natural language explanation of the reasoning path that led to the evaluation that a given component or architectural element is in violation of the code.

9.4   SCALED EVALUATION: SAFEQUAL

SafeQual is an operational, commercially available KBES that can be used to assist in prequalifying or selecting contractors for a construction project on the basis of their expected safety performance [Levitt 1989a]. SafeQual reasons about the past safety performance and current safety practices of each contractor and can provide any of the following as output: a numerical safety evaluation; a qualitative evaluation (excellent, good, moderate, poor, unacceptable); and a set of safety concerns to be addressed if the contractor is awarded the project.

9.4.1 Motivation for SafeQual

The motivation for SafeQual was a 1981 study in which it was demonstrated that construction buyers experienced better safety performance on those projects for which they prequalified or selected contractors on the basis of expected safety performance, with substantial attendant savings in capital costs [Levitt 1987c]. Yet the evaluation of the past accident experience and current safety practices of a contractor requires a level of expertise beyond what is typically available in the procurement departments of many construction buyers. SafeQual was thus an attempt to use KBES techniques to make construction safety expertise accessible to the procurement departments of construction buyers.

9.4.2 Architecture of SafeQual

SafeQual was developed as an inference net in which the top-level hypothesis is "This contractor is expected to work safely" (see Figure 9-6). Supporting this hypothesis are pieces of evidence (ideas) such as "This contactor's past safety record is good" or "This contractor provides adequate safety training for its employees." SafeQual was implemented using the Deciding Factor expert system shell [Campbell 1985]. This shell, which is PC-based, does its reasoning through an inference net (see Section 5.6) with some interesting features that add to its expressive power.

Each of these items of evidence for the top-level hypothesis is itself a hypothesis, supported by additional lower-level evidence (see Figure 9-6). Note, however, that the inference net in SafeQual is not strictly hierarchical. SafeQual exploits a feature from the Deciding Factor called the **same-as idea**, in which an idea somewhere in the net can be declared to be the same as an evidence or hypothesis elsewhere in the tree. The belief provided or computed for the original evidence is then assigned to the same-as evidence, although the latter might be given different weights in support of a competing hypothesis or might provide control for the consultation or for issuing warning statements (see Section 9.4.4).

The leaf nodes of SafeQual's tree contain a series of relatively objective items of evidence which are turned into questions for the user. Typical questions are "Does the contractor send all new supervisors to a safety training program such as the AGC Line Foreman Safety Program at the time they are first appointed?" or "How frequently does senior management see reports of project accident statistics—weekly, monthly, quarterly, annually?" These questions have binary and multiple choice answers,

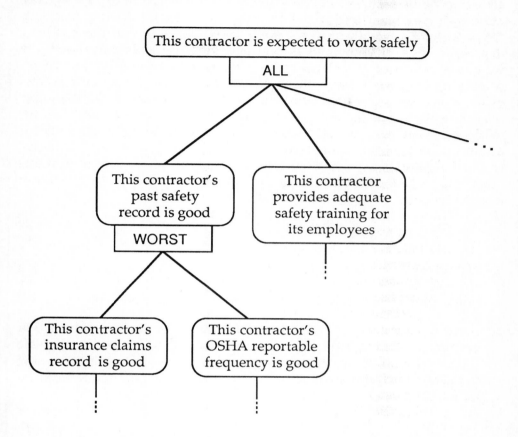

Figure 9-6 A portion of the SafeQual inference net (after Levitt [1989a]).

respectively.   Another question asks for the contractor's Interstate Experience Modification Rating, the answer to which is the ratio of the number of the contractor's actual workers' compensation claims to the average for like work.

9.4.3   Reasoning in SafeQual

SafeQual reasons with the user-supplied answers as follows. The real, interval, or binary answers supplied by the user are mapped to a degree of belief for the evidence along a scale of belief that runs from –5 (positively false) to +5 (positively true). An "unknown" or missing answer is assigned a degree of belief of 0. Beliefs for the evidence supporting a given hypothesis are then multiplied by the weight that evidence has been assigned for its hypothesis (on a scale of –1.0 to +1.0), and the resulting degree of belief is combined in one of several possible ways with the weighted beliefs of other evidence for the same hypothesis. For BEST combining logic, only the highest-weighted belief of any of the pieces of evidence is used to determine the belief in the hypothesis; for WORST logic, only the lowest. For ALL logic, a weighted sum is computed from all of the evidence, positive or negative, associated with the hypothesis. Belief is accumulated in this manner up the tree to the top-level hypothesis, combining the belief contributions of evidence for each hypothesis according to the logical operator specified for the hypothesis. The results of a consultation with SafeQual are as follows.

1. A numerical degree of belief that the contractor will be safe (on a scale from –5 to +5).

2. A qualitative evaluation corresponding to this score. For example, a score of +3.5 or higher results in the statement "Based on its current safety management practices, this contractor is expected to be very safe."

3. A series of warnings or recommendations to the construction buyer. For example, "Although this contractor is expected to be moderately safe (+1.85), the contractor currently conducts no safety training for new workers. It is recommended that the contractor be required to institute formal orientation and training of new workers immediately."

9.4.4   Control in the SafeQual System

The control structure of SafeQual is basically depth-first backward chaining. The top-level hypothesis establishes each of its evidences as subgoals (subhypotheses). The first evidence listed for the top-level hypothesis becomes the first subhypothesis to be evaluated. Its items of evidence are expanded next, starting with the first one listed, and so on, until the first evidence listed for a subhypothesis is a leaf node with no evidence below it. This evidence is then turned into a question which is posed to the user. The way in which questions are posed to the user has been customized in SafeQual to include natural language and graphics, and several of the more important questions have attached to them detailed explanations which are available on request to assist the user in answering them.

The flow of control in SafeQual is also data-driven in places. Besides supporting different ways to combine the evidence for a given hypothesis, the Deciding Factor allows the knowledge engineer to set **kill values** for any idea (evidence or hypothesis) in the system. If a user provides evidence that falls outside of a range delimited by kill values for a given question, or if in its process of "rating and weighting" evidence SafeQual finds that an intermediate level piece of evidence falls outside of its legal range, then the hypothesis supported by that evidence is "killed"—that is, its belief is set to a value of –5.0, corresponding to absolutely false. These kill values can simply shut off a line of questioning by immediately killing a hypothesis low in the net, or they can cascade through the net, affecting the entire flow of control in the program.

For instance, an unacceptably high response to a question about the contractor's interstate experience modification rating will kill the next hypothesis up in the tree, that the contractor's experience modification rate is acceptable. Since this hypothesis has a kill value of –4.5, setting it to –5.0 will, in turn, kill the hypothesis above it that the contactor's past safety performance is acceptable. This will kill the top-level hypothesis, causing the contractor to be excluded from bidding on the project.

Kill values are also used with a special type of logic termed **conditional logic,** which, when an answer falls out of range, stops a line of questioning but does not kill the hypothesis [Campbell 1985]. A simple example of the use of conditional logic is that if accident records are not kept, there is no point in asking how frequently management sees them. Thus the evidence about whether accident records are kept is made a conditional question, and this question is asked at the beginning of a series of questions dealing with accident reporting.

Same-as values, together with conditional logic, are used to activiate conclusions at the end of the consultation. The value determined earlier for a same-as idea is checked against the allowable range in its matching conditional evidence. If it is in the range, the program continues to provide the explanation or warning stored in the next "dummy" question; if not, this line of reasoning terminates and the program checks the next conclusion or warning. Thus, if the contractor performs no safety training but otherwise passes the evaluation, a warning about the importance of safety training will be presented as part of SafeQual's conclusions.

Same-as values for ideas, alternative combination logics, and the use of kill values (alone or in conditional statements) permit a richness of reasoning and representation not immediately evident in what appears at first glance to be a simple tree-structured rating and weighting system.

9.4.5   Present Status of SafeQual

Unlike the LSC Advisor, which reads a CADD database for much of its input, SafeQual must be given all of its input by the user at the keyboard. In fact, the user of SafeQual keys in responses from a questionnaire previously filled out by the prospective contractor. In this respect, SafeQual acts like an intelligent form entry system: it enables purchasing clerks to interpret data which had previously proved to be too subjective for them to classify correctly, and it provides an evaluation and recommendations. As mentioned in Chapter 5, the inference net style of evaluation KBES has found widespread usage in the financial services sector, where it is employed to support workers who evaluate loan applications, assess insurance risks, and perform similar tasks involving some computation and some judgement.

9.4.6   Recapitulation of Evaluation KBESs

The two evaluation systems described in Sections 9.3 and 9.4 show how KBES techniques can be used to develop decision support systems for evaluation tasks. A binary evaluation system such as the LSC Advisor ("Does this architectural design violate any aspect of the Life Safety Code?") was implemented using external data, procedures with rules to enhance them, and additional rules to evaluate the transformed data. A scaled evaluation such as SafeQual ("How safe is this contractor?"), like the PROSPECTOR mineral evaluation systems from which it is descended ("How likely is it that this prospect contains an economic mineral deposit?"), was implemented using a standard "rating and weighting" inference net approach.

Of course, a document like the Life Safety Code might contain ambiguities or contradictions—and building a KBES is a sure way to force them to the surface. Such errors or omissions can take many hours of frustrating work to resolve, but the code is improved as a result of the debugging efforts generated in the course of formalizing it. Another pragmatic difficulty in building evaluation KBESs is that the knowledge for making an evaluation may be difficult or impossible for the expert to articulate, as in the "day-old chicken sexing" example provided by [Dreyfus 1986]. In spite of such pragmatic difficulties, however, the inference structure and knowledge engineering tools for representing and reasoning about evaluation knowledge are mature and well understood. Thus, evaluation systems, like diagnosis systems, are relatively straightforward to implement in terms of KBES tools and techniques.

9.5   MONITORING AND CONTROL: PLATFORM

The task of monitoring and control includes some or all of the following elements.

❑   **Observe** an ongoing process by receiving data about salient dimensions of system performance,

❑   **Interpret** data from the process to detect deviations from normal or desired behavior,

❑   **Predict** the future state of the system to identify developing emergency or alarm conditions,

❑   **Diagnose** the causes of malfunctions, and

❑   **Select** actions to correct the malfunctions or shut down the process until the malfunction can be corrected.

Monitoring and control tasks thus involve elements of several classification problem types. As a result, KBESs that address monitoring and control applications typically involve several discrete KBES subsystems that exchange data in some of the ways that we have discussed in Chapters 7 and 8. In this section and the next we will describe two systems that fall into this category. PLATFORM, described in Section 9.5, is a system designed to monitor and control construction projects. Guardian, described in Section 9.6, is a monitoring and control system for intensive care units.

The PLATFORM system was initiated to explore the potential of AI techniques in the domain of engineering project management [Levitt 1985]. Ideas from PLATFORM have subsequently found their way into a number of proprietary systems for factory scheduling.

9.5.1   Goals of the PLATFORM Project

Traditional network-based project planning tools provide computer support for the analysis of project plans and schedules that have been generated by human experts. Network-based tools such as CPM or PERT can represent and manipulate only the final result of the planning process, not the knowledge that went into generating the plan. Thus, as a project's status changes sufficiently to require replanning—this can be monthly, weekly, or even hourly for some kinds of projects—the same kinds of high-level expertise must be repeatedly applied to create meaningful revisions to the plan. Of course, the experts who possess this scarce planning knowledge typically become embroiled in day-to-day crises once the project is under way, so it is difficult or impossible for them to devote the needed time to replanning. Because of this dilemma, tools like CPM and PERT have proved valuable as decision support tools primarily during the early planning stages of projects and have tended to be used mainly for archival purposes once a project has commenced.

The goal of the PLATFORM project was to use KBES techniques to capture some of the knowledge employed by human planners during the planning stages of projects in order to use this knowledge again to support later planning iterations. Specifically, the project sought to use qualitative correlations among risk factors identified as having affected past performance to reforecast the durations of remaining activities on a project. PLATFORM was implemented using the KEE hybrid rule/frame/OOP KBES development tool.

9.5.2   Representation in PLATFORM

PLATFORM was implemented using frames to represent activities and risk factors that could affect their durations. Activity frames contain the same kinds of information about activities that might be stored in a PERT project database: description, optimistic duration, pessimistic duration, most likely duration, expected duration, actual duration, early and late start and finish times, and resources used.

Each activity frame inherits from its parent class, ACTIVITIES, the standard PERT procedure or method to compute its expected duration from (1) the user input values for most likely, optimistic, and pessimistic durations; and (2) a method written in OOP style to perform critical path calculations on the network by message passing.

The innovative aspect of PLATFORM was the inclusion of one other type of qualitative information not usable by conventional network analysis programs. Each activity frame has an attribute, RISK_FACTORS, whose value is a list of the risk factors that could affect the activity's duration. These are the names of frames, one for each risk factor which is a member of a class called RISK_FACTORS. RISK_FACTORS frames inherit the attribute ROLE, whose value is restricted to be (ONE_OF KNIGHT, VILLAIN, DRONE). A risk which has been determined (using the reasoning approach described in Section 9.5.3) to shorten completed activity durations is dubbed a KNIGHT; one which has been found to delay completed activity durations is dubbed a VILLAIN; and one with no identified effect remains at its default value of DRONE.

9.5.3 Reasoning in PLATFORM

Reasoning in PLATFORM is performed by just four rules containing variables which bind to activities and risk factors in the abstraction hierarchy. The four rules in PLATFORM are (1) identify KNIGHTS; (2) propagate KNIGHT effects to remaining activities, that is, revise their durations downward toward the optimistic duration; (3) identify VILLAINS; and (4) propagate VILLAIN effects by lengthening the durations of affected downstream activities.

The PROPAGATE_VILLAIN rule is shown in Figure 9-6 as an example. The other rules employ a similar syntax. (The reader may want to try and write them as an exercise.) First, note that clauses in this rule use the system's standard syntax (the ATTRIBUTE of OBJECT is VALUE). This allows the rule to read and write values from and to slots of frames. Second, note that the special KEE syntax (?X IS_IN_CLASS_Y) for a rule premise causes the rule to fire repeatedly with different variable bindings for ?X, one for each member of the class Y. This is how rule/frame integration can economize on the number of rules and simultaneously structure search in a KBES.

```
(RULE   (PROPAGATE_VILLAIN

(IF       ((?ACTIVITY IS IN CLASS ACTIVITIES)
          AND (THE COMPLETION_STATUS OF ?ACTIVITY IS
              INCOMPLETE)
          AND (A RISK_IMPACT OF ?ACTIVITY IS ?RISK_FACTOR)
          AND (THE ROLE OF ?RISK_FACTOR IS VILLAIN)
          AND (THE PESSIMISTIC_DURATION OF ?ACTIVITY IS
              ?DURATION))

THEN    (THE EXPECTED_DURATION OF ?ACTIVITY IS ?DURATION))))
```

Figure 9-6 The PROPAGATE_VILLAIN rule of PLATFORM [Levitt 1989a].

9.5.4 Control in PLATFORM

Control in the PLATFORM application is very simple. It combines strict ordering of goals to be tested with depth-first backward chaining in the set of production rules available to test the goals. The user is asked to confirm all hypotheses (for example, "Concrete productivity is believed to be a VILLAIN, because . . . Do you agree with this diagnosis?"). Thus the user is kept in the control loop in PLATFORM. The PLATFORM system was not designed to learn from these interactions. If the user disagrees with a conclusion, the conclusion is simply invalidated.

The conclusion of the PROPAGATE_KNIGHTS rule is established as the first goal. It chains backward to the rule for identifying KNIGHTS. If any KNIGHTS are found, the PROPAGATE_KNIGHTS rule's premises are satisfied, so it fires, shortening the durations of affected downstream activities. The conclusion of the PROPAGATE_VILLAIN rule is then invoked as a second goal. It works in a similar fashion, chaining back to the IDENTIFY_VILLAIN rule.

This ordering is deliberate: the expert whose knowledge was incorporated in PLATFORM thought that VILLAINS would vanquish KNIGHTS; that is, if any risk factor was exerting a lengthening effect on the duration of an activity, this would override the shortening effect of a KNIGHT. This seemed quite plausible to PLATFORM's developers and was incorporated into PLATFORM's reasoning by controlling the order in which rules fire.

9.5.5 Knowledge-Based Interactive Graphics in PLATFORM

Subsequent extensions focused on allowing the user to interact with the knowledge in PLATFORM, creating a powerful facility for interactive decision support which its developers dubbed **knowledge-based interactive graphics** [Levitt 1987b]. A live Gantt chart was created which allows the user to select and move activities around within their float windows, that is, the period from their earliest legal start to their latest legal finish. As activities are moved around in this live Gantt chart, demons perform several functions: they watch the start times of weather-sensitive activities, adjusting their durations as needed; they move successor or predecessor activity start times to maintain precedence constraints; and they revise resource usage histograms. The input and live output of this simulation by the user are portrayed graphically using demons to read and write active images. This kind of capability is available in a number of the high-end AI development tools.

Thus, in PLATFORM, KBES tools have been used to provide new kinds of graphic decision support for humans rather than to automate a task previously done by humans. The PRIDE and SightPlan systems, described in Chapter 10, are two more examples of using KBES technology for intelligent synergy of interactive graphics with the things that humans do best.

9.6   REAL-TIME MONITORING AND CONTROL: GUARDIAN

The last system that we will describe in this chapter is a KBES framework called Guardian that is being developed for intelligent, real-time monitoring and control applications [Hayes-RothB 1989]. Its first application was for monitoring patients in the intensive care unit of a hospital; ongoing work is extending its use to manufacturing automation and to process plant condition monitoring for maintenence planning.

9.6.1   Goals of the Guardian System

The Guardian framework is intended to be a high-level tool for implementing intelligent real-time monitoring and control applications for complex dynamic systems. Such applications cannot be implemented using control theory alone since direct mappings between sensor data and needed response actions are impossible to specify or compute algorithmically. For many engineering applications in manufacturing and project management, system behavior must be interpreted and predicted from sensed data; exceptional events must be diagnosed; and the system should react, respond, and plan ongoing events with appropriate levels of urgency, allocating available resources as it proceeds, both for computing and for suggested interventions.

9.6.2   Guardian's Architecture

Guardian is implemented as a blackboard system using the BB1 blackboard environment (see Section 8.3) for reasoning about control [Hayes-RothB 1985]. It contains several modules which exchange data asynchronously via a series of blackboards. An interesting feature of this system is that it is implemented on multiple networked Lisp machines which are in constant communication with one another, using an interrupt-driven protocol for doing so [Hayes-RothB 1987b].

9.6.3   Representation in Guardian

All objects and concepts which define the state of Guardian's problem and evolving solution, as well as the knowledge sources (akin to rules) and procedures which provide Guardian's intelligent behavior, are represented as frames within the BB1 architecture. These frames can be browsed and edited graphically as hierarchies with arbitrary links, including, but not limited to, the usual abstaction links for classes and instances. A number of separate blackboards are used to hold related groups of frames in global memory for inspection by domain and control knowledge sources that reason about their changing attribute values.

9.6.4 Reasoning in Guardian

Knowledge sources in Guardian perfom the following kinds of tasks, competing for execution by the scheduler on each cycle.

❑ **Data filtering.** Guardian currently handles up to 10 data readings per second from 20 sensors. Much of this data is unexceptional, and a system would be overloaded by attempting to analyze all of it. Yet random sampling might miss important trends in a very dynamic system. The data-filtering knowledge sources in Guardian continuously adjust both the sampling rates and the thresholds of attention for incoming data to support the system's ongoing monitoring and control reasoning.

❑ **Data abstraction.** Data are abstracted to identify significant events or changes in system behavior.

❑ **Problem identification.** Events or states of the system are heuristically associated with likely causes.

❑ **Causal reasoning about diagnosis.** Explicit structure/function models of several kinds of physical processes have been implemented within Guardian to confirm and supplement its heuristic reasoning capabilities. These follow the model-based reasoning paradigm discussed in Chapter 8 and employ explanatory graphics for Guardian's users. Modules of this type developed to date include ones for fluid flow (to model breathing) and diffusion (to model oxygen and carbon dioxide diffusion in the lungs). Although the initial applications for these causal models are in patient monitoring, they have been developed in the same layered style as the BB1 system so that their reasoning capabilities can easily be applied elsewhere, for example, to process plants or other kinds of systems.

❑ **Intervention planning.** Guardian identifies standard actions that should be taken to address commonly diagnosed problems using heuristics. The response-planning knowledge sources in Guardian are its least mature knowledge sources at the time of writing.

Since diagnosis is such an an integral part of monitoring and control, it is not surprising that the second, third, and fifth modules listed above correspond to the three steps in the heuristic classification model of diagnosis described in Section 9.2.1 [Clancey 1985].

9.6.5   Control in Guardian

Guardian uses the standard BB1 blackboard control architecture for its reasoning, although the many knowledge sources in Guardian and its use of multiple distributed processors add complications that are beyond the scope of this discussion.

As explained in Chapter 8, the blackboard paradigm permits multiple knowledge sources with specialized kinds of knowledge to collaborate by allowing all knowledge sources to read the blackboards containing current information about the state of the system, the evolving solution, and the strategy currently being pursued. Knowledge sources that can contribute to the evolving solution post recommended actions to an agenda, and a scheduler selects the one for execution in each cycle that best matches its current solution strategy. Guardian's problem-solving metaphor of task delegation to specialists—coupled with centralized control of decision making by a manager with a global perspective of the solution strategy—appears to provide a good fit for intelligent monitoring and control applications.

9.6.6   Status of Guardian

The fourth version of Guardian was implemented as a monitoring system for intensive care patients in 1989. The system is still being developed and is used together with a patient simulator which provides sensor data. The simulator will continue to be the primary development environment of the system for a variety of reasons, including practicality, cost, and the opportunity to study the effects of alternative control decisions. However, it is intended that Guardian will begin monitoring real patient data from a hospital during 1990. The Guardian system will be generalized to process plant and manufacturing automation applications during the early 1990s.

9.7   SUMMARY

In this chapter, we have presented a series of examples of KBES applications to classification problems. The example applications and the discussions of them were intended to serve two separate purposes: first, to ground the material on fundamentals (in Part I of the book) and on representation and reasoning paradigms (in Part II); and second, to serve as models and to provide guidelines for engineers planning to implement KBES applications of their own.

Classification applications represent a mature field for the application of KBES technology. They are generally straightforward in terms of inference structure, and currently available tools provide excellent development shells in which to prototype and refine applications efficiently. Thousands of applications of this type are already in routine use by organizations of all types and sizes, and many more are under development. Intelligent real-time monitoring and control applications that involve model-based diagnosis and data filtering for dynamic systems probably pose the most significant challenges for KBES among classification problems. However, even these appear to be yielding to generic architectures as systems like Guardian evolve toward generic frameworks.

Chapter 10

KNOWLEDGE-BASED SYSTEMS
FOR DESIGN

In this first of two chapters on applications of KBESs to formation tasks in engineering, we now turn to a discussion of design. This is perhaps one of the most challenging tasks performed by engineers. It is a task that requires both large amounts of domain-specific knowledge and considerable skill in solving problems. Thus, the potential for successfully applying KBES technology seems clear. Because design itself is an open-ended subject with no universally accepted definition or vocabulary, comprehensive KBES design applications are hard to develop. However, as we shall see, we can use the notions of representation, search, and deduction to effectively describe—and model within KBESs—many interesting and important design tasks.

10.1 ENGINEERING DESIGN: TAXONOMIES AND PRESCRIPTIONS

10.1.1 Definitions of Engineering Design

We have noted that there is no universally accepted definition of design. In fact, there are many, many definitions of design, and at a high enough level of abstraction, they sound very much alike. We shall mention only a few here. One definition is that design is a goal-directed activity, performed by humans, and subject to constraints. The product of this design activity is a plan by which goals are realized [Agogino 1988]. Another widely quoted definition seems more closely related to engineering concerns: the objective of the design activity is the production of a "... description of an artifice in terms of its organization and functioning—its interface between inner and outer environments" [Simon 1981].

There is one characteristic of engineering that distinguishes design in this domain from design in other domains. In some domains, such as graphics or type design, the designer actually produces the artifact directly. In engineering design, the end product is not, typically, an artifact; rather, it is a set of specifications for an artifact. This implies that a major aspect of engineering design is the development of ways to describe these specifications clearly, concisely, and unambiguously [Fenves 1988; Rehak 1988]. This tells us that representation is an important design issue, although perhaps with an emphasis on the translation of the original design objectives and constraints into some version of the specification language, and on the recognition that the specifications provide the starting point for a construction or fabrication process [Dym 1991b].

A definition of engineering design should also account for the fact that design is a cooperative human activity or process, with all that is thus entailed about context and language. At the same time, as noted above, design must focus on the idea that plans are going to be produced from which an artifact can be realized. Thus, a definition of engineering design must be broad enough to encompass a variety of concerns [Dixon 1988] but not so abstract as to have no obvious practical implementation. A definition of engineering design that includes—albeit somewhat implicitly— consideration of design as a process is taken from [Dym 1991b].

> Engineering design is the systematic, intelligent generation and evaluation of specifications for artifacts whose form and function achieve stated objectives and satisfy specified constraints.

This definition incorporates many assumptions whose expression we will see in the applications presented later in this chapter. Some of these assumptions include the following (see [Dym 1991b] for a more complete elaboration).

1. We can find a successful representation for both form and function, and we can compute—in terms of this representation—their interaction. Also, the original statement of a design problem, that is, its objectives and the applicable constraints, can be cast in terms of this representation.

2. We can find problem-solving techniques to exploit this representation to generate and enumerate design alternatives which can, in turn, be translated into a set of specifications for fabrication.

3. We can state criteria for evaluating designs in terms of the same representation used to generate and test design solutions.

We are saying here that representation is inherently and unavoidably involved in every part of the design process. From the original statement of a design problem, through its mapping and solution, to its specification and evaluation, the intended artifact must be described; it must be "talked about." Thus, representation is a key issue in our consideration of design.

Even if we were to agree on a single definition of design—whether one of the above or one of the countless others that appear in the literature—we would not be much closer to detailed understanding of what designers do, and especially that part of what designers do that can be encapsulated within a knowledge-based system. Thus, in the remainder of this section we shall try to describe the tasks of engineering design in a way that sets the stage for applying KBES technology to aid in the design process; characterize the process of design; outline the pieces of an organization or taxonomy of the field of design; and identify roles for computation—especially with KBESs—in design.

We also note in passing that it has been argued that the distinction between specifications and constraints is ephemeral [Simon 1975]. The distinction seems to depend on demarking those attributes of the designed artifact which we choose to optimize from those for which satisficing is acceptable (see Section 2.3.5). The former we term specifications, the latter constraints. Inasmuch as the distinction is maintained in most of the literature on design, we shall continue to use it in our own discussions.

Note that in carrying out the above agenda we are only scratching the surface of the discipline of design. We do not intend—nor are we capable of—a complete explication of the subject, so well discussed in so many other books and papers [Brown 1989; Cline 1990; Coyne 1990; Dixon 1986a, 1987b, 1988; Dym 1991b; Gero 1987; Levitt 1991; Lien 1987; Mittal 1986a, 1986b, 1987; Morjaria 1989; Mostow 1985; Pugh 1988; Rychener 1988; Simon 1981; Smithers 1989; Srinivasan 1989]. What we do intend here is a description sufficient to lay the foundation for some applications of expert systems to engineering design.

10.1.2 The Spectrum of Engineering Design Tasks

As we begin to look at descriptions of the design process, we will be able to recognize within them three generic tasks that are performed repeatedly—in an iterative fashion—within each of the various phases of the design process [Asimow 1962; Levitt 1991].

❑ **Synthesis.** The synthesis task consists of assembling a set of partial designs or primitive design elements into a configuration that clearly and obviously satisfies a few key specifications and constraints.

❑   **Analysis.** The analysis task is that of performing the calculations or deductions needed to assess whether the current synthesis—as reflected in its components and their attributes and relationships—satisfies other, less obvious specifications and constraints.

❑   **Evaluation.** The evaluation task consists of predicting the behavior of the current design synthesis—that is, deriving the values of all relevant performance measures—to determine whether, in terms of the stated design specifications and objectives, the current synthesis is acceptable. The statement that a given synthesis is unacceptable typically prompts a new synthesis aimed at correcting the unmet specifications or violated constraints.

We introduce these task descriptions now because they are ubiquitous within the different phases of design and because they provide a general statement about *what* we are actually doing when we design an artifact. These task definitions will form a useful backdrop for our discussions of taxonomies of design as well as for our descriptions of KBES applications (Sections 10.3–10.6).

10.1.3   A Taxonomy of Design: Routine versus Creative Design

We have now defined, at least tentatively, what we mean by design, and we have described the principal tasks of design. In so doing we have begun to identify some of the ways in which problem-solving strategies could be employed in the design process. Now we turn to outlining two taxonomies of design which allow us to classify design problems according to certain characteristics and, at the same time, facilitate the organization of the knowledge, reasoning, and representation schemes that might be useful in modeling different kinds of design. We believe that a more scientific theory of design cannot be developed without such a taxonomy [Dixon 1987b]. We note also that various taxonomies have been proposed (see, for example, [Dixon 1988]) and there is considerable overlap among them.

We will describe first a taxonomy that is based on asking whether a design is *routine* or whether it is *creative*. This classification, first proposed by Brown [1983], devolves into an assessment of the difficulty of generating design choices. This assessment is based in part on the completeness of the generating knowledge—especially as regards specificity of form, goals, and constraints—and the availability of the auxiliary knowledge required for testing. Another major factor in the assessment of design complexity has to do with the difficulty of controlling the search process [Brown 1989]. Before presenting the specifics of this taxonomy, we review some of the realities that motivate it.

We know that experience with previous attempts to design the same or similar artifacts allows an engineer to more quickly solve a problem. Some of this experience can be viewed as knowledge that relates some of the requirements to parts of the artifact that carry out those requirements. Similarly, past experience teaches us how to configure independent parts to achieve a desired overall behavior. Such cases involve relatively routine design in which the problem-solving task is largely a process of matching the requirements to previous attempts at meeting the same set of requirements. And while we might have to iterate over this process several times to arrive at an acceptable design, it is still a relatively simple task.

The design activity becomes more complex when the goal is an artifact that is markedly different from previous efforts, the number of alternatives to be considered is very large, or the artifact is completely new (truly creative design). These situations are typically characterized by large, complex design spaces. In some cases the space of possible designs may not even be clearly defined. Any attempt to enumerate the possible designs and then test them will therefore require a prohibitively long time. Thus, a more powerful problem solver is needed either to generate novel candidate solutions or to efficiently control the search through a large space of possible designs. In these situations, then, we would expect that knowledge—obtained from experience or a deeper understanding of the domain—plays an essential role in guiding a search of highly plausible design alternatives [Mittal 1986a]. Such expert knowledge may also be used to modify a design if some of the design choices turn out to be undesirable.

Three classes of design are identified in this taxonomy [Brown 1989].

Class 1: Creative design. Creative design is characterized by goals that are vaguely specified, a paucity of effective problem decompositions, and a scarcity of designs for subproblems. This kind of design requires considerable problem solving even in its auxiliary processes. Class 1 design is innovative, rare, and almost certainly not susceptible to encapsulation with current KBES technology—largely because we do not understand the origins or form of true creativity.

Class 2: Variant design. The distinguishing mark of Class 2 design is the availability of powerful decompositions. In such design, it is the modification or replacement of components that makes the design hard to complete. As a classic example, consider the continuous revisions in automobile design [Brown 1989]. The basics are still the same, but the individual components are certainly quite different—and much more complex—than their counterparts of even a decade ago.

Class 3: Routine design. In relatively routine design, we have effective problem decompositions, compiled plans for designing the components, and failure analysis information that can be usefully applied. Still, Class 3 problems require significant amounts of design domain knowledge because of complex interactions between subgoals and between components, as a consequence of which we must anticipate the complexities both of plan selection and ordering and of backtracking to undo failures. Thus, even in this "simple" class of routine design, there is more than ample scope for deploying design knowledge.

It is not surprising, given the above taxonomy, that most KBES applications in design have reflected attempts to build expert systems for carrying out Class 3 (routine) design tasks. We shall describe a few of these applications later in this chapter, but first we turn to another taxonomy of design, based on steps in the product life cycle.

10.1.4 The Design Process: Phases and Prescriptions

We have already noted that to describe design we must describe the artifact to be designed and, at the same time, we must look at the process itself. We will do so now, briefly, and we will see that from the analysis of the process there will emerge implications both for the architectures of design-oriented KBESs (as we anticipated in Chapter 8) and for the reasoning and representations used therein. And while our focus is on the process, we are beginning to discuss the specifics of engineering design tasks and their encapsulation within KBESs. Now, in describing the design process, we can identify several distinct stages [Levitt 1991; Rychener 1988], some of which are described in detail below.

Conceptual design is the most open-ended part of the design process, in which discussion is relatively abstract and the focus is on high-level tradeoffs between conflicting goals. In this stage the focus is much more strongly on the function of an artifact than on its form, except to the extent that those involved in the design process see the artifact as a variant or mutation of some known object. At this early stage, too, it is virtually impossible to predict how subsystems will interact, what subgoals might conflict, what options may have to be ruled out because of local conditions, and so on.

Conceptual design can be thought of in terms of knowledge-guided search of a large space of possible designs [Mittal 1986a]. Since the space is likely to be large and complex, we don't want to look for solutions in an ad hoc fashion; we may miss good solutions or, at best, take a very long time to find them. Knowledge from previous designs can be very useful in this process by suggesting solutions which worked well in the past or by quickly rejecting ones which failed in the past. KBESs may turn out to be a very suitable means for collecting and transferring this knowledge. The tireless nature of computers ensures that a piece of knowledge, once articulated, could be systematically used in all future designs. Thus, we may be able to do a more systematic, more complete, and faster search of the design space if we can bring to bear large amounts of domain-specific knowledge.

There are several general problem-solving strategies that are potentially applicable for conceptual design—indeed, for design in general. Perhaps the most generally applicable is the idea of **decomposition** or "divide and conquer" [Rich 1983]. The basic idea is self-evident; that is, if we can find a way to reduce a large problem into a set of smaller—and presumably easier—subproblems, we can usually facilitate the solution of the problem. Of course, in this process we will then have to keep in mind the interactions between the subproblems, and we have to monitor their individual solutions to ensure that they do not violate the assumptions or constraints of the other, complementary subproblems.

Another approach is to follow a strategy of **least commitment**, that is, to express component attributes only in terms of other component attributes—without specifying particular values—because the available data are both very abstract and very uncertain [Stefik 1982a]. Other important strategies include reasoning by analogy [Johnson 1988] and **case-based reasoning**, that is, examining prior cases from which lessons might be inferred [Howard 1989b] or from which acceptable design mutations might be drawn [Gero 1987].

This early part of the design cycle is also the one most likely to require negotiation between diverse stakeholders: manufacturing engineers versus financial specialists, marketing analysts versus quality control analysts, specialist designers—all must resolve perfomance goals and other tradeoffs. This points to the need for the high-level interaction of multiple

experts or sources of knowledge, both humans and computer programs—
perhaps through the blackboard and related architectures we described in
Chapter 8.

Preliminary design is the part of the process in which design proposals are
first "fleshed out"—that is, the time for hanging the meat of preliminary
choices upon the abstract bones of the conceptual design. Here we begin to
select and size the major subsystems on the basis of performance
specifications and the operating requirements. Thus, we begin here the
process of synthesis [Rychener 1988]. In so doing, we have begun to use—
even if only implicitly—the strategies of decomposition and of generate-
and-test.

This phase of the design process makes extensive use of rules of thumb that
reflect the designer's experience. For example, in the design of a chemical
process plant, the designer puts together a preliminary block flow diagram
that reflects the different technologies (drying, catalysis, etc.) that will be
used to transform the feedstock into the desired output [Lien 1987]. In
preparing the rough flow diagram, the designer may use various estimates,
back-of-the-envelope calculations, and algorithms, as well as rules about
size, efficiency, and so on. The resulting rough design represents a
synthesis of the parts and processes required to achieve the desired goals.

In doing preliminary design we are concerned first with generating
candidate solutions and then with testing or evaluating them [Dym 1985a;
Stefik 1982a]. The testing is largely directed at ensuring conformance with
design objectives and applicable constraints. The evaluation would most
likely be focused on rank ordering preliminary designs against some
metric—for example, cost—that supports a choice among satisficing
designs. Thus, in terms of reasoning and representation, a common
strategy is generate-and-test, although we must guard against a
combinatorial explosion of candidate designs. We must also work to
narrow the search space or, as we described it in our discussion of search in
Chapter 2, prune the search tree. Strategies for doing this include
hierarchical pruning and constraint propagation.

In preliminary design we also see more clearly the interaction of subsystems
whose interdependent behavior is vital to successful design. When teams of
people are collaborating on preliminary design tasks, they often try to
achieve successful coordination with frequent meetings of the designers of
individual components and subsystems [Levitt 1991]. However, as
experience with the PRIDE project has indicated (see Section 10.3), an
automated designer's assistant provides a very efficient mechanism for

allowing subsystem designers to check on conformity with and satisfaction of subsystem interaction constraints. In this respect, we can also envisage an increasing role for the CDPS architectures we described in Chapter 8: we can model a collection of subsystem designers as a network of semi-autonomous agents who must interact to achieve a global goal without perfect knowledge of each other's requirements and resources.

In **detailed design** the concern shifts to refinement of the choices made in preliminary design. Here the early choices are articulated in much greater detail, typically down to specific part types and numbers. This phase of design is procedural in nature, and much of the relevant knowledge is expressed in rather specific rules as well as in formulas, handbooks, algorithms, databases, and catalogs. In fact, detailed design also becomes increasingly decentralized—that is, left almost completely to the component specialists—as the design comes closer and closer to being an assemblage of standard components.

Detailed design could be characterized as procedural in flavor. This is because we are, by now, fairly far down in the design search tree. The decompositions and their interactions are well understood and easily manageable. Consequently, detailed design is very rule-intensive in terms of its application of heuristic domain knowledge. Because these heuristics derive in large part from design codes or manuals which reflect local experience, we should expect that much of the knowledge applied can be traced to an institutionalized understanding of past failures, either of individual subsystems or of interactions among them. Dysfunctional behavior often occurs in this context because there is a strong temptation to discard a solution that previously has failed, even if it failed for a reason that no longer holds!

In the **analysis and optimization** stage of the design process, we focus on verifying and evaluating all aspects of a design [Rychener 1988]. This phase is almost entirely algorithmic, even though it is typically computationally intensive; the role for symbolic computation is most likely limited to decision support, especially as it pertains to the intelligent use of large, complex algorithmic programs (e.g., large-scale FEM packages). We address elsewhere the issue of weaving together KBES technology and algorithmic or graphics computing (see Sections 8.1, 8.2, and 10.1.5).

Documentation and detailed project planning is another phase of design with which we shall not really concern ourselves here, although we shall have occasion in Section 10.5 and Chapter 11 to discuss some KBES work on documentation and project management.

10.1.5 An Information-Processing Model of Design

The overview of the design process just presented is not the only process-oriented model of design. An alternative, information-processing model has been suggested in which design tasks and subtasks are proposed and analyzed in terms of the information they use [Brown 1989]. This particular view is important because it helps us refine the prescriptions for modeling various aspects of design with KBES techniques. In information-processing assessment, two basic processes are noted, somewhat analogous to the division between *generate* and *test*. The first set of processes consists of those that *propose* design choices. The second is the collection of *auxiliary* processes that *provide information* in support of generating or testing a design choice or commitment. These two sets of processes can then be further delineated as follows. (See Brown [1989], whose discussion we follow here, for further details.)

Processes that propose design commitments. There are four basic information processes that are used to generate choices or commitments to design specifics.

❑ **Decomposition.** As we have already noted, decomposition is ubiquitous in design. The basic idea is to reduce a large problem into a set of smaller subproblems. These subproblems are, in turn, such that previously compiled solutions are already known, or else they require searches of much smaller solution spaces. Reasoning will be required both for the decomposition/recomposition process and for solving the individual subproblems. In the latter case, the ideas of constraint posting have been found to be quite effective [Stefik 1981a].

❑ **Design planning.** Design is viewed through the prism of setting out a plan of steps to be taken to produce the specifications for an artifact. These plan steps may be set out in terms of goals to be achieved (see, for example, the discussion of PRIDE in Section 10.3) or in terms of the parts or components of the artifact. The reasoning may be characterized as **instantiate and expand**—that is, specify particular goals or parts as the plan unfolds.

❑ **Design modification.** Here we explicitly recognize the existence of libraries of previous designs that we can modify to meet current goals and constraints. The reasoning involves matching, critiquing, and modifying previous designs. Thus, we need to have criteria for choosing those designs which seem closest to the current problem, perhaps reasoning by means-ends analysis (see Section 2.3). And we need to be able to assess both why an old design fails to meet current needs and what to modify so that the old design can be adapted.

❑ **Constraint processing.** If the structure of the artifact is known and the design process can be reduced to the selection of variable and parameter values, then the processing of constraints becomes a viable tool for design. This is sometimes done algorithmically because there is enough structure to the problem to make numerical modeling approaches such as optimization useful. Constraint processing can be combined with heuristic reasoning in order to expand the solution space of overconstrained problems [Chan 1987] or to reduce the number of feasible solutions in underconstrained problems [Maher 1984a; Levitt 1989b].

Processes that provide auxiliary information.   Again we can identify four basic types of information processing [Brown 1989].

❑ **Subproblem goal and constraint generation.** The issue here is the translation and reification of high-level goals and constraints into more detailed versions appropriate to the subproblems of the original decomposition. Again, the idea of constraint posting could be quite effective here.

❑ **Recomposition.** This is the process of assembling the subproblem solutions into the coherent solution to the overall problem. The kind of information required might be explanatory in nature, that is, concerned with explaining how the pieces fit together.

❑ **Design verification.** This is the test part of the cycle, wherein we verify that the design meets goals and constraints. This portion is often algorithmic in nature, although qualitative considerations do occasionally enter.

❑ **Design criticism.** The information required here is that pertaining to identifying failures and suggesting modifications to overcome them. We shall describe an analyze/advise/modify cycle in our discussion of PRIDE (see Section 10.3).

It is worth observing, as regards the above model of information processing in design, that the auxiliary information processes are not unique to design; rather, they are fairly typical problem-solving skills that can be—and are—equally well invoked in analysis problems. However, the processes involved in generating design choices are rather unique to design, where the idea is to create an artifact or specifications for an artifact. It is this recognition that sets the stage for outlining an integrated taxonomy of design.

10.2 KBES-BASED APPROACHES TO ENGINEERING DESIGN

In Chapter 1 we drew a distinction between classification and formation problems and asserted that design is a formation problem, that is, one for which unique solutions have to be formed rather than selected from a menu of predefined solutions. A closer look at the tasks of design (as well as the descriptions of the design process and the taxonomies already presented) shows that this may be an oversimplified assertion. Humans clearly have trouble generating—on demand—creative new solutions for complex, open-ended problems. Design would be difficult to do, therefore, if it involved the continuous formation of unique solutions. In fact, design tasks at every stage—conceptual, preliminary, and detailed—often involve a style of problem solving that combines elements of both selection and formation.

In Section 10.1.2 we identified three engineering design tasks: synthesis, analysis, and evaluation. Of these three design tasks, synthesis comes closest to being a formation task, although it can very often be seen as a series of selection tasks done in some specific order. In Section 10.1.5 we presented a taxonomy of AI search prescriptions in which we identified the potential or demonstrated applicability of these search techniques to the various classes and phases of design. Thus, as we proceed to explore the use of KBES techniques in design, we must recognize the importance of (1) synthesis as a task which can be implemented through selection, and (2) applying appropriate search techniques. In this light we now suggest solution methods for various classes of design.

10.2.1 Solution Methods for Design Problems

As noted, many kinds of design synthesis can be viewed as a series of selection tasks applied in a specific sequence. The following approaches to a synthesis task show that design can range from pure selection to pure formation. This section describes several approaches from a taxonomy of methods for solving arrangement problems [Hayes-RothB 1987c]. We present this abstraction of that taxonomy in increasing order of specificity to parallel the creative versus routine taxonomy outlined in Section 10.1.

Analogy and mutation. We have already noted that generating syntheses for truly unique products—that is, products which are not assembled from libraries of elementary components in relatively standard ways—is quite difficult. While we can point to some recent research attempts to employ cognitive processes such as analogy [Carbonell 1986; Dyer 1986; Johnson 1988] and mutation [Lenat 1982] to generate truly innovative designs using computers, creative design is still largely the province of human designers. Case-based and analogic reasoning have been applied, respectively, in the RESTCOM system [Howard 1989b] and the TRANALOGY system [Johnson 1988]. This is an area where there is more potential than demonstrated applicability.

Assembling unique solutions from elementary components. This approach is used for design problems whose solutions are too different from one another to use protoypes economically. In such problems, solutions must be assembled from elementary components—or in some cases, literally formed from bulk materials—to achieve a synthesis that satisfies all goals and constraints at some level of acceptance. This type of synthesis is complicated by the fact that the attributes of the elementary components invariably interact with one another in significant ways—not only geometrically, but also functionally—so that there are numerous constraints to be satisfied among the components themselves. The assembly approach to design requires knowledge of all elementary components and their attributes, including their behavior (to simulate system performance) and their constraints with respect to other components. Reasoning about assembly design tasks typically involves some form of constraint propagation and satisfaction. Systems to aid in this type of design have recently emerged from the research environment into practice. They can be implemented with logic programming techniques such as Prolog [Chan 1987]; production rules [McDermottJ 1981]; or high-level OOP tools such as those described in Section 10.5, where we outline the Intelligent Boiler Design System (IBDS) [Riitahuhta 1988]. This approach is feasible for both the preliminary and detailed stages of engineering design for semicustom products.

Hierarchical generation, testing, elimination, and evaluation of solutions. This approach to design, which can also be used for prototype refinement, is exemplified by HI-RISE [Maher 1984a]. It involves generating all possible solutions at some relatively high level of abstraction, heuristically eliminating most of them, generating all solutions at the next level of abstraction for those that survive the first elimination, and so on. Finally, all surviving solutions are ranked using a set of evaluation criteria. This approach employs less search than pure selection (see below), since the solution space is progressively pruned so that it explores only a small number of branches after the first level of the search tree. However, it does require a hierarchically decomposable problem and knowledge of heuristic elimination rules. The most notable example of success with heuristic selection is the R1/XCON system used to configure VAX systems at the Digital Equipment Corporation [McDermott] 1981; Barker 1989]. Constraint-based approaches have been applied in PRIDE [Mittal 1986a]; SightPlan [Levitt 1989b]; and Molgen [Stefik 1981a, 1981b]. (We discuss both PRIDE and SightPlan later in this chapter.) The generation, testing, and elimination parts of this process can be implemented with production rules alone, albeit with difficulty. A frame-based representation can help to control the search and to propagate component behavior. The evaluation part of this process is easily handled by using an inference net approach to rate and weight subjective criteria. The HI-RISE system for preliminary structural design is an exemplar of a hierarchical generate, test, and evaluate system [Maher 1984a]. Both PRIDE and Molgen contain elements of hierarchical generate, test, and evaluate procedures.

Prototype selection and refinement (diagnosis and repair). The idea that prototypes are the very stuff of design has been forcefully argued by several researchers, including Friedland [1985] and Gero [1987]. In many kinds of semicustom design, designers have available to them a library of prototype solutions which can serve as starting points for a solution to a new design problem. If there are heuristics for selecting an initial prototype solution which allow us to abstract given problems to classes of design problems for which solutions—or at least solution strategies—might apply, we call this approach **case-based design**. Having selected a good candidate as a prototype solution, we can then test a series of attributes of the candidate design solution and modify those that fail to meet the imposed constraints. We can do this by using either an exhaustive search or a hierarchical search which checks conformity with specifications at a high level of abstraction before exploring more detailed reasons for failure to comply. This approach requires (1) a library of prototype solutions, together with heuristics for selecting one to use as a starting point; and (2) rules or methods for consistency checking of prototype attributes and for component substitution or modification to address failures. Prototype refinement is a form of diagnosis and repair and can be implemented with rules, although frames provide additional power. This approach is feasible at any stage of the design of relatively standard products.

Pure selection. This involves satisfying the imposed constraints by selecting an arrangement (or synthesis) from an already enumerated set of alternatives. An example of this would be choosing an oxygen supply system for a process plant from a set of standard vendor-supplied system configurations to meet a set of imposed capacity, purity, pressure, safety, and reliability requirements. This approach requires knowledge of all—or many—alternatives, including the values of those attributes of each alternative which are needed to check whether that alternative meets the imposed specifications.   It requires a great deal of search—the entire solution space must be covered—and a great deal of testing. It is feasible for selection of standard components or subsystems in the detailed design stage of semicustom products, and it can be incorporated into any CADD system that can interface with production rules. For this class of design problems, the role of heuristic selection is self-evident.

10.2.2   Roles for Knowledge-Based Tools in Engineering Design

The foregoing discussion suggests that there is sufficient scope for interesting engineering design applications of KBES techniques. Most of the work has been on systems to perform—or assist in the performance of— routine design. It is worth mentioning some of the pioneering work here. One of the earliest KBES projects related to design was the R1/XCON project, which was a rule-based system to configure VAX systems in accord with customer requirements [McDermottJ 1984; Barker 1989]. In fact, this system is often cited as one of the premier KBES success stories and is now viewed as the pioneering configuration system (see Section 10.3). Another early KBES project suggested an architecture for doing mechanical design which was applied to standard V-belt drive design [Dixon 1984]. That model was based on the observation that in some routine design tasks one can perform a complete preliminary design, evaluate it, and then iterate this process if the evaluation is not satisfactory. This approach, which is essentially generate-and-test, would be computationally intractable on any but the simplest design tasks because even the smallest failure in a design leads to discarding the entire design and starting from scratch. Another system based on the generate-and-test paradigm is the HI-RISE system for doing the preliminary structural design of high-rise buildings [Maher 1984a]. A more powerful model for handling these kinds of designs addressed questions about how to represent knowledge about routine designs in terms of formulating design plans, selecting between these plans, and managing the design modification process [Brown 1983]. The PRIDE system that we discuss in Section 10.3 was a pioneering design system that moved in the direction of nonroutine design, in which a complex configuration task was modeled [Mittal 1986a].

Now, given the diversity and complexity of the design tasks performed by engineers, we can expect multiple roles for knowledge-based tools in the spectrum of design tasks. We have discussed some of these roles elsewhere in the book (see Chapter 1 and especially Chapter 8), but it is useful to list some other roles with particular reference to engineering design [Mittal 1986a].

Integration with analysis tools. Once a candidate design (partial or complete) has been identified, we often perform a detailed analysis to determine whether performance constraints and goals are satisfied. However, the analysis techniques are not always known or accessible to an engineer. For example, analysis techniques such as finite element methods are implemented as large programs which are not always easy to apply. Knowledge-based analysis tools can be used as expert design checkers. A step in this direction was the SACON system for providing consultation on the use of the MARC package [Bennett 1978]. One can go beyond providing an interface to an analysis package by integrating design and analysis knowledge in the same knowledge base. A key benefit of this integration is that designs can be systematically checked at each stage instead of at the end. Furthermore, the reasons for the failure of the evolving design, as determined by specific analyses, can be used to provide pointers toward ways to modify and fix the design solution developed thus far, thus obviating the need to start over.

Collaborative design. Another important aspect of the design activity is its communal nature. Real-world complex systems are often designed by a team of engineers. One aspect of the team effort is the decomposition of a complex system into smaller subsystems. However, the designs are not carried out in isolation. Often, an engineer who is unable to meet his or her performance requirements negotiates with engineers designing interfacing modules in an attempt to relax the requirements. Thus, engineers have to engage in exploring choices and balancing different sets of constraints. We have suggested some architectures for addressing these concurrent design issues in Chapter 8.

Community knowledge bases. Another aspect of team effort is the distribution of expertise among the team members. For example, in the early knowledge acquisition phase of the PRIDE project it was found that different engineers often had specialized knowledge about specific subtasks (see Chapter 12 and [Mittal 1985]). Knowledge-based systems provide an opportunity to bring the expertise from many different specialists together. In effect, one could create a community knowledge base which has more expertise than any single expert [Mittal 1984, 1985; Stefik 1986]. Clearly, much work remains to be done before this vision can be realized. Indeed, one of the motivations for the PRIDE project was the establishment of such a community knowledge base that could be expanded over time, and shared across the company [Mittal 1986a].

10.3 CONFIGURATION: THE PRIDE SYSTEM

In this section we describe a knowledge-based system called PRIDE for the design of paper-handling systems inside copiers and duplicators. The PRIDE system uses a large knowledge base which explicitly describes the different elements of design knowledge, such as what steps to perform, dependencies between them, how to carry them out, constraints on the solutions, analyses for testing the solutions, and advice on modifying the design when the requirements are not satisfied. A prototype version of the system was successfully tested on real design problems, and PRIDE is now in routine use as a designer's assistant. The description of PRIDE presented here is adapted from [Mittal 1986a].

10.3.1 PRIDE: A Sophisticated Configuration System

A paper copier has several paper-handling systems, such as paper transports or paper feeders which move paper from one part of a copier to another. The PRIDE system focuses on one kind of paper transport, namely, the kind that uses pinch rolls to move the paper (as opposed to using belts, say). A paper transport must meet a large set of requirements. These include geometric properties, such as input (paper entrance) and output (paper exit) locations and angles (see Figure 10-1); paper properties, including size, weight, stiffness, and curl; timing requirements and constraints, including entrance and exit speeds; and permissible skew. There may also be constraints on the tolerances of various engineering parameters, cost, and so on. Many other requirements may be optionally imposed, depending on the interfacing systems.

Design of a paper transport can be typically decomposed into subproblems, such as designing a smooth path between the input and output locations; deciding the number and location of pinch roll stations to be placed along this path; designing a "baffle" to be placed around the paper path to guide the paper; designing the sizes of various pinch rolls (drivers and idlers); selecting the proper materials for the pinch rolls and baffle; making decisions about velocities and forces; calculating the time needed to move the various sizes of paper; and calculating the various performance parameters and ensuring that they satisfy the requirements.

Typically it takes a trained engineer many weeks to completely design a paper transport. One reason is the sheer diversity of the task: it involves making decisions about geometry, spatial layout, timing, forces, jam clearance, and so on. Rarely does a single engineer know enough to make all of the design choices and analyses; collaboration with other specialists is

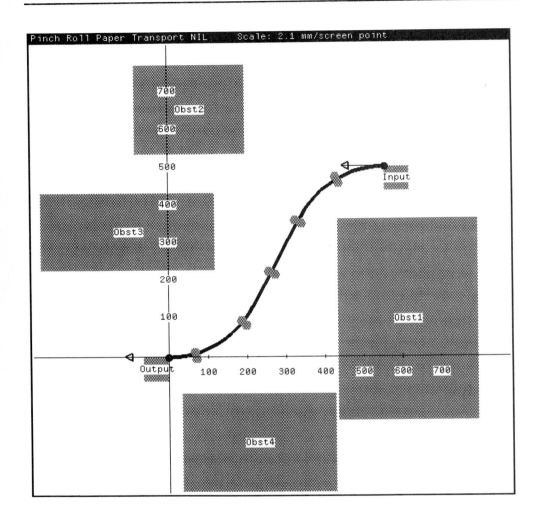

Figure 10-1 A stylized view of the paper path design problem in PRIDE as seen in the user interface [Mittal 1986a; Morjaria 1985]. Shown are the input and output locations and angles, various obstructions that must be avoided, the path drawn, and the positions of roll stations.

essential. The same transport has to be able to handle different sizes and weights of paper—often presenting conflicting constraints. For example, if the lengths (or widths) of the different sizes of paper are far apart, then the constraint on the maximum separation of neighboring roll stations for the smallest paper conflicts with the constraint on not having more than two stations guiding the paper for the longer papers. The design of the paper path is complicated by the presence of obstructions which have to be avoided and strict requirements on the smoothness, continuity, and manufacturability of the baffle, which takes the shape of the paper path [Morjaria 1985]. There are tight constraints related to buckling and stubbing of the paper, which affect the design of the baffle, the pinch rolls, the paper path, and the velocities. The subproblem of deciding the number and location of roll stations to be placed along the paper path to guide the paper is again a constraint-driven problem with a large search space [Mittal 1986c].

10.3.2   The Origins of PRIDE

The PRIDE project was originally undertaken (in early 1984) as a demonstration of technology transfer, that is, with the intent of showing that KBES technology could play a useful role in helping perform complex engineering tasks. The issues included demonstrating that the technology itself could make a contribution and that it could be ported into an engineering environment. It was also a project for which there were ample intellectual reasons to be involved. It concerned elements of nonroutine design in a very large design space defined by many variables—some continuous, some discrete; some found from analytical formulas, some modeled numerically—and dozens of parameters. Thus, it would clearly require serious AI research on the role of automated guided search in a complex domain.

One of the most critical parts of any KBES project is knowledge acquisition. This is the process whereby detailed knowledge is acquired from the domain experts for representation in a knowledge base inside the computer. Another interesting aspect of the PRIDE project was that it produced an unusual—if somewhat informal—study of the roles of multiple experts in the knowledge acquisition phase. We detail the PRIDE knowledge acquisition process in Section 12.4 (see also [Mittal 1985, 1986a]).

10.3.3   Architecture of PRIDE

PRIDE is an expert system in the traditional sense because its knowledge base contains the same knowledge that an expert engineer uses in designing paper-handling systems. However, unlike the case in a typical expert system, the knowledge base is not manipulated by a single, uniform inference mechanism such as backward or forward chaining of production rules. As we describe in Section 10.3.4, the knowledge base contains objects (represented as frames) which are organized into well-defined classes with appropriate protocols of behavior. In simple terms, one can think of each class of objects as following a separate problem-solving protocol.

A design session in PRIDE starts with the specification of a new design problem or the selection of a previously stored problem. The PRIDE problem solver uses the knowledge base to develop a paper transport. The problem solver can be thought of as following a generate-test-analyze-advise-modify paradigm. The knowledge base defines a plan for the steps to be carried out in a design. Each step describes both how to refine the design further and how to verify that the design is progressing along in a satisfactory direction based on the analysis applicable so far.

Whenever the design runs into trouble—that is, when some requirement is not satisfied—the problem solver analyzes the current partial design and tries to come up with suggestions to overcome the violations. PRIDE invokes two complementary methods for modifying a partial design in response to problems encountered at later stages. The first is heuristic, capturing designer's prior experience in fixing similar problems. These heuristics encode knowledge about how to change the design in response to various constraint violations. This seems to be sufficient for many routine design problems. The second method is based on a more general problem-solving approach which uses dependencies between the different parts of a design and the problem solver's ability to analyze the design knowledge to suggest modifications that go beyond the knowledge directly represented in PRIDE's knowledge base.

PRIDE also has the capability for maintaining multiple designs simultaneously and for switching between different partial designs [Mittal 1986b]. Thus, designers (or the system) can explore different options in parallel. A designer can also selectively undo a design or impose additional constraints. These exploratory capabilities and the ability to critique designs and suggest modifications allow PRIDE to act as a designer's assistant. It seems likely that design engineers working in conjunction with systems such as PRIDE can often find suitable designs faster than either a KBES or an engineer could have working alone.

10.3.4   Representation Issues in PRIDE

The knowledge base in PRIDE is structured as a generalized design plan. The plan defines the design space and provides guidance on how to carry out the design. The elements of a plan are the steps to be carried out, coupled with information about ordering the steps, how to perform each step, how to detect failures in the design requirements, and suggestions for fixing the failures. The plan is generalized because all designs in PRIDE are obtained from the same plan when executed for a different set of requirements.

A plan is structured around design goals which decompose the process of design into simpler steps. Thus, there is a top-level goal in the knowledge base for designing the paper transport as well as goals for subproblems such as deciding the number of roll stations, deciding the diameter of the driver at a particular station, and designing the baffle gap. Figure 10-2 shows the top-level design goals in a goal browser. As the design is carried out, more goals are added to the browser, reflecting a sort of top-down structure of the design plan. A **design goal**, as represented in PRIDE, is both a description of some part of the overall design and a concept around which knowledge is organized. Each design goal is responsible for designing (and redesigning) a small set of design parameters which describe some part or aspect of the artifact being designed. In the domain of paper transports, some of the design parameters are paper path segments; paper path length; number of roll stations; diameter, width, and material of each pinch roll; baffle gap; baffle material; and time taken by each size of paper during transport. All the alternative ways for making a decision about a design parameter are attached to the same goal. Such decision-making knowledge is encoded in design methods. Similarly, the knowledge for verifying that the solution is indeed acceptable at this stage in design is attached to the goal in design constraints. It is useful, therefore, to think of a design goal as a small, autonomous specialist, similar in many ways to the notion of a design specialist [Brown 1985].

Figure 10-3 shows a simplified representation of the goal for deciding the number and location of roll stations. In the rest of this section we will briefly describe some of the elements in representing a goal. Variables such as descriptor and name are used to describe the goal to the human users; designMethods is an ordered list of alternative methods for achieving the goal. In this example there is only a single method, which specifies that the way to carry out this goal is to achieve four subgoals. These subgoals are represented the same way, allowing a recursively nested plan. Notice that in this example, the method for carrying out the goal is itself a plan. However, there are many other kinds of methods, described later, which directly specify how to make decisions about the design parameters of the associated goal.

A **design method** specifies how to carry out a goal. The representation of design methods is crucial to the problem-solving ability of PRIDE because

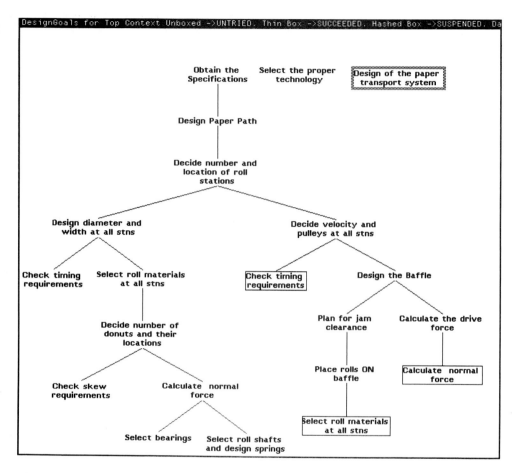

Figure 10-2 A snapshot of the goal browser when the design has just begun, showing the top-level goal and some of its immediate subgoals [Mittal 1986a]. The lines connecting the subgoals indicate some of the dependencies between the subgoals. The dependencies are automatically computed by the system on the basis of descriptions contained in the goals.

they not only specify how to perform one design; they collectively specify all possible designs. Thus their representation is designed to serve multiple purposes. Here we provide only a brief description (see [Mittal 1986a] for further details). Ideally, one would like each design method to specify the parameters (design variables) which will be assigned new values by it; any extra preconditions before the method can be run; how to generate a

type	SimpleGoal
name	Goal5
descriptor	"Decide number and location of roll stations"
status	INIT
anteGoals	"Design Paper Path"
inputPara	"PaperPath", "length of PaperPath"
outputPara	"Number of RollStations", "location of AllRolls"
designMethods	(SubGoals
	Goal51: "Decide min number of rollStns"
	Goal52: "Decide Abstract Placing"
	Goal53: "Generate Concrete Location"
	Goal54: "Build RollStn Structure")
constraints	(Constr8: "First Stn <= 100 mm."
	Constr17: "Dist. between adj. stn <= 160mm."
	. . .
	Constr24: "Dist. between adj. stn >= 50mm.")

Figure 10-3 Simplified representation of the goal Decide number and location of roll stations [Mittal 1986a]. This goal has only one method, which decomposes the goal into four subgoals. For simplicity we have directly shown the subgoals, even though they are embedded inside a design sequence method object. This goal has associated with it many other objects, such as Constr8, Constr17, and Goal51, each of which has its own structure and behavior.

suitable value the first time; how to revise the value at future times; what the value depends on; and so on. Unfortunately, not every design parameter can be designed in this fashion. Some parts of the design need very complex calculations that cannot be represented in such a declarative fashion. Others may need a complex procedure to be followed. Yet others may need the user to interact with the system to arrive at some suitable design (see [Morjaria 1985] for more on the need for interactive design). In recognition of this diversity in knowledge for carrying out design, PRIDE provides different kinds of design methods. These follow a common minimum protocol which allows them to interact with the attached design goals. We shall illustrate the different kinds of design methods by way of examples.

The most powerful design methods from the point of view of capturing many design alternatives are the **design generators**, which are all capable of generating different values for the same (or a small set of related) design parameter(s). These methods allow the incorporation of heuristic knowledge for making a "good" guess about the initial value to be generated. They also specify the ranges of possible values and increments. Figure 10-4 shows a design generator for the goal Design driver diameter, which generates diameters for the drivers from a database of acceptable driver diameters. This type of generator belongs to the class InstanceSetGenerator because the database is represented as instances of different classes of objects. The generated objects here are instances of DriverDiameter. The method also specifies that a good starting value is a diameter of 10 millimeters because the experts have found this to be a good default choice. Finally, it specifies that this instance object becomes the value of the design parameter DriverDiameter.

---

type	InstanceSetGenerator
name	SetGen1
descriptor	"Generate standard driver diameters"
assignTo	(DesignObject defRollPair driver diameter)
initValue	"Find a diameter of 10mm"
classes	DriverDiameter
soFar	NIL
status	INIT

Figure 10-4 A simplified description of a method for generating the driver diameter by looking up a database of standard diameters [Mittal 1986a].

Constraints is a list of design constraints which must be satisfied for the goal to be successful (see Figure 10-3). In this example there are many different constraints, each encoding some requirement on the placement of the roll stations along the paper path. Finally, there are three variables—anteGoals, inputPara, and outputPara—which are used to relate this goal to other goals and to the object being designed. Direct dependencies between goals are represented via anteGoals (antecedent goals). Thus, because we know that the decision about roll placement can be made only after designing the paper path, we make the former depend on the latter. The problem solver ensures that a goal will not be executed unless its antecedent conditions (which include anteGoals and inputPara) are satisfied. The variables inputPara and outputPara are used to describe the input and output behavior of a goal with respect to the artifact being designed. Thus, inputPara describes parts of a paper transport which should be designed prior to attempting this goal. In Figure 10-3, the input design parameters are the PaperPath and length of PaperPath. The outputPara describe the parts of the design carried out by this goal. In Figure 10-3, the output design parameters are the Number of RollStations, location of AllRolls, and the actual objects representing each roll station. In many cases the dependency information cannot be expressed statically but needs to be computed dynamically. For example, depending on the actual design method which is tried, the design decisions at a goal may depend on different sets of design parameters. The PRIDE representation allows dependencies to be expressed in different ways.

Sometimes the same basic design steps have to be repeated, once for each member of a set of similar objects. For example, the design goals for designing different aspects of roll stations (widths, diameters, materials, velocities, skew, and so on) contain the same (possibly parameterized) knowledge which then is copied for each roll station. These goals are represented as **macrogoals** which when executed expand into a set of subgoals, one for each of the enumerated objects. A macrogoal is defined by an abstractGoal (the goal being copied) and an enumeration expression.

In some cases, the knowledge for making design decisions requires matching some set of conditions and can be more easily expressed as a set of rules. The **design rule group** is a representation for such knowledge. A rule group contains a set of rules and some control description, such as FIRST (stop at the first rule whose conditions are satisfied) or ALL (execute all rules whose conditions are satisfied). Each rule is a set of conditions followed by actions which are themselves design methods. Thus, the actual design knowledge is ultimately contained in other kinds of methods, with the rule methods providing some extra control information on which methods to use. Note that this representation explicitly separates the knowledge about the different ways to make the design decisions (encoded as the methods in the action part) from the control knowledge for selecting from these alternatives (encoded in the condition part). This allows advice to be sent to the relevant methods even though the method capable of responding may be embedded inside more than one level of control. Also, note that since the action part of a rule can be any method, one can nest rule groups inside other rules and rule groups, allowing knowledge to be more easily shared. Figure 10-5 shows the rule group for deciding on the number of roll pairs at each station.

type	DesignRuleGroup
name	RuleG1
descriptor	"Decide number of roll pairs per station"
control	FIRST
rules	(Rule1 Rule2 Rule3 Rule4)
status	INIT

Figure 10-5 Description of the rule group for deciding the number of roll pairs for each station [Mittal 1986a]. This rule group is run separately for each station.

So far we have talked about decomposing a complex design step into simpler design steps without describing the mechanism in PRIDE for representing such decomposition. Decomposition of a goal into subgoals is handled by the use of a design sequence method which says, in effect, that the way to perform this goal is to execute a set of subgoals. In other words, goals do not have subgoals directly. The only way to decompose a goal into subgoals is to embed the subgoals inside a design sequence method and make this be one of the methods of the goal. This method only specifies a default sequence on the subgoals it contains. The actual order is computed by the problem solver on the basis of the inputPara and anteGoals, as discussed above. One consequence of embedding subgoals inside a method is that it becomes possible to easily specify alternative sets of subgoals for carrying out the same goal or to have alternative ways of performing some goal, only some of which involve decomposition into subgoals.

Some of the other kinds of design methods allowed in PRIDE are **calculations** (calculating a value from other sets of values) and **procedures** (some closed piece of Lisp code which cannot be reasoned about). The latter make a sort of escape valve in the representation in the sense that they allow escape to the full power of Lisp in a still somewhat principled way. Thus, even though the design of the paper path requires a large and complex piece of Lisp code, it can still be reasoned about to some extent and used in a principled way by encapsulating it inside a design procedure. For example, the system can reexecute this procedure with some advice if the paper path needs to be modified or it can wait till the procedure is complete before continuing.

The design methods are responsible only for suggesting a plausible design, which is not necessarily the best or even a correct one. The knowledge about testing and validating a proposed solution is contained in the various design constraints attached to the goals. There are many reasons for making this separation. First, it helps to explicitly describe what in fact are two different, albeit related, aspects of the design process. An immediate implication of this separation is that it allows the same validation knowledge to be applied regardless of which method produces the solution (or how the solution was produced). At the same time, it does not preclude methods from making use of the constraints in generating solutions. Some of the design methods in the PRIDE knowledge base actually use some kind of constraint satisfaction algorithm in generating possible solutions. This is made possible by the explicit attachment of constraints to the same goal that the design methods are attached to. A second important reason for this separation is that in some cases a constraint can only be applied after two or more design parameters have been designed. Thus, instead of making a commitment about the order in which the variables should be designed, we can place a constraint on some later goal which only requires that all the relevant design parameters are designed prior to running the goal (recall that inputPara serves this purpose in the representation of design goals).

Figure 10-6 shows a simple constraint from the PRIDE knowledge base. The applyWhen variable is used to describe the conditions under which a constraint is applicable. The constraint in Figure 10-6 is always applicable, but there are other constraints which depend either on the specifications of the particular design problem or on the nature of the interfacing systems. The variable mustSatisfy is used to specify whether the constraint can be relaxed if it is not satisfied.

The variable paraConstrained is used to describe the dependent variables which are constrained by this constraint object. In this case, even though two variables are mutually constrained, we know (from the domain experts) that the width of the idler is the dependent variable. Since this is an example of a constraint on a single variable (as indicated by the type), the actual constraint expression is composed from the predicate, paraConstrained, and the testExp (test expression) variables. Other kinds of constraints have other ways of composing the constraint expression.

Some very complex analyses might be behind the test expression used to constrain the designed variables. The PRIDE representation scheme provides an explicit way to describe the calculations behind such validation analyses. This allows, for example, some advice for fixing a constraint violation to be recursively back-propagated through the calculation expression. In other words, the advice on some constraint whose variables

type	SingleConstraint
name	Constraint29
description	"Idler width >= 1.2 times driver width"
applyWhen	ALWAYS
mustSatisfy	YES
abstractable	YES
paraConstrained	(DesignObject defRollPair idler width)
predicate	GEQ
testExp	(TIMES 1.2
	(GetPara DesignObject defRollPair driver width))
adviceCntxt	ALWAYS
advice	(Increase (DesignObject defRollPair idler width))
	(Decrease (DesignObject defRollPair driver width))

Figure 10-6 Stylized description of the constraint Idler width >= 1.2 times driver width [Mittal 1986a]. The actual advice and advice context are represented by separate objects.

are themselves calculated can be converted into further advice based on an analysis of the calculation expression. Another advantage for explicitly representing the calculation is that any explanation that is produced for the design choice can state the mathematical formula instead of just computing the value.

What should happen when a constraint fails? Answers to this question are crucial to the system's ability—as a designer's assistant—to help a designer. In generate-and-test models (e.g., [Dixon 1984]), a failure leads to a new round of design activity where the system can presumably generate a new design to be tested again. More sophisticated approaches employ some kind of backtracking mechanism to unwind to a prior decision point and continue from there. For example, in dependency-directed backtracking schemes [de Kleer 1979b], the problem solver maintains an explicit record of the dependencies between a decision and the basis for making the decision. These dependencies can be used to unwind to a relevant prior decision point. The advantage is that only a small part of the design needs to be undone when some constraint violations are detected. However, most of these approaches do not address the issue of how to modify a decision that is subsequently identified as the culprit in some design failure or the cause of a contradiction in deductive reasoning.

10.3.5   Control Issues in PRIDE

The problem solver in PRIDE is based on dependency-directed backtracking, with an important extension: PRIDE allows advice to be sent to the problem solver by the constraint that failed (see Figure 10-7). In many cases, this advice is meant for some prior decision point, telling it how to modify its decision. In more complex cases, the advice can affect many decision points or even the problem solver itself. Often it happens that more than one piece of advice is applicable at some point, and the system (or the user) might want to explore the consequences of following the advice in parallel. This is enabled in PRIDE by a multiple contexts mechanism which allows a tree of related contexts to be created. In order to follow the advice, the problem solver has to figure out which goal to advise, how to minimally undo the dependent design, how to preserve the context of the original failure, and how to select from competing or partially satisfactory advice. It is important, however, to point out that the approaches typically taken (e.g., [Brown 1985]) finesse many of these issues by making two simplifying assumptions. First, it is assumed that the target of the advice is always known in advance. This assumption is valid only when the structure of the designed artifact is fixed in advance. Clearly, this is not true for artifacts such as paper transports which have a variable structure; that is, the structure is itself designed. Second, it is assumed that the advice will be carried out successfully, thus obviating the need for maintaining the context or making choices. This assumption is again untenable for many real design problems, where the process of finding one or more suitable designs involves an exploration of choices.

How is advice generated and represented in PRIDE? Sometimes advice is obtained from the domain experts in advance because they learn from experience what the typical failures are and how some of them may be fixed. These can be represented in PRIDE via the adviseCntxt and advice attached to each constraint: adviseCntxt contains knowledge for analyzing the failure and advice contains suggestions for fixing the failure. For example, in the constraint shown in Figure 10-6, there is only one context, namely, ALWAYS, which contains two different pieces of advice. These, respectively, advise the problem solver to try to increase the width of the idler or decrease the width of the driver.

In order to provide a more general framework for exploring the design space—something that we believe will provide important leverage to a designer—the system must be able to go beyond the advice explicitly made available by the experts. In effect, the system must be able to reflect on its knowledge, analyze the cause of the failure, and then automatically

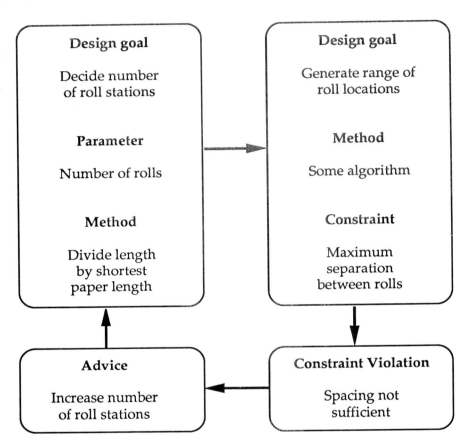

Figure 10-7 An illustration of the PRIDE advice mechanism showing that the advice is triggered by the violated constraint (after [Mittal 1986b] and [Morjaria 1989]).

generate advice (or a plan in more complicated cases) to repair the failure. This requires being able to analyze constraint expressions and the calculations underlying those constraints to automatically generate advice over and beyond what was provided by the experts. The mechanisms and knowledge representations required to support this kind of reasoning are beyond the scope of this chapter (see [Mittal 1986b, 1987; Frayman 1987]).

There are many other unresolved issues relating to the role of constraints in the design process. Some of these issues deal with maintaining the consistency of a design under a set of constraints. In other words, once some design choices have been made which satisfy a set of constraints, how can we ensure either that none of those choices will be modified individually or that the effect of modifying one of the choice variables will be propagated to all the other constrained variables? PRIDE was an excellent test bed for investigating some of these issues. Another issue deals with efficiently generating all possible solutions under a set of constraints so that they can be examined by other more complex constraints. Some of the early results on this problem are described in [Mittal 1986c].

10.3.6   Current Status of PRIDE

PRIDE is implemented in the LOOPS environment [Bobrow 1983; Stefik 1983], one of the earliest general-purpose representation languages (see Chapters 4 and 12) running on a Xerox 1100-series Lisp machine. LOOPS is a multiparadigm knowledge programming language implemented in and as an extension of the Interlisp-D dialect of Lisp [Sannella 1983]. Among the many facets of LOOPS exploited in PRIDE's knowledge representation scheme, as described earlier, is the use of object-oriented programming. As we have seen, each design goal, method, constraint, adviseContext, advice, and calculation was represented as a distinct object. Furthermore, the paper-handling system being designed was itself represented as a collection of interconnected objects.

The behavior attributed to these objects, described in Sections 10.3.1 through 10.3.5, was made operational by defining (and implementing) a set of messages by which these objects communicate with each other. This style of knowledge programming—variously called message passing, active values, or demons—is very different from the rule-based approaches. It offers more flexibility in representing different kinds of knowledge and enables a knowledge programmer to make explicit the role of some piece of knowledge in a problem-solving activity. Forcing all knowledge into the form of rules and running a uniform inference procedure over them often obscures the intent and impedes the use of the same knowledge for different purposes.

The current knowledge base in PRIDE for pinch roll paper transports is largely complete and is composed of more than a thousand objects. The knowledge base objects, along with all the supporting Lisp code, take up over 2 megabytes of memory, over and beyond that occupied by LOOPS and Interlisp-D. Part of the reason for the size of the system is the complexity and size of the design domain. A large part of the code (at a rough estimate, some 40 percent), however, was taken up by the many user interface facilities which were developed either to support a design engineer during a design session or to support a knowledge programmer in the creation and maintainence of the object-oriented knowledge base.

PRIDE was initially tested on over a dozen real paper transport problems from previous and current copier projects. It produced satisfactory designs in many of those cases. In fact, engineers working with the PRIDE system have been able to come up with more than one satisfactory design for some of the problems. In a test involving an ongoing copier project, PRIDE's creators were able to modify PRIDE to first accept the design produced by the project engineers and then test it. The analysis produced by PRIDE showed some key drawbacks in the design which were later confirmed by the project engineers. Later, PRIDE was able to come up with a different design which satisfied the design considerations in its knowledge base. PRIDE is now routinely used in ongoing copier projects [Morjaria 1989].

Another measure of a system's effectiveness is the time required to produce a design and the thoroughness of the analyses performed on the design. Experience with PRIDE suggests that such systems are effective in this regard. PRIDE can produce in 30 minutes a design that typically takes an engineer many weeks to perform. Furthermore, PRIDE's analysis and the report generated are more complete than is usual in current practice.

In fact, PRIDE proved to be sufficiently useful that the user organization (the Reprographics Business Group—the copier unit—of Xerox) set up its own support group for the PRIDE system. It is unlikely that statistical comparisons of PRIDE's performance with that of design engineers will prove to be very helpful by themselves. Success of systems such as PRIDE will be determined as much by technical competence as by the creation of a user community which can collectively play a role in defining the scope of the system, validating the knowledge, and in other ways using the system as an effective knowledge medium.

10.4 SYNTHESIS: THE SIGHTPLAN SYSTEM

Spatial reasoning with KBESs poses significant challenges for knowledge engineers. There is considerable evidence that humans perfom spatial reasoning using right-brain cognitive processes, which differ significantly from the left-brain cognitive processes through which we perform deductive or associative tasks such as language understanding and mathematical computations. Right-brain processing is still the subject of fundamental AI research in areas like image interpretation. Nevertheless, as we discussed in Chapter 7, some progress has been made in building KBESs that reason about space.

The SightPlan system is a blackboard KBES that was developed to provide computer support for the task of locating temporary facilities on a construction site [Tommelein 1989a, 1989b]. SightPlan locates objects in a two-dimensional space where objects have constraints with respect to the site and its context (roads, prevailing wind direction, and so on) and with respect to other objects on the site. SightPlan thus carries out constraint-based spatial reasoning. In addition, site layout involves several different kinds of concerns, including minimizing travel time for workers on the site; providing access for large equipment or prefabricated components; and meeting a variety of labor relations, safety, security, and other concerns, each of which is typically addressed by specialists. SightPlan therefore also has to address the challenge of combining multiple sources of expertise in an integrated system.

The description of the system provided in this section is intended to show how SightPlan addresses the concerns of constraint-based spatial reasoning and integration of multiple sources of expertise. This discussion of SightPlan is abstracted from [Levitt 1989b].

10.4.1   The Origins of SightPlan

Despite several previous attempts to formalize the site layout process, field construction managers have resisted using tools such as operations research, cutout templates, and other models to help them in their task. Managers find the formulation of the input for such methods tedious and difficult to achieve with the limited amounts of information at hand, and they mistrust the solutions generated by the "black box" that constitutes the implementation. Indeed, this "black box" does not provide any means for them to get insight into the process or to intervene and follow intuitions that might lead to an acceptable solution. SightPlan's developers believed that in this respect AI programming techniques could contribute to the development of better tools.

The SightPlan project was initiated by a team of civil engineering and computer science researchers at Stanford University, who had four major research goals. The researchers sought first to understand the knowledge used by construction managers for laying out construction sites, in order to formalize this area of field construction practice. The second goal was to build a model to reproduce the problem-solving strategies employed by these human experts in designing site layouts. A third goal was to test the power and generality of the BB1 blackboard architecture (see Chapter 8) on a realistic design problem in a new and challenging domain. The fourth goal of the SightPlan project, as with PRIDE, PLATFORM, and other projects described in this book, was to explore the potential of using knowledge-based interactive graphics to integrate the bookkeeping and computational strengths of a computer system like SightPlan with the spatial perception and reasoning strengths of a person engaged in this spatial layout task.

SightPlan's scope was carefully defined to make the project feasible while preserving as much realism as possible.

❏ **SightPlan was developed for a single class of projects.** Its target application would be remotely located fossil fuel power plants. Several such projects were under construction and site managers appeared to be available to the research team as potential sources of site layout knowledge. Furthermore, empirical guidelines had already been formalized for such projects in the form of field construction manuals and a few articles describing concerns for site layout.

❏ **SightPlan arranges about fifty predefined temporary facilities.** This is about the level of detail at which designers and construction managers currently lay out temporary buildings and long-term laydown areas on such sites.

❏ **SightPlan limits its layout to two dimensions**. Ignoring topography on the site and assuming that only one facility could be located on each (x, y) element of the site appeared to be an acceptable limitation for a first pass at this problem.

❏ **SightPlan assumes rectangular objects.** SightPlan also limits all constraints to be rectilinear; that is, minimum and maximum distances between objects are measured horizontally or vertically. The computation done by the geometry engine developed to manipulate constraints in SightPlan was thereby greatly simplified, and thus the computation costs were low.

❏ **SightPlan considers time implicitly or in discrete intervals.** When locating an object needed for only part of the project, SightPlan does not reason about reuse of its assigned area at other times. (A second, extended version of SightPlan reasons about time explicitly.)

The limitations imposed on SightPlan result in a realistic representation of site layout that approaches the grain size that would be needed in a practical decision support tool for construction site layout.

10.4.2   Architecture of SightPlan

As noted, SightPlan was implemented in the BB1 architecture that we described in Chapter 8 [Hayes-RothB 1985]. There were several reasons for this choice. First, the spatial arrangement of objects under constraints defines a class of problems which humans find very challenging. Since humans cannot hold more than a small number of constraints in short-term memory at any one time, they must generally solve such problems by assembling solutions incrementally, examining partial solutions for acceptance and changing strategy along the way. The BB1 control architecture was specifically designed to represent and reason opportunistically with the kind of metaknowledge (strategic knowledge about how to order steps in problem solving) that humans use to guide such planning and design tasks [Hayes-RothB 1985].

Second, BB1 supports frame-based representation. Much of SightPlan's knowledge falls naturally into this representation, in which attributes and links can be inherited from one or more related frames. BB1 also provides excellent facilities for browsing and editing knowledge bases. Furthermore, earlier application developments in BB1 established the idea of layering the various knowledge bases in the system hierarchically, so other applications—including SightPlan—could easily reuse the appropriate frame hierarchies [Hayes-RothB 1987a]. BB1 molds rulelike structures into frames, but BB1's inference mechanism does not employ conventional forward or backward chaining of these. Instead, these frames represent independent units called knowledge sources (KSs). As we explained in more detail in Chapter 8, knowledge sources are triggered by information changes on a blackboard which is maintained and updated at every cycle of problem solving. This provides opportunistic reasoning capabilities and modularly distributed knowledge, both of which fit SightPlan's needs.

Third, BB1 separates **domain KSs** (in SightPlan, those KSs that describe how a specific object can be positioned in a specific arrangement with a specific constraint) from **control KSs** (in SightPlan, the set of KSs that capture the strategy pursued by a field manager laying out a site), permitting explicit formalization of a layout strategy. An important ingredient of the research approach was to decompose the problem in order to avoid manipulating massive constraint sets—the Achilles heel of several prior attempts to employ constraint satisfaction in solving complex design problems. The researchers wanted to define compound objects (consisting of groups of facilities highly constrained with respect to each other); arrange them internally; locate them as a single object on the site; and then consider remaining detailed constraints with objects on the site from within the compound object. The BB1 control architecture facilitates modeling multilevel control strategies for this kind of problem solving and is able to manipulate multiple and hierarchical partial arrangements to store multiple descriptions of the problem's solution.

For all of these reasons, the BB1 blackboard architecture provided a good fit for the demands of this problem. Moreover, the developers of BB1 had already applied it to what they thought was a related problem: synthesis of protein molecules from nuclear magnetic resonance constraint data. A prototype of the PROTEAN system for protein molecule synthesis was already completed before the start of the SightPlan project [Hayes-RothB 1986]. Because this application of BB1 to a spatial arrangement problem was developed in a layered software architecture, its developers believed that much of PROTEAN's spatial reasoning capability could be exploited for the SightPlan problem. In fact, the desire to test this hypothesis about the generality of the opportunistic reasoning and spatial arrangement language used in PROTEAN was a primary motivation for the AI researchers' involvement in the SightPlan project.

The layered architecture of the SightPlan system—including the Lisp environment; BB1; the ACCORD language (or "framework") for solving arrangement and assembly problems in BB1; the GS2D constraint engine developed to manipulate the rectilinear constraints between SightPlan's objects; and the SightPlan domain and control knowledge sources—is shown in Figure 10-8 along with the components of the PROTEAN system. Note that SightPlan uses all of the components of PROTEAN except its 3-D constraint engine. This greatly facilitated development of SightPlan.

10.4.3 Representation Issues in SightPlan

Concepts in the BB1/SightPlan world are represented in a conceptual graph [Sowa 1984]. The underlying BB1 scheduler then makes the appropriate inferences. Concepts are represented by frames that can have any kind of user-defined attributes or links to other objects and which can inherit attributes over specific links. For the sake of clarity and flexibility the conceptual graph is layered; that is, concepts specific to a particular application domain are grouped in a blackboard. A schema representing various layers and how they relate conceptually to one other is given in

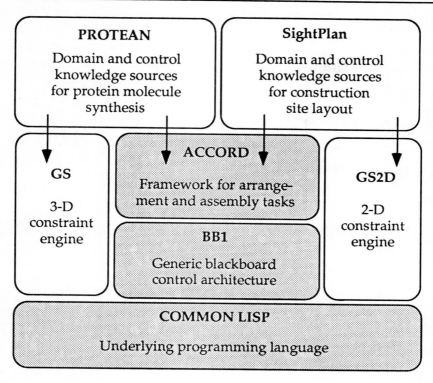

Figure 10-8 The layered architecture of the SightPlan and PROTEAN systems (after [Levitt 1989b]). The shaded components of the architecture are shared with the PROTEAN system.

Figure 10-9, which illustrates how multiple application systems can coexist in the same conceptual graph representation. PROTEAN is the biochemistry application. Intermountain and American 1 are two separate SightPlan implementations in the domain of construction site layout. With the system organized in layers, it is easy to build a new application by substituting only the needed blackboards (BBs).

The most abstract concepts, from which domain-specific concepts stem, are grouped on the CONCEPT blackboard. Those that define objects (e.g., those related to site layout and construction management) are grouped on the SITE blackboard, and objects on the SITE blackboard, in turn, can be specialized to concepts related to power plant construction on the POWER_PLANT blackboard. Finally, those examples of specific objects

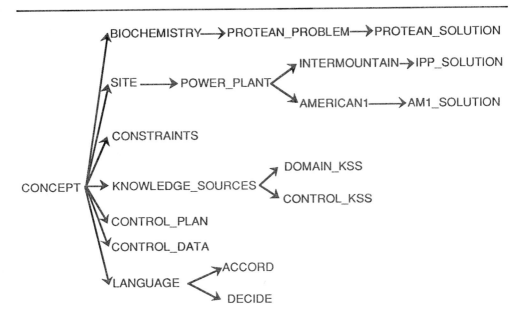

Figure 10-9 Schema of layered BBs in SightPlan's conceptual graph [Levitt 1989b]. Each of the nodes in this graph represents a blackboard that groups frames representing concepts. The nodes in the topmost line represent PROTEAN BBs that are not used by the SightPlan system.

that exist on one particular site—here, for instance, the site of the Intermountain Power Project—are on the INTERMOUNTAIN blackboard; those that exist on another site, the American 1 site, are on the AMERICAN1 blackboard. The system generates solutions in terms of instances of example objects, and these instances are stored on the solution blackboards (PROTEAN_SOLUTION, IPP_SOLUTION, AM1_SOLUTION). In this way, the concepts on the CONCEPT blackboard can be specialized to accommodate any representation of more specialized worlds. This abstraction hierarchy makes use of *can_be_a*, *exemplified_by*, and *instantiated_by* links and their inverse links for inheritance of attributes and relationships.

In SightPlan's current implementation, all simple objects are represented by single rectangles. For instance, POWER_UNIT_1 is a simple object: the values of its attribute DIMENSIONS give the dimensions of the rectangular area that it occupies. SightPlan represents all legal locations of the object by a series of zero or more rectangles (termed **essential areas**) in which the center point of the object can be located. Thus, a single point defines a fixed location for the object; one or more rectangles with finite sizes define regions in which the object's center point can be located while satisfying all known constraints.   This representation turns out to be efficient for manipulation of constraints.

While a simple object has a predefined area and shape, an aggregate object—which includes several parts that have constraints with each other—may be undimensioned. Thus, SightPlan reasons about the size and shape of aggregate objects before positioning them in an arrangement. An example aggregate object is the CONSTRUCTION_ENTRANCE, including the craft parking lot, two security offices, two "brass alleys," a welder qualification building, and a weld test building.

Depending on the types of constraints among the components of an aggregate object, SightPlan will dimension and locate it in one of two ways. One way to meet constraints among the components of an aggregate object is to build a separate arrangement, including the parts, and solve this layout independent of possible constraints between the parts and other objects outside of the aggregate or of possible constraints between the aggregate and other objects. This results in a layout of which the boundaries provide the size and shape of a single rectangle for the aggregate. The other way is to heuristically estimate the dimensions and the shape of the aggregate object, locate it on the site, and then attempt to arrange its component objects within the boundaries of the aggregate object SightPlan has created. The flexibility to attack aggregate objects in either of these two ways illustrates the flexibility and power of BB1's opportunistic control structure.

Constraints, knowledge sources, and all other concepts in SightPlan are represented as frames, organized into a series of layered blackboards that collectively make up the SightPlan knowledge base. Descriptions of all of these frame types, with examples, are provided in [Levitt 1989b].

10.4.4   Control Issues in SightPlan

Control in SightPlan is implemented using the BB1 knowledge source activation records (KSARs) and scheduling mechanism described in detail in Section 8.3.5. At any cycle there can be multiple executable KSARs, and the scheduler chooses among competing proposed actions according to a numerical rating representing a strategy match. When a BB1 application employs a high-level application language such as ACCORD, the rating is established using a matching scheme implied by the language. Figure 10-10 illustrates how a focus sentence that uses an ACCORD template matches a

KSAR's action sentence. When a noun and/or a verb in the KSAR's action sentence is of the same type as those of the focus sentence, a rating value of 100 is assigned; otherwise, a value of 0 is assigned. If modifiers precede a noun or verb in the focus, then the modifying function (the value of an attribute of a modifier) is applied to the matching noun or verb in the KSAR's action and a value between 0 and 100 is returned. Thus, TURBINE_GENERATOR_1 is rated R80 in terms of the modifier TIME_CRITICAL, whereas MECH&PIPING_UNIT scores only R60 against this modifier. This results in the top KSAR being rated higher than the bottom one against the ACCORD focus sentence in the center of Figure 10-10. If these were the only two KSARs under consideration, the scheduler would choose the top KSAR for execution in the current cycle.

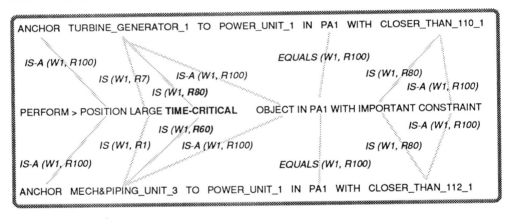

Figure 10-10 Rating two contending domain actions against an ACCORD focus in SightPlan [Levitt 1989b]. The ACCORD focus that is currently active is shown in the center of the figure. Above it and below it are two KSARs that have been proposed by SightPlan knowledge sources.

10.4.5 The GS2D Constraint Engine

When an action executes, SightPlan passes the constraint and the object pair with their current essential areas to a constraint engine, called GS2D, for the computation of constraint satisfaction. For each object, GS2D then returns the subset of essential areas which meet the constraint. Note that only constraint satisfaction between object pairs is handled by GS2D, acting as a procedure called by SightPlan. Issues such as constraint propagation or truth maintenance are dealt with and reasoned about by the SightPlan system itself. GS2D is a procedural system, implemented in Common Lisp, which solves geometric constraints between rectangular objects in a two-dimensional world, using a bounded interval representation [Confrey 1988]. It is a two-dimensional adaptation of the three-dimensional GSD constraint engine that was used for PROTEAN.

The fundamental decision in the design of a geometric constraint engine is its representation of space. Given the implementation of objects within SightPlan—objects are rectangles—an orthogonal bounded interval representation was selected to model the possible positions of an object. Objects' axes must be aligned on a single global Cartesian coordinate system; thus they are allowed a 0- and a 90-degree orientation. Each bounded interval pair within GS2D describes a rectangular set of legal locations for the center point of an object, which we call the essential area. A fixed object is therefore described by a single point. An object that is not fixed has dimensions and a set of orthogonal bounded intervals for each of its two possible orientations.

SightPlan limits constraints to be rectilinear. That is, the distance between two objects is, by choice, the minimum of the horizontal or the vertical absolute distances between their edges. The implementation of constraints is thus simplified to a series of expansion and intersection operations on sets of rectangles. This greatly speeds the operation of the constraint engine at the cost of reduced precision in computing distance.

Figure 10-11 shows how GS2D reduces the sets of possible positions of two objects to allow only for positions where the objects are CLOSER_THAN a given distance to each other. Those unfamiliar with GS2D need to get used to the fact that GS2D computes on rectangles representing sets of possible locations for the center point of each entity rather than on the entities themselves. Also, the definition of distance used in GS2D may be counter-intuitive.

The constraints that SightPlan uses are obviously all supported by GS2D, but the SightPlan and GS2D programs are implemented as totally independent modules. GS2D is available for use by other application systems, and SightPlan could easily make use of another constraint engine if it needed to. (See [Confrey 1988] for a more detailed account of GS2D.)

10.4.6 SightView: An Interactive Graphic Interface for SightPlan

The initial version of SightPlan used the TI Explorer's graphic Lisp primitives to provide a graphic display of the site, permanent facilities, and sets of possible locations for temporary facilities currently included in a

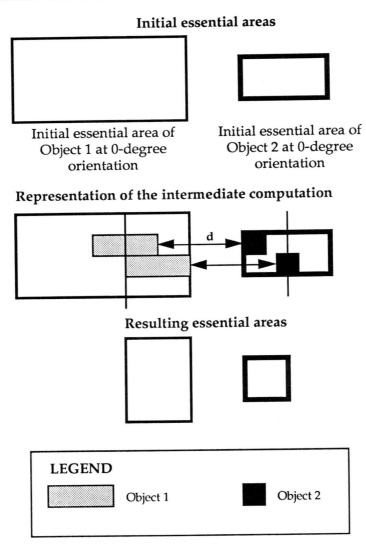

Figure 10-11 Application of the CLOSER_THAN constraint to two objects in SightPlan's GS2D constraint engine (after [Levitt 1989b]).

solution. Although of considerable value in debugging and explanation, this method had only limited resolution and was of little value in distinguishing between the essential areas of different temporary facilities once any significant number of them were being displayed. Moreover,

SightPlan spent a significant number of cycles and much processing time on reasoning about display.

A color graphic display running on an Apple Macintosh II computer was thus developed for SightPlan. This high-resolution color display permits a user to discern far more detail about the state of a solution under development. The display system running on the Macintosh II, called SightView, is connected via an Ethernet connection and a communication interface to SightPlan running on a TI Explorer. Each time SightPlan updates an object's essential area, that information is passed within the same action to SightView for display. In this way, the SightPlan expert system itself spends a minimum amount of time on handling display information (see Figure 10-12).

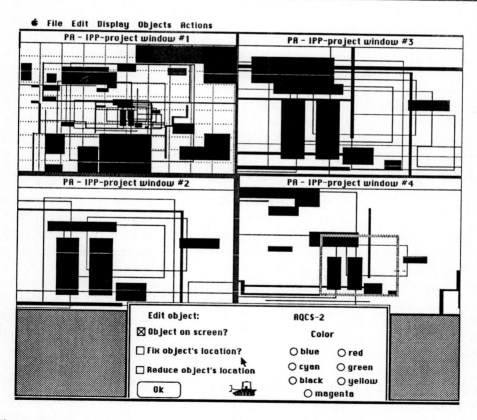

Figure 10-12 Four views of the same site in the SightView graphic display system of SightPlan [Levitt 1989b].

The representation of objects and their positions is consistent throughout the SightPlan system: the object data structure used by GS2D (essential areas) and by SightPlan (state families) is also used for data transfer to the Macintosh display.

The SightView user can open multiple windows and can set each individually to view any portion of any partial arrangement at any scale and to display a selected subset of the facilities. By selecting the temporary facilities of interest in different windows and choosing colors to provide contrast between them, the user can obtain a vivid and intuitive understanding of the state of a solution.

Window 1 in Figure 10-12 shows the whole site, 3 a close-up, 2 and 4 different facilities of interest. In window 4 the existing legal location of the air quality control system (AQCS-2) is highlighted with the shaded gray line. The open dialog box permits the user to decide whether or not to display the object in the window, to change the color of the object's essential area display, to reduce the object's essential area, or to fix the object's location.

SightView has been designed to interact with SightPlan. A user can select a temporary facility and give it a precise location somewhere within the facility's set of currently legal locations. Alternatively, a facility's set of legal locations can be arbitrarily reduced within existing legal limits to satisfy some user preferences about the region of its ultimate location.

 When the user restricts the possible locations of a temporary facility via the Macintosh's graphic interface, that information is sent back to SightPlan. SightPlan then checks to see which constraints need to be reapplied with other objects so that it can further restrict their legal positions. The new essential areas for all objects are then redisplayed, and the user can make additional positioning decisions. Alternatively, the user can decide not to intervene and can allow SightPlan to proceed with the position actions it selects using its stored knowledge of site layout. In this way, the user is involved as one more knowledge source in the SightPlan system, a source whose suggestions receive an infinitely high rating.

A SightPlan user is not allowed to choose a location for a temporary facility that lies outside the boundaries of its current essential area. Permitting this would imply relaxing a previously met constraint, and the system would need a dependency-directed backtracking mechanism, or some other form of truth maintenance capability, to determine which constraints needed to be reapplied or relaxed to permit the desired positioning of the facility.

Implementing this capability is a potential extension to the SightPlan system that is feasible (since BB1 keeps records of all of its actions, including the application of constraints), and it may be attempted in the future.

10.4.7   Current Status of SightPlan

To explore the strengths and weaknesses of human versus computer approaches to spatial reasoning, SightPlan applied different strategies to the Intermountain power plant site: one of early commitment (implemented as the expert strategy); one of least commitment (in which specific location decisions were delayed as long as possible); and one of postponed commitment (implemented as the computational strategy). In the following paragraphs we discuss the advantages and disadvantages of each.   A detailed discussion of the cognitive science aspects of SightPlan is provided in [Tommelein 1989b].

Early commitment. The expert model demonstrated that an early commitment strategy can succeed for laying out construction sites. Yet such a strategy may not always result in a solution, even if one exists. Many alternative solutions are excluded by following this strategy. It was found that if provided with alternatives, the expert could rank legal solutions, thereby providing additional knowledge that could be used for generating solutions.

Least commitment. The least commitment strategy, which SightPlan applied as its preliminary computational strategy, models a brute force approach. The brute force approach has the advantage that it will produce a solution if one exists. In the case of the underconstrained Intermountain problem, SightPlan's strategy resulted in an explosively large number of alternative arrangements.   When faced with all these alternative arrangements, we prefer applying some evaluation or discrimination criteria in order to differentiate between them, rather than picking one at random.   Not only is it expensive to generate (almost exhaustively) all possible combinations of objects in a layout; the cost of differentiating between the results may be prohibitive as well. A system should therefore balance the costs incurred for generating alternatives with the benefits of finding a better arrangement.

Postponed commitment. SightPlan's developers proposed that problems are often stated in highly underconstrained terms. People opportunistically add constraints before or during problem solving in order tighten the problem specifications and to narrow the set of potential solutions.   To explore this concept, the developers crafted a postponed commitment strategy for SightPlan that generates a reasonable subset of all possible solution layouts by using additional preference constraints.

The postponed commitment strategy, implemented as the second computational strategy, strikes a balance between heuristically pruning the solution space and flexibly generating alternatives. SightPlan heuristically applies some user preference constraints, samples sets of possible locations of objects, and generates a set of coherent instances. When constraining and sampling succeed in cutting out extraneous locations, instance generation is fast and a small number of solution layouts can be returned to the user for evaluation. This strategy may not find a solution even if one exists, but its probability of success is higher than that of the early commitment strategy.

User-interactive model. SightPlan's developers experimented with a user-interactive model and explored the implications of such an improved model on managers' practice. Implicit in their approach was the desire to explore whether it might be possible to build an interactive decision support system that could permit a human expert using a computer to exploit the strengths of humans (in spatial visualization) and of machines (in data storage and retrieval and in constraint bookkeeping) to plan for better designs than either of these could do alone. (See our discussion of knowledge-based interactive graphics in Chapter 8.) A computer screen with multiple colors can easily represent possible object locations on a planar site. Graphics might thus be an especially powerful medium for human-machine communication in this domain. The interactive graphic interface developed for this project combines three modalities of computing that provide significant leverage to one another: (1) BB/KBES reasoning to choose which temporary facilities to position on the site and which constraints to apply to them; (2) a procedural constraint engine for processing constraints efficiently and for updating the state of the solution, both on the SightPlan solution blackboard and on the graphic display; and (3) graphic display of solution status and input of user choices.

The main objective for the SightPlan project was to explore AI architectures for solving the class of spatial arrangement problems to which site layout belongs. It was found that by using carefully selected domain knowledge and a flexible reasoning mechanism, SightPlan could show significant advantages over generic and more rigid heuristic construction methods for layout design.

10.5 SYNTHESIS: INTELLIGENT BOILER DESIGN SYSTEM (IBDS)

We stated in Chapter 8 that AI techniques for design synthesis are just now entering into commercial application. In this section we provide a brief case study to show how one company is using a knowledge-based design automation system—the Intelligent Boiler Design System (IBDS)—to automate the preliminary design of semicustom products, that is, power generation boilers. We include this case study because it demonstrates the integrated and operational use of state-of-the-art KBES techniques in a real engineering environment.

10.5.1 Background of IBDS

Tampella Power Industries of Tampere, Finland, designs and manufactures boilers and other components of power plants. Since April 1987 the company has been using Design++, a high-level design automation AI language that follows the model-based reasoning (MBR) paradigm described in Chapter 8 for boiler design. The boiler design expert system developed using Design++ is integrated with a ComputerVision CAD system, a VAX-based engineering analysis system, and an Oracle relational database system [Riitahuhta 1988]. Another application study conducted by Tampella addressed the design of upper circulation piping (Figure 10-13). Here, the upper circulation pipes refer to the water-collecting pipes of the boiler furnace walls which return the boiler water into the drum. Modeling for the IBDS pipe layout system was divided into three stages.

❑ Defining the positions of the drum connections,

❑ Defining the positions of the connections of the wall collecting headers, and

❑ Defining the routing of the pipelines from the drum connections to the corresponding connections of the wall collecting headers.

In principle, the layout of the drum connections is determined by standard construction, but the number and positions of the connections have to be determined separately for each project. The positions of the connections for a given boiler are dictated by the need to avoid interference with the downcomers. There are construction standards for the layout of the wall connections. Solutions for the particular project are provided again by the specific obstructions resulting from different boiler sizes. Tampella has not

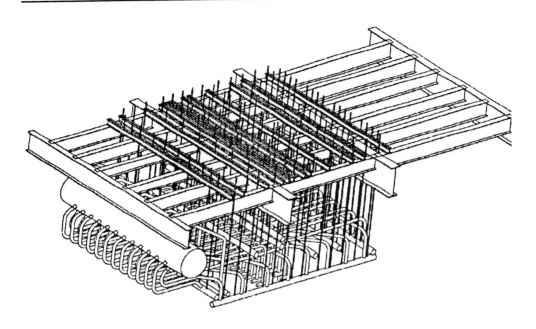

Figure 10-13 The upper circulation pipework for a power plant boiler (after [Riitahuhta 1988]). Design++, a high-level AI design automation language, was used to generate the component layout for this boiler using the MBR approach described in Chapter 8.

been able to standardize these structures; rather, the structure is determined for each project using design rules.

There are several obstructions, including the upper headers, the weld joints, and the lifting lugs of the header needed for hanging both the header and the furnace wall it supports from the upper support structures. Boiler downcomers, boiler suspension rods, parallel circulation pipes, and other piping systems are additional obstructions. With the aid of design rules implemented in Design++, the positions of the drum connections and wall collecting header connections are determined and the boiler pipes are positioned automatically, one at a time, to avoid all of these obstacles.

10.5.2 Architecture of IBDS

The Design++ framework is implemented as a knowledge base in IntelliCorp's KEE, which runs under Common Lisp. IBDS is made up of a series of linked knowledge bases implemented on top of Design++. The original version of the IBDS was implemented on a Symbolics AI workstation and interfaced to other computers. The current version of Design++ runs in a UNIX environment on Sun workstations. This allows applications like IBDS to interface and share data with relational databases, document preparation software, engineering analysis programs, CADD programs, and other applications in the UNIX environment.

10.5.3   Representation in IBDS

Tampella first developed a set of frames to represent boiler components. (Design++ is developed using KEE, so these components are stored as KEE frames similar to the ones illustrated in Chapter 6.) Design++ uses a "pretty printed" (hierarchically indented) text file to represent product part-of hierarchies. Tampella made up a part-of hierachy (whose elements can recursively reference more detailed part-of hierarchies) for each type of power or other boiler that it wished to design. Configuration knowledge was represented in rules defined at the level of generic components, or at the level of particular product models where generic rules were customized.

10.5.4   Reasoning in IBDS

Attribute values are propagated via demons. Rules fire as components are defined to propagate constraints from the attributes of one component to the relevant attributes of others. For instance, as a pump is selected, its power consumption is propagated to conductors, transformers, circuit breakers, or other electrical components that need this information to select or size themselves; its weight is propagated to structural components that provide it support; its output diameter is propagated to the pipe and flange that connect to its output side; and so on. This is classic object-oriented programming (OOP) as described in Chapter 6.

The high-level design rule language used in Design++ facilitates the implementation of spatial reasoning (e.g., about clearances) and some kinds of electromechanical reasoning in terse rules; any other desired relationship among component attributes can be defined in Lisp as part of such demons. Substantial Lisp methods are used to carry out some of the more complex types of geometric reasoning in IBDS (e.g., routing of pipes).

10.5.5   Explanation in IBDS

The current version of Design++ uses AutoCad as an internal visualization tool. This permits the user to see the evolving design in three dimensions, colored by layers or subsystems, as desired. The design visualization can be rotated, panned, zoomed, and so on from within AutoCad, so the user can inspect the results of design decisions made to date. The user can backtrack to make changes, and all affected components are automatically redesigned. This permits consideration of multiple alternatives, each of which is guaranteed to be consistent with all design rules in the system, in a fraction of the time that would be required with conventional CADD systems.

Design++ has the ability to represent reports as assemblies of components (paragraphs, subsections, and so on). Also, there are interfaces between Design++ and document processing languages such as InterLeaf. These two features allow the automatic generation of reports, such as bills of quantities, specifications, warranties, procedure manuals, and so on, based upon the design model. AutoCad images can be pasted into such reports. The AutoCad model can be used to produce preliminary or working drawings or to generate CAD files for other three-dimensional CADD systems via its DXF interchange format. Finally, the model can be used to generate manufacturing instructions in numerical control (NC) format for robotic pipe benders or other automated manufacturing equipment.

10.5.6 Current Status of IBDS

The power of the IBDS system is based on the large amount of knowledge of the domain that can be captured in the design rule language, project structure model, and component libraries in Design++. When the amount of knowledge increases, knowledge management becomes a significant problem. In this system, the knowledge management problem has been solved by utilizing an object-oriented approach to component descriptions and by exploiting relational databases.

The benefit obtained through automation in the design of the upper circulation pipes is summarized by Tampella's engineering staff [Riitahuhta 1988] as follows (emphasis added).

- ❑ Using manual design, the design work took two *months*.

- ❑ With ComputerVision's conventional plant design software, design took two *weeks*.

- ❑ Using the IBDS expert system together with the ComputerVision CADD system, a design can be completed in two *days*.

Thus, AI techniques have been exploited to automate many aspects of routine design for a semicustom product. The techniques used in this case study parallel very closely the MBR approach. There currently exist a number of off-the-shelf design automation tools like Design++ (including ICAD and Concept Modeler) that can facilitate the development of applications like this. The best of these design automation tools not only provide rules, frames, and OOP for representation and reasoning; they also serve as the "glue" to integrate CADD, analysis, database, document preparation, and manufacturing automation software tools.

10.6 SUMMARY

What have we learned from all these definitions, process descriptions, taxonomies, solution methods, and examples? Can we now confidently model engineering design tasks with KBES technology? Some particular points do seem to emerge from the foregoing discussion. First of all, design problems are hard, and the closer we get to true creativity, the further we are—with the current state of the art—from being able to build successful KBES tools. Second, for all intents and purposes, our interests must perforce focus largely on routine (Class 3) design and occasionally on nearly routine or variant (Class 2) design. In terms of the selection/synthesis taxonomy, we would seem to be able to build KBESs to do all but creative design with at least some measure of success. Thus there is a useful role for KBES technology in modeling serious, practical design.

To bring that role into focus, we conclude with a limited but pragmatic taxonomy of design, couched in terms of applying the processes of selection and design to components and configurations [Morjaria 1989]. That is, there are four design tasks we understand well enough to model in a KBES.

❑ **Component selection.** Here we simply choose a component from among a set of available components. The search space is defined by the number of components. Production rule methods can readily be used to implement tasks of this type.

❑ **Component parameter design.** This activity focuses on choosing values of parameters for a component in order to meet some requirements. The component being designed typically has a small number of known parameters, which number defines the size of the search space. V-belt drive design is an example of component parameter design [Dixon 1984].

❏ **Configuration selection.** In this case the task is to organize or assemble a known set of components into a topological structure to meet some performance specification. The search space is defined by the combinatorics of the number of feasible combinations of the components. Examples of configuration include the R1/XCON system [McDermottJ 1981; Barker 1989] and the Cossack system [Frayman 1987]. Further, the SightPlan system we discussed at length is certainly an example of sophisticated configuration selection [Levitt 1989b], as is the IBDS, which we outlined briefly [Riitahuhta 1988].

❏ **Configuration design.** This is the most complicated task of the four in this pragmatic taxonomy, as it encompasses the other three. What distinguishes this task is that the structure into which the components are to be inserted may not be rigidly defined in advance. Further, the components may often have to be designed rather than selected. Also, the number of parameters could be very large and their values might vary continuously as a result of being determined analytically (as opposed to being chosen from a restricted listing of finite possibilities). Thus, the search space could be quite large, and the role for knowledge-based tools to guide the search could be very significant. The PRIDE system that we discussed in Section 10.3 is just such a complex configuration design task [Mittal 1986a].

Thus, we can in fact achieve a great deal with KBES approaches to design. Design is, as we have repeatedly noted, a challenging task to model, but the advent of KBES techniques has dramatically improved our understanding of design—and so, too, our ability to model it and teach it.

Chapter 11

KNOWLEDGE-BASED SYSTEMS
FOR PLANNING

Planning and scheduling the activities required to design or manufacture an engineered product constitute the second set of formation applications of KBESs that we address in this book. **Planning** can be defined as "generating a linear (i.e., sequential) or parallel (i.e, concurrent) set of actions that will transform some initial state of the world into a desired goal state" [Levitt 1987b]. We will call the output of a planning process a **plan**. **Scheduling** can be defined as assigning resources to the activities in a plan; computing the durations of activities, the start and finish times, and the associated float or slack, for each activity in the plan; and computing the utilization of resources over time [Levitt 1987b]. We will term the output of the scheduling process the **schedule**. Planning and scheduling are two of the core tasks in predicting and controlling the use of the resources—including people, time, materials, equipment, and capital—needed to implement engineered systems.

Management of the resources consumed by engineering projects includes two other tasks associated with planning and scheduling: **objective setting** (making tradeoffs among competing goals or objectives at the early stages of the project) and **project control** (monitoring progress, forecasting production rates and productivities for remaining activities, and taking appropriate corrective actions to correct unacceptable deviations from plans). Levitt [1987a] provides a broad overview of the potential of AI techniques to assist in all four of these tasks of project management; we will focus our discussion in this chapter on KBES applications to planning.

11.1 OVERVIEW OF AI PLANNING RESEARCH

Planning is a difficult task for people—or computers—to perform. The space of possible solutions for any realistically complex planning problem is so large that brute force search techniques are useless and generally applicable heuristic search techniques are difficult to define and implement. Planning problems were among the first to be tackled by artificial intelligence researchers in the early 1960s, yet little progress was achieved in terms of practically useful planning systems by the late 1980s. It is instructive to reflect on this experience.

Research on planning has been an important part of mainstream AI research. Early attempts at building computer systems to generate plans had as their goal the development of generic approaches to planning that could be employed in any domain. For planning, as in the case of other areas of AI, the **knowledge principle** was found to apply: *In the knowledge lies the power* [Feigenbaum 1977]. Just as narrowly scoped expert systems proved to be more powerful than general problem-solving systems for tasks like medical diagnosis or mineral prospecting, domain-specific planning systems were able to produce realistic plans for tasks like offshore platform maintenance and job shop scheduling while general-purpose planning systems were still struggling to solve small block-stacking problems.

The Molgen system showed that domain-specific knowledge for a narrowly scoped planning problem—knowledge about the equipment and materials used in molecular biology experiments—permitted a drastic pruning of the plan solution space [Stefik 1981a, 1981b]. After the success of Molgen, a number of researchers—quickly followed by practitioners—began to pursue this knowledge-intensive approach to KBES for planning during the mid-1980s. **Domain-specific planning systems** such as LIFT use the techniques of rules, frames, and inheritance to encode large amounts of knowledge that is specific to a particular domain [Bremdal 1987]. That domain knowledge is then used to identify and order tasks or activities in that planning domain.

However, the knowledge principle is a two-edged sword. Recall our discussion of knowledge mesas in Chapter 8. Most of the knowledge in an expert planning system like Molgen, LIFT, or PLANEX is not applicable to even a slightly different domain. For instance, Molgen's knowledge of mloecular biology is of little use in planning chemistry experiments. Thus, there is little potential for leveraging the effort that goes into the development of an expert planning system.

The goal of achieving both generality and power in a planning system motivated attempts to develop model-based reasoning (MBR) approaches to planning, employing the type of architecture and representation described in Chapter 8. As for design tasks, MBR appears to be a fruitful approach for developing KBESs that support or perform planning tasks.

Successful prototypes of two such systems, PIPPA [Marshall 1987] and OARPLAN [Darwiche 1989], have already been developed, and we expect that MBR-based planning shells will be available by the early 1990s.

In this chapter, we begin by reviewing the attempts of AI researchers to develop general-purpose planning systems, and we explain why researchers have failed to produce useful planners for engineering applications. We briefly discuss a few of the expert planning systems developed in the mid-1980s. We then give an extensive discussion of the architecture, representation, and reasoning of OARPLAN, a third-generation KBES planning system developed using the MBR approach. We conclude that these MBR planning systems have the potential to evolve into powerful knowledge-based planning shells that can interface with conventional or KBES computer systems used in engineering design.

11.2   GENERAL-PURPOSE AI PLANNING SYSTEMS

Research on **general-purpose planning systems** started with the General Problem Solver (GPS) [Newell 1960] and evolved through a series of planning systems that extended that system's basic concepts: STRIPS [Fikes 1971]; ABSTRIPS [Sacerdoti 1973]; NOAH [Sacerdoti 1975]; NONLIN [Tate 1976]; and TWEAK [Chapman 1987]. In this section, we briefly discuss this line of planners and comment on the reasons why they have failed to become practically useful planning tools for engineers.

11.2.1   The Evolution of AI Planning Systems

Planners belonging to this line of AI planning systems assume a state-based repesentation of the world and are referred to as **classical planners** or **STRIPS-style planners** in the AI literature. The input for such a planner consists of the set of simple facts or literals (e.g., block A is on block B, block C is on the table) to represent the initial state of the world and a second set of literals to represent the goal state. A set of possible actions or **operators** is then defined, with **preconditions** of each action (literals that must be true before executing the action) and **effects** of the action on the world state (defined by addition and/or deletion of literals).

These AI planning systems search through available actions and use heuristics to select for execution of an action that will maximally reduce the difference between the current state and the goal state (the heuristics that guide this type of search are termed **means-end** heuristics). Using means-end search repeatedly, such systems instantiate a sequence of actions that will transform the initial state to the goal state. Some of these planners work backward, generating subgoals from the goal state; others plan in a forward direction or in both directions simultaneously. STRIPS-style plan operators are analogous to production rules in the sense that production rules chain together forward or backward by matching the literals contained in rule premises and conclusions, while STRIPS operators chain forward or backward by matching the literals contained in preconditions and effects.

A major challenge that faced the developers of these AI planners was that the *effects* of one action can delete one or more of the *preconditions* of a subsequent action in the sequence of actions, rendering the plan invalid. Means-end heuristics do not detect such interferences among actions. As a result, the early STRIPS-style planners failed to find optimal plans—or any correct plans—even for simple block-stacking tasks like the Sussman anomaly problem shown in Figure 11-1, whose solution is obvious to a human. Successive AI planners introduced increasingly powerful and general ways to detect and correct such plan interferences (see [Tate 1976] or [Levitt 1987b] for more specifics).

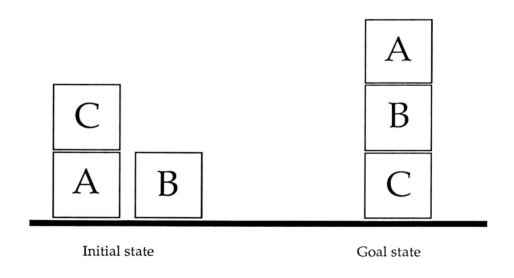

Initial state   Goal state

Figure 11-1 The Sussman anomaly problem (after [Sussman 1975]). Early AI planners were unable to generate the optimal plan—or, in some cases, any plan—to solve this simple block-stacking problem.

The assumption of plan linearity was a major limitation of the early planning systems. The first generation of AI planners, starting with STRIPS (Stanford Research Institute Planning System [Fikes 1971]) and ending with ABSTRIPS (Abstraction-Based STRIPS [Sacerdoti 1973]), configures a plan as a linear or strictly ordered sequence of actions; no parallel actions are allowed. The assumption of linearity is realistic when planning for a single agent such as a robot arm, but it is unrealistic in many real-life manufacturing or construction applications in which multiple actions can occur in parallel. Moreover, the linearity assumption imposes unneeded linear constraints between actions, constraints that might prevent the system from finding a solution or might result in additional backtracking and searching.

The second generation of AI planners adopted a **least commitment approach** to planning, in which decisions are delayed until the planner has as much useful information as possible for making them. The least commitment approach was first introduced in NOAH (Nets of Action Hierarchies), which avoided commitments by using nonlinear plans— containing parallel sequences of actions—to postpone ordering decisions [Sacerdoti 1975].

Logic programming is an alternative approach for general-purpose AI planners and has been used in several research efforts. Preiss [1989] describes two logic-based planning systems, one built in Prolog for single-agent process planning and a second in Concurrent Prolog for multiagent process planning. These planners use a STRIPS-style state representation and heuristics to select process plan actions. GEMPLAN represents planning knowledge as first-order logic constraints on the timing and relative sequence of domain events (actions); the planner tries to generate a plan that satisfies these constraints [Lansky 1988]. In this way, the problem is decomposed into subproblems for which planning can proceed independently, with constraint propagation serving to communicate interdependencies among subplans (as in Molgen, described in Section 11.6). GEMPLAN's constraint-based approach to planning seems to be more appropriate to the requirements of engineering project planning than the STRIPS operator approach. The system has been used to generate plans for building construction projects containing about 50 activities.

11.2.2   Limitations of Classical AI Planners

As detailed in [Tate 1976], AI planning systems had evolved by the mid-1970s so that they could both detect plan interferences and generate parallel or "nonlinear" plans. Even with these enhancements, however, STRIPS-style AI planners remain ill suited for planning in most engineering domains. We discuss some of the reasons here in an abbreviated version of the critique of AI planners in [Darwiche 1989].

Actions. In block-stacking and similar planning problems, it is always assumed that a complete set of primitive actions is available and that the preconditions and effects of each action are known. This assumption works with robot planning because the number of possible actions is small and detailed knowledge about actions is part of the robot's specifications. In manufacturing, construction, and other tasks involving more flexible human agents, however, we usually do not have either a complete enumeration of possible primitive actions or a precise definition of their preconditions and effects.

Classical AI planners define the literals involved in the preconditions and effects of actions as the only way to represent such domain knowledge. Minor errors or omissions in defining actions thus have major effects on the correctness of the final plan. We argue that planning knowledge for engineering projects is not naturally or commonly expressed in the form of action preconditions and effects, but rather should be expressed as a set of more fundamental principles representing the transformation of objects or assemblies as well as the underlying causes of precedence between actions. MBR planners such as OARPLAN overcome this limitation with a richer representation of actions and constraints ([Darwiche 1989]; see Section 11.7).

State abstraction. Classical planners are state-based; they assume a state representation of the world, so they must express a problem as sets of literals defining an initial and a final state (see Chapter 2 for a discussion of state space search). For a robot's plan, defining the initial state of the world is both relevant and possible; for a manager's plan, it may be both more difficult and less useful. The kind of plan needed by a project manager is not affected by the exact location of a particular beam at the beginning of construction; a precise definition of initial state at this level of detail is therefore not needed. Since it is not feasible to represent infinite amounts of knowledge, we have to be selective about how to abstract the minimum information required to do things. This is especially true for engineering tasks performed by humans using machines, where the actions are not so clearly defined in terms of their preconditions and effects. Classical planners lack a theory of **state abstraction**; that is, they provide no guidance for determining the level of detail at which to abstract such complex real-world states.

Hierarchical planning. A hierarchical planner can discover dead ends in a high-level (abstract) plan before generating a more detailed expansion of the plan, for which search and backtracking will be more time-consuming. When hierarchical planning was first introduced, it was intended to reduce the amount of search that a planner needs to do. However, it turns out that there is no way of producing a plan which is guaranteed to be correct—in the classical sense—at one level of abstraction without verifying that correct plans can be generated at all lower levels of detail. This is a very important weakness of AI planning systems. It undermines the notion of hierarchical planning—at least in the way classical planners define it—since we have to do a complete depth-first search to ensure soundness.

Plan correctness. The notion of plan correctness in classical planners makes more sense in the case of robot plans than in managerial plans. For a managerial plan, correctness is a subtle notion. A manager will measure a plan's correctness against its ability to represent, predict, and control the use of resources on the project. It is not clear how the classical planning notion of logical correctness can ensure that a plan will meet this requirement. Failure to satisfy some action's precondition can prevent a robot from achieving the goal of its task but may have no major effect on the correctness of an engineering manager's plan.

11.2.3   Representation: The Achilles Heel of AI Planners

The underlying cause of these limitations of classical AI planners is inadequate representation. They use only literals—either in propositional logic or first-order predicate logic syntax (recall the discussion in Chapter 3)—to define both the knowledge about the problem and the operators which are the building blocks for solving it. Initial states and goal states must be described by lists of literals. Further, each operator is defined only as a list of literals that constitute its preconditions and a second list of literals whose addition or deletion constitute its effects.

We have asserted in several places in this book that representation and problem solving are intimately connected. The situation after thirty years of experience with AI planning systems illustrates this point clearly. An impoverished form of representation for planning knowledge has consigned classical AI planners to the role of solving toy problems in introductory AI classes, while knowledge-based planning systems are solving real manufacturing problems by employing rules, frames, and MBR techniques to represent and reason with a variety of knowledge about objects, actions, and resources in specific domains. The Molgen

[Stefik 1981a, 1981b] and SIPE-2 [Wilkins 1988] systems, which are described in Section 11.3, provided important extensions to both the representation and reasoning capabilities of classical AI planners and laid the groundwork for later MBR planners such as PIPPA and OARPLAN, which we describe in Section 11.7.

11.3 NARROWLY SCOPED EXPERT PLANNING SYSTEMS

General-purpose planners require no a priori assumptions about the domain to which they will be applied. In contrast, special-purpose planners are built with a specific, narrow planning domain in mind, with the result that they resemble expert systems in the selected planning domain. Among the special-purpose planners that have been developed to date are some developed for engineering applications. Because these systems employ large amounts of domain-specific knowledge, they have generally proved to be more powerful at generating plans in their area of applicability than general-purpose planners. Moreover, several of them have also attempted to automate parts of the scheduling task; that is, they assign resources and durations to activities in a plan. These expert planning systems usually accept as their input a description of the facility to be manufactured. Using this input, the kinds of planning and scheduling tasks attempted by such expert planning systems include

❑   Selecting manufacturing methods;

❑   Generating a list of project activities (rather than having these provided as a set of operators as in general-purpose planners), typically as a relatively straightforward expansion of the components contained in the artifact to be created;

❑   Ordering the activities in the plan;

❑   Estimating activity durations and costs; and

❑   Producing and maintaining schedules that meet different project constraints.

There is much activity currently under way in implementing expert planning and scheduling systems in various domains. Some recent examples include planning for subsea maintenance of oil platforms [Brysland 1988]; scheduling airline crews [Martins 1988]; scheduling an automobile factory [Jain 1989]; and process planning for machine parts

[Cutkosky 1989]. Numerous other commercial—and hence proprietary—knowledge-based planning and scheduling systems are under development or have been implemented in organizations that manufacture products as diverse as process plants, semiconductors, aircraft, machine parts, and trucks, and in service organizations like airlines and hospitals.

We now briefly describe two representative expert planning systems. They employ large amounts of domain-specific knowledge implemented in rules and frames, but their applicability is limited to narrow classes of problems. Molgen is a system to plan experiments in molecular biology. LIFT is another expert planning system. It plans effectively for offshore platform outfitting, but it has no general planning capabilities outside of the specific domain of installing deck modules in offshore platforms of a particular type.

11.3.1   Molgen

The **Molgen** system [Stefik 1981a, 1981b] was an attempt to use domain-specific knowledge about the actions and objects employed in molecular biology experiments to plan in that domain. Molgen introduced the notion of planning at multiple levels of abstraction using hierarchies of both actions and objects; used constraint propagation to communicate among almost independent subproblems; and used a layered control structure similar to the one found in BB1 [Hayes-RothB 1985]. This system and its subsequent extensions provided the first convincing evidence that knowledge-rich planning systems could produce plans comparable to those of human experts in challenging, real-world planning domains. We will present a detailed discussion of the Molgen system in Section 11.6.

11.3.2   LIFT

The **LIFT** system developed by Bremdal [1987] for planning the offshore installation of deck modules on offshore platforms with floating cranes was one of the first expert planning systems implemented in an engineering domain. LIFT sequences the installation of deck modules on an offshore platform by incorporating heuristics to take account of geography, season, wind, waves, tide, ocean bottom conditions, water depth, oil platform characteristics, and crane characteristics.

The first version of LIFT was a proof-of-concept prototype, developed as a rule-based system using a custom inference engine developed from scratch in Lisp and Flavors. The second version of LIFT—called LIFT-2—greatly expanded upon the amount of knowledge encoded as heuristics and was implemented using rules in the OPS5 production rule language [Brownston 1985] to improve its efficiency and portability.

The search process in LIFT-2 is close to the one described for the HI-RISE design system [Maher 1984a] mentioned in Chapter 10 and to Friedland's extension of Molgen [Friedland 1985]. LIFT employs hierarchical generate/test/eliminate, refining a skeletal plan as it proceeds down the hierarchy of detail. LIFT also makes use of a context tree in which variables in rules are instantiated from their context (see Section 5.3.2) in order to reduce the number of rules needed.

The third version of LIFT was implemented using a blackboard approach to represent knowledge normally applied in solving this problem by the platform owner, engineer, and contractor. The blackboard approach enabled LIFT to use the same kind of opportunistic problem-solving control strategy used in the SightPlan system described in Chapter 10 [Tommelein 1989a]. This approach is also similar to the approach used in the Callisto system described in Section 11.4.1 [Sathi 1985]. Work on the LIFT system is continuing.

We draw these parallels between design and planning systems to show that KBESs for formation tasks as far apart as offshore platform construction, high-rise building design, and construction site layout can use many of the same architectures and paradigms for knowledge representation and reasoning.

11.4 TOWARD KBES PLANNING SHELLS

Developers of KBESs for diagnosis and evaluation attempted to develop shells or generic problem-solving architectures by abstracting high-level representation and reasoning concepts from a series of domain-specific applications. Developers of planning systems have tried to do likewise. ISIS and Callisto were two of the earliest attempts at planning shells; they were developed for job shop scheduling and project management, respectively. We review these briefly. The CONSTRUCTION PLANEX system is a prototype of a planning shell of this type that has been successfully used to generate plans for building construction and wire harness assembly—a considerable range of problem types [Zozaya-Gorostiza 1989]. We provide a somewhat more detailed description of the PLANEX system.

11.4.1   ISIS and Callisto

The **ISIS** system employs a frame-based knowledge representation language for modeling activities and their constraints; it applies constraint-directed search to solve job shop scheduling problems [Fox 1984]. ISIS makes extensive use of constraints to prune an otherwise vast search space of planning solutions for job shop scheduling. The sequence of machining operations to be applied to a particular part is known in advance in this domain; the problem is to allocate scarce machine, material, and operator resources in a way that best satisfies a set of objectives for on-time completion of criticial parts (or lots of parts) while optimizing resource allocation in the shop. ISIS is thus a scheduling rather than a planning system in that it devotes few resources to deriving needed actions or their precedence relationships.

The Callisto project was an attempt to extend some of the ideas from ISIS to address the demands of managing large-scale development projects at Digital Equipment Corporation (DEC) [Sathi 1985]. The first prototype of Callisto was implemented as a rule-based system for configuration tracking. Subsequent work continued in several areas: resource management (scheduling); activity management (relevant to our current discussion of planning); and configuration management. We will discuss the activity management aspects of Callisto here.

Callisto represents knowledge about a project in four layers of abstraction in the same frame-based system used in ISIS [Wright 1983]. This is the same abstraction idea used in Molgen, so it will not be further elaborated here. Callisto uses a rich representation of activities, including slots, to represent the aggregation and abstraction of activities as well as temporal and causal constraints. Callisto extends somewhat the STRIPS representation of causality in which states enable actions and actions change states, but Callisto falls far short of representing causality in the qualitative reasoning style discussed in Chapters 7 and 8.

The approach that Callisto uses for plan generation is that the user inputs activities and constraints interactively and proposes an initial sequence. Callisto then uses structural rules (e.g., pointing out a missing constraint) or heuristic rules (e.g., suggesting revision of an inappropriate duration) to critique the user-submitted plan. After the plan has been debugged by Callisto's (internal) critics, it carries out scheduling in a forward "dispatch" mode (rather than in a backward "reservation" mode). As it sets up the schedule, Callisto uses one of four algorithms to assign priorities to activities competing for overconstrained resources. The system can schedule multiple projects simultaneously over the same resource pool.

The most interesting contribution of Callisto is arguably in the area of configuration management, where Callisto introduces some novel approaches to constraint-directed negotiation for resolving design interface clashes by a series of mini-Callisto systems, each representing a different member of a project team [Sathi 1986].

Although Callisto has very limited capabilities for plan generation, we have discussed it here because it begins to introduce the notion of an integrated, high-level AI shell for designing, planning, and managing projects; it also uses a layered frame architecture for representation, and it uses inheritance, rules, and procedures for reasoning.

11.4.2 CONSTRUCTION PLANEX

CONSTRUCTION PLANEX is a knowledge-based system that was originally developed to carry out both planning and scheduling in the construction excavating domain; it was then generalized to plan for other areas of building construction and for electrical wire harness assembly [Hendrickson 1987; Zozoya-Gorostiza 1989]. PLANEX was developed in the KnowledgeCraft rule/frame/OOP AI development language.

PLANEX accepts as its input a description of the elementary components in a facility, coded according to an industry-standard numbering system termed the MASTERFORMAT system. This permits aggregation of elements into subsystems or systems by dropping the trailing digit of the code at each level. The actions associated with each component are bound to elementary components to generate a list of **element activities**.

Element activities are then rolled up into **project activities**—the level of aggregation at which plans and schedules will be generated—using the MASTERFORMAT code. At this point the system attempts to introduce appropriate precedence relationships among project activities. It does this by having project activities inherit rules about precedence constraints from their component superclasses. Since editing frame slots directly in a text mode is extremely tedious, rules are implemented as decision tables to facilitate knowledge acquisition and debugging.

CONSTRUCTION PLANEX represents much more knowledge about its planning domain than the operators in STRIPS-style planners can do. It can produce useful plans in the construction domain, but much of its knowledge must be replaced in order for PLANEX to plan in even a related construction domain, and particularly for the wire harness planning problem. This is because the knowledge about precedence between activities and the decomposition and aggregation of activities is hard-wired into PLANEX rather than being derived causally from first principles like topological enclosure or gravity support. At the same time, PLANEX has extensive capabilities for scheduling and resource assignment and has a well-developed user interface. Thus, PLANEX's principal strength, like Callisto's, is more in aiding or automating scheduling than in plan generation.

A more broadly applicable knowledge-based planning shell requires representing and reasoning with fundamental knowledge about the reasons for including activities in a plan, as well as for determining precedence among the activities so included. The MBR planning systems described in Section 11.5 begin to approach this goal.

11.5 MBR PLANNING SYSTEMS

Model-based reasoning (MBR) involves qualitative reasoning about causality in engineering systems (see Chapters 7 and 8). In the case of planning, this translates into reasoning causally about both the inclusion of activities in a plan and the ordering of those activities. Several planning systems that were implemented during the late 1980s can claim to embody MBR concepts. We describe four of them briefly in this section and expand upon the OARPLAN system as our second major example in Section 11.7.

11.5.1 SIPE-2/SIPE

SIPE-2 [Wilkins 1989] is the latest in the line of STRIPS-style AI planners, but with some significant extensions that address the representational weaknesses of earlier AI planners. The original SIPE system is an extension of STRIPS-style AI planners [Wilkins 1984, 1988]. It employs a means-end search in generating plans, but it extends the Molgen approach of using constraints in planning by providing an explicit, general set of constraints that can be used in many domains and by allowing constraint variables to be evaluated before being instantiated. SIPE also provides a frame hierarchy in which objects can inherit attributes from superclasses; thus it greatly expands upon the representational capabilities of earlier planners.

SIPE was designed to generate plans efficiently for single-agent tasks. However, the heuristics employed to speed up search resulted in overconstrained plans for multiple agents—highlighting the age-old tradeoff between processing speed and optimality of solutions. **SIPEC** was an attempt to extend SIPE into a high-level planning shell for multiagent planning problems in the construction domain [Kartam 1990]. To support SIPEC and other real-world planning applications of SIPE (including a brewery planning system), Wilkins modified the original SIPE heuristics used to expand plan goals so that SIPE could generate logically correct, least constrained plans for multiple agents. There have been many other minor improvements in SIPE-2. These include extended temporal reasoning, extended resource reasoning, and a vastly improved graphic interface. However, from our perspective, the primary difference in SIPE-2 is its ability to produce least constrained, parallel plans for multiple agents.

SIPEC uses fundamental knowledge akin to first principles to derive precedence relationships among activities, rather than having activity precedences hard-wired into preconditions or decision tables. This knowledge is used in SIPEC to order activities such that components have gravity support and are protected from weather (if required) at the time that they are installed; workers satisfy safety constraints related to falls; components are protected from materials or activities that could damage them after being installed; and so on.

SIPEC has also been integrated with a CADD system (AutoCad Version 10.0) in the style described in Chapter 8 so that component descriptions, including topology, can be read in from the CADD database [Ito 1989]. Because it reasons from first principles at the *component level*, SIPEC can generate plans for additional projects of the same type, and even for other kinds of constructed facilities that employ the same components and activities, with no additional knowledge. Moreover, as the library of generic activities and components included in SIPEC is expanded, its versatility increases.

Experiments with SIPEC have demonstrated that SIPE-2, an extended and customized classical AI planner, can generate correct plans for a fairly broad range of construction projects—including an office building, a single-family house, and an offshore oil platform—from descriptions of components' attributes and the topology of each project [Kartam 1990]. SIPEC thus points the way to knowledge-based planning shells that can be used for planning problems across a much broader range of applications than the expert planning systems described in Section 11.4.

11.5.2 GHOST: Using Critics to Constrain a Plan

GHOST is a planning system that reasons about attributes of and relationships among objects in the construction planning domain to define project activities and precedence relations [Navinchandra 1988]. GHOST starts with the assumption that all activities can be executed in parallel, then uses a series of critics to introduce precedence constraints among activities. A related system, BUILDER, generates plans for interior partition construction by reasoning about graphic objects defined in an object-oriented CADD system [Cherneff 1988].

GHOST starts with a high-level set of tasks, all of which it assumes can be executed in parallel. It uses its **refinement critics** to expand the high-level activities into subnetworks. Activities in subnetworks inherit object descriptions from the high-level activities. Next, GHOST introduces **physical critics** and **construction critics** to introduce precedence constraints among the detailed activities in the parallel subplans. Finally, GHOST uses a **redundancy critic** to eliminate redundant constraints which are likely to be introduced by the other critics to give a least constrained, logically correct plan.

The control structure in GHOST involves a simple blackboard architecture that reasons about when to apply the modular rule sets (critics). Critics fire on the basis of matches between their premises and facts in the problem description and in the current solution state, stored in a common data structure of frames. Since GHOST's critics reason causally about precedence on the basis of enclosure, support, and so on, we consider it to be an MBR planner. It has no scheduling capability.

11.5.3 PIPPA: A Hierarchy of Actions Applied to Objects

The **PIPPA** planning system and the **XPERT** expediting system introduce a clear and rich definition of activities [Marshall 1987]. They have been used to develop and expedite plans for manufacturing flight simulators, for constructing foundations, and for planning the tasks involved in submitting tenders for furnace installation. PIPPA and XPERT are implemented in the Rule-Based Frame System (RBFS) rule/frame/OOP environment which we described in Chapter 6 [Kellett 1989].

The PIPPA system synthesizes the object and action abstraction ideas from Molgen into a clean yet powerful framework for planning, based upon the notion that an activity in a plan consists of an action-object pair. This hardly seems revolutionaryin the light of the current discussions, but the way in which PIPPA implements this idea results in a remarkably uncluttered planning framework with considerable power.

PIPPA employs both object and action abstraction and product and project models. Objects are described in a hierarchy of objects and inherit many of their properties and behavior, including those needed to generate plans, from superclasses. Similarly, actions are defined in a hierarchy of action types and inherit planning knowledge from the project action hierarchy. Activities can be defined at any level of abstraction by creating a link from an object in the object hierarchy to an action in the action hierarchy.

PIPPA uses rules and demons to instantiate plans at any level of detail, by attaching a specific set of components (the specific plan) to a generic object model of the product. The specific product instantiates itself properly using "when accessed" demons to modify the attributes inherited from the generic model as needed. As explained in our discussion of MBR in Chapter 8, naming conventions are important to ensure that this happens correctly.

Work is under way to extend and refine the capabilities and interface of PIPPA to make it a powerful and easily used planing shell for a variety of planning applications. The modeling of structure and function in the object hierarchy, and the causal reasoning about activity elaboration and refinement in the action hierarchy, make PIPPA an attractive planning system for building MBR planning KBESs.

11.5.4 OARPLAN: Planning as Model-Based Reasoning

The OARPLAN system adopts the activity representation in PIPPA and extends it to incorporate resources as a third constituent of activities [Darwiche 1989]. It has been implemented as part of an integrated design and construction planning environment in which designs produced using AutoCad are read into an object-oriented model of product structure. OARPLAN reads this model and produces a construction plan. Subsequent changes in design are reflected in modified construction plans.

Like GHOST, OARPLAN reasons with knowledge of first principles to derive its precedence relationships among activities. Like PIPPA, it uses models of product and project structure and function as part of its reasoning. And like SIPEC, it draws its problem definition directly from CADD project component descriptions and topology. Section 11.7 contains a detailed description of OARPLAN, the second planning system that we will describe in depth in this chapter.

11.6 MOLGEN: HIERARCHICAL PLANNING WITH CONSTRAINTS

Molgen (<u>Mol</u>ecular <u>Gen</u>erator) is a knowledge-based planner that assists molecular geneticists in planning experiments. It represents an important advance over earlier AI planners [Stefik 1981a, 1981b].   Molgen makes extensive use of the notions of constraint propagation [Stefik 1981a] and metaplanning [Stefik 1981b]. The core idea in Molgen is that planning problems can be treated by decomposing them into nearly independent subproblems for which plans can be developed separately, while using constraint formulation, constraint propagatation, and constraint satisfaction to manage the interdependencies that exist among subplans.

11.6.1   Philosophy of Molgen

Molgen employs two important ideas in its planning:

❑   *Abstraction hierarchies* of both objects and actions in this domain, and

❑   A *least commitment* approach to planning, in which constraints are used to progressively restrict the range of legal values for the operators and objects involved in plan steps.

11.6.2   Representation in Molgen

Molgen represents operators, objects, and constraints as frames, using the Units Package, an early frame representation language with OOP capabilities (from which KEE, LOOPS, and several other commercial AI programming environments are descended).

The most general operator in Molgen is called LAB OPERATOR. At the next level of abstraction there are 4 fundamental molecular biology operators: MERGE, AMPLIFY, REACT, and SORT. The final level has 13 specific operators that are instances of the 4 at the second level. Similarly, LAB_OBJECTS is the most generic object about which Molgen can reason. The next level contains 6 objects: ANTIBIOTIC, CULTURE, DNA_STRUC, ENZYME, and SAMPLE. The object hierarchy continues to specialize objects through 6 levels with 74 kinds of objects.

11.6.3   Reasoning in Molgen

Molgen begins its planning by proposing high-level operations on abstract objects. This allows the plan to be developed at an abstract level with less searching and backtracking.

Constraints in Molgen represent domain-specific knowledge that can be used to deal with interacting subproblems. For example, the application of the abstract object BACTERIUM can be restricted with the constraint

(RESISTS BACTERIUM_1 ANTIBIOTIC_4). In applying this constraint, Molgen limits the possible values for BACTERIUM_1 to the set of bacteria which resist ANTIBIOTIC_4, but Molgen does not yet commit to a specific value which might violate other constraints.

Constraints in Molgen play several roles. First, they serve to eliminate large numbers of potential solutions at each step of the plan (as in our example above). Second, they serve as partial descriptions of objects or operators (mostly of objects in Molgen). Third, they serve to communicate interdependencies among subproblems during plan elaboration.

11.6.4 Control in Molgen

Molgen also introduced the notion of **metaplanning**, planning about planning [Stefik 1981b]. The layered architecture for control in Molgen reasons at the lowest level, the "laboratory space," about domain actions or specific plan steps that can be implemented in the laboratory. The next level, the "design space," contains knowledge about designing plans to implement specific plan steps; that is, it reasons about the order in which such steps should be attempted. The objects that Molgen reasons about at this level are CONSTRAINTS, DIFFERENCES, REFINEMENTS, and so on. The operators are PROPAGATE_CONSTRAINT, REFINE_OBJECT, and so on. The design space communicates with objects in the laboratory space by sending messages to objects in that space. Similarly, the strategy space plans at the highest level, communicating as needed with objects in the design space.

At the highest level, Molgen reasons both logically and heuristically. It attempts to plan by successively propagating constraints, introducing new steps in the plan, or resuming previously suspended steps. It resorts to heuristics when it gets stuck, that is, when it runs out of least commitment steps to take. It makes guesses to find values for underconstrained variables and undoes constraints to find legal values for overconstrained variables.

Molgen was extended in Friedland's Molgen Planner and SPEX, which use the planning strategy of looking up and refining appropriate skeletal plans [Friedland 1985]. The idea here is analogous to the concept of using case-based reasoning to select design prototypes and then applying rules to refine the prototypes for the specific requirements of a given application (which we discussed in Chapter 10). SPEX uses abstractions of an experiment's goals as the basis for selecting an appropriate skeletal plan and then refines the plan hierarchically, employing qualitative simulation of the experiment being planned to test the validity of the plan. SPEX also integrates Molgen's layered control structure for controlling reasoning.

11.6.5   Contributions of Molgen

Attentive readers will have noticed the similarity of ideas in Molgen to those in the BB1 blackboard system described in Chapter 8 [Hayes-RothB 1985], as well as to the design interpreter described in Chapter 4 [Chan 1987]. The similarity with BB1 is no coincidence; their developers exchanged ideas extensively. And Chan's design interpreter drew heavily on the Molgen work while attempting to implement these ideas in Prolog.

The domain-specific knowledge incorporated in Molgen's constraints; the way in which Molgen can plan at multiple levels of abstraction (in terms of the specificity of actions to be executed, and of objects involved in those actions); and its layered control knowledge—all these provide a powerful demonstration that richer forms of knowledge representation for domain-specific knowledge in a given applications area (e.g., molecular biology experiments) and of control knowledge for a class of problems (e.g., experiment design) can greatly increase the power of a planning system.

SPEX incorporates causal reasoning and is implemented in a way that facilitates its extension to other domains. It is thus a forerunner of MBR planning systems. The OARPLAN system, described next, builds on many of the ideas in Molgen and SPEX.

11.7   OARPLAN: THE OBJECT-ACTION-RESOURCE PLANNER

OARPLAN, the Object-Action-Resource Planner, is an attempt to combine the generality and high performance of prior general-purpose and expert planning systems, respectively, to generate project plans based on facility descriptions. OARPLAN can be viewed as an MBR planner in that

❑   OARPLAN obtains its problem definition in the form of product component properties and topology extracted from a CADD database and placed into an object-oriented product model that employs abstraction hierarchies and part-of hierarchies synergistically; and

❑   OARPLAN carries out true causal reasoning about precedence based upon first principles like topological enclosure and structural support.

A planning problem is presented to OARPLAN as a facility description. A facility is defined as a set of physical components. Each component has its specifications, such as material type, surface finish, and paint. Components of a facility are related through different kinds of relationships, the most important being spatial ones. Since an OARPLAN planning problem is defined by a set of physical components with their specifications and interrelationships, it is possible to extract such a description from a three-dimensional CADD model of the facility. The task of the planner is to produce a plan for constructing the facility described by its CADD model.

The plan produced by OARPLAN consists of a list of activities and their sequential relationships which, when executed, achieve the overall project objective: constructing the facility. It is important to note that there is a continuum of plans that meet the above objective. At the most abstract level, we may generate an **executive-level plan**—the type of plan that is needed by a high-level manager for project estimation and control. At the other extreme, we may generate a motion plan that is to be used by a robot for automatic construction. Levitt [1987b] defines executive, work package, and task levels as three levels of plan abstraction used by managers of construction facilities. OARPLAN tries to generate plans at these levels.

The OARPLAN system is intended to be embedded in a networked workstation design environment where it can be accessible to all of the participants in a facility design team—humans and computers [Howard 1989b]. OARPLAN was thus designed to interface with industry-standard software: AutoCad for design description input and MicroPlanner for visualization and analysis of plans produced by OARPLAN [Ito 1989].

The initial version of OARPLAN was implemented in 1988 using the BB1 blackboard environment on a TI Explorer workstation. In order to facilitate interfacing OARPLAN with CADD and project management software, a second version was implemented during 1989 using FrameKit and RuleKit (frame and production rule shells implemented in Common Lisp) to run on a Macintosh II computer. Sections 11.7.1 and 11.7.2 describe OARPLAN's current representation and reasoning capabilities [Darwiche 1989; Ito 1989].

11.7.1   Representation in OARPLAN

In this section we describe how OARPLAN represents the product (a building, in this case); the plan; and the activities in the plan.

Description of the facility in OARPLAN. The user of OARPLAN describes the building for which it will develop a plan by simply designing the building in AutoCad using CIFECAD [Ito 1989], a high-level building design interface developed for OARPLAN within AutoCad's embedded

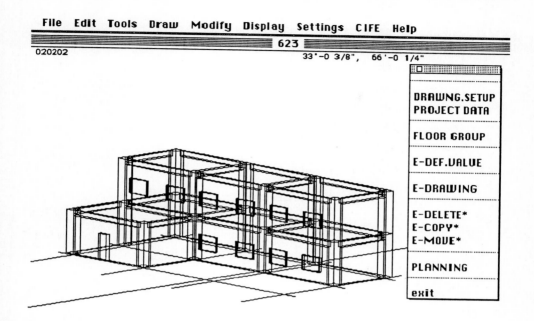

Figure 11-2 The CIFECAD design interface. Much of the component property and relationship information needed to generate construction plans can be automatically captured as a building is designed in AutoCad using this interface.

AutoLisp language. Figure 11-2 shows the CIFECAD interface as it appears on a Macintosh II computer.

As additional components are created in CIFECAD, the following kinds of information are generated with little user input by a combination of default values, overriding entries in dialog boxes, and computation, then stored in AutoCad blocks for transfer to the project model (see Figure 11-3).

❑ **Component classes,** such as floors, beams, columns, and walls, along with further classification of these components (e.g., external and internal walls), are defined in PMAP, an object-oriented product model that serves as an interface between CIFECAD and OARPLAN [Ito 1989]. CIFECAD menus for component definition enforce PMAP's naming conventions for components so that they will be correctly attached to the frame-based product model later.

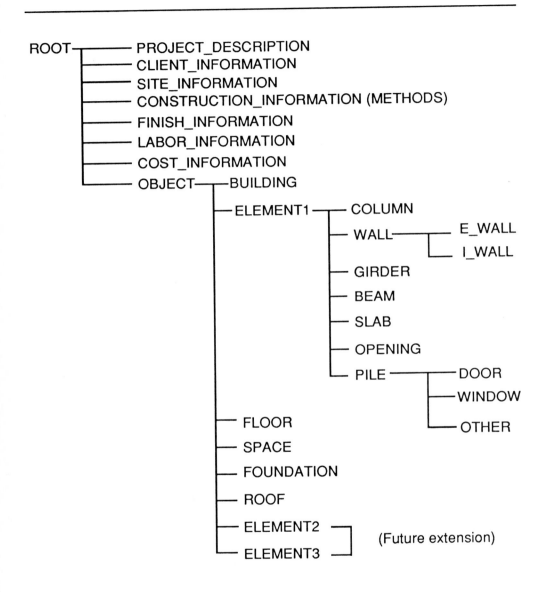

Figure 11-3 Elements of the OARPLAN product model in PMAP (adapted from [Ito 1989]).

❑ **Component properties**, such as dimensions, material composition, and finish specifications, are provided when OARPLAN accepts default values, which are correct in many cases. As project definition proceeds,

OARPLAN dynamically adjusts these values or overrides defaults with new local values. The component property data are stored in AutoCad's "blocks" data structure and are retrieved later for transfer to OARPLAN via PMAP.

❑ **Component geometric and topological relationships** (e.g., SUPPORTED_BY, ENCLOSED_BY, ADJACENT_TO) are generated automatically when components are created using CIFECAD. For example, a beam must be attached to a column, and a simple procedure deduces that a beam is supported by the columns at its ends and below it. (This default computation can also be overridden—for example, for a cantilever beam.) Component relations are stored in AutoCad blocks along with properties.

Representation of a plan in OARPLAN. In OARPLAN, the concept of a plan is modeled around that of an activity. A plan is defined as a collection of activities connected by a number of different types of relations [Sathi 1985]. One kind of relation involves sequential dependency, that is, **before** or **after**; these reflect the ordering among activities. There are other useful relationships among activities, including **subactivity** and **superactivity**, reflecting the different levels of abstraction or elaboration of a project plan.

These two kinds of activity relationships serve different purposes. Within a given level of detail of a plan, sequential dependency relations are needed in order to perform network time calculations. Aggregation of activities through superactivity relationships can be used to infer responsibility for completion of the activity, among other things. Activity elaboration is needed to reduce the scale of activities and to allow better estimation and control of project time and cost.

Representation of activities in OARPLAN. An activity is a core concept of project planning. Examples of activities are pouring concrete, erecting a wall frame, and constructing a column. The means of representing an activity in OARPLAN is adapted from PIPPA [Marshall 1987]. In PIPPA an activity is defined as an action that applies to a product component and that needs resources. Our representation is essentially the same; in OARPLAN we define an activity as the following triple.

<ACTION><OBJECT><RESOURCES>

Each element of this triple is called an **activity constituent**. For example, *painting a wall* can be defined as the *action* <PAINT> being applied to the *object* <WALL> using the *resources* <PAINT, LADDER, PAINTER>. Other examples are <WELD><MECHANICAL_PIPE><WELDER>; <LEVEL> <GROUND><DOZER, DOZER_OPERATOR>; and <CONSTRUCT> <BUILDING><ABC_COMPANY_RESOURCES>.

It is important to notice the difference between this notion of an activity and the STRIPS notion of an action schema or operator, such as PutOn (x, y). An operator is defined as an action, PutOn, augmented by a number of arguments, (x, y), that could represent anything—for example, an object or a resource used by the action. There are no predefined semantics for these arguments. Associated with an operator are the action's preconditions and effects. An OARPLAN activity corresponds to a STRIPS operator with the constituents—action, object, and resource—represented uniformly and having fixed semantics. Also, no preconditions or effects of an activity are specified a priori in OARPLAN; elaboration and dependency knowledge sources (discussed below and in Section 11.7.2) are used to deduce them.

Activities can be represented at different levels of abstraction based on the levels of abstraction of the included actions, objects, and resources. The activity <CONSTRUCT><BUILDING><CONTRACTOR'S_RESOURCES> is a very abstract one because of the abstraction levels of its constituents, <CONSTRUCT>, <BUILDING>, and <CONTRACTOR'S_RESOURCES>. The relative degree of abstraction of an action or an object is defined by its position in an abstraction hierarchy. (In version 1.0 of OARPLAN, only action and object constituents are represented and used in reasoning; resources will be represented in the next version of the system.)

Actions are either simple or compound. **Simple actions** are those that can be performed directly without refinement, like *installing* a bolt in a steel connection. **Compound actions** are those that can be elaborated to lower-level ones; for example, *placing concrete* can be elaborated to pouring, curing, and finishing concrete. It is important to keep in mind that there is no predefined set of primitive activities; depending on the size of the object concrete_1 , <PLACE><CONCRETE_1> might be a good primitive activity. On the other hand, if the size of concrete_1 is too large for a given level of precision in cost or schedule estimating or control, <PLACE> <CONCRETE_1> may need to be elaborated to <POUR><CONCRETE_1>, <CURE><CONCRETE_1>, and <FINISH><CONCRETE_1>.

Similarly, object constituents of activities can be of different types and grain size. There are **simple objects** and **compound objects**. In the same example, building construction, OARPLAN has simple objects such as steel bolts and compound ones such as concrete beams. Classifying an object as being simple or compound depends on the level of reasoning to be performed on it. When installing a steel bolt, we are interested only in the bolt itself and not in its more detailed physical properties. In the case of a concrete beam, we may want to reason about the components of the beam, such as the type of concrete that is used and the number and diameter of reinforcing steel bars. In the latter case, we can classify concrete and reinforcing steel bars as simple objects that are PART_OF the compound object, CONCRETE_BEAM.

To illustrate how this distinction is used, consider how an elaboration of the activity <CONSTRUCT><CONCRETE_BEAM> might include the activities <CONSTRUCT><FORM>, <PLACE><REBARS>, <POUR><CONCRETE>, and <CURE><CONCRETE>. In the case of a precast concrete beam supplied by a subcontractor, classifying it as a simple object might be more appropriate.

Compound objects are of many types and are defined as collections of other compound or simple objects that we call its **components**. The type of a compound object depends on the common property that relates the components. The group of columns located on a given floor can be viewed as a compound object that can be a constituent of an activity. A compound object is usually specified by a predicate that filters instances of a certain generic type as either being in the group or not. Different predicates yield different group instances. If the components are contained within a defined space, then the compound object is a **zone**. (For example, a building floor is a zone and all the objects within the floor are its components.) If the components are parts of a physical object, then it is an **assembly**. (The reinforcing steel bars and concrete are parts of a concrete beam, the assembly in this case.) Defining compound objects is a way of grouping objects, which is a common way of aggregating activities.

The generic language of OARPLAN is aimed at allowing the user to communicate easily about activity constituents, both actions and objects. To this end, OARPLAN provides the user with various grouping predicates specific to the domain and different object properties or relationships that can be extracted from a CADD system.

11.7.2 Reasoning in OARPLAN

OARPLAN starts at the first level of the plan with a high-level activity, such as <CONSTRUCT><BUILDING_1>. Different knowledge sources (KSs) contribute to the development of the plan by either elaborating each activity or posting some sort of a dependency onto it. Elaborating activities creates multiple levels of a plan, each with a different level of abstraction.

Dependency constraints apply to activities at the same level of a plan. When KSs cannot post any further modifications to a plan, the resulting plan is final.

Activity elaboration. A main activity A_m can be elaborated to a group of activities $[A_1, ..., A_n]$, which is called the **elaboration set**. Each one of these A_ks will be an **elaboration of** A_m. If activities $A_1, ..., A_n$ are completed, then so is activity A_m. Each member of the elaboration set is a **subactivity** of the main one, the **superactivity**.

OARPLAN has elaboration KSs which reduce the level of abstraction of higher-level activities. These KSs vary in their generality. Some apply to a wide range of activities, while others only apply to specific ones. Whenever an activity is included in a plan, elaboration KSs of OARPLAN try to elaborate it by introducing other, smaller-scale ones. Activity elaboration can be viewed as scale reduction.

The scale of an activity can be reduced along several dimensions, each of which serves a different purpose. We may reduce the scale to enhance the precision of time/cost estimation and control. In other cases we may not be satisfied with the overall project duration; elaborating some activities enables us to exploit potential parallelism among their subactivities and thus reduce the overall project time.

In some cases, the included action remains constant and the scale of the included object is reduced. For example, when elaborating the activity <CONSTRUCT><BUILDING_1>, the following KS (stated in pseudo-English) applies.

If	the activity includes:
action:	CONSTRUCT and
object: of class	ASSEMBLY

Then	elaborate the activity to activities including:
action:	CONSTRUCT and
object:	part of the ASSEMBLY.

Applying this KS will result in the activities <CONSTRUCT><FLOOR_1>, <CONSTRUCT><FLOOR_2>, and so on, as an elaboration of the higher-level activity <CONSTRUCT><BUILDING_1>.

Another KS can elaborate an activity <CONSTRUCT><ZONE>. It does so by generating activities that construct the objects included in a zone. An example of this is elaborating <CONSTRUCT><FLOOR_1>, which will yield the activities that construct all the objects included in the floor. The above elaboration KS and the one immediately following are examples of generic KSs, because they apply to actions involving abstract objects such as zones and assemblies.

In other cases, the scale of the action is reduced while the object remains the same. A specific elaboration KS that does this is

If	the activity includes:
action:	PLACE and
object:	CONCRETE

Then	elaborate the activity to the ordered activities:
action:	POUR, object: CONCRETE;
action:	FINISH, object: CONCRETE;
action:	CURE, object: CONCRETE.

Elaboration KSs may or may not introduce orderings among the elaboration set. The concrete KS imposed some ordering among activities, but the assembly and zone KSs did not. Other examples of elaboration KSs are those for a wall and a slab. *Specific* elaboration KSs refer to activities that are constant across different projects (Figure 11-4a). Slab construction remains relatively constant across projects in terms of the activities that elaborate it. Such KSs are more like subplans that the system knows about. *Generic* KSs apply to activities which can vary across projects depending upon the specific objects that make up each project and the relationships between them (Figure 11-4b). These KSs know how to perform scale reduction, such as breaking the included object along the ENCLOSED_BY or PART_OF relations. OARPLAN thus uses two methods to deal with activity inclusion: activity subplans and activity scale reduction. Note that elaboration KSs introduce activities that are less abstract than their superactivities.

Activities are elaborated in OARPLAN until no more KSs are applicable. In general, this does not produce optimal results. Extensions to OARPLAN will formalize the notion of an activity's scale and relate it to the needed grain size for estimation and control. Constructs that deal with activity

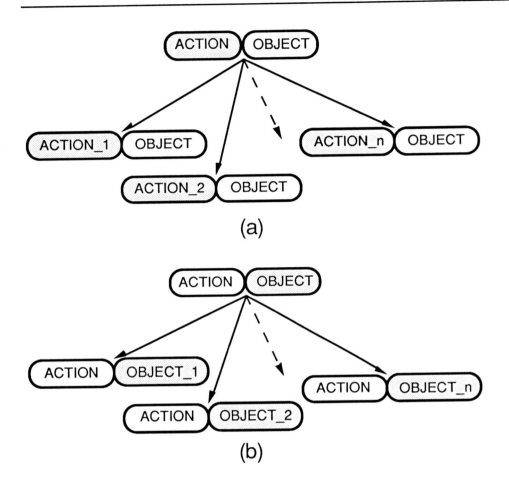

Figure 11-4 Activity elaboration in OARPLAN. (a) Elaboration of an activity by introducing scaled-down actions in its subactivities. (b) Elaboration of the original activity by reducing the scale of its constituent object. (Source: [Darwiche 1989])

scale are provided as part of the user language. The user can thus specify declaratively the needed scale for different activities, which will be used by the planner to decide when to stop elaborating. This is needed because, as we mentioned, elaborating activities based on object scale reduction may proceed unneccessarily far for some activities. If the user is not satisfied with the overall project cost or with the level of uncertainty in the current cost estimate, further elaboration of relevant activities can be requested.

GHOST [Navinchandra 1988] and PLANEX [Hendrickson 1987] start with activities at the component level and aggregate upward. OARPLAN, in contrast, embodies a top-down approach for elaborating activities. Construction planning is *product-oriented* in the sense that the final goal is to produce some product that meets certain requirements. The product here is a facility consisting of components. OARPLAN begins with a plan that includes activities at the component level, such as <CONSTRUCT> <COMPONENT_1>, and then elaborates down—by reducing action and object scale—until it reaches an activity scale that the user has defined to be appropriate.

Then OARPLAN can start working from the bottom up by combining activities in other ways based on aggregation KSs—similar to elaboration KSs—until a level of aggregation is reached that meets some user's organizational criteria.

Activity dependencies. Any dependency between two activities has some underlying reason. OARPLAN follows an MBR approach in asserting that this reason is related to the nature and properties of the activity in the context of a given project. OARPLAN therefore adopts the notion of activity constituents to capture the nature of the activity and reflect its important properties in its context. In this way, dependencies and elaborations can be inferred by deep causal reasoning, rather than being hard-wired into the activity description across all projects. In fact, in OARPLAN the activity name is just a label for a set of linked activity constituents.

With enough knowledge about constituents, a planner should be able to attribute any dependency between two activities to the relations or interactions among their constituents. OARPLAN's current representation of activities has action and object constituents. Accordingly, logical or technical dependencies are attributed to action or object relations.

One of the main sources for activity dependency is the interaction among their constituent actions. *Inspecting* something has to happen after *installing* it, *curing* concrete has to come after *finishing* it, and so on. This is a very common type of activity dependency and is usually not flexible. Both PIPPA [Marshall 1987] and PLANEX [Zozaya-Gorostiza 1989] use this sort of action dependency to infer activity dependencies.

A second important source of activity dependency is the presence of relations between object constituents. OARPLAN has dependency KSs of the following general form (stated in pseudo-English).

If   (ACTIVITY_1 and ACTIVITY_2 are in the plan and

        ACTIVITY_1 consists of action A_1, object O_1 and

        ACTIVITY_2 consists of action A_2, object O_2 and

        object O_1 is related to object O_2 by relation R)

Then   (introduce relation D between ACTIVITY_1 and ACTIVITY_2).

This is a simple form of KS. Others may have as their premise a condition on the relation between the included actions or their superclasses. The general form of a premise is some relation among activity constituents or their superclasses. An important goal of the OARPLAN research is to provide the user with a rich set of domain constituent relations that replace R in the above rule. Current relations include SUPPORTED_BY, ADJACENT_TO, ENCLOSED_BY, and IN_SAME_FLOOR. Figure 11-5 illustrates how OARPLAN introduces an activity precedence constraint using the SUPPORTED_BY relation of the activities' object constituents.

OARPLAN also provides the user with a set of useful activity relations to replace D in the above rule. Currently it has only BEFORE and AFTER relations; other important ones are REQUIRES, CAUSES, and LAGS. REQUIRES and CAUSES are, respectively, similar to AFTER and BEFORE. The difference is that they force ACTIVITY_2 in the above rule to be included in the plan, if it is not already included. The LAGS relation requires some lag between the two activities—which subsumes BEFORE and AFTER relations.

The REQUIRES and CAUSES relations are of special importance. They represent another way for introducing activities in a plan. We pointed out that OARPLAN starts with a plan that has activities at the facility component level and elaborates the plan from these activities. The problem with this approach, however, is that a complete plan often requires supporting activities (e.g., scaffolding, cleanup, or excavation activities) which are not directly related to any of the project's components. These relations can be used to introduce such activities and others that are not directly elaborated from components.

It is both natural and easy to express dependency rules in the form of such object or action constraints. The experience of OARPLAN's developers indicates that it is natural for an expert to provide planning knowledge in this form; and the knowledge, once captured, is easily understood and learned by novice users, because it relates the activity dependency causally to some meaningful relationship that exists among the activity constituents.

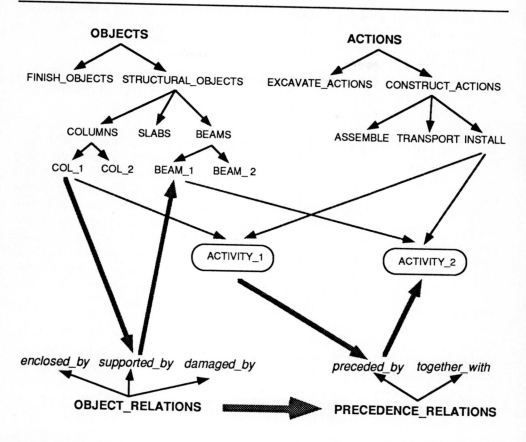

Figure 11-5 Reasoning from object relationships to activity dependency in OARPLAN.

Some specific examples of the dependency rules that the OARPLAN prototype system utilizes to develop plans for low-rise frame buildings are

☐ **Supports constraint.** Columns must be placed before the beams they support. The relation between the object constituents of the activities for installing columns and installing beams is *supported_by*.

☐ **Safety constraint.** In steel-framed buildings, do not start work on the members of floor *n* until the slabs of floor *n–1* or floor *n–2* are constructed. The relation here between activity objects is that *they belong to floors that are one or two levels apart.*

❑ **Interior wall–slab constraint.** Do not start constructing a wall until all (one or both) of the floor slabs adjacent to it are constructed. The relation here is that the slabs are *adjacent to the wall*.

❑ **Interior wall–exterior wall constraint.** Within a given floor, do not construct interior walls until all external walls have been constructed. The relation here is that the two walls *belong to the same floor*.

The current OARPLAN system utilizes mainly object relations. Dependencies that result from relations among action constituents are reflections of methodological or technical dependencies. Those that result from object relations reflect the spatial and topological description of the building. Both kinds are considered to be hard dependencies since they must be satisfied by all "legal" plans and are shown in the same way on the precedence diagram produced by the OARPLAN prototype. Future versions of the system will investigate other constituent relations, such as resource relations, which will result in "soft" or preference dependencies that apply to a plan. The latter will be represented differently in screen and hardcopy outputs of project plans produced by OARPLAN.

In summary, OARPLAN infers dependencies in two ways. The first is by utilizing predefined dependencies that are inherited from activity subplans, such as placing concrete. These are of the type that are constant across projects and about which little reasoning is needed. The second is by inferring dependencies through applying dependency KSs which reason about the constituents of activities. Since these vary across projects as a function of the objects, actions, and resources of a given project, extensive project-specific data are needed for each of the plans that OARPLAN produces. The data acquisition problem is solved via an automated interface to a high-level building design interface implemented in AutoCad.

11.7.3 Control in OARPLAN

Within the BB1 blackboard environment [Hayes-RothB 1985], OARPLAN runs several blackboards. The **facility blackboard** contains the description of the facility with all of its components and their relations. Entities on this blackboard represent object abstractions, which become more specific as we go down until we reach object instances. The **action blackboard** contains a similar hierarchy of actions. The **plan blackboard** contains the activities of the plan with the *before, after, subactivity,* and *superactivity* relations existing among them. Each activity is linked to an object on the facility blackboard and an action on the action blackboard. Finally, the **elaboration and dependency blackboards** contain the elaboration and dependency KSs. In

Note that 42 percent of the code is devoted to the user interface, while only 30 percent of Dipmeter Advisor's code is devoted to the obvious KBES components, the knowledge base and the inference engine. This emphasis on the user interface is not unusual in KBES design. In the PRIDE system, for example, about 40 percent of the code is dedicated to the user interface [Mittal 1986a].

We thus see here an interesting example of how technical and institutional implementation issues interact, and it speaks directly to the issue of how resources are allocated as an expert system is being built. It is important to recognize that the software (and the delivery platform) must create an environment that will be consistent with the way the expertise is exercised and comfortable for the intended user to use. That is, the knowledge engineers must design an interface that can be easily exercised by the domain experts and by the potential users. For example, we could look at the starting point in the design process captured in the PRIDE system. The interface allows the designer/user to "sketch" a path for a paper-handling subsystem in a way that is very close in feeling to how it would have previously been done on a drawing board [Morjaria 1985; Mittal 1986a]. And it is an interface that can be manipulated without requiring the user to know anything about Lisp, the language in which it was programmed, or about the intricacies of knowledge representation.

It is also interesting to look at the successful systems with a view toward the time required to complete them. Let us start, again, with Dipmeter Advisor, and let us see how much time was required for its development and evolution. It began as a research project in 1978, and the first protype was completed in 1980. The prototype, containing 245 kilobytes of DEC 2020 Lisp code and another 450 kilobytes of VAX Fortran code, was too slow. The second implementation was completed in 1983, running on a Xerox workstation with 650 kilobytes of Interlisp-D code. The 1983 implementation was considered sufficiently fast and robust for testing [Smith 1984]. (Recall the discussions of Lisp and other AI languages in Chapter 4, including the remarks on their history and their dialects; this should help explain some of the terms we have just used.)

Another well-known KBES also started as a research project in 1978 [Barker 1989; McDermottJ 1981]. The R1/XCON system began at Carnegie Mellon University in that year, with the first prototype being delivered to DEC in 1980. However, it was not put into regular use there until 1982, and even now it requires a very large support and maintenance staff. (Some 50 people work on this and related projects at DEC.) However, it does successfully configure 97 percent of all VAX orders, and thus its economic return is quite substantial.

Dipmeter Advisor and R1/XCON are often cited to make the point that building a large and robust expert system is a long and expensive process. Both of these projects required years of research and experimentation before they were adopted for regular use. Development of these systems began long before the kinds of tools that we now take for granted were available and understood, and both were developed to the point where they could be put into active, day-to-day use in commercial settings. Whereas the kinds of AI programming environments available today are far superior to those used in these early KBES applications and can significantly enhance the productivity of knowledge engineers in encoding expert knowledge, the process of knowledge acquisition for all but the most simple classification applications is still a time-consuming process that has not yielded significantly to automation or even acceleration.

As a general guide, it appears that a working prototype that addresses the key representation, reasoning, explanation, and validation problems for a significant KBES application can be built by a small team within one to two years. This was true for the prototypes of both Dipmeter Advisor and R1/XCON, as well as for the LSC Advisor, Platform, PRIDE, and SightPlan research projects. Note that, for commercial applications, a large part of the total expense of developing the KBES goes into the conversion of the system from a working or research prototype to an "industrial-strength" system that is put on-line in an organization and routinely used to support serious decisions.

One of the less obvious costs in building such systems is that of the experts' time. Clearly, the time devoted by the experts to a system-building project is typically time taken away from what they would otherwise be doing in their various organizations. Further, without the experts' active, enthusiastic, and continuing interaction with the knowledge engineers and other system builders, the knowledge cannot be successfully explicated and captured in the system. Thus, major commitments must be made both by the experts and by their organizations. Without such commitments, which obviously can be very expensive, serious system-building endeavors should not be undertaken.

Another aspect of system building that requires a major institutional commitment is the life of the system *after* its development. A KBES is—or at least should be—a dynamic system that receives active maintenance and updating. New cases and situations provide further experience that can be added to the knowledge base. The user interface and other features of the system can also be refined. (Remember that one of the real advantages of the separation of knowledge and control in expert system programming is that it facilitates the addition of chunks of knowledge [Dixon 1986b; Dym 1985a].) This requires a commitment by management to maintain and support the system, which really means that the system should provide a continuing benefit sufficient to justify to its sponsoring organization this continuing expense. (Recall our discussion of maintenance and support.)

Given even this relatively short itemization of the costs to an organization of building a KBES, we might well ask what benefits are to be gained in return for these expenditures. The answers are several [Bobrow 1986b; Dym 1985a]. The most obvious benefit is that the knowledge encapsulated within a KBES becomes available for use by people other than the originating experts, in a variety of circumstances. For instance, the knowledge can be used for propagating an approach to a problem (e.g., a design style) across a geographically dispersed collection of users. The KBES may be useful for retaining some aspect of corporate memory, perhaps the expertise of a retiring expert, for future use. A KBES can also be used as a training device, serving to initiate novices into areas of expertise with which they are unfamiliar. Thus, there are several ways in which a KBES can provide a significant return on investment for a corporation. ([Feigenbaum 1988] provides a series of case studies that illustrate dramatic benefits of recent KBES applications.)

Some of the benefits are more subtle, and perhaps more personal than increased corporate profits. One result of the knowledge acquisition process is the increase in understanding gained by the domain experts as their knowledge is elicited. It is now almost universally taken as a given that the experts derive a much sharper and deeper understanding of how they exercise their expertise, as well as the roots of that expertise in both experience and fundamental domain principles. And while it used to be thought that experts would be afraid of being replaced by KBESs based on their expertise, what usually happens is almost the precise opposite. Experts find that they enjoy the process and that they like having their experience and knowledge made the foundation of a good KBES. There are clearly psychic rewards here for the experts, and for many it turns out that they are then freed of the chore of having to repeatedly exercise the expertise that has been encapsulated. This in turn allows them to go on to new and more creative activities. It has even been argued convincingly that attempting to formalize the knowledge in a field highlights those areas of the field where knowledge is weakest, thus helping to focus research and advance science.

12.8.2 Who Owns the Knowledge in a KBES?

We have discussed how problems are selected and how knowledge is acquired for incorporation in a KBES application. Although this book is not intended as a legal treatise, we consider it worthwhile to discuss briefly the questions of who owns, and who is responsible for, the knowledge encoded in a KBES application.

Labor economists recognize two kinds of human capital based upon knowledge that individuals acquire in the course of their careers: knowledge about a class of problems in an industry sector, and knowledge about an organization's procedures, personnel, and modus operandi. The former is potentially of value to other firms in the industry and is taken with an employee if she or he leaves the employer; the latter is typically of little value to anyone other than the current employer and does not add to the employee's human capital in the marketplace.

KBESs incorporate both kinds of knowledge held by experienced individuals in an organization. If an individual's general, industry-sector knowledge has been incorporated in a KBES, it might be construed that something of value has been appropriated from an employee by his or her employer, in spite of employment agreements that assign all work products of the employment relationship to the employer. If this sounds extreme or unfair, readers should remember that courts frequently overrule language in an agreement if they it find to be in conflict with either party's—or some third party's—fundamental rights. An employee's industry-sector knowledge encapsulated in a KBES retained by the employer may thus become the subject of future litigation. The authors are not aware of any cases where claims have been filed by departing employees for royalties or other compensation for their knowledge that has been incorporated into a KBES, but it may be expected that such claims will be filed in the future. Companies—and experts who provide knowledge for KBESs—would be well advised to consider the intellectual property issues carefully, and to watch trends that develop in the law or in future litigation of this type.

12.8.3 Who Is Responsible for the Knowledge in a KBES?

In similar vein, we can discuss the issue of who is responsible for losses or damage arising from a third party's use of the knowledge in a KBES. Once again our discussion is primarily philosophical; it is not intended as a substitute for serious legal study of each situation—our standard disclaimer.

In the vast majority of past cases involving claims against software developers for damages or losses arising from the use of the software by professional end users, the users of software have been held liable. Courts have insisted that lawyers, doctors, accountants, engineers, and other professional users of software have a professional responsibility to be aware of and take into account any assumptions or limitations of the software that might affect its adequacy for the purposes for which it is being used. This seems to us to be a reasonable standard. The alternative would drive all software developers out of business under a storm of liability suits. In the case of KBESs, however, some observers have believed that the experts whose knowledge is incorporated in the systems, together with the knowledge programmers who incorporated the knowledge, should be held to a higher standard of liability. The rationale for this suggestion is that KBESs make specific diagnoses or recommendations, based on domain-specific knowledge, rather than delivering numerical solutions whose interpretation is left to the end user.

There is a counterargument, however, that carries some weight. Unlike conventional computer programs, such as finite element analysis packages, which are delivered in the form of "black boxes" made up of compiled binary code, KBESs are "glass boxes" that can "turn themselves inside out" to explain the knowledge that they incorporate to end users (see Chapter 6 for a discussion of this). Thus it can be argued that it is rather easy for end users to understand the underlying assumptions and the reasoning steps that KBES applications perform. The role of the user as a professional is then to evaluate for the client whether the program is appropriate for its intended use and to use the KBES technology where it is the best approach for delivering the professional engineering design, analysis, or management service. Following this line of reasoning, we might even project that there will come a time when engineers might be found liable for *not* using KBES technology in situations where analysis or design knowledge has been formulated in a KBES and has received validation by the profession. This validation could be explicit through acceptance by professional societies or regulatory authorities, or implicit through widespread use by leading practitioners in the profession.

Although there is merit in the latter philosophy, we must remind readers that the legal system in the United States—with its contingency-fee approach to tort claims, and its tendency to compensate accident victims by digging into any "deep pocket" that might have even a tangential share of liability—will undoubtedly generate litigation (and perhaps awards of damages) against KBES developers during the 1990s. It is therefore especially important that KBES applications be marketed and distributed with clear descriptions of their intended use, and of the range of cases for which their performance has been validated.

12.8.4   The Changing Roles of KBES Users

Professions have historically been flexible enough to redefine their goals and content as technology and social needs have evolved. Doctors became increasingly specialized as the body of medical knowledge grew beyond the reach of a single mind; the dental profession moved rapidly into preventive and cosmetic care after fluoride supplements became available; accountants moved into management consulting as bookkeeping became automated; and draftspeople will likely go the way of printing technicians. How will engineers adapt to the transformation of their profession as many tasks that were thought of as core tasks of engineers are partially or fully automated with KBES technology?

Clearly, some low-level engineering functions such as plant monitoring and design detailing will be largely assumed by intelligent machines. Diagnosis and repair planning will be automated using KBES technology for routine problems and assisted by KBES technology for novel or unusual problems. Design will become partially automated: routine and semicustom design will be done by KBESs, while human designers will use MBR design and simulation tools to help them assess the feasibility of innovative design solutions to new problems. Management of engineering projects and enterprises will still require many uniquely human skills, although KBESs for planning, scheduling, monitoring, and control will be valuable decision support tools for engineers in these roles. Even legal and personnel management tasks will be aided by KBES technology—indeed, this is already happening in some areas of these professions.

In a review of the impact of factory automation technology on human operators, Zuboff [1988] asserts that information technology can be used in two ways: to **deskill** tasks so that in effect humans become sensors and data entry operators for computers, or to **informate** tasks so that the information technology is used to provide human decision makers with a broader and deeper understanding of the systems that they build and operate. KBES technology clearly has the potential to be used in both ways.

We can already see some examples of deskilling KBESs in place—the early consultation-style expert systems are especially prone to be viewed in this way by both employers and users. Employers have powerful incentives to deskill tasks. Sometimes skilled people are just not available, so deskilling tasks allows employers to operate with less skilled but available employees. Moreover, even where skilled workers are available, employers under competitive pressures may elect to use less skilled—and hence lower-paid—workers to do the same tasks. In many cases this is probably a short-term solution, since less skilled workers are less adaptable to future changes and may be less likely to propose improved work methods or products. However, many firms live in a world that requires them to maximize profits in the short run.

At the same time, there are encouraging examples of informating KBESs. The notion of knowledge-based interactive graphics exhibited in KBESs like PRIDE [1986a], PLATFORM [Levitt 1987b], SightPlan [Tommelein 1989a], and the Intelligent Boiler Design System [Riitahuhta 1988] provide users with computer support tools that can rapidly compute and display the implications of the users' planning or design choices. The users can rapidly generate and test multiple solutions for problems on the formation end of our problem continuum.

Whether KBES will be used to deskill tasks so that they can be "run by the ghosts of experts past"—a quotation from a Swedish hydropower engineer who attended a short course offered by one of the authors—or to informate tasks, allowing workers to generate innovative and cost-effective solutions to engineering problems, is under the control of the next generation of computer-literate engineers like yourselves. The social and economic implications of this choice are as profound as any we can imagine. Using KBESs primarily for deskilling engineering work will hasten the arrival of the two-tier economy—programmers and robot technicians versus leisure industry workers and janitors—about which many social critics have already warned us. In contrast, exploiting KBESs and other emerging information technologies as powerful new tools for educating workers and informating work has the potential to generate broadly dispersed, enduring economic gains for all workers.

12.9   SUMMARY

This chapter has been devoted to a discussion of the implementation of a KBES, that is, of how to make it happen. In the process, we have raised many important issues, some technical, some institutional, some social, and some interactive across these three dimensions. It may be useful to close this discussion—and the book—with some maxims or warnings about KBES development, as well as with a listing of some of the advantages accruing to an organization that sponsors the development of an expert system. (An extended list of maxims about the process of system building can be found in [Buchanan 1983a].) The maxims, the list of benefits, and the potential roles for KBESs together summarize the main points of this chapter.

It is worth remembering the maxims that

❑ Expert systems cannot do the impossible (e.g., cure cancer).

❑ Expert systems cannot do the extraordinary (e.g., make money continuously on the stock market).

❑ Knowledge is expensive.

❑ It takes time to build a serious, robust expert system.

❑ A single knowledge representation scheme is often inadequate.

❑ Much more is known about developing diagnostic and interpretive expert systems than about planning and design systems.

Then why invest in an expert system? Because

❑ Expert systems do not get tired. They can perform routine tasks with high reliability and consistency.

❑ The knowledge acquisition process deepens and sharpens the experts' own understanding of knowledge—and it limits—in a domain.

❑ Expert systems allow the experts to concentrate on rarer, more interesting tasks.

❑ Expert systems can be used to train neophytes.

❑ Expert systems provide a community memory for sharing and propagating knowledge.

❑ Expert systems, with networking, permit the widespread standardization of techniques, methods, requirements, and so on.

And how will KBESs be used? They can be used in two ways.

❑ **Deskilling workers.** Using KBES technology in this way may appear cost-effective in the short term but has some unattractive long-term implications for both employers and workers.

❑ **Informating workers.** This approach to the use of KBES and other information technologies empowers knowledge workers by using the techniques and tools to disseminate and propagate—rather than to encapsulate and hide—what is arguably our scarcest resource: knowledge.

REFERENCES

[Agogino 1988]   A. M. Agogino, personal communication, 18 June 1988.

[Amarel 1968]   S. Amarel, "On Representations of Problems of Reasoning About Actions," in D. Michie (Editor), *Machine Intelligence 3*, Edinburgh University Press, Edinburgh, 1968.

[Amarel 1978]   S. Amarel, "Basic Themes and Problems in Current AI Research," in V. B. Ceilsielske (Editor), *Proceedings of the Fourth Annual AIM Workshop*, Rutgers University Press, Rutgers, NJ, 1978.

[Anderson 1987]   J. R. Anderson, A. T. Corbett, and B. J. Reiser, *Essential LISP*, Addison-Wesley, Reading, MA, 1987.

[Arbib 1987]   M. A. Arbib and A. R. Hanson (Editors), *Vision, Brain and Cooperative Computation*, MIT Press, Cambridge, MA, 1987.

[Asimow 1962]   W. Asimow, *Introduction to Design*, Prentice-Hall, Englewood Cliffs, NJ, 1962.

[Banares-Alcantara 1983]   R. Banares-Alcantara, A. W. Westerberg, and M. D. Rychener, *Development of an Expert System for Physical Property Predictions*, Technical Report, Design Research Center and Robotics Institute, Carnegie Mellon University, Pittsburgh, PA, 1983.

[Barber 1987]   G. R. Barber, "Lisp vs. C for Implementing Expert Systems," *AI Expert* 2 (1), 1987.

[Barker 1989]   V. E. Barker and D. E. O'Connor, "Expert Systems for Configuration at Digital: XCON and Beyond," *Communications of the ACM* 32 (3), 1989.

[Barr 1981]   A. Barr and E. A. Feigenbaum (Editors), *The Handbook of Artificial Intelligence*, Vol. 1, William Kaufmann, Los Altos, CA, 1981.

[Baugh 1989]   J. W. Baugh, Jr., and D. R. Rehak, "Implementation of a Finite Element Programming System: A Declarative Approach," *Proceedings of the 1989 ASCE Structures Congress*, San Francisco, 1989.

[Bennett 1978]   J. Bennett, L. Cleary, R. Englemore, and R. Melosh, *SACON: A Knowledge-Based Consultant for Structural Analysis*, Report No. STAN-CS-78-699, Department of Computer Science, Stanford University, Stanford, CA, 1978.

[Bennett 1984]   J. S. Bennett and R. S. Englemore, "SACON: A Knowledge-Based Consultant for Structural Analysis," *Proceedings of AAAI-84*, 1984.

[Bjork 1987]   B-C. Bjork, *RATAS: A Proposed Finnish Building Product Model*, Studies in Environmental Research No. T6, Helsinki University of Technology, Otaniemi, Finland, 1987.

[Bobrow 1977]   D. G. Bobrow and T. Winograd, "An Overview of KRL, A Knowledge Representation Language," *Cognitive Science* 1 (1), 1977.

[Bobrow 1983]   D. G. Bobrow and M. J. Stefik, *The LOOPS Manual*, Xerox Palo Alto Research Center, Palo Alto, CA, 1983.

[Bobrow 1985a]   D. G. Bobrow (Editor), *Qualitative Reasoning about Physical Systems*, MIT Press, Cambridge, MA, 1985.

[Bobrow 1985b]   D. G. Bobrow, "If Prolog Is the Answer, What Is the Question? or What It Takes to Support AI Programming Paradigms," *IEEE Transactions on Software Engineering* SE-11 (11), 1985.

[Bobrow 1986a]   D. G. Bobrow and M. J. Stefik, "Perspectives on Artificial Intelligence Programming," *Science* 231 (8), 1986.

[Bobrow 1986b]   D. G. Bobrow, S. Mittal, and M. J. Stefik, "Expert Systems: Perils and Promise," *Communications of the ACM* 29 (9), 1986.

[Bobrow 1988]   D. G. Bobrow, L. G. DeMichiel, R. P. Gabriel, S. E. Keene, G. Kiczales, and D. A. Moon, "The Common Lisp Object System," *Lisp and Symbolic Computation* 1 (3, 4), 1988.

[Bond 1988]   A. H. Bond and L. Gasser (Editors), *Readings in Distributed Artificial Intelligence*, Morgan Kaufmann, San Mateo, CA, 1988.

[Bonissone 1983]   P. P. Bonnisone and H. E. Johnson, *Expert System for Diesel Electric Locomotive Repair*, Knowledge-Based Systems Report, General Electric Company, Schenectady, NY, 1983.

[Bonissone 1987]   P. P. Bonnisone, "Plausible Reasoning," in S. C. Shapiro (Editor), *Encyclopedia of Artificial Intelligence* 2, John Wiley, New York, 1987.

[Brachman 1983]   R. J. Brachman, "What are Expert Systems?" in F. Hayes-Roth, D. A. Waterman, and D. B. Lenat (Editors), *Building Expert Systems*, Addison-Wesley, Reading, MA, 1983.

[Brachman 1985]   R. J. Brachman and H. J. Levesque (Editors), *Readings in Knowledge Representation*, Morgan Kaufmann, Los Altos, CA, 1985.

[Bremdal 1987]   B. A. Bremdal, "Control Issues in Knowledge-Based Planning System for Ocean Engineering Tasks," *Proceedings of the Third International Expert Systems Conference*, London, June 1987.

[Brown 1983]   D. C. Brown and B. Chandrasekaran, "An Approach to Expert Systems for Mechanical Design," in *Trends and Applications '83*, IEEE Computer Society, National Bureau of Standards, Gaithersburg, MD, 1983.

[Brown 1985]   D. C. Brown and B. Chandrasekaran, "Expert Systems for a Class of Mechanical Design Activity," in J. S. Gero (Editor), *Knowledge Engineering in Computer-Aided Design*, North Holland, Amsterdam, 1985.

[Brown 1989]   D. C. Brown and B. Chandrasekaran, *Design Problem Solving*, Pitman, London, and Morgan Kaufmann, Los Altos, CA, 1989.

[Brownston 1985]   L. Brownston, R. Farrell, E. Kant, and N. Martin, *Programming Expert Systems in OPS5*, Addison-Wesley, Reading, MA, 1985.

[Brysland 1988]   C. Brysland and K. J. MacCallum, "A Knowledge Based Assistant for the Scheduling of Subsea Maintenance," in J. S Gero (Editor), *Artificial Intelligence in Engineering: Robotics and Processes*, Elsevier Science Publishers, Amsterdam, 1988.

[Buchanan 1983a]   B. G. Buchanan et al., "Constructing an Expert System," in F. Hayes-Roth, D. A. Waterman, and D. B. Lenat (Editors), *Building Expert Systems*, Addison-Wesley, Reading, MA, 1983.

[Buchanan 1983b]   B. G. Buchanan and R. O. Duda, "Principles of Rule-Based Expert Systems," in M. C. Yovits (Editor), *Advances in Computers* 22, Academic Press, New York, 1983.

[Buchanan 1984]   B. G. Buchanan and E. H. Shortliffe, *Rule-Based Expert Systems*, Addison-Wesley, Reading, MA, 1984.

[Campbell 1982]   A. N. Campbell, V. Hollister, R. O. Duda, and P. E. Hart, "Recognition of a Hidden Mineral Deposit by an Artificial Intelligence Program," *Science* 217 (3), 1982.

[Campbell 1985]   A. N. Campbell and S. Fitzgerrell, *The Deciding Factor Users' Manual*, Power-Up Software, San Mateo, CA, 1985.

[Carbonell 1986]   J. Carbonell, "Derivational Analogy: A Theory of Reconstructive Problem Solving and Expertise Acquisition," in R. Michalski, J. Carbonell, and T. Mitchell (Editors), *Machine Learning II: An Artificial Intelligence Approach*, Morgan Kaufmann, Los Altos, CA, 1986.

[Chan 1987]   W-T. Chan and B. C. Paulson, Jr., "Exploratory Design Using Constraints," *Artificial Intelligence for Engineering Design, Analysis and Manufacturing* 1 (1), 1987.

[Chandrasekaran 1983]   B. Chandrasekaran and S. Mittal," Conceptual Representation of Medical Knowledge for Diagnosis by Computer: MDX and Related Systems," in M. C. Yovits (Editor), *Advances in Computers* 22, Academic Press, New York, 1983.

[Chandrasekaran 1984]   B. Chandrasekaran and S. Mittal, "Deep versus Compiled Knowledge Approaches to Diagnostic Problem-Solving," in M. J. Coombs (Editor), *Developments in Expert Systems*, Academic Press, London, 1984.

[Chang 1988]   T.-C. Chang, C. W. Ibbs, and K. C. Crandall, "A Fuzzy Logic System for Expert Systems," *Artificial Intelligence for Engineering Design, Analysis and Manufacturing* 2 (3), 1988.

[Chapman 1987]   D. Chapman "Planning for Conjunctive Goals," *Artificial Intelligence* 32, 1987.

[Charniak 1985]   E. Charniak and D. McDermott, *Artificial Intelligence*, Addison-Wesley, Reading, MA, 1985.

[Cherneff 1988]   J. Cherneff, *Automated Generation of Construction Schedules from Architectural Drawings*, M.S. Thesis, Department of Civil Engineering, Massachusetts Institute of Technology, Cambridge, MA, 1988.

[Clancey 1985]   W. J. Clancey, "Heuristic Classification," *Artificial Intelligence* 27 (3), 1985.

[Cline 1990]   T. Cline, H. Abelson, and W. Harris, "Symbolic Computing in Engineering Design," *Artificial Intelligence for Engineering Design, Analysis and Manufacturing* 4 (1), 1990.

[Clocksin 1984]   W. F. Clocksin and C. S. Mellish, *Programming in Prolog*, 2d edition, Springer-Verlag, New York, 1984.

[Cohen 1985] P. R. Cohen, *Heuristic Reasoning about Uncertainty: An Artificial Intelligence Approach,* Pitman, London, and Morgan Kaufmann, Los Altos, CA, 1985.

[Cohen 1987a] P. R. Cohen, M. Greenberg, and J. Delisio, "MU: A Development Environment for Prospective Reasoning Systems," *Proceedings of AAAI-87,* Seattle, WA, 1987.

[Cohen 1987b] P. R. Cohen, G. Shafer, and P. P. Shenoy, "Modifiable Combining Functions," *Artificial Intelligence for Engineering Design, Analysis and Manufacturing* 1 (1), 1987.

[Cohen 1988] P. R. Cohen and A. E. Howe, "How Evaluation Guides AI Research," *AI Magazine* 9 (4), 1988.

[Confrey 1988] T. Confrey and F. Daube, *GS2D: A 2-D Geometry System,* Report No. KSL-88-15, Knowledge Systems Laboratory, Department of Computer Science, Stanford University, Stanford, CA, 1988.

[Corkill 1986a] D. D. Corkill, K. Q. Gallagher, and K. E. Murray, "GBB: A Generic Blackboard Development System," *Proceedings of AAAI-86,* Philadelphia, PA, 1986.

[Corkill 1986b] D. D. Corkill, K. Q. Gallagher, and P. M. Johnson, *From Prototype to Product: Evolutionary Development within the Blackboard Paradigm,* Technical Report 86-46, Department of Computer and Information Science, University of Massachusetts, Amherst, MA, 1986.

[Coyne 1990] R. D. Coyne, M. A. Rosenman, A. D. Radford, M. Balachandran, and J. S. Gero, *Knowledge-Based Design Systems,* Addison-Wesley, Reading, MA, 1990.

[Cruse 1988] T. A. Cruse, *Boundary Element Analysis in Computational Fracture Mechanics,* Kluwer Academic Publishers, Dordrecht, The Netherlands, 1988.

[Cunningham 1988] J. J. Cunningham and J. R. Dixon, *Designing with Features: The Origin of Features,* MDA Technical Report No. 3-88, Department of Mechanical Engineering, University of Massachusetts, Amherst, MA, 1988.

[Cutkosky 1990] M. R. Cutkosky and J. M. Tenenbaum, "A Methodology and Computational Framework for Concurrent Product and Process Design," *Mechanism and Machine Theory* 25 (3), 1990.

[Dahl 1966] O-J. Dahl and K. Nygard, "SIMULA: An Algol-Based Simulation Language," *Communications of the ACM* 9 (9), 1966.

[Darwiche 1989]   A. Darwiche, R. E. Levitt, and B. Hayes-Roth, "OARPLAN: Generating Project Plans by Reasoning about Objects, Actions and Resources," *Artificial Intelligence for Engineering Design, Analysis and Manufacturing* 2 (3), 1989.

[DavisE 1987]   E. Davis, "Commonsense Reasoning," in S. C. Shapiro (Editor), *Encyclopedia of Artificial Intelligence* 2, John Wiley, New York, 1987.

[DavisR 1984]   R. Davis, "Diagnostic Reasoning Based on Structure and Behavior," *Artificial Intelligence* 24, 1984.

[de Kleer 1979a]   J. de Kleer, "Qualitative and Quantitative Reasoning in Classical Mechanics," in P. H. Winston and R. H. Brown (Editors), *Artificial Intelligence: An MIT Perspective*, MIT Press, Cambridge, MA, 1979.

[de Kleer 1979b]   J. de Kleer, J. Doyle, G. L. Steele, and G. J. Sussman, "Explicit Control of Reasoning," in P. H. Winston and R. H. Brown (Editors), *Artificial Intelligence: An MIT Perspective*, MIT Press, Cambridge, MA, 1979.

[de Kleer 1984]   J. de Kleer and J. S. Brown, "A Qualitative Physics Based on Confluences," *Artificial Intelligence*, 24 (1–3), 1984. (Repro-duced in [Bobrow 1985].

[de Kleer 1987a]   J. de Kleer, "Qualitative Physics," in S. C. Shapiro (Editor), *Encyclopedia of Artificial Intelligence* 2, John Wiley, New York, 1987.

[de Kleer 1987b]   J. de Kleer, "Dependency Directed Backtracking," in S. C. Shapiro (Editor), *Encyclopedia of Artificial Intelligence* 1, John Wiley, New York, 1987.

[Dixon 1984]   J. R. Dixon and M. K. Simmons, "An Architecture for the Application of Artificial Intelligence to Design," *Proceedings of the ACM/IEEE 21st Annual Design Automation Conference*, Albuquerque, NM, 1984.

[Dixon 1986a]   J. R. Dixon, C. D. Jones, E. C. Libardi, Jr., S. C. Luby, and E. H. Neilsen, "Knowledge Representation in Mechanical Design Systems: Issues and Examples," *Proceedings of the SAE International Conference and Exhibition*, Detroit, MI, 1986.

[Dixon 1986b]   J. R. Dixon and C. L. Dym, "Artificial Intelligence and Geometric Reasoning in Manufacturing Technology," *Applied Mechanics Reviews* 39 (9), 1986.

[Dixon 1987a]   J. R. Dixon, J. J. Cunningham, and M. K. Simmons, *Research in Designing with Features*, MDA Technical Report No. 4-87,

Department of Mechanical Engineering, University of Massachusetts, Amherst, MA, 1987.

[Dixon 1987b]   J. R. Dixon, "On Research Methodology Towards a Scientific Theory of Design," *Artificial Intelligence for Engineering Design, Analysis and Manufacturing* 1 (3), 1987.

[Dixon 1988]   J. R. Dixon, M. R. Duffey, R. K. Irani, K. L. Meunier, and M. F. Orelup, "A Proposed Taxonomy of Mechanical Design Problems," *Proceedings of the ASME Computers in Engineering Conference*, San Francisco, CA, 1988.

[Dixon 1989]   J. R. Dixon, E. C. Libardi, Jr., and E. H. Nielsen, *Unresolved Research Issues in Development of Design-with-Features Systems*, MDA Technical Report No. 2-89, Department of Mechanical Engineering, University of Massachusetts, Amherst, MA, 1989.

[Doyle 1979]   J. Doyle, "A Truth Maintenance System," *Artificial Intelligence* 12, 1979.

[Doyle 1983]   J. Doyle, "Methodological Simplicity in Expert System Construction: The Case of Judgements and Reasoned Assumptions," *AI Magazine* 4 (2), 1983.

[Dreyfus 1986]   H. L. Dreyfus and S. E. Dreyfus, *Mind Over Machine: The Power of Human Intuition and Expertise in the Era of the Computer*, Free Press, New York, 1986.

[Duda 1979]   R. O. Duda, J. Gaschnig, and P. E. Hart, "Model Design in the Prospector Consultant System for Mineral Exploration," in D. Michie (Editor), *Expert Systems in the Micro-Electronic Age*, Edinburgh University Press, Edinburgh, 1979.

[Duda 1987]   R. O. Duda, P. E. Hart, R. Reboh, J. Reiter, and T. Risch, "Syntel: Using a Functional Language for Financial Risk Assessment," *IEEE Expert* 2 (3), 1987.

[Durfee 1986]   E. H. Durfee, *An Approach to Cooperation: Planning and Communication in a Distributed Problem Solving Network*, Technical Report No. 86-09, Department of Computer and Information Science, University of Massachusetts, Amherst, MA, 1986.

[Durfee 1989]   E. H. Durfee, V. R. Lesser, and D. D. Corkill, "Trends in Cooperative Distributed Problem Solving, " *IEEE Transactions on Knowledge and Data Engineering* KDE-1 (1), 1989.

[Dyer 1986]   M. Dyer, M. Flowers, and J. Hodges, "EDISON: An Engineering Design Invention System Operating Naively," in D. Sriram and R. Adey (Editors), *Applications of Artificial Intelligence to Engineering Problems*, Springer-Verlag, New York, 1986.

[Dym 1980]
C. L. Dym and E. S. Ivey, *Principles of Mathematical Modeling*, Academic Press, New York, 1980.

[Dym 1985a]
C. L. Dym, "Expert Systems: New Approaches to Computer-Aided Engineering," *Engineering with Computers* 1 (1), 1985.

[Dym 1985b]
C. L. Dym (Editor), *Applications of Knowledge-Based Systems to Engineering Analysis and Design*, American Society of Mechanical Engineers, New York, 1985.

[Dym 1987]
C. L. Dym, "Issues in the Design and Implementation of Expert Systems," *Artificial Intelligence for Engineering Design, Analysis and Manufacturing* 1 (1), 1987.

[Dym 1988]
C. L. Dym, R. P. Henchey, E. A. Delis, and S. Gonick, "Representation and Control Issues in Automated Architectural Code Checking," *Computer-Aided Design* 20 (3), 1988.

[Dym 1989]
C. L. Dym and S. E. Salata, "Representation of Strategic Choices in Structural Modeling," *Proceedings of the 1989 ASCE Structures Congress*, San Francisco, 1989.

[Dym 1991a]
C. L. Dym and R. E. Levitt, "Toward the Integration of Knowledge for Engineering Modeling and Computation," *Engineering with Computers* 7, 1991.

[Dym 1991b]
C. L. Dym, "Representation and Problem Solving: The Foundations of Engineering Design," *Planning and Design: Environment and Planning B*, 18 (2), 1991.

[El Ayeb 1988]
B. El Ayeb and J-P. Finance, "On Cooperation Between Deep and Shallow Reasoning: SIDI: An Expert System for Troubleshooting Diagnosis in Large Industrial Plants," in J. Gero (Editor), *Artificial Intelligence in Engineering: Diagnosis and Learning*, Elsevier, Amsterdam, 1988.

[Elishakoff 1983]
I. Elishakoff, *Probabilistic Methods in the Theory of Structures*, John Wiley, New York, 1983.

[Enderton 1972]
H. B. Enderton, *A Mathematical Introduction to Logic*, Academic Press, New York, 1972.

[Ericsson 1984]
K. A. Ericsson and H. A. Simon, *Protocol Analysis: Verbal Reports as Data*, MIT Press, Cambridge, MA, 1984.

[Erman 1980]
L. D. Erman, F. Hayes-Roth, V. R. Lesser, and D. R. Reddy, "The Hearsay-II Speech Understanding System: Integrating Knowledge to Resolve Uncertainty," *ACM Computing Survey* 12, 1980.

[Feigenbaum 1977]   E. A. Feigenbaum, "The Art of Artificial Intelligence: Themes and Case Studies of Knowledge Engineering," *Proceedings of IJCAI 77*, Cambridge, MA, 1977.

[Feigenbaum 1983]   E. A. Feigenbaum and P. McCorduck, *The Fifth Generation*, Addison-Wesley, Reading, MA, 1983.

[Feigenbaum 1988]   E. A. Feigenbaum, P. McCorduck, and H. P. Nii, *The Rise of the Expert Company*, Times Books, New York, 1988.

[Fenves 1982]   S. J. Fenves, "Expert Systems in Civil Engineering," Invited Lecture, *MIT Workshop on Microcomputers in Civil Engineering*, Massachusetts Institute of Technology, Cambridge, MA, 1982.

[Fenves 1988]   S. J. Fenves, personal communication, 28 June 1988.

[Fikes 1971]   R. E. Fikes and N. J. Nilsson, "STRIPS: A New Approach to the Application of Theorem Proving to Problem Solving," *Artificial Intelligence*, 2, 1971.

[Fikes 1985]   R. Fikes and T. Kehler, "The Role of Frame-Based Representation in Reasoning," *Communications of the ACM* 28 (9), 1985.

[Forbus 1981]   K. D. Forbus, *A Study of Qualitative and Geometric Knowledge in Reasoning about Motion*, Report No. TR 615, AI Laboratory, Massachusetts Institute of Technology, Cambridge, MA, 1981.

[Forgy 1979]   C. L. Forgy, *On the Efficient Implementation of Production Systems*, Ph.D. Dissertation, Department of Computer Science, Carnegie Mellon University, Pittsburgh, PA, 1979.

[Forgy 1982]   C. L. Forgy, "Rete: A Fast Algorithm for the Many Pattern/Many Object Pattern Match Problem," *Artificial Intelligence* 19 (1), 1982.

[Fox 1984]   M. S. Fox and S. F. Smith, "ISIS—A Knowledge-Based System for Factory Scheduling," *Expert Systems* 1 (1), 1984.

[Fox 1987]   M. S. Fox, *Constraint-Directed Search: A Case Study of Job-Shop Scheduling*, Morgan Kaufmann, Los Altos, CA, 1987.

[Frayman 1987]   F. Frayman and S. Mittal, "COSSACK: A Constraints-Based Expert System for Configuration Tasks," *Proceedings of the Second International Conference on Applications of AI to Engineering*, Boston, MA, 1987.

[Friedland 1985]   P. E. Friedland and Y. Iwasaki, *The Concept and Implementation of Skeletal Plans*, Report No. KSL 85-6, Knowledge Systems Laboratory, Department of Computer Science, Stanford University, Stanford, CA, 1985.

[Gabriel 1985]   R. P. Gabriel, *Performance and Evaluation of Lisp Systems*, MIT
                      Press, Cambridge, MA, 1985.

[Gaschnig 1981]   J. Gaschnig, R. Reboh, and J. Reiter, *Development of a Knowledge-
                      Based System for Water Resources Problems*, Technical Report No.
                      1619, SRI International, Menlo Park, CA, 1981.

[Geissman 1988]   J. R. Geissman and R. D. Schultz, "Verification and Validation of
                      Expert Systems," *AI Expert* 3 (2), 1988.

[Genesereth 1985]   M. R. Genesereth and M. L. Ginsberg, "Logic Programming,"
                      Communications of the ACM 28 (9), 1985.

[Genesereth 1987]   M. R. Genesereth and N. J. Nilsson, *Logical Foundations of
                      Artificial Intelligence*, Morgan Kaufmann, Los Altos, CA, 1987.

[Gero 1985]   J. S. Gero (Editor), *Design Optimization*, Academic Press,
                      Orlando, 1985.

[Gero 1987]   J. Gero, "Prototypes: A New Schema for Knowledge-Based
                      Design," working paper, Architectural Computing Unit,
                      University of Sydney, Australia, 1987.

[Goel 1988]   V. Goel, "A Cognitive Strategy for Structuring Space," *Artificial
                      Intelligence for Engineering Design, Analysis and Manufacturing* 2
                      (2), 1988.

[Goldberg 1983]   A. Goldberg and D. Robson, *Smalltalk-80: The Language and Its
                      Implementation*, Addison-Wesley, Reading, MA, 1983.

[Grant 1986]   T. J. Grant, "Lessons from O.R. for A.I.: A Scheduling Case
                      Study," *Journal of the Operational Research Society* 37 (1), 1986.

[Gruber 1987]   T. R. Gruber and P. R. Cohen, "Design for Acquisition: Principles
                      of Knowledge System Design to Facilitate Knowledge
                      Acquisition," *International Journal of Man-Machine Studies* 26 (1),
                      1987.

[Hajek 1988]   J. Hajek and C. Haas, "Applications of Artificial Intelligence in
                      Highway Pavement Maintenance," in J. Gero (Editor), *Artificial
                      Intelligence in Engineering: Diagnosis and Learning*, Elsevier,
                      Amsterdam, 1988.

[Hardt 1987]   S. L. Hardt, "Naive Physics," in S. C. Shapiro (Editor),
                      Encyclopedia of Artificial Intelligence 2, John Wiley, New York,
                      1987.

[Harmon 1985]   P. Harmon and D. King, *Expert Systems*, John Wiley, New York,
                      1985.

[Hart 1982]   P. Hart, "Directions for AI in the Eighties," *SIGART Newsletter* (79), 1982.

[Hayakawa 1978]   S. I. Hayakawa, *Language in Thought and Action*, 4th edition, Harcourt Brace Jovanovich, San Diego, 1978.

[Hayes 1977]   P. J. Hayes, "On Semantic Nets, Frames and Associations,"*Proceedings of IJCAI-77*, Cambridge, MA, 1977.

[Hayes 1984]   P. J. Hayes, "Naive Physics II: Ontology for Liquids," in J. R. Hobbs and R. C. Moore (Editors), *Formal Theories of the Commonsense World*, Ablex, Norwood, NJ, 1984.

[Hayes-RothB 1979]   B. Hayes-Roth, F. Hayes-Roth, S. Rosenschein, and S. Cammarate, "Model Planning as an Incremental Opportunistic Process," *Proceedings of IJCAI 79*, 1979.

[Hayes-RothB 1985]   B. Hayes-Roth, "A Blackboard Architecture for Control," *Artificial Intelligence* 26, 1985.

[Hayes-RothB 1986]   B. Hayes-Roth et al., "PROTEAN: Deriving Protein Structure from Constraints," *Proceedings of AAAI-86*, Philadelphia, PA, 1986.

[Hayes-RothB 1987a] B. Hayes-Roth and M. Hewett, "Building Systems in the BB* Environment," in R. Engelmore and A. Morgan (Editors), *Blackboard Systems*, Addison-Wesley, London, 1987.

[Hayes-RothB 1987b] B. Hayes-Roth, A *Multi-Processor Interrupt-Driven Architecture for Adaptive, Intelligent Systems*, Technical Report KSL-87-31, Department of Computer Science, Stanford University, Stanford, CA, 1987.

[Hayes-RothB 1987c] B. Hayes-Roth, A. Garvey, V. Johnson, and M. Hewett, *A Modular and Layered Environment for Reasoning about Action*, Technical Report No. KSL 86-38, Department of Computer Science, Stanford University, Stanford, CA, 1987.

[Hayes-RothB 1989]   B. Hayes-Roth, R. Washington, R. Hewett, M. Hewett, and A. Seiver, "Intelligent Real-Time Monitoring and Control," *Proceedings of IJCAI 89*, Minneapolis, MN, August 1989.

[Hayes-RothF 1983]   F. Hayes-Roth, D. A. Waterman, and D. B. Lenat (Editors), *Building Expert Systems*, Addison-Wesley, Reading, MA, 1983.

[Hayes-RothF 1985]   F. Hayes-Roth, "Rule-Based Systems," *Communi-cations of the ACM* 28 (9), 1985.

[Hendrickson 1987]   C. Hendrickson et al., "Expert System for Construction Planning," *ASCE Journal of Computing in Civil Engineering* 1 (4), 1987.

[Hillier 1980]   F. S. Hillier and G. J. Lieberman, *Operations Research*, Holden-Day, San Francisco, CA, 1980.

[Hillis 1985]   W. D. Hillis, *The Connection Machine*, MIT Press, Cambridge, MA, 1985.

[Hoffman 1987]   R. R. Hoffman, "The Problem of Extracting the Knowledge of Experts from the Perspective of Experimental Psychology," *AI Magazine* 8 (2), 1987.

[Howard 1989a]   H. C. Howard, J. Wang, F. Daube, and T. Rafiq, "Applying Design-Dependent Knowledge in Structural Engineering Design," *Artificial Intelligence for Engineering Design, Analysis and Manufacturing* 3 (2), 1989.

[Howard 1989b]   H. C. Howard, R. E. Levitt, B. C. Paulson, J. G. Pohl, and C. B. Tatum, "Computer-Integrated Design and Construction: Reducing Fragmentation in the AEC Industry," *ASCE Journal of Computing in Civil Engineering* 3 (9), 1989.

[Howard 1989c]   H. C. Howard and D. R. Rehak, "KADBASE: Interfacing Expert Systems with Databases," *IEEE Expert* 4 (3), 1989.

[Hsu 1989]   W.-L. Hsu, M. Prietula, and D. Steier, "Merl-Soar," *Proceedings of the Third International Conference on Expert Systems and the Leading Edge in Production and Operations Management*, Hilton Head, SC, 1989.

[Huhns 1987]   M. N. Huhns (Editor), *Distributed Artificial Intelligence*, Pitman, London, and Morgan Kaufmann, Los Altos, CA, 1987.

[Ishizuka 1981]   M. Ishizuka, E. L. Hutchinson, and L. Weitzman, *SPERIL-I: Computer Based Structural Damage Assessment System*, Report CE-STR-81-36, School of Civil Engineering, Purdue University, Lafayette, IN, 1981.

[Ito 1989]   K. Ito, U. Yasumasa, R. E. Levitt, and A. Darwiche, *Linking Knowledge-Based Systems to CAD Design Data with an Object-Oriented Building Product Model*, Working Paper No. 7, Center for Integrated Facility Engineering, Stanford University, Stanford, CA, 1989.

[Jain 1989]   S. Jain, K. Barber, and D. Osterfield, "Expert Simulation for On-Line Scheduling," *Proceedings of the Winter Simulation Conference*, London, UK, 1989.

[Jain 1990]   D. Jain, personal communication, 3 February 1990.

[Johnson 1988]   M. Vaughan Johnson and B. Hayes-Roth, *Learning to Solve Problems by Analogy*, Report No. KSL-88-01, Department of Computer Science, Stanford University, Stanford, CA, 1988.

[Kaehler 1986]   T. Kaehler and D. Patterson, "A Small Taste of Smalltalk," *BYTE* 11 (8), 1986.

[Kartam 1990]   N. A. Kartam and R.E. Levitt, "Intelligent Planning of Construction Projects with Repeated Cycles of Operation," *ASCE Journal of Computing in Civil Engineering* 4, 1990.

[Kellett 1989]   J. M. Kellett, G. Winstanley, and J. T. Boardman, "A Methodology for Knowledge Engineering Using an Interactive Graphical Tool for Knowledge Modelling," *Artificial Intelligence in Engineering* 4, (2), 1989.

[Knuth 1973]   D. Knuth, "Computer Science and Mathematics, *American Scientist* 61 (6), 1973.

[Korf 1988]   R. E. Korf, "Search: A Survey of Recent Results," in H. E. Shrobe and AAAI (Editors), *Exploring Artificial Intelligence*, Morgan Kaufmann, San Mateo, CA, 1988.

[Kunz 1989a]   J. C. Kunz, *Concurrent Knowledge Systems Engineering*, Working Paper No. 005, Center for Integrated Facility Engineering, Stanford University, Stanford, CA, 1989.

[Kunz 1989b]   J. C. Kunz, M. J. Stelzner, and M. D. Williams, "From Classic Expert Systems to Models: Introduction to a Methodology for Building Model-Based Systems," in G. Guida and C. Tasso (Editors), *Topics in Expert System Design*, North-Holland, Amsterdam, 1989.

[Laird 1986]   J. E. Laird, A. Newell, and P. S. Rosenbloom, "Soar: An Architecture for General Intelligence," *Machine Learning* 1 (1), 1986.

[Laird 1987]   J. E. Laird, P. S. Rosenbloom, and A. Newell, "Chunking in Soar: The Anatomy of a General Learning Mechanism," *Artificial Intelligence* 33 (1), 1987.

[Lambert 1988]   H. Lambert, L. Eshelman, and Y. Iwasaki, "Using Qualitative Physics to Guide the Acquisition of Diagnostic Knowledge," in J. Gero (Editor), *Artificial Intelligence in Engineering: Diagnosis and Learning*, Elsevier, Amsterdam, 1988.

[Lansky 1988]   A. Lansky, "Localized Event-Based Reasoning for Multiagent Domains," *Computational Intelligence*, 4 (4) 1988.

[Lathrop 1985]   Lathrop, J. K. (Editor), *Life Safety Code Handbook*, 3d edition, National Fire Protection Association, Worcester, MA, 1985.

[Lenat 1982]   D. Lenat, "An Artificial Intelligence Approach to Discovery in Mathematics as Heuristic Search," in R. Davis and D. Lenat (Editors), *Knowledge-Based Systems in Artificial Intelligence*, McGraw-Hill, New York, 1982.

[Lenat 1986]   D. B. Lenat, M. Prakash, and M. Sheperd, "CYC: Using Commonsense Knowledge to Overcome Brittleness and Knowledge Acquisition Bottlenecks," *AI Magazine* 6 (4), 1986.

[Lenat 1987]   D. B. Lenat and E. A. Feigenbaum, "On the Thresholds of Knowledge," *Proceedings of IJCAI 1987*, Milan, Italy, 1987.

[Lesser 1975]   V. R. Lesser, R. Fennell, L. D. Erman, and D. R. Reddy, "Organization of the HEARSAY-II Speech Understanding System," *IEEE Transactions on Acoustics, Speech and Signal Processing* ASSP-23 (1), 1975.

[Lesser 1985]   V. R. Lesser, "Cooperative Distributed Problem Solving," Presentation at IBM–Bethesda, Bethesda, MD, 1985.

[Lesser 1987]   V. R. Lesser and D. D. Corkill, "Distributed Problem Solving," in S. C. Shapiro (Editor), *Encyclopedia of Artificial Intelligence* 1, John Wiley, New York, 1987.

[Level 5 1987]   Level 5 Research, *Insight 2+ User's Manual*, Melbourne Beach, FL, 1987.

[Levitt 1985]   R. E. Levitt and J. C. Kunz, "Using Knowledge of Construction and Project Management for Automated Schedule Updating," *Project Management Journal* 16 (5), 1985.

[Levitt 1986]   R. Levitt, "HOWSAFE: A Microcomputer-Based Expert System to Evaluate the Safety of a Construction Firm," in C. Kostem and M. Maher (Editors), *Expert Systems in Civil Engineering*, Proceedings of ASCE Spring Convention, Seattle, WA, April 1986.

[Levitt 1987a]   R. E. Levitt, "Expert Systems in Construction," in M. L. Maher (Editor), *Expert Systems for Civil Engineering: Technology and Applications*, American Society of Civil Engineers, New York, 1987.

[Levitt 1987b]   R. E. Levitt and J. C. Kunz, "Using Artificial Intelligence Techniques to Support Project Management," *Artificial Intelligence for Engineering Design, Analysis and Manufacturing* 1 (1), 1987.

[Levitt 1987c]   R. Levitt and N. Samelson, *Construction Safety Management*, McGraw-Hill, New York, 1987.

[Levitt 1989a]   R. E. Levitt, *SAFEQUAL: A Knowledge-Based System for Prequalification or Selection of Construction Contractors Based on Expected Safety Performance*, Building Knowledge Systems, Inc., Stanford, CA, 1989.

[Levitt 1989b]   R. E. Levitt, I. D. Tommelein, B. Hayes-Roth, and T. Confrey, *SightPlan: A Blackboard Expert System for Constraint Based Spatial Reasoning About Construction Site Layout*, Technical Report No. 020, Center for Integrated Facility Engineering, Stanford University, Stanford, CA, 1989.

[Levitt 1991]   R. E. Levitt, C. L. Dym, and Y. Jin, *Knowledge-Based Support for Concurrent, Multidisciplinary Design*, Working Paper No. 10, Center for Integrated Facility Engineering, Stanford University, Stanford, CA, 1991.

[Lien 1987]   K. Lien, G. Suzuki, and A. W. Westerberg, "The Role of Expert Systems Technology in Design," *Chemical Engineering Science* 42 (5), 1987.

[Logcher 1979]   R. D. Logcher and R. E. Levitt, "Organization and Control of Engineering Design Firms," *ASCE Engineering Issues* 105 (EI1), 1979.

[Luce 1957]   R. D. Luce and H. Raiffa, *Games and Decisions*, John Wiley, New York, 1957.

[Luger 1989]   G. F. Luger and W. A. Stubblefield, *Artificial Intelligence and the Design of Expert Systems*, Benjamin/Cummings, Redwood City, CA, 1989.

[Maher 1984a]   M. L. Maher, *HI-RISE: A Knowledge-Based Expert System for the Preliminary Design of High Rise Buildings*, Ph.D. Dissertation, Department of Civil Engineering, Carnegie Mellon University, Pittsburgh, PA, 1984.

[Maher 1984b]   M. L. Maher, D. Sriram, and S. J. Fenves, *Tools and Techniques for Knowledge-Based Expert Systems for Engineering Design*, Technical Report No. DRC-12-22-84, Design Research Center, Carnegie Mellon University, Pittsburgh, December 1984.

[Maher 1987a]   M. L. Maher (Editor), *Expert Systems for Civil Engineers: Technology and Application*, American Society of Civil Engineers, New York, 1987.

[Maher 1987b]   M. L. Maher and R. H. Allen, "Expert Systems Components," in M. L. Maher (Editor), *Expert Systems for Civil Engineers:*

Technology and Application, American Society of Civil Engineers, New York, 1987.

[Malin 1985]   J. Malin and N. Lance, "An Expert System for Fault Management and Automatic Shutdown Avoidance in a Regenerative Life Support System," *ISA 1985 Proceedings*, ISA Paper No. 85-0333, 1985.

[Marcot 1987]   B. Marcot, "Testing Your Knowledge Base," *AI Expert* 2 (8), 1987.

[Marshall 1987]   G. Marshall, T. J. Barber, and J. T. Boardman, "A Methodology for Modelling a Project Management Control Environment," *IEEE Proceedings* 134 (Pt. D, 4), 1987.

[Martins 1987]   J. Martins, "Belief Systems," in S. C. Shapiro (Editor), *Encyclopedia of Artificial Intelligence* 1, John Wiley, New York, 1987.

[Martins 1988]   J. P. Martins and E. M. Morgado, "CREWS: Scheduling Airline Crews," in J. S. Gero (Editor), *Artificial Intelligence in Engineering: Robotics and Processes*, Elsevier Science Publishers, New York, 1988.

[Mayer 1988]   A. K. Mayer and S. C-Y. Lu, "An AI-Based Approach for the Integration of Multiple Sources of Knowledge to Aid Engineering Design," *Journal of Mechanisms, Transmission, and Automation in Design* 110 (3), 1988.

[McCorduck 1979]   P. McCorduck, *Machines Who Think*, W. H. Freeman, New York, 1979.

[McDermottD 1984]   D. V. McDermott, "Reasoning about Plans," in J. R. Hobbs and R. C. Moore (Editors), *Formal Theories of the Commonsense World*, Ablex, Norwood, NJ, 1984.

[McDermottD 1987]   D. V. McDermott, "Spatial Reasoning," in S. C. Shapiro (Editor), *Encyclopedia of Artificial Intelligence* 2, John Wiley, New York, 1987.

[McDermottJ 1981]   J. McDermott, "R1: The Formative Years," *AI Magazine* 2 (2), 1981.

[McLaughlin 1987]   S. McLaughlin and J. S. Gero, "Acquiring Expert Knowledge from Characterized Designs," *Artificial Intelligence for Engineering Design, Analysis and Manufacturing* 1 (2), 1987.

[Minsky 1975]   M. Minsky, "A Framework for Representing Knowledge," in P. H. Winston (Editor), *The Psychology of Computer Vision*, McGraw-Hill, New York, 1975.

[Mittal 1984]   S. Mittal, D. G. Bobrow, and J. de Kleer, *DARN: A Community Memory for a Diagnosis and Repair Task,* Technical Memorandum, Xerox Palo Alto Research Center, Palo Alto, CA, 1984.

[Mittal 1985]   S. Mittal and C. L. Dym, "Knowledge Acquisition from Multiple Experts," *AI Magazine* 6 (2), 1985.

[Mittal 1986a]   S. Mittal, C. L. Dym, and M. Morjaria, "PRIDE: An Expert System for the Design of Paper Handling Systems," *IEEE Computer* 19 (7), 1986.

[Mittal 1986b]   S. Mittal and A. Araya, "A Knowledge-Based Framework for Design," *Proceedings of AAAI-86*, Philadelphia, PA, 1986.

[Mittal 1986c]   S. Mittal and M. J. Stefik, *Constraint Compaction: An Approach for Generating All Solutions from a Set of Constraints,* Technical Memorandum, Xerox Palo Alto Research Center, Palo Alto, CA, 1986.

[Mittal 1987]   S. Mittal and F. Frayman, "Making Partial Choices in Constraint Reasoning Problems," *Proceedings of AAAI-87*, Seattle, WA, 1987.

[Miyasato 1986]   G. H. Miyasato, W. Dong, R. E. Levitt, and A. C. Boissonnade, "Implementation of a Knowledge Based Seismic Risk Evaluation System on Microcomputers," *Journal of Artificial Intelligence in Engineering* 1 (1), 1986.

[Mohan 1989]   S. Mohan and M. L. Maher (Editors), *Expert Systems for Civil Engineers: Education,* American Society of Civil Engineers, New York, 1989.

[Morjaria 1985]   M. Morjaria, S. Mittal, and C. L. Dym, "Interactive Graphics in Expert Systems for Engineering Applications," *Proceedings of the 1985 International Computers in Engineering Conference and Exhibit,* Boston, MA, 1985.

[Morjaria 1989]   M. Morjaria, *Knowledge-Based Systems (KBS) for Engineering Design,* Technical Report No. X8900555, Xerox Corporation, Webster, NY, 1989.

[Mostow 1985]   J. Mostow, "Toward Better Models of the Design Process," *AI Magazine* 6 (1), 1985.

[Mullarkey 1985]   P. W. Mullarkey, *CONE—An Expert System for Interpretation of Geotechnical Characterization Data from Cone Penetrometers,* Ph.D. Dissertation, Department of Civil Engineering, Carnegie Mellon University, Pittsburgh, PA, 1985.

[Mullarkey 1987]   P. W. Mullarkey, "Languages and Tools for Building Expert Systems," in M. L. Maher (Editor), *Expert Systems for Civil*

Engineering: Technology and Applications, American Society of Civil Engineers, New York, 1987.

[Navinchandra 1988]   D. Navinchandra, D. Sriram, and R. Logcher, "GHOST: A Project Network Generator," *ASCE Journal of Computing in Civil Engineering* 2 (3), 1988.

[Newell 1960]   A. Newell, J. C. Shaw, and H. A. Simon, "Report on a General Problem Solving Program for a Computer," *Proceedings of the International Conference on Information Processing*, UNESCO, Paris, 1960.

[Newell 1963]   A. Newell and H. A. Simon, "GPS: A Program that Simulates Human Thought," in E. A. Feigenbaum and J. Feldman (Editors), *Computers and Thought*, McGraw-Hill, New York, 1963.

[Newquist 1988]   H. P. Newquist III, "Struggling to Maintain," *AI Expert* 3 (8), 1988.

[Nii 1982]   H. P. Nii, E. A. Feigenbaum, J. Anton, and A. Rockmore, "Signal-to-Symbol Transformation: HASP/SIAP Case Study," *AI Magazine* 3 (2), 1982.

[Nii 1986]   H. P. Nii, "Blackboard Systems: Part I and Part II," *AI Magazine* 7 (2, 3), 1986.

[Nii 1989]   H. P. Nii, "Blackboard Systems," in A. Barr, P. R. Cohen, and E. A. Feigenbaum (Editors), *Handbook of Artificial Intelligence*, 4, Addison-Wesley, Reading, MA, 1989.

[Nilsson 1980]   N. J. Nilsson, *Principles of Artificial Intelligence*, Morgan Kaufmann, Los Altos, CA, 1980.

[Ogawa 1984]   H. Ogawa, K. S. Fu, and J. P. Yao, "An Expert System for Damage Assessment of Existing Structures," *Proceedings of the First Conference on Artificial Intelligence Applications*, IEEE Computer Society, 1984.

[O'Keefe 1987]   R. M. O'Keefe, O. Balci, and E. P. Smith, "Validating Expert System Performance," *IEEE Expert* 2 (4), 1987.

[Papoulis 1965]   A. Papoulis, *Probability, Random Variables and Stochastic Processes*, McGraw-Hill, New York, 1965.

[Parsaye 1988]   K. Parsaye and M. Chignell, *Expert Systems for Experts*, John Wiley, New York, 1988.

[Pascoe 1986]   G. A. Pascoe, "Elements of Object-Oriented Programming," *BYTE* 11 (8), 1986.

[Pearl 1987]   J. Pearl, "Bayesian Decision Methods," in S. C. Shapiro (Editor), *Encyclopedia of Artificial Intelligence* 1, John Wiley, New York, 1987.

[Pedersen 1989]   K. Pedersen, *Expert Systems Programming: Practical Techniques for Rule-based Systems,* John Wiley, New York, 1989.

[Pospesel 1974]   H. Pospesel, *Introduction to Logic: Propositional Logic,* Prentice-Hall, Englewood Cliffs, NJ, 1974.

[Pospesel 1976]   H. Pospesel, *Introduction to Logic: Predicate Logic,* Prentice-Hall, Englewood Cliffs, NJ, 1976.

[Preiss 1989]   K. Preiss and O. Shai, "Process Planning by Logic Programming," *Robotics and Computer-Integrated Manufacturing,* 5 (1), 1989.

[Prerau 1985]   D. S. Prerau, "Selection of an Appropriate Domain," *AI Magazine* 6 (2), 1985.

[Pugh 1988]   S. Pugh and I. E. Morley, *Total Design,* Design Division, University of Strathclyde, Strathclyde, U.K., 1988.

[Rehak 1985]   D. R. Rehak and S. J. Fenves, "Expert Systems in Civil Engineering, Construction and Construction Robotics," *1984 Annual Research Review,* Robotics Institute, Carnegie Mellon University, Pittsburgh, 1985.

[Rehak 1988]   D. R. Rehak, personal communication, 10 August 1988.

[Reich 1989]   Y. Reich and S. J. Fenves, "The Potential of Machine Learning Techniques for Expert Systems," *Artificial Intelligence for Engineering Design, Analysis and Manufacturing* 3 (3), 1989.

[Rich 1983]   E. Rich, *Artificial Intelligence,* McGraw-Hill, New York, 1983.

[Richards 1989]   T. Richards, *Clausalform Logic: An Introduction to the Logic of Computer Reasoning,* Addison-Wesley, Reading, MA, 1989.

[Riitahuhta 1988] A. Riitahuhta, "Systematic Engineering Design and Use of an Expert System in Boiler Plant Design," *Proceedings of the ICED International Conference on Engineering Design,* Budapest, Hungary, 1988.

[Rosenschein 1985] J. S. Rosenschein, *Rational Interaction: Cooperation Among Intelligent Agents,* Ph.D. Dissertation, Department of Computer Science, Stanford University, Stanford, CA, 1985.

[Rychener 1988]   M. D. Rychener (Editor), *Expert Systems for Engineering Design,* Academic Press, Boston, 1988.

[Sacerdoti 1973]   E. D. Sacerdoti, "Planning in a Hierarchy of Abstraction Spaces," *Proceedings of IJCAI-73*, Palo Alto, CA, 1973.

[Sacerdoti 1975]   E. D. Sacerdoti, "The Nonlinear Nature of Plans," *Advance Papers IJCAI-75*, Tbilisi, U.S.S.R., 1975.

[Sannella 1983]   M. Sannella (Editor), *Interlisp Reference Manual*, Xerox Special Information Systems, Pasadena, CA, 1983.

[Sathi 1985]   A. Sathi, M. S. Fox, and M. Greenberg, "Representation of Activity Knowledge for Project Managment," *IEEE Transactions on Pattern Analysis and Machine Intelligence* PAMI-7 (5), 1985.

[Sathi 1986]   A. Sathi, T. E. Morton, and S. F.Roth, "Callisto: An Intelligent Project Management System," *AI Magazine* 7 (4), 1986.

[Schank 1972]   R. C. Schank, "Conceptual Dependency: A Theory of Natural Language Processing," *Cognitive Psychology* 3 (4), 1972.

[Sedgewick 1983]   R. Sedgewick, *Algorithms*, Addison-Wesley, Reading, MA, 1983.

[Shames 1985]   I. H. Shames and C. L. Dym, *Energy and Finite Element Methods in Structural Mechanics*, Hemisphere, New York, 1985.

[Sheil 1983]   B. Sheil, "Power Tools for Programmers," *Datamation* 29 (2), 1983.

[Shoham 1987]   Y. Shoham and D. V. McDermott, "Temporal Reasoning," in S. C. Shapiro (Editor), *Encyclopedia of Artificial Intelligence* 2, John Wiley, New York, 1987.

[Simon 1975]   H. A. Simon, "Style in Design," in C. M. Eastman (Editor), *Spatial Synthesis in Computer-Aided Building Design*, Applied Science Publishers, London, England, 1975.

[Simon 1981]   H. A. Simon, The *Sciences of the Artificial*, 2d edition, MIT Press, Cambridge, MA, 1981.

[Smith 1984]   R. Smith, "On the Development of Commercial Expert Systems," *AI Magazine* 5 (3), 1984.

[Smithers 1989]   T. Smithers, "AI-Based Design versus Geometry-Based Design," *Computer-Aided Design* 21 (3), 1989.

[Sowa 1984]   J. C. Sowa, *Conceptual Structures: Information Processing in Mind and Machine*, Addison-Wesley, Reading, MA, 1984.

[Sridharan 1987]   N. S. Sridharan, "Report on the 1986 Workshop on Distributed Artificial Intelligence," *AI Magazine* 8 (3), 1987.

[Srinivasan 1989]   S. Srinivasan and R. H. Allen, "Partitioning and Guided Search: A Generalized Approach to Problem Solving in Preliminary Design," in W. P. Seering (Editor), *Proceedings of the First International Conference on Design Theory and Methodology*, American Society of Mechanical Engineers, New York, 1989.

[Sriram 1989]   D. Sriram et al., "Knowledge-Based System Applications in Engineering Design: Research at MIT," *AI Magazine*, 10 (3), 1989.

[Stachowitz 1987]   R. Stachowitz, et al., "Building Validation Tools for Knowledge-Based Systems," *SOAR Conference*, NASA/JSC, Houston, TX, 1987.

[Stallman 1977]   R. M. Stallman and G. J. Sussman, "Forward Reasoning and Dependency-Directed Backtracking in a System for Computer-Aided Circuit Analysis," *Artificial Intelligence* 9 (2), 1977.

[Stankovic 1984]   J. A. Stankovic, "A Perspective on Distributed Computer Systems," *IEEE Transactions on Computers* C-33 (12), 1984.

[Steele 1984]   G. Steele, *Common Lisp: The Language*, Digital Press, Bedford, MA, 1984.

[Stefik 1981a]   M. J. Stefik, "Planning with Constraints (Molgen: Part 1)," *Artificial Intelligence* 16, 1981.

[Stefik 1981b]   M. J. Stefik, "Planning and Meta-Planning (Molgen: Part 2)," *Artificial Intelligence* 16, 1981.

[Stefik 1982a]   M. J. Stefik, J. Aikins, R. Balzer, J. Benoit, L. Birnbaum, F. Hayes-Roth, and E. Sacerdoti, *The Organization of Expert Systems: A Prescriptive Tutorial*, Technical Report No. VLSI-82-1, Xerox Palo Alto Research Center, Palo Alto, CA, 1982.

[Stefik 1982b]   M. J. Stefik and L. Conway, "The Principled Engineering of Knowledge," *AI Magazine* 3 (3), 1982.

[Stefik 1983]   M. J. Stefik, et al., "Knowledge Programming in LOOPS," *AI Magazine* 4 (3), 1983.

[Stefik 1984]   M. J. Stefik, personal communication, February 1984.

[Stefik 1986]   M. J. Stefik, "The Knowledge Medium," *AI Magazine* 7 (1), 1986.

[Stefik 1990]   M. J. Stefik, *Introduction to Knowledge Systems*, Xerox Palo Alto Research Center, Palo Alto, CA, 1990.

[Sterling 1986]   L. Sterling and E. Shapiro, *The Art of Prolog: Advanced Programming Techniques*, MIT Press, Cambridge, MA, 1986.

[Stonebraker 1986]   M. Stonebraker and L. Rowe, "The Design of POSTGRES," *Proceedings of the ACM SIGMOD Conference*, 1986.

[Subrahmanian 1987]   E. Subrahmanian and J. Davis, *Validation of Expert Systems: Two Perspectives*, Technical Report No. EDRC-05-11-87, Engineering Design Research Center, Carnegie Mellon University, Pittsburgh, PA, 1987.

[Sussman 1975a]   G. J. Sussman and R. M. Stallman, "Heuristic Techniques in Computer Aided Circuit Analysis," *IEEE Transactions on Circuits and Systems* CAS-22 (11), 1975.

[Sussman 1975b]   G. J. Sussman, *A Computer Model of Skill Acquisition*, Elsevier, New York, 1975.

[Tatar 1987]   D. Tatar, *A Programmer's Guide to Common Lisp*, Digital Press, Bedford, MA, 1987.

[Tate 1976]   A. Tate, *Project Planning Using a Hierarchic Nonlinear Planner*, Research Report No. 25, Department of Artificial Intelligence, University of Edinburgh, Edinburgh, 1976.

[Thompson 1967]   J. Thompson, *Organizations in Action*, McGraw-Hill, New York, 1967.

[Tommelein 1987]   I. D. Tommelein, M. Johnson, B. Hayes-Roth, and R. E. Levitt, "SightPlan—A Blackboard Expert System for the Layout of Temporary Facilities on Construction Sites," in J. S. Gero (Editor), *Computer-Aided Design*, North Holland, Amsterdam, 1987.

[Tommelein 1989a]   I. D. Tommelein, *SightPlan: An Expert System that Models and Augments Human Decision-Making for Designing Construction Site Layouts*, Ph.D. Dissertation, Department of Civil Engineering, Stanford University, Stanford, CA, 1989.

[Tommelein 1989b]   I. D. Tommelein, *Comparing Design Strategies of Agents with Limited Resources*, M.S. Thesis, Department of Computer Science, Stanford University, Stanford, CA, 1989.

[Touretzky 1984]   D. S. Touretzky, *LISP: A Gentle Introduction to Symbolic Computation*, Harper & Row, New York, 1984.

[Walters 1988]   J. R. Walters and N. R. Nielsen, *Crafting Knowledge-Based Systems*, John Wiley, New York, 1988.

[Waterman 1986]   D. A. Waterman, *A Guide to Expert Systems*, Addison-Wesley, Reading, MA, 1986.

[Whyte 1986]   E. Whyte and R Malloy (Editors), "Object-Oriented Programming," *BYTE* 11 (8), 1986.

[Wilkins 1984]   D. E. Wilkins, "Domain-Independent Planning: Representation and Plan Generation," *Artificial Intelligence* 22 (3), 1984.

[Wilkins 1988]   D. E. Wilkins, *Practical Planning: Extending The Classical AI Planning Paradigm*, Morgan Kaufmann, Los Altos, CA, 1988.

[Wilkins 1989]   D. E. Wilkins, *Can AI Planners Solve Practical Problems?*, Technical Note 468R, Stanford Research Institute AI Center, Menlo Park, CA, 1989.

[Winston 1984a]   P. H. Winston, *Artificial Intelligence*, 2d edition, Addison-Wesley, Reading, MA, 1984.

[Winston 1984b]   P. H. Winston and B. K. P. Horn, *LISP*, 2d edition, Addison-Wesley, Reading, MA, 1984.

[Wright 1983]   J. M. Wright and M. S. Fox, *SRL: Schema Representation Language*, Technical Report, Robotics Institute, Carnegie Mellon University, Pittsburgh, PA, 1983.

[Woods 1975]   W. A. Woods, "What's in a Link: Foundations for Semantic Networks," in D. Bobrow and A. Collins, eds., *Representation and Understanding: Studies in Cognitive Science*, Academic Press, New York, 1975

[Zadeh 1975]   L. A. Zadeh, "Fuzzy Logic and Approximate Reasoning," *Synthese* 30, 1975.

[Zozaya-Gorostiza 1989] C. Zozaya-Gorostiza, C. Hendrickson, and D. R. Rehak, *Knowledge-Based Process Planning for Construction and Manufacturing*, Academic Press, Boston, 1989.

[Zuboff 1988]   S. Zuboff, *In the Age of the Smart Machine*, Basic Books, New York, 1988.

INDEX

A* algorithm, 54–55
Abduction, 78
Abstraction hierarchies, 131–138
  in frame systems, 141
  with Molgen, 311
Abstraction of data, 7, 216, 240
ABSTRIPS planning system, 297, 299
ACCORD language, 278, 281–282
Act phase for rules, 112
Action blackboard with OARPLAN, 326
Actions and activities
  in OARPLAN, 317–324
  in planning problems, 300
  in PLATFORM, 236
  with situation-action rules, 99
Active values
  with PRIDE, 273
  in slots, 145
Administrative information for
    components, 183
Admissible changes in time, 176
Advice, validation of, 346–348
Aggregate objects in SightPlan, 281
AI (artificial intelligence), 10–11, 94
Algorithms, 8
  directed search, 49–55
  distance, 225–227
  exhaustive search, 41–49
Amarel, S., 2–3
Analogy and mutation approach for
    design, 254–255
Analysis and analytic models, 5
  for design, 246, 251
  for structural mechanics, 165
AND connective and operator, 61–63, 67–
    68, 106
Antecedents in rules, 101
Architectures, 14–18
  blackboard, 190–198

CDPS, 203–208
  of Guardian, 239
  of IBDS, 290–291
  of LSC Advisor, 220–222
  model-based reasoning, 181–190
  of PRIDE, 261–262
  of Prolog, 89
  requirements of, 179–181
  for rule-based representation, 113–116
  of SafeQual, 230–231
  of SightPlan, 277–278
Arguments
  Lisp, 83
  of predicates, 66–67
  with rules, 106
Arity of predicates, 66
Arrows with taxonomic hierarchies, 130–
    132
ART environment, 150, 350
Artificial intelligence, 10–11, 94
Artificial Intelligence for Engineering, 19
*Artificial Intelligence for Engineering Design,
    Analysis, and Manufacturing*, 19
Assembly approach
  to design, 255
  to planning, 319
Assistants, computers as, 8, 10, 250–251,
    262
Associative conclusions, 181
Associative heuristics, 214
Associative triples, 108–109
Asynchronous searches, 202
Atomic propositions, 60
Atoms, Lisp, 82–83
Attribute-value pairs in frames, 141–142
Attributes
  of components with OARPLAN, 316–317
  in frame-based systems, 142–144
  in Lisp, 84–85

of rule-based systems, 115–116
in semantic nets, 132–136
AutoCad program
  with IBDS, 291–292
  with OARPLAN, 314
  with SIPEC, 308
Automated design assistants, 250–251
Automatic explanations, 157–158
Axioms, frame, 170–172

Backtracking
  with belief revision systems, 171
  with PRIDE, 270–271
  with searches, 49
Backward chaining and reasoning, 36–38,
  91, 101–105
Bayesian probability, 116–120, 125
BB1 blackboard system, 192–197, 241
  for Guardian, 239
  for Molgen, 313
  for OARPLAN, 326–327
  (*See also* SightPlan system)
Behavior
  inheritance of, 145–147, 184–185
  modeling of, 165
  simulation of, 186–189
Belief revision systems, 169–173
Best-first searches, 52–53
Bidirectional implication connective, 62–
  63, 68
Bidirectional searches, 38, 40, 104
Binary evaluation system, 218–229
Bindings with Prolog, 92
Blackboard architectures, 17–18, 190–198
  vs. CDPS, 199
  for GHOST, 309
  for Guardian, 239
  for LIFT, 304
  for Molgen, 313
  for OARPLAN, 326–327
  (*See also* SightPlan system)
Blind searches, 31, 40
Boilers, design of, 289–293
Boolean operators with rules, 106
Brachman, R. J., 13–14
Branch-and-bound searches, 53–54
Branches, tree search, 35–37
Breadth-first searches, 32, 42–43
Bremdal, B. A., 303
Buchanan, B. G., 120, 123, 334

BUILDER system, 309
Building of KBES (*see* Life cycle of KBES)
Building safety evaluation, 218–229

C programming language, 150, 352–353
C++ programming language, 150
CADD systems
  and component selection, 182–184
  with LSC Advisor, 220–221, 228–229
  with OARPLAN, 310
  with SIPEC, 308
Calculations (*see* Computation and
  computers)
Callisto planning system, 304–306
CAR primitive (Lisp), 84
Cardinality facets, 144
Case-based reasoning strategy, 249, 256
Cases, libraries of, 333–334, 338, 347–348
CATS-1 system, 355
Causal reasoning, 164, 240
  abduction for, 78
  modeling for, 181–182
  in probability, 118
  rules for, 101
CDR primitive (Lisp), 84
Certainty and uncertainty
  in explanation of reasoning, 157–158
  inference nets for, 124–126
  representation of, 116–124
Chaining, 101–105
Chan, W. T., 313
Characteristics of problems, 38–39
Characterized designs, 343
Charniak, E., 170
Child nodes, 27, 35
Chronological backtracking, 49, 171
Chunking, 343
CIFECAD system, 314–315
Clancey, William, 215
Classes
  component, with OARPLAN, 315–316
  Lisp, 84–85
  with taxonomic hierarchies, 130–132
Classical planners, 297–301
Classification problems, 2–3
  characteristics of, 213–214
  diagnosis, 215–218
  Guardian for, 239–241
  LSC Advisor for, 218–229
  PLATFORM for, 235–239

SafeQual for, 229–234
Clauses, 73–74
  in Prolog, 90–91
  for rules, 105–106
Closed nodes, 35
CNTXT variable (SACON), 109–110
Code application phase for LSC Advisor, 220–221
Collaborative design, 258
Colmerauer, Alain, 88
Combinatorial explosion, 24
Combining of evidence, 123–126
Common Lisp Object System (CLOS), 85, 150
Common Lisp programming language, 88, 352–354
Commonsense reasoning, 166
Communication with CDPS, 206
Community knowledge bases, 258
Compact units, 145
Compiled knowledge, 10–11, 100
Components
  descriptions of, 182–184
  function deduction by, 185–187
  hierarchies of, 136–138
  inheritance of behavior by, 184–185
  libraries for, 291
  with OARPLAN, 315–317, 319
Compound actions in OARPLAN, 318
Compound propositions, 60
Computation and computers, 81
  with CDPS, 206
  in engineering, 7–10
  higher-level languages for, 93–95
  issues involving, 353–354
  for knowledge, 8–9
  Lisp for, 82–88
  with PRIDE, 268–270
  Prolog for, 88–93
  and semantic nets, 138–140
Conceptual dependency theory, 139
Conceptual design phase, 248–249
Conceptual graphs for blackboard architecture, 194
Conceptualization stage for system building, 332
Concurrent knowledge system development, 349
Concurrent Prolog for planners, 299
COND function (Lisp), 85

Condition-action statements, 36
Conditional logic
  connective for, 62–63, 68
  in Lisp, 85–86
  with SafeQual, 233
Conditional probability, 118–119
CONE application, 18
Configuration tracking, Callisto for, 305–306
  (See also PRIDE system)
Conflict resolution for rules, 112–113
Confluences, 167–168
Conjunctive symbol, 61
Connected_to predicate in semantic nets, 135
Connectives, 60–63, 67–68
CONPHYDE application, 18
CONS primitive (Lisp), 84
Consequents in rules, 101
Constant symbols, 68
Constraints, 25, 47–49
  and backward reasoning, 38
  and design commitments, 253
  and goal states, 38–39
  in Molgen, 311–312
  in planning systems, 308–309
  in PRIDE, 266–267, 269–270
  in Prolog, 92
  in SightPlan, 281–284
Construction critics, 309
CONSTRUCTION PLANEX planning system, 19, 296, 304, 306–307, 323
Consultation systems, 93
Context trees, 108–109, 111
Contractors, selection KBES for, 229–234
Contradictory propositions with TMS, 173
Control
  in blackboard architecture, 195–196
  CDPS for, 200
  in classification problems, 214
  in Guardian, 241
  in LSC Advisor, 227–228
  in Molgen, 312–313
  in OARPLAN, 326–327
  in OOP languages, 147–149
  in PLATFORM, 237–238
  in PRIDE, 271–273
  in SafeQual, 232–233
  in SightPlan, 277, 281–282
  vs. knowledge, 12, 17, 115

Control knowledge, 42
  in blackboard architecture, 195
  in SightPlan, 277
Conventional programming, 12–13
Cooperative distributed problem solving
    (CDPS), 198
  architectural considerations in, 203–208
  characteristics of, 202–203
  motivation and applications for, 199–201
Coordination networks, 200–201
CPM tool and PLATFORM, 235–236
Creative design, 246–247
Criteria for task selection, 333–334
Criticism in design, 253
Critics in GHOST, 308–309
Cutoff depth for depth-first searches, 44–
    45

Data
  abstraction of, 7, 216, 240
  checking of, in frame-based systems,
    144–145
  filtering of, in Guardian, 240
  ordering of, for conflict resolution, 113
Data-driven reasoning, 36–38, 101–105
Databases with LSC Advisor, 228–229
Deciding Factor shell, 94, 230, 233, 351
Declarative knowledge, 12, 41
Decomposition of problems strategy, 40,
    104
  by experts, 337–338
  in CDPS, 198, 202
  in design, 249, 252
  in PRIDE, 259, 268
  in routine design, 248
  in SightPlan, 277–278
  in variant design, 247–248
  task, 204–205
  with rules, 111–112
Deduction, 75–79
  of function by components, 185–187
  with Lisp, 84
Deep knowledge, 10
Defining of functions with Lisp, 83–84
DEFUN function (Lisp), 83
Delivery of KBES, 349–356
DELTA application, 18
Demons, 145, 273
Demonstrations by experts, 337–338, 341
Dempster-Shafer theory, 121–122

Dependencies with OARPLAN, 323–326
Dependency-directed backtracking, 49,
    171–172, 271
Depth-first, backward chaining with
    Prolog, 91
Depth-first iterative deepening (DFID)
    searches, 44–46
Depth-first searches, 43–46
Derivation tasks, 2–3
Descendant nodes, 35
Design, 3
  applications, 19
  definitions of, 243–245
  information-processing model of, 252–
    254
  Intelligent Boiler Design System, 289–293
  for knowledge acquisition, 344
  phases and prescriptions for, 248–251
  in PRIDE, 259–274
  in SightPlan, 274–288
  roles for, 257–258
  as search problem, 34
  solution methods for, 254–257
  tasks of, 245–246
  taxonomy for, 246–248
Design++ language, 289–293
Design with features approach, 175
Designer's assistant, 250–251, 262
Deskill tasks, 362–363
Detailed design phase, 251
Diagnosis, 2
  applications for, 18
  in classification problems, 213
  in Guardian, 240
  in LSC Advisor for evaluation, 218–229
  MBR for, 189–190
  medical systems for, 215–218
  in monitoring and control systems, 235
  as search problem, 33
DICE blackboard architecture, 196
Differential equations, 167
Dipmeter Advisor, 18
  prototype for, 358
  user interface for, 356–357
Directed arcs, 27, 35
Directed searches, 31, 40, 49–55
Direction of searches, 36–38
Disjoint activities, 205
Disjunction symbol, 62
Distributed planning and control, 200

Divide and conquer strategy, 40, 249
Documentation design phase, 251
Domain-independent frameworks, 350–351
Domain knowledge, 14–15, 17
  in blackboard architecture, 195
  in SightPlan, 277
Domain-specific planning systems, 296
Domain vocabulary, 335
Dym, C. L., 2–3
Dynamic cutoff depth for depth-first searches, 44–45
Dynamic memory management with Lisp, 86–87
Dynamic nature of KBES, 355
Dynamic programming principle, 55

Early commitment strategy in SightPlan, 287
Edinburgh Prolog, 89
8–Puzzle, 30–33
EL system, 172
Elaboration sets and blackboard in OARPLAN, 320–322, 326
Element activities in CONSTRUCTION PLANEX, 306
ELSE Boolean operator, 106
Emulation of problems, 215
EMYCIN systems, 94, 116, 121–124, 351
Engineering
  computation in, 7–10
  KBES in, 18–19
  practice and tasks of, 1–4
Environments, 94
EQUAL TO (=) operator, 106
Essential MYCIN systems, 94, 116, 121–124, 351
Evaluation
  binary, 218–229
  in classification problems, 214
  in design, 246, 251–252
  of expressions in Lisp, 83
  functions for, 31–32
  in PRIDE, 269
  of safety codes, 218–229
Example-based learning, 343
Execution cycles for blackboard architecture, 195–196
Executive-level plans, generation of, 314
Exhaustive searches, 41–49, 228

Existential quantifiers, 70–72
Existential queries in Prolog, 90
Expanded nodes, 27
Experience, learning from, 343
EXPERT framework, 351
Expertise as knowledge, 11
Experts
  cost of, 358
  interviewing of, 341–343
  and KBES ownership, 360
  number needed, 336–341
Explanation of reasoning, 15–16, 156–161, 291–292
Explicit goals and backward reasoning, 38
Expressions in Lisp, 83
Expressive power, 99
Extensibility of rule-based systems, 115

Facets and slots, 144–145
Facility blackboard and description in OARPLAN, 314–315, 326
Factors with inference nets, 125
Facts in Prolog, 89–90
Feigenbaum, E. A., 191
FEM (finite element method), 7–8, 102
Filtering of data in Guardian, 240
Fire protection codes, evaluation of, 218–229
Firing
  of methods in OOP, 147–149
  of rules, 11, 101
First-order predicate logic, 58–59, 65–73
First principles, 5, 164
Flavors programming language, 150
Focuses for blackboard architecture, 195
Foothill problem, 52
FOR_ALL quantifier, 70
FOR_SOME quantifier, 70
Formal logic systems, 57
  and deduction, 76–79
  first-order predicate logic, 65–73
  interpretation in, 75–76
  propositional, 58–65
  unification and resolution in, 73–75
Formalization stage for system building, 332
Formulation of problems, 2–3, 6, 24–34
Fortran programming language, 353
Forward chaining and reasoning, 36–38, 101–105

Frame problem of mathematical logic, 170
Frames and frame-based knowledge
    representation, 140–146
 axioms for, 170–172
 hierarchies with, 156
 in ISIS, 305
 in SightPlan, 277
 integration of, 151–155
Frameworks, 93–94, 304–307, 350–351
Friedland, P. E., 312
FROB system, 175
Functions
 decomposition of, 204–205
 deduction of, by components, 185–187
 Lisp, 83–84
 for predicate logic, 68–69
Fuzziness and uncertainty, 117, 121
Fuzzy set theory, 121

Garbage collection in Lisp, 86–87
Gaschnig, J., 12
GBB blackboard architecture, 196
GEMPLAN planning system, 299
General Problem Solver (GPS), 297
General-purpose planning systems, 297–
   302
General-purpose programming
   languages, 94, 350
Generality ordering for conflict resolution,
   113
Generate-and-test strategy, 29, 39–40, 46–
   47
Generators in PRIDE, 265–266
Geometry of components, 183
GET function (Lisp), 85
GHOST planning system, 308–309, 323
Goal-driven reasoning, 36–38, 91, 101–105
Goals
 and design, 243, 253
 in PRIDE, 263–264, 266–269
 reduction strategy for, 40
 states for, 25, 28, 30
Granularity and CDPS, 202–203
Graphs and graphics
 for rules, 159–160
 for searches, 34–36
 knowledge-based interactive, 160–161
 in PLATFORM, 238–239
 in SightPlan, 283–287

GREATER THAN (>) operator, 106
Green, C., 88
Ground facts with Prolog, 91
GS2D constraint engine, 278, 282–284
Guardian system, 190, 193, 217, 239–241
Guided searches, 31, 40, 49–55

Hardware environments, 349–354
HASP project, 190
Hayes, P., 88
HEARSAY system, 18, 190, 193, 351
Heterarchical structure, 205
Heuristics, 5
 associative, 214
 for blackboard architecture, 195
 and classification, 215–216
 and evaluation functions, 50
 and knowledge, 31–33, 181
 and rules, 100
 and searches, 49–50
 for structural mechanics, 165
HI-RISE system, 19, 255–257, 304
Hierarchies and hierarchical structures
   abstraction, 131–138, 141, 311
 for backtracking, 49
 for design, 255–256
 for generate-and-test searches, 47
 vs. heterarchical structures, 205
 for matches, 40
 for planning, 192–196, 301
 taxonomic, 130–132
Higher-level programming languages, 93–
   95
Hill-climbing searches, 50–52
Histories for temporal reasoning, 177
Horn clauses, 73, 90–91
Hospital patients, monitoring of, 239–241
HOWSAFE system, 217, 340
Human organization analogy for
blackboard architecture, 191–193
Hypotheses
 in early KBESs, 181
 with inference nets, 125
 with rules, 102

Ideas with inference nets, 125
Identification of problems, 221, 240
Identification stage of system building,
   332

IEEE Computer, 19
IEEE Expert, 19
IF clauses and connectives, 68, 101
IFF connective, 62–63, 68
Implementation stage of system building, 332
Implicit goals and backward reasoning, 38
IMPLIES connective, 62–63, 68
In rules, 63–64
Inconsistent information and CDPS, 205–206
Incremental problem-solving, 193
Independent agents, design of, 204
Induction, 78–79, 343
Inference engines, 12, 14–16, 346
Inference nets, 124–126, 160
Inference rules, 63–65
Inference structure for diagnostic system, 215–217
Infix convention, 66
Informate tasks, 362–363
Information-hiding with frames, 140–141
Information-processing model of design, 252–254
Information sharing in blackboard architectures, 192–196
Inheritance
  of attributes, 85, 134, 139, 142–144
  of behavior, 145–147, 184–185
Inheritance lattices, 134
Initial states, 25, 35
Initiation files, Lisp, 84
Inlist propositions in TMS, 172–173
Input/output facilities, 14
Insight 2+ shell, 94
Instances
  of classes in Lisp, 85
  of products, 183
  with taxonomic hierarchies, 130–132
Instantiated constraint variables, 49
Institutional impacts of KBES, 356–363
Integration
  of analysis tools for design, 258
  of rules, frames, and procedures, 151–155
Intelligent assistants, 8, 10, 250–251, 262
Intelligent Boiler Design System (IBDS), 289–293, 363
Interacting effects and probability, 120
Interaction of systems in preliminary design phase, 250

Interactive graphics
  in PLATFORM, 238–239
  for reasoning, 160–161
  in SightPlan, 283–287
Interdependence in CDPS, 201
Interfaces for engineering KBESs, 180
Internal representation of knowledge, 14
Interpretation, 2
  applications for, 18
  CDPS for, 200
  in classification problems, 214
  in formal logic systems, 75–76
  in monitoring systems, 235
  as search problem, 33
Intervention planning in Guardian, 240
Interviewing of experts, 341–343
ISIS planning system, 19, 304–305

Job shop scheduling, ISIS for, 305
Justifications in TMS, 172–173

KAS framework, 351
KEE environment, 150, 350, 352
  compact units in, 145
  frame hierarchies in, 156
  and LSC Advisor, 222
  rules as frames in, 153–154
Kill values in SafeQual, 233
KMS/KES framework, 351
Knowledge and knowledge bases, 6–7, 10–12, 14–15, 334–344
  with CDPS, 207–208
  community, 258
  control, 42, 195, 277
  vs. control, 12, 17, 115
  declarative, 12, 41
  facilities for, 15–16
  for interactive graphics, 160–161, 238–239
  in PRIDE, 261–262
  representation of (*see* Representation of knowledge and problems)
  for rule-based systems, 113
  sources for, 192–196, 277
Knowledge-based systems
  architectures of, 14–18
  definitions for, 10–18
  in engineering, 18–19
  programming styles for, 12–14
Knowledge engineering, 17, 216–217
Knowledge mesas, 191

Knowledge principle, 296
Knowledge source activation records in
    SightPlan, 281–282
Knuth, D., 8
Korf, R. E., 43
Korzybski, A., 7
Kowalski, R., 88

Languages for symbolic computation, 81
  higher-level, 93–95
  Lisp, 82–88
  Prolog, 88–93
Last in first out default scheduler choice,
    196
Layered architecture, 278–279
Leaf nodes, 35
Least commitment strategies, 249, 287,
    299, 311
Left-brain cognitive processes, 274
Legal issues, 360–361
LESS THAN (<) operator, 106
Levitt, R. E., 314
Liability issues, 361
Libraries
  of cases, 333–334, 338, 347–348
  of components, 187, 291
  of prototype solutions, 256
Life cycle of KBES, 331
  delivery in, 349–356
  institutional and social impacts in, 356–
    363
  knowledge acquisition in, 334–344
  and maximum anxiety heuristic, 348–349
  stages of development in, 332–333
  task selection criteria for, 333–334
  verification and validation in, 344–348
LIFT planning systems, 296, 303–304
Likelihood ratio, 119
Links, 25–28, 35
Lisp programming language, 81–88, 150,
    350, 354
Lists in Lisp, 82–84
Literals in Prolog, 91
Logic (*see* Formal logic systems;
    Reasoning)
Logical inference, 99–101
Logical variables in Prolog, 90
LOOPS environment, 111, 150, 160, 273,
    350, 352

LSC Advisor system, 175, 190, 218–229,
    341, 358

McCarthy, John, 82, 350
Macrogoals in PRIDE, 267
Maintenance and support of KBESs, 354–
    356, 358–359
MARC package, 108, 258
Martins, J., 172
MASTERFORMAT system, 306
Matching
  with IF THEN clauses, 101, 104–105
  for rule-based systems, 114
  strategy for, 40
Maximum anxiety heuristic, 348–349
MDX project, 337
Means-ends analysis, 40, 297
Medical diagnosis systems, 215–218
Meeting emulation in blackboard
    architecture, 193–196
Memory, 14
  for breadth-first searches, 43
  for depth-first searches, 44–45
  issues involving, 353–354
  with Lisp, 86–87
  for rule-based systems, 113
Message passing
  in OOP, 147–149
  in PRIDE, 273
Metaplanning, 312
Metarules, 112
Methods
  in OOP, 146–149
  with PRIDE, 263–265
MicroPlanner system, 314
Missionaries-and-cannibals problem, 24–
    30
Model-based reasoning, 181
  applications of, 189–190
  component descriptions for, 182–184
  deduction of function in, 185–186
  Design++ for, 289
  inheritance of behavior in, 184–185
  for planning, 296–297, 307–310
  system behavior in, 186–189
  (*See also* OARPLAN planning system)
Models, 4–7
  for behavior, 165
  and logic systems, 76

for qualitative physics, 168–169
for reasoning, 335
solution, for design, 254–257
Modification and design commitments, 252–253
Modularity, 115, 149
Modus ponens rule, 64
Modus tollens rule, 64
Molgen planning system, 256, 296, 301–303, 310–313
Monitoring and control, 2, 235–239
applications for, 19
in classification problems, 214
real-time, 239–241
as search problem, 33
Multiple experts, advantages of, 336–338
Multiple inheritance, 144
Mutation approach to design, 255
MYCIN system, 93–94, 111–112

Naive physics, 166
Narrowly scoped planners, 302–304
Neats, 57
Negation connective, 61, 63
Negation of quantifications, 72
Networks, granularity of, 203
NEWTON system, 175, 177
NEXPERT OBJECT environment, 159, 350, 352
Nii, H. Penny, 339
NIL value (Lisp), 83
Nilsson, N. J., 42
No-function-in-structure principle, 169
NOAH planning system, 297, 299
Nodes, 25–29
in state space searches, 35
with taxonomic hierarchies, 130–132
NONLIN system, 176
NOT connective and operator, 61, 63, 106
Numerical representations, 5, 165

OARPLAN planning system, 190, 297, 300, 302, 310, 313
control in, 326–327
essential features of, 327
reasoning in, 319–326
representation in, 314–319
Object-oriented programming (OOP), 141, 146–150

Objective C programming language, 150
Objective probabilities, 118
Objective setting, 295
Observation in monitoring systems, 235
Obviation conditions in blackboards, 195
One expert, working with, 339–341
Open nodes, 35
Operating systems, 353
Operators
with classical planners, 297
with rules, 106
with state space searches, 34–36
Opportunistic Planning Model (OPM), 192–193
OPS5 production rule language, 304
Optimization of solutions, 40–41, 44–45
OR connective and operator, 61–64, 68, 106
Organization
with CDPS, 205
of rule-based systems, 113–115
of rules, 108–113
Organizations, issues for, 356–362
Out rules, 63–64, 71, 139
Outlist propositions in TMS, 172–173
Ownership of KBES, 360

Parallelism with CDPS, 202
Parent nodes, 35
Pareto optimization, 343
Part-of hierarchies, 136–138, 185–188
Part-whole representation, 174
Pascal programming language, 150, 353
Pathfinding problems, 38
Pattern matching with rules, 105, 114–115
Persistences for temporal reasoning, 177
PERT tool and PLATFORM, 235–236
Phases for design, 248–251
Phenomenological models, 5, 165
Physical critics, 309
Physical properties of components, 183
PIPPA planning system, 297, 302, 309–310
Plan blackboard in OARPLAN, 326
PLANEX planning system, 19, 296, 304, 306–307, 323
Planning, 3
applications for, 19
CDPS for, 200
and design commitments, 252

general-purpose, 297–302
in Guardian, 240
MBR systems for, 307–310
Molgen for, 310–313
narrowly scoped, 302–304
OARPLAN for, 313–327
overview of research for, 295–297
and PLATFORM, 235–236
with PRIDE, 262–263
as search problem, 33
shells for, 304–307
Plateaus in searches, 52
PLATFORM system, 19, 235–239, 358, 363
Plausible inference, 99–101
Pospesel, H., 71
Possibility theory, 121
Postponed commitment strategy, 287–288
SightPlan system
Power tools, 94
Precalculation phase for LSC Advisor,
    220, 222
Preconditions, 31
  in blackboard architecture, 194
  with classical planners, 297–298, 300
Predicates, 66–68
  Lisp, 83
  with rules, 102, 106
Prediction tasks
  in classification problems, 214
  in monitoring and control systems, 235
Prefix notation, 66, 107
Preiss, K., 299
Preliminary design phase, 250–251
PRIDE system, 19, 238–239, 256–261
  architecture of, 261–262
  control in, 271–273
  current status of, 273–274
  as design assistant, 250, 262
  as informating KBES, 363
  knowledge acquisition in, 336–338
  origins of, 261
  representation in, 262–270
  rules in, 111
  user interface for, 357
Primitives, Lisp, 84
Probability and uncertainty, 116–122
Problems and problem-solving, 2–3
  characteristics of, 38–39
  in design, 244
  formulation and representation of, 23–34

identification of, 221, 240
and modeling, 4–7
in PRIDE, 262
strategies for, 39–40
Procedural knowledge, 42
Procedural programming, 12–13, 150, 353
Procedures
  in detailed design phase, 251
  integration of, 151–155
  with PRIDE, 268
Programming languages and styles, 12–
    14, 81, 150, 350–354
  higher-level, 93–95
  Lisp, 82–88
  Prolog, 88–93
Project activities in CONSTRUCTION
    PLANEX, 306
Project control, 295
Project planning design phase, 251
Prolog programming language, 75, 88–93,
    350, 299
Properties
  of components in OARPLAN, 316–317
  in frame-based systems, 142–144
  in Lisp, 84–85
  of rule-based systems, 115–116
  in semantic nets, 132–136
Proposition of design choices, 252–253
Propositional logic, 58–65
Propositions in TMS, 172–173
PROSPECTOR system, 18, 125
PROTEAN system, 278–279
Protocol analysis, 341–343
Prototypes, 256, 358
Pruning of search branches, 40, 47
Pseudovariables in OOP, 146
Pure selection with design, 256–257
PUTPROP function (Lisp), 84

Qualitative physics and reasoning, 163–
    165
  definitions for, 166–168
  model for, 168–169
Quantifiers for predicate logic, 69–72
Quantity space, 167
Queries in Prolog, 89–90
Questions in interviewing of experts, 342

R1/XCON system, 111, 116, 174, 257, 355,
    357–358

Randomness and uncertainty, 117
RATAS building product model, 186
Real-time monitoring and control systems, 239–241
Reasoning, 14–15
  in blackboard architecture, 194–195
  data-driven and goal-driven, 36–38
  deductive, 75–79
  development of, 335
  explanation of, 15–16, 156–161, 291–292
  in Guardian, 240–241
  in IBDS, 291
  in LSC Advisor, 223–225
  in Molgen, 311–312
  in OARPLAN, 319–326
  in PLATFORM, 237
  qualitative, 163–169
  vs. representation, 348–349
  in SafeQual, 231–232
  with semantic nets, 138–140
  spatial, 173–176
  temporal, 176–177
Recency ordering for conflict resolution, 113
Recognize phase for rules, 112
Recomposition in design, 253
Recursion
  in Lisp, 86
  in Prolog, 91
Redundancy, 205, 207, 309
Refinement critics, 309
Relational databases with Prolog, 91
Relational operators with rules, 106
Relationships, representation of, 129–140
Reliability in CDPS, 207
Repeated nodes, 29
Representation of knowledge and problems, 6–7, 24–34
  in blackboard architecture, 194
  in design, 244–245
  frame-based, 140–146
  in Guardian, 239–240
  in IBDS, 291
  in LSC Advisor, 223–225
  in Molgen, 311
  numerical, 5, 165
  in OARPLAN, 314–319
  in planners, 301–302
  in PLATFORM, 236–237
  in PRIDE, 262–270

  vs. reasoning, 348–349
  and relationships, 129–140
  rule-based (*see* Rule-based representation)
  in SightPlan, 278–281
Research on planning, 295–297
Resolution
  of conflicts, 112–113
  in logic systems, 73–75
  with Prolog, 91
Resource tradeoffs with CDPS, 206
Responsibility for KBESs, 360–361
RESTCOM system, 255
Rete match algorithm, 115
Revision of belief systems, 169–173
Ridge problem in search, 52
Right-brain cognitive processes, 274
Roles of KBES users, 362–363
Root nodes, 27, 35
Rosenschein, J. S., 206
Route-finding, 175–176
Routine design, 246–248
Rule-based frame systems (RFBS), 154–155, 309
Rule-based representation, 154–155, 309
  architecture for, 113–116
  forward and backward chaining, 101–105
  and inference nets, 124–126
  logical and plausible inference in, 99–101
  organization of, 108–113
  of uncertainty, 116–124
  writing of, 105–108
Rules
  for conflict resolution, 113
  decomposition of, 111–112
  firing of, 11, 101
  graphs of, 159–160
  and heuristics, 5
  inference engines for, 15
  integration of, 151–155
  interpreter for, 114
  precedence networks for, 113
  for predicate logic, 71–73
  in Prolog, 90–91
  selection of, 112–114
  tracing of, 156–157
Rules of thumb in preliminary design, 250

SACON system, 18, 94, 108–111, 258
SafeQual system, 229–234

Same-as values feature, 230, 233
Satisficing of solutions, 40–41
Scaled evaluations, SafeQual for, 229–234
Scaling and granularity, 202
Scheduling, 295
  in blackboard architecture, 193
  CONSTRUCTION PLANEX for, 306–307
  ISIS for, 305
  planners for, 302–304
Scientific method, 79
Scoping in Lisp, 82–83
Scruffies, 57
Searches, 23–34
  and CDPS, 202
  chaining with, 101–105
  for classification problems, 215
  directed, 31, 40, 49–55
  exhaustive, 41–49, 228
  with Lisp, 84
  with LSC Advisor, 228
  for problem formulation, 6
  with Prolog, 91
  state space, 34–41
  trees and graphs for, 34–36
Selection, 2
  in classification problems, 213
  in LSC Advisor, 221
  in monitoring and control systems, 235
  as search problem, 33
SELF variable in OOP, 146–147
Semantic nets, 129–140, 194
Semantics
  in formal logic, 58
  and interpretation, 76
Sentence symbols, 60
Sentential logic, 58–65
Separation of knowledge from control, 12,
    17, 115
Sequential dependency, 317
Shape representation, 174
Sharing of information in blackboard
    architectures, 192–196
Shells, 93–94, 304–307, 350–351
SightPlan system, 175, 197, 238–239, 274
  architecture of, 277–278
  constraint-based approaches in, 256
  constraint engine for, 282–283
  control issues in, 281–282
  current status of, 287–288
  graphic interface for, 283–287

  as informating KBES, 363
  origins of, 275–277
  prototype for, 358
  representation issues in, 278–281
SightView interface, 197, 283–287
Simple actions in OARPLAN, 318
SIMULA simulation language, 146
Simulation of behavior in MBR, 186–189
Singular statements, 66–67
SIPE-2 planning system, 302, 307–308
SIPEC planning system, 308
Situation-action rules, 99, 194
Slots in frames, 141–145, 153
Smalltalk programming language, 146
Soar system, 343–344
Social impacts of KBES, 356–363
Software environments, 349–354
Solutions
  models for, 254–257
  in preliminary design phase, 250
  searching for, 23–34
Spatial decomposition vs. functional, 204
Spatial distribution of sensors with CDPS,
    201
Spatial reasoning, 173–176
  (*See also* SightPlan system)
Special-purpose planners, 302–304
Specifications as design goal, 244
Speed issues, 353–354
SPERIL applications, 18
SPEX system, 312–313
State abstraction with planners, 300
State space searches, 34–41
Stefik, M. J., 2–3, 7, 340
Strategies for problem-solving, 39–40
  in blackboard architecture, 195
  case-based reasoning, 249, 256
  decomposition (*see* Decomposition of
    problems strategy)
  divide and conquer, 40, 249
  generate-and-test, 29, 39–40, 46–47
  least commitment, 249, 287, 299, 311
STRIPS planning system, 171–172, 176–
    177, 297–300
Strong search methods, 49–50
Structural mechanics, taxonomy for, 164–
    166
Structured English algorithms, 42–43
Structured meeting emulation in
    blackboard architecture, 193–196

Structures of frames, 141–142
Subclasses
  inheritance of behavior by, 145–146
  with taxonomic hierarchies, 130–132
Subjective probabilities, 118–119
Subproblem generation in design, 253
Subsystem hierarchies, 136–138
Successor nodes, 35
Sufficiency of rules, 119
Support requirements for KBESs, 354–356,
    358–359
Surface knowledge, 10
Sussman anomaly problem, 298
Symbols
  constant, for predicate logic, 68
  in KBS, 11–12
  representation by, 6–7
  sentence, 60
Synchronization with CDPS, 207
Syntax
  in formal logic, 58
  of methods in OOP, 146–147
  for rules, 105–108
  in searches, 42
Synthesis, 2–3
  for design, 245
  IBDS for, 289–293
  MBR for, 189
  (*See also* SightPlan system)

Tasks
  decomposition of, 204–205
  for design, 245–246
  engineering, 2–4
  for system building, 332–334
Taxonomy
  for design, 246–248
  of engineering knowledge, 164–166
  hierarchies of, 130–132
Technical specifications for components,
    183
Temporal reasoning, 176–177
Terminal predicates with rules, 102
Terms in predicate logic, 68–69
Test cases for task selection criteria, 333
Testing
  with deductions, 76–77
  in design, 251–252
  in generate-and-test strategy, 29, 39–40,
    46–47

of KBES, 344–346
in PRIDE, 269, 274
in system building, 332
THEN statements with rules, 101
Time
  and exhaustive searches, 44, 46
  and reasoning, 176–177
Tip nodes, 35
Tools, 94, 351–352
Topological information, 182–183, 317
Tracing of rules, 156–157
TRANALOGY system, 255
Transparency of reasoning, 16, 116, 157–
    158
Travel distance algorithms, 225–227
Trees
  context, 108–109, 111
  search, 34–36
Trigger conditions in blackboards, 194
Truth maintenance systems (TMS), 49,
    172–173
Truth tables, 62–63
TWEAK planning system, 297
Two-player games, 38
Two-way interactive graphics for
    reasoning, 160–161

Uncertainty
  inference nets for, 124–126
  representation of, 116–124
Unification
  in logic systems, 73–75
  with Prolog, 91
Universal quantifiers, 70–71, 139
UNIX operating system, 353
Upward inheritance, 144
User-interactive model in SightPlan, 288
User interfaces, 356–357
Users, changing roles of, 362–363

Validation of KBES, 346–348
Value class facets, 144
Variables
  in Lisp, 86–87
  in OOP, 146–147
  for predicate logic, 68–71
  in Prolog, 89–90
Variant design, 247–248
Verification
  in design, 251, 253

Verification (*Cont.*)
 of KBES, 344–346
Volume descriptions, 174

Weak exhaustive search methods, 42
Weaker reasoning methods, 14
Weight of belief with subjective
     probabilities, 119–120, 126
WFF (well-formed formulas), 60, 63–64

White box testing, 345
Working memory, 14, 113
Writing of rules, 105–108

XCON system, 111, 116, 174, 257, 355, 357–
 358
XPERT expediting system, 309

Zones in OARPLAN, 319